Charles
III

Also by Robert Hardman

Monarchy: The Royal Family at Work
Our Queen
Queen of the World
Queen of Our Times

New
KING
New
COURT

Charles
III

THE INSIDE
STORY

ROBERT
HARDMAN

MACMILLAN

First published 2024 by Macmillan
an imprint of Pan Macmillan
The Smithson, 6 Briset Street, London EC1M 5NR
EU representative: Macmillan Publishers Ireland Ltd, 1st Floor,
The Liffey Trust Centre, 117–126 Sheriff Street Upper,
Dublin 1, D01 YC43
Associated companies throughout the world
www.panmacmillan.com

ISBN 978-1-0350-2741-5 HB
ISBN 978-1-0350-2748-4 TPB

3 5 7 9 8 6 4

A CIP catalogue record for this book is available from the British Library.

Typeset by Palimpsest Book Production Ltd, Falkirk, Stirlingshire
Printed and bound by CPI Group (UK) Ltd, Croydon, CR0 4YY

Visit **www.panmacmillan.com** to read more about all our books
and to buy them. You will also find features, author interviews and
news of any author events, and you can sign up for e-newsletters
so that you're always first to hear about our new releases.

For my godchildren

Contents

Introduction

Like Elizabeth II before him, King Charles III is content to be judged on his record and will not be giving periodic interviews from the throne. Having interviewed him and spoken to him many times when he was Prince of Wales, I had formed a clear and rounded impression of the heir to the throne long before his accession. Similarly, I had also met the then Duchess of Cornwall on frequent occasions, whether on royal tours or at her Clarence House events for her many causes or interviewing her for documentaries. Both of them would always be the genuine article. You did not, as with some in the public eye, wonder which persona might greet you on any given day.

At the time of the death of Elizabeth II, people frequently asked what the new King and Queen were 'really like'. The answer lay before us already. They were never going to undergo some sort of character bypass or transplant.

But how would they respond to events for which no one could ever be fully prepared? No previous monarch had taken on the role at this stage in life (it is worth considering that when Elizabeth II was the same age, she was approaching her Golden Jubilee). How would the couple rise to this monumental challenge? In this new and even more scrutinized existence, what would they think of us and we of them?

1

Charles III

I have been allowed inside to follow it all – the trauma, the transition and the establishment of the new modus vivendi. Now and then, I have been alongside a television camera, more often with just pen and notebook. I have not sought to write a full-life biography. This is a contemporary portrait of our new monarch and his new court. It is also a ringside account of what happens when you take over from the most famous woman in the world to lead Britain's pre-eminent institution; to be the head of its most famous family; and also to become sovereign of a greater area of the planet than any other head of state on Earth.

Chapter One

C-Rex

The King is making his rounds of Windsor Great Park. Since succeeding to the throne at the age of seventy-three, he has had much to absorb both as head of state and head of the most famous family in the land. Among his new responsibilities – an optional rather than a hereditary one – is that of Ranger of the Great Park, a royal hunting ground for deer since the days of William the Conqueror. Today, the Ranger's duty is to protect the wildlife, along with everything else in these 5,000 acres of parkland, woods and gardens. Together with his full-time Deputy Ranger, the King is slowly nudging towards a herd of red deer shielding from a gale in a small copse. He is particularly struck by a group of stags. 'The weight on their heads is amazing,' reflects the King. 'The strength of their necks to support those antlers . . .'

It's an interesting observation from a man who is coming to terms with a considerable weight on his own shoulders, both figuratively and, in actual fact, a few months from now, at Westminster Abbey. It's a scene to pique the artistic imagination – the metaphor of the stag as monarch; the awesome, uneasy burden on 'the head that wears the Crown.'[1]

Being a new monarch in the twenty-first century is not the perilous existence it was in Shakespeare's time, but it still carries multiple challenges.

Charles III

A former private secretary points out one in particular. Charles III has to deal with a world that constantly needs to be reminded of the merits of monarchy. 'There were no doubts when the Queen came to the throne. It was just accepted,' he says. 'Now, people do have doubts. They may want a monarchy but they also feel the need to be convinced.'[2] Moreover, the King is conscious, says his ex-aide, that the survival of the British monarchy was never an inevitability but that it has enjoyed a uniquely lucky set of historical circumstances: 'The things which can bring a monarchy to an end have not happened in the two centuries since the French showed us that there could be an alternative. We haven't lost any major wars. We haven't had any huge economic disruption. And we haven't had a monarch who's behaved really disgracefully. It also helped that for more than fifty-five per cent of the time, the monarch has been a woman.'

The more that the late Queen continued to set new royal records, so the same was true of her eldest son. In 2015, for example, Elizabeth II overtook Queen Victoria to become the longest-serving monarch in British history. By then, the Prince of Wales had already broken Edward VII's record as the longest-serving heir to the throne a good four years earlier. In 2013, the Prince also became the oldest heir (at the age of sixty-four) when he overtook William IV.

It made him, by some margin, the oldest person in history to succeed to the throne. Seventy-three on his accession and seventy-four at his Coronation, his mother had been, respectively, twenty-five and twenty-seven.

Some had predicted that his tenure would only be a 'caretaker' administration in between the longest-reigning monarch in British history and a younger, more glamorous generation led by King William V. Over almost three decades, opinion polls would periodically show equal numbers or even a majority of the public 'preferring' Prince William to his father as the immediate successor to Elizabeth II.[3] These polls overlooked one essential point. Prince William had zero interest in displacing his father. As he told me shortly before the 2012 Diamond Jubilee, he tried 'desperately hard' not to think about the destiny that lay ahead.[4] 'That can wait until I'm a bit older,' he added. Given the longevity of both Charles III's parents as well as the King's own levels of fitness and relatively abstemious lifestyle, it is more than likely that the new Prince of Wales will be waiting well into his sixties before he himself becomes sovereign. Not only does the King feel that he has earned his position after the longest apprenticeship in history, he also has no intention of imposing such a burden on his son any earlier than the Almighty ordains.

A regular refrain in those first few days of the new reign was: 'Well, Charles has certainly had plenty of time to think about it.' This was, plainly, true. The Princess Royal sees this as one of his great strengths. 'It's perspective,' she explains. 'He's covered a lot of the country, he's well informed. He's had more chance to be able to see more. I always thought that must have been a huge disadvantage for my mother because [she was] literally thrown into it in a rather unexpected way and had not had the chance to have that broader experience.'[5]

However, over all those years (much like his mother), the new King had given very little away about what he was actually thinking. Even his own family were not entirely sure of his plans for the monarchy.

What has become clear from the start is that Charles III did have well-developed views on the style and tone of his monarchy, although he preferred to keep most of these in his head. There was no detailed masterplan locked away in a drawer, waiting to be enacted. Indeed, as will be seen, he was profoundly reluctant to discuss the details even with his own advisers, let alone to engage in wider discussions, while Elizabeth II was alive. 'Tempting fate' and 'commendably diffident' are two explanations offered by close sources. Everyone would simply have to wait and see when the time came. Hence, the catalogue of confident predictions which have now quietly been shelved and forgotten: that Charles III would never live at Windsor Castle; that he would find it hard to curtail his opinions; that he would stray into politics and compromise his constitutional neutrality; that he would show no interest in the world of racing; that he would not share his late mother's commitment to the Church of England; that he would 'slim down' the monarchy; that he had no time for ancient flummery like the Gold State Coach.

On one point, however, the pundits were spot on. The era of the corgi has, indeed, come to an end. The age of the Jack Russell has begun.*

'The way he looks at it is rather like the legal profession and the way lawyers can be barristers and then judges,' says one of the King's senior aides. 'You can be a barrister and then you can become a judge. It is a completely different job but you change when the time comes and that is accepted.'[6]

According to one of his inner circle, he also appreciates that any organization is at its most vulnerable in transition. 'Change is always a moment of weakness. So when there is change, you've got to be even better than usual,' says one, adding that the King, like his mother before him, believes there are two main components to good leadership. They are trust and visibility. With regards to the former, Charles III, like Elizabeth II, is seen as authentic. Whether or not people like the idea of a hereditary monarchy (or even Charles the man), he is seen to

---

* Queen Camilla has two Jack Russells, Beth and Bluebell, both rescue dogs from Battersea Dogs & Cats Home.

be, genuinely and consistently, himself. As for visibility, Prince Charles was raised on his mother's mantra that 'I have to be seen to be believed.' Immediately after her death, it became clear that he would abide by this. Duties and conventions which might have been spread over many months at the start of the previous reign kicked in almost immediately. His first broadcast as monarch was recorded within twenty-four hours (Elizabeth II's first broadcast, which was by radio, came ten and a half months into her reign). There would be visits to all the home nations within days. Court mourning, which continued for two and a half months after the state funeral of George VI, would end precisely one week after that of Elizabeth II. In less than three weeks, the King's cypher, 'CIIIR' (Charles III Rex), was ready and released for immediate use on post boxes, military uniforms and official documents. It had taken more than five months before the design for 'EIIR' was approved in 1952. Investitures were up and running again within the month.

The British monarchy prides itself on being a force for stability and continuity (it says so at the very top of its own website) – hence its sensitivity to any threat of transitional weakness. There was no such problem when Elizabeth II succeeded her father, whereas the threat had been very real for George VI. Witness the speed with which his coronation was organized immediately after the abdication of his elder brother. There was another factor driving the pace in the case of Charles III. He both needs and wants to get on with making his mark, with Queen Camilla at his side. 'It's quite hard to begin this new phase of their lives when they're both in their mid-seventies,' says the Queen's friend and companion, the Marchioness of Lansdowne. 'I know, particularly, the King has got so many things he wants to do and achieve. And I don't think there's ever going to be enough hours in the day for him.'[7]

The clue was in his first broadcast, when he pledged to follow his late mother's 'unswerving devotion' to duty 'throughout the remaining time God grants me'. He has accepted that if he wants to get things done at speed, then it is best not to shake up the monarchical machinery too much. 'There used to be those stories – and *The Crown* peddled this idea, too* – that he was desperate for the Queen to abdicate, but that was always nonsense,' says a good friend. 'After she died, I heard him say: "I always wondered if it would ever come but I never wanted it a minute sooner, either. And now I know what I want to do". He might do some things differently, of course. But he feels, as monarch, that he is still a lot closer to her way of doing things than the next generation is going to be.'[8]

In some regards, his guiding light is not so much his late mother as his grandfather. One close friend of the family says that, shortly after his accession, she was offering her condolences to the new monarch and assured him that both his mother and the Queen Mother would be 'looking after' him from somewhere up on high. 'That's very kind of you,' he replied, 'but the person whose hand I feel on my shoulder is the King.'[9] For George VI has always loomed large in his mind. There are now only two people alive who were in Sandringham House on the night the King died in his bed there in February 1952. Prince Charles, aged three, and Princess Anne, aged one, were staying with their grand-parents while Princess Elizabeth and the Duke of Edinburgh were in Africa, at the start of their round-the-world Commonwealth tour. The little prince heard the news of the King's death from his grandmother. As the Queen Mother later told James Pope-Hennessy, she explained to Prince Charles that the King had been found by his valet when delivering his early

---

* The fifth series of the Netflix drama *The Crown* imagined that the Prince of Wales was pushing for an abdication, pressing his mother to step aside.

morning cup of tea. Charles listened gravely before asking: 'Who drank the tea?'[10] More than half a century later, the historian Kenneth Rose was introduced to the Prince of Wales at a Welsh Guards event on what happened to be the Prince's birthday. 'I offered him my congratulations as you would,' Rose later told me, 'and he said the most extraordinary thing. He replied: "I am today of the same age that my grandfather was when he died". Which indeed he was but it was sort of chilling really.'[11]

That capacity for gloomy introspection, so familiar to his friends and family during the Prince's middle years, now seems to have lifted. He is unquestionably more cheerful these days. Even in more melancholy times, he always had a robust sense of humour and of the absurd. Now, though, he laughs a lot more, whether at the Archbishop of Canterbury fluffing his lines during Coronation rehearsals or discovering a pie crust depicting his face at the Sandringham Flower Show. 'More like Wallace and Gromit,' he chuckled. The new mood has even permeated his wardrobe. Finding gifts for the man who really does have everything might be tricky but, since his accession, his family have given the King several new ties. A particular favourite, seen on numerous occasions, from church at Sandringham to a walkabout in Manchester, is of pale pink silk with a light blue *Tyrannosaurus rex* pattern printed all over it. Is the T-Rex motif a humorous, coded play on C-Rex? 'I couldn't possibly comment,' says one of his team with a grin, suggesting strongly that it might be. Like his mother, who thoroughly enjoyed being Queen, even during some very dark days, Charles III is, simply, very happy being monarch.

'I think that when you know a change is coming, there's a kind of suspension, isn't there, of what you do and the things you worry about before it happens,' says the Princess Royal. 'Then the change happens and you go: "Okay, it's me. Now I have to do things this way. I have to get on with it." That allows you to take ownership of that role instead of being one step back.'[12] Another reason for this new-found royal contentment, say those around the King, is a subtle shift in public attitude. There is the inevitable change of aura which comes with promotion to the top job but there is also a fresh awareness of all the things he has been – in his own words – 'banging on about' for years. 'Those who follow the royals closely might have known about all his work but a lot of people are discovering it for the first time,' says one of his team. 'That would make anyone happy.'[13]

Another common media perception is that the King and his staff spend much if not most of their time worrying about how to 'slim down' the monarchy and what to do with the two difficult Dukes. In reality, the King has learned over long years of royal domestic trauma how to compartmentalize issues over which he has little control. Queen Camilla has also been instrumental in lifting the mood.

The departure of the Duke and Duchess of Sussex from royal life in 2020 and their subsequent sensational attacks on the institution, on camera and in print, have hurt. 'Of course the King is extremely sad about Harry and Meghan but there is a sense of exasperation, that he has done what he can and now he is King, there are many more things to think about,' says one friend. 'He has tried listening. Now he just says: "I don't want to know what the problem is. I'm just getting on with my life".' Nothing is final, however. 'You'd always like your child back,' says a senior official. 'But when your child has decided that, at the moment, they want to do things differently, you have to give them the space to do that. The door is always open, though.'

The one positive upshot is a closer rapport with the Prince of Wales, who has his own set of issues with the Sussexes' public airing of private grievances. Now that the King is using Windsor

Castle at least two days a week, he also sees much more of his British-based grandchildren since they live beneath the ramparts.

As for the Duke of York, eternally tainted by his association with the dead sex offender Jeffrey Epstein and the ongoing legal aftermath,* it had been expected that the King would take a much tougher line. The late Queen had always provided a security shield for her second son. There were expectations, after her death, that the Duke would be swiftly moved out of Royal Lodge, the spacious former Windsor home of the Queen Mother. Contrary to reports that the King wanted to give it to the Prince of Wales (who, in any case, was not looking for another house move), it is more a question of cost. Royal Lodge sits outside the main Windsor security cordon and requires separate protection. Since the Duke's withdrawal from public life, this has no longer been regarded as a legitimate public expense and was being funded by the late Queen. The King's position, according to one source, is quite simple. His brother can either foot the bill or move inside the Windsor cordon, where the Duke of Sussex's old home, Frogmore Cottage, is available. For now, the Duke is still to be found riding around the Windsor estate by way of something to do. When there are family gatherings away from the public gaze, he is still welcome. In March 2023, he was not only invited to the quadrennial service for the Royal Victorian Order at St George's Chapel, Windsor, but the King allowed him to wear his GCVO** robes. The media were not admitted and so the moment was not captured. He is still invited to the non-public elements of the annual gathering of the Order of the Garter, too. 'The King will not just cast his brother adrift. He is very fond of his nieces [Princesses Beatrice and Eugenie].

---

* In 2022, the Duke paid a reported £10 million to settle a claim of sexual assault from Virginia Roberts. The same allegation has since appeared in other US court documents.
** Knight Grand Cross of the Royal Victorian Order

Also, Andrew could be far more damaging on the loose outside the loop and at least he hasn't been disloyal,' says one source. 'But any return to public life is out of the question. His legal problems are not resolved, the public don't want him and many people still remember his rudeness last time round.'[14] Privately, within diplomatic circles or the county lieutenancies, it is seldom long before mere mention of the Duke prompts a rolling of the eyes and a less than flattering anecdote.

The question of 'slimming down' the monarchy might have made sense five years earlier when there were fifteen members of the family regularly undertaking public duties. Since that number had reduced to ten regulars by 2023, with six of those well past retirement age and no prospect of new recruits for at least a decade, the idea has been shelved. 'I think "slimmed down" was said in a day when there were a few more people to make that seem like a justifiable comment,' the Princess Royal has observed. 'It doesn't sound like a good idea from here. I'm just not sure what else we can do.'[15]

Every phase of King Charles's life has been chronicled exhaustively in films, press articles and books. Much of it has also been reimagined and dramatized for stage or screen. It is a story so well known that we often overlook the extent to which it broke the royal mould.

Prince Charles was the first future monarch to have a conventional education starting at Hill House, a London day school. He then followed the path laid down by his father, becoming a boarder at Cheam preparatory school in Berkshire before moving on to Gordonstoun in Scotland. Unlike his younger brothers, he did not enjoy it one bit, later describing his time there as 'a prison sentence.'[16] Being in the Highlands was no great hardship for a boy who adored Balmoral. However, the Prince had to endure what one contemporary, John Stonborough, described as 'virtually institutionalized' bullying from those who thought it amusing to abuse the future monarch. In any rugby scrum, there would be someone who wanted to claim that they had roughed up the heir to the throne. 'I never saw him react at all,' Stonborough told Sally Bedell Smith, recalling: 'He was very stoic.'[17]

The highlight of his schooldays was a six-month interlude at Geelong Grammar School in Victoria, Australia. Despite a similar emphasis on outward-bound character-building, the Prince found he was treated like anyone else and thrived on all the challenges, before returning to Gordonstoun for his final exams. He left with two A-Levels and 'without a twinge of regret.'[18] He could also be grateful for several lasting life skills. He had acquired a taste and a talent for appearing on stage, had developed a love of Shakespeare and knew how to write a good essay. Of the 4,000 candidates sitting the Oxford and Cambridge Exam Board's special history paper that year, the Prince came out in the top 6 per cent. He continued to enjoy acting at Trinity College, Cambridge, where he read Archaeology and Anthropology before switching to History. 'He was always intelligent, cultured, very considerate and very controlled,' says his Cambridge contemporary Richard (now Lord) Chartres. The student Prince's serious side, he adds, did him no favours. 'He worked very hard and was popular. But if he had actually been more of a playboy, people would have regarded him in an even more favourable light.'[19]

Once again, there was a break in his studies when he spent a term at the University College of Wales in Aberystwyth learning Welsh, prior to his investiture as Prince of Wales in 1969. 'It was quite intense but it set a tone for what he was going to do next,' says the Princess Royal. 'I certainly remember the aftermath of the investiture at Caernarfon. We were sent off to Malta for him to recover. He really did need to recover.' The Princess recalls that the constant walkabouts had left her brother so exhausted that he was doing them in his sleep. 'He woke up trying to speak to people.'[20]

He returned to Cambridge to complete his studies, graduating with a 2:2 (second-class) degree. Both the university and the King himself remain proud that he was the first future monarch to 'earn' a degree,[21] unlike Edward VII and George VI, who had merely 'studied' there. Similarly, there were no special exceptions made after the Prince went on to follow family tradition and join the Royal Navy in 1971.

There was, inevitably, forensic media interest in any girlfriends, including a certain Camilla Shand, but the Prince was in no rush to embrace married life. In 1976, as he turned twenty-eight, he left the Royal Navy to take up full-time royal duties. Despite great privilege, he felt he had been properly tested at every stage of his life, more so than any of his predecessors, and was, therefore, entitled to have some say in his own future. 'I was sent off to do all these so-called ordinary things,' he told me at the time of his sixtieth birthday. 'They can't really expect me, having done all that and having to fight to show I could do it as well as everybody else, then not to get stuck into all the things I mind about.' The Prince's Trust and a multitude of other causes and passions would be the beneficiary of a new form of royal activism. The Duke of Edinburgh, with projects like his award scheme and the World Wildlife Fund, had revived the sort of hands-on, executive style of royal patronage pioneered by Prince Albert. The Prince of Wales took it to a new level. While he understood the constitutional rules, he was happy to stir up debates. If these had a common theme, it was not a craving to change things so much as a determination to protect precious things from the impact of change – be they climate, rainforests and old buildings or, in the case of his trust, the life opportunities of disadvantaged young people.

His press secretary from those days, the Australian diplomat John Dauth, says that various career plans were considered. 'There was a lot of talk about getting him "a proper job", but the Prince didn't want to be at a desk from nine to five.' Among the suggestions which were rejected was a senior role with the British Council. Dauth also remembers a separate discussion about his boss's approach to royal duties: 'The Prince said: "I want to be seen as a modern man but not too modern. Just behind the curve." I've always remembered that – "just behind the curve".'

The Prince's marriage to Lady Diana Spencer in 1981, the biggest global royal event since the Queen's coronation, was followed by the birth of their sons, William, in 1982, and Harry, in 1984. For almost a decade, Charles and Diana were the most glamorous couple in international public life. The eventual collapse of their marriage, leading to separation in 1992 and divorce in 1996, dominated the media. It eclipsed almost all other royal activity, including some of the most important state visits of the Queen's reign. Leaked phone calls, television interviews by both the Prince and Princess plus relentless media speculation led to a polarization of opinion among some sections of the public and a wider sense of disenchantment with royalty in general. The Prince's 1994 on-camera admission that his youthful romance with Camilla Parker Bowles (née Shand) had resumed after his marriage 'became irretrievably broken down'[22] led many to side with the Princess. Positions became more entrenched a year later after the BBC's Martin Bashir used faked documents to lure her into the now-debased *Panorama* interview in which she cast doubts on the Prince's prospects as king. Their divorce mirrored the failed marriages of more than a quarter of British couples who wed during the 1980s,* plus those of two of the Prince's siblings and his aunt. Yet the collapse of the marriage remained the chief faultline in public perceptions of the heir to the throne long after the tragic early death of the Princess in a Paris car crash in 1997. From that moment on, the Prince suddenly found himself a single parent with two young sons, combining royal duties with the stewardship of one of Britain's largest charitable networks.

In 2005, he finally married Camilla Parker Bowles, heralding a new chapter in his life. Royal fortunes in general continued on a slow but steady upward trajectory. The marriage of Prince William to Catherine Middleton, in 2011, and the Queen's Diamond Jubilee, in 2012, marked further turning points. At the same time, Elizabeth II was gradually delegating more duties to the Prince of Wales. After she stopped long-distance travel in 2013 and all overseas travel in 2015, the Prince was Britain's senior royal emissary. After the retirement of the Duke of Edinburgh from public duties in 2017, the Prince would either accompany or stand in for his mother at major occasions, be it a state visit or Remembrance Sunday at the Cenotaph. In 2018, he was endorsed as future Head of the Commonwealth by all the member states. Yet, through it all, he was still careful to ensure that nothing undermined the ultimate authority of the Queen. 'He didn't want to enter an area into which his day had not yet come,' is how one former courtier sums it up.[23]

When family crises unfolded, not least those involving the removal of the Dukes of York and Sussex from public duties (the former under compulsion, the latter of his own volition),

---

* Office for National Statistics figures show that 28 per cent of couples married in the 1980s were divorced by their thirteenth anniversary. (*The Guardian*, 4 March 2016)

the Prince of Wales would help the Queen make some painful decisions. He would also help her uphold them, while never trying to usurp her position. That was clear enough after the Duke of York started to row back on his withdrawal from public life, just hours after this had been announced in the wake of his catastrophic 2019 BBC interview on *Newsnight*. The Duke let it be known that he would still be pressing ahead with a business visit to Bahrain. Buckingham Palace did not, initially, intervene. With the Prince of Wales away on a tour of New Zealand, the Duke had been to see the Queen and had plainly secured his mother's acquiescence to his plan. No sooner had dawn broken in New Zealand, however, than the Duke's Bahrain trip was very firmly off. The Prince had seen to that. 'When you get an issue like a *Newsnight*, which will suddenly get worse, you just have to be brutal and fast,' says a senior Palace aide. 'Charles knows that.'[24]

During the Covid pandemic, which might have been a very grave threat to an institution rooted in public interaction, the Royal Family found a new way of operating through video messages and arms-length engagements, led by the Queen. The Prince, who caught and recovered from the virus early on, held back. After the death of the Duke of Edinburgh in 2021, the spotlight still remained firmly on the Queen as head of state, with her family in a supporting role. In 2022, laid low by what the Palace called recurrent 'mobility issues', the Queen asked the Prince of Wales to open Parliament. Here was a very significant moment. On all previous occasions when monarchs had been unable to read the Speech from the Throne (Victoria and Elizabeth II included), the task had been delegated to one of the Lords Commissioners, usually the Lord Chancellor. The Queen decided that this duty and honour should fall to the Prince of Wales. She even issued new Letters Patent to that effect. For once, that overused word 'unprecedented' was called for. Had it been commonly supposed that the Prince was itching to take charge, this might well have been interpreted as some sort of regency-by-stealth. It was not.

During the celebrations for the Queen's seventieth year on the throne in 2022, it was the Prince who stood in when her declining health meant she could not be there in person, be it the Platinum Jubilee service of thanksgiving at St Paul's Cathedral or her Jubilee pageant.* The public, however, always had a sense that she was there in spirit. This was quite an achievement on the part of both the Queen and her son. Short of signing Acts of Parliament and a weekly chat with the prime minister, the Prince was de facto monarch in almost every regard. Save one – and a crucial one. The Queen's authority remained not just solid but even enhanced. 'It was remarkable but the frailer she became in her later years, the greater her authority,' says one of her most senior officials.[25] 'It was never questioned.' The Prince himself had been assiduous in ensuring that such a question was not asked. When the time finally came, however, no one in history had been more ready.

One of his most senior advisers points to an unsung virtue of the King. It is hardly one which he can espouse on the royal. uk website, but that does not make it any less valid. It is one familiar to many who have inherited great fortunes or titles, and thus a sense of 'noblesse oblige', though this is on an entirely different scale. This adviser calls it 'the humility of the hereditary principle', explaining: 'There is an argument that if you have someone who has fought to get to the top, you are

---

* The Queen came onto the palace balcony after the pageant, her last public appearance in the capital.

more likely to get an egomaniac. For people who get to the top of their profession, it's always a competitive business – rightly so. But they often have embedded in them the feeling that they are better than everyone else. The other side of that coin, in the case of a monarch, is that becoming head of state isn't competitive. People may say: "It's terrible someone who's done nothing to deserve it gets plonked in as head of state just because they are someone's son or daughter". For that reason, you get people who have a fantastic focus on duty – if they're good people. They can be very competitive in their own areas – sport or whatever – but they still think to themselves: "Bloody hell, what have I done to be here? It's even more of an incentive for me to make sure I do it properly". So the fact that the Prince wasn't at all pushy in terms of taking over as King was a good thing.'[26]

It helps, too, that the King shares his late father's capacity for taking on extra tasks which others might prefer to delegate. That, perhaps, explains why, a few weeks after becoming monarch, he was not reassigning responsibilities so much as simply acquiring new ones. One such was that appointment of himself to succeed his father as Ranger of Windsor Great Park. For a passionate gardener and countryman, it might be no great burden but it still means more meetings, more briefing notes and more decisions.

The King also shares his late mother's capacity to absorb endless quantities of paperwork. One change which staff have noticed since the accession of Charles III is an increase in the amount of red box traffic between the monarch and the private secretaries. The Queen used to receive two different types of red box. All would contain a mix of state papers, Cabinet minutes, ambassadorial despatches, nominations for honours and much else for her attention and approval. On most weekdays, though, her officials would try to limit this to the contents of a 'reading box', a smaller model roughly the size of a large shoebox. At weekends, they would send her a 'standard', a larger briefcase-sized box. Whatever the size, the paperwork would be completed and the box returned to the private office in time for the next working day. These days, it is almost always a 'standard' box which goes to Charles III. Sometimes, there are several of them. It is not because there are suddenly more state papers for this head of state. It is that he asks for more information. 'The Queen was wonderfully dutiful and she read everything she had to,' says one who worked for them both. 'He, on the other hand, reads a lot of stuff he doesn't need to read. He might complain about some things, but work isn't one of them. Having a lot on his plate is what he likes. Having too much on his plate is never going to worry him.' This is just as well, given that the King has little choice, as his sister points out.

'There's a huge amount that goes on and always has done. And what comes in the red boxes doesn't stop,' says the Princess Royal. 'It's the regularity and the amount that goes into that more public side of life that impinges on the other things that he used to do. I don't envy him. To assume you can go on doing the things that you did before – it's probably not going to work because you suddenly find you just don't have that time available. Monarchy is a 365-days-a-year occupation. And it doesn't stop because you change monarchs for whatever reason.'

It also helps that Charles III is a monarch who regards correspondence as a form of relaxation. 'When other people like watching television, I actually like going for a walk and also, funnily enough, writing letters,' he told me. 'I write a lot – therapeutic exercise which helps to retain my sanity!'[27]

The late Queen, though a busy letter-writer, preferred to unwind in front of the television, especially the *BBC News at Six* and dramas such as *Downton Abbey* and *Midsomer Murders*. Not only was she heard swapping notes on the latter with fellow fan and German Chancellor Angela Merkel, but one official recalls the evening she spotted *Midsomer* star John Nettles at a Palace reception: 'She went straight up to him and said: "There have been an awful lot of murders in your village".'[28] Enthralled at a young age by the post-war production of *Oklahoma!*, Elizabeth II always loved West End musicals and Hollywood. Hence Barack Obama's decision to seat her between himself and the actor Tom Hanks at his banquet for the Queen (at the US embassy residence) during his 2011 state visit.

Charles III prefers radio, especially BBC Radio 4, and also audiobooks. His other forms of 'therapy' include gardening, classical music, opera and theatre (especially Shakespeare). When the Royal Family wanted to celebrate the late Queen's seventieth birthday in 1996, they arranged a small dinner cooked by Michel and Albert Roux.* When Charles III (then still Prince of Wales) reached the same age, there was an evening of Shakespeare, poetry and music at Buckingham Palace. Introducing the birthday boy, the compere, Stephen Fry, declared: 'Everyone who works in the field of arts in this country knows how extremely and freakishly lucky we are that our Prince of Wales has such a genuine knowledge of, unquenchable thirst for, and understanding of the role and value of the arts in our public and our personal lives.' Four and a half years later, Fry could be heard voicing identical thoughts in a loud stage whisper to fellow guests in the North Transept of Westminster Abbey as the King arrived for his Coronation.

---

* The dinner was due to take place at the Roux brothers' restaurant, the Waterside Inn at Bray. After word leaked out to the media, the dinner – sole, lamb and raspberry soufflé – was switched to Frogmore House in the grounds of Windsor Castle.

When asked what he would do if he could take a few days off being royal, the King has said he would like to immerse himself in art. 'In many ways it would be lovely to have a sabbatical and find out a bit more about the origins of the Royal Collection,' he told me some years ago, 'and do a bit more studying in Italy because it is always rather fun.'[29]

There is another form of relaxation which, say members of his team, is taking up more, not less, of his time since becoming King. That is his love of planting trees. 'It's become something of an obsession,' says one. 'Whenever someone asks where he is, we joke that he is probably tree-planting. Then it turns out that he is.' It is not just about leaving something for posterity. The King still has vivid childhood memories of the countryside covered in elm trees, particularly in Gloucestershire. He has talked of family trips to stay at Badminton House, seat of the Dukes of Beaufort, for the famous horse trials. When he made Gloucestershire his home in 1979, with the purchase of Highgrove, he was dismayed to find more than a hundred dead or dying elms on the estate and decided, in his words, to 'reclothe the landscape.'[30] These days, that mission to 'reclothe' now extends to the landscapes of all the royal estates, and at a brisk pace, too.

The King is in good physical shape. He has spent much of his life adhering to a short, daily exercise regime developed for the Royal Canadian Air Force and has inherited an iron self-discipline from his late parents when it comes to food and drink. Indeed, he has gone one step further, removing lunch from his daily routine on the basis that it is superfluous if one has had a decent breakfast. This can prove challenging for organizers of royal visits, who still need to factor in occasional refuelling points for other members of the entourage. The King is certainly not frugal when it comes to feeding his guests, though. If a formal luncheon is called for, he will sit down with everyone else. 'It can be a bit disconcerting,' says one house guest. 'You can be seated next to him, your food arrives and you are expected to tuck in while he sits there with an empty plate. But he's very nice about it.' When he does pick up a knife and fork, say friends, he eats sparingly and prefers fish to red meat. Left to his own devices, adds one, the King could exist quite happily for the rest of his days on a daily diet of 'something eggy with spinach.'*

His favourite form of physical recreation, apart from long walks and shovelling soil over tree roots, is skiing (an enthusiasm which he does not share with his wife). He has been a regular visitor to the Swiss resort of Klosters since he first took up the sport in 1978, staying with his friends Charles and Patty Palmer-Tomkinson, and he adores the relative privacy he enjoys there. The media have largely left him in peace of late, having covered family trips in previous years. One year, the photographers presented the Prince with a bright new ski suit in the hope of taking a picture of him in something other than the same two elderly outfits he had been wearing for as long as they could recall. The following day, they were both disappointed and amused to see the King, as ever, in his trusty grey one-piece while their colourful gift was being worn by his protection officer.

Several years ago, the village named its main cable car 'HRH The Prince of Wales' (and then renamed it 'King Charles III' in 2022). The King knows many of the locals by name. In 2018, they threw a party to mark the fortieth anniversary of his arrival with several emotional speeches thanking him for his loyalty. He

---

* The King's suggestion for an official dish to mark his crowning moment was 'Coronation Quiche', made with eggs, spinach, broad beans and tarragon. Though well-received it has yet to overtake its 1953 counterpart, 'Coronation Chicken', in the nation's affections.

replied with a speech full of love and gratitude not just for Klosters but for Switzerland, noting that it had been a Swiss surgeon who had inserted a Swiss plate in his arm after a serious riding accident in younger days. He joked that many centuries hence, when some archaeologist or revolutionary breaks into his tomb, all they will find is a pile of dust and a titanium plate saying 'Made in Switzerland'. It brought the house down.

A stylish and fearless skier, he has no qualms about tackling the hardest off-piste terrain, despite a narrow escape in 1988 when an avalanche killed his equerry, Hugh Lindsay, and seriously injured Patty Palmer-Tomkinson. However, he decided to forgo his usual week in the Alps in 2023. This was not just because even a small accident might have ruined his Coronation plans. It was also because the country was enduring a winter energy and economic crisis. The lasting reputational damage suffered by the King of Holland after taking his family on holiday to Greece in 2020, while new lockdown measures were coming in at home, is well-remembered at Buckingham Palace. 'Look at that disaster with the Dutch royals. They went to Greece and everyone was furious even though it was actually legal,' says a senior official. 'You could get the same reaction if, say, the King was at his farm in Romania and there was another Grenfell disaster.' There is every expectation that he will be back in Klosters one day, but only after careful consideration.

Nor has he entirely given up on another potentially hazardous pursuit. The King no longer rides at the breakneck speed he did in his younger days, whether as a polo player or as an amateur jockey. Yet he cherishes the memories. He still keeps

---

* The fire which destroyed the Grenfell Tower in North Kensington on 14 June 2017 cost seventy-two lives.

a picture of his favourite mare, Reflection, on his dressing-room table at Highgrove and has never forgotten Allibar, his much-loved steeple-chaser who carried him to a second-place finish at Ludlow but collapsed and died on the gallops at Lambourn in 1981.[31] These days, his riding is mainly ceremonial, though his calm control of the neurotic newcomer he rode during the 2023 Birthday Parade shows he has lost none of his skill.

His sporting tastes reflect a fondness for speed, as does his driving, according to those who have shared a car with him. 'He is fast but he is actually a very good driver, unlike his father,' says one who has travelled with them both, and still shudders at the memory of careering off an Aberdeenshire road with the Duke of Edinburgh at the wheel.

That the King has a temper is well known among staff and family who have been on the receiving end. Occasionally, signs of impatience and irritation spill over in public – famously so when having problems with his pen in the days after his accession (something which he has since joked about himself). His critics sometimes accuse him of being an old fuss-pot with a propensity to whinge. 'He does whinge from time to time, like we all do,' says one who worked with him for many years, 'but the interesting thing is he only whinges about small things that don't matter. It's never about the things that really do matter.'

That attention to the smaller details is also an asset. An elderly close friend of Elizabeth II, who had not been well enough to attend her funeral or service of committal, had watched it all on television at home. A few days later, she was astonished to receive a delivery of flowers with a personal note from the King saying how sorry he was that she had not been able to be there. Just a fortnight before the Coronation, the Australian comedian and writer Barry Humphries was seriously ill in hospital in Sydney.* The creator of Dame Edna Everage was suddenly handed the phone and told that the King (who had checked the time difference) was on the line.[32] Cabinet Minister Penny Mordaunt, whose prominent role (and striking blue outfit) as the sword-wielding Lord President of the Council drew much comment during the Coronation, was struck by a moment at the end of the service. 'He was very kind to me when he left the abbey – after going through all of that and what he had to do. He took the time to turn to me, as I was doing the final guard of honour, and said: "You look great, you know". He's got many qualities. When you meet him, you get an impression of kindness.'

His old university friend, Lord Chartres, points out that the occasional flash of temper is hardly surprising, given the stifling and often stilted bonhomie of the average engagement. 'The two problems facing royalty are trust and the anodyne, genial statement. You've just got to be so damned nice to everybody all the time and everybody is nice and genial back to you,' he says. 'But geniality kills in the end. And being royal, you also don't know who to trust. Yet you can't spend your whole life in suspicion, always thinking: "What do they want?" That's one of the reasons why Queen Camilla is so marvellous. She can be robust in her views and that allows him to relax. When things go wrong and you have to keep being nice, you need an intimate who can talk you down.'[33]

Those who once argued that the future King Charles III would need to be a carbon copy of his mother are now realizing that this will not be the case. Nor should it be, as the Princess Royal is the first to point out: 'People are different.'

The King is unquestionably his own man. However, he knows

---

* Humphries died two days later.

that the success of the longest reign in history depended on the loyalty of others, notably himself. Now that it is his turn, he will hope for the same in return. 'I'm his closest in age and, you know, we don't always agree,' says the Princess Royal. 'But we both understand what is important about the monarchy. We both agree on that. It's understanding that the team has to pull together to make it work.'

Chapter Two

Queen Camilla

Rishi Sunak was worried he was perhaps being just a little too loud at the Balmoral dinner table. It was his first visit to the monarch's Highland retreat, following the traditional invitation for the prime minister of the day (plus spouse) to spend a weekend there. As the houseparty sat down for cheese soufflé followed by turbot, Sunak was delighted to find himself next to Queen Camilla. She was certainly not worried about the noise, however, since she was equally responsible for it herself.

'She was an incredible host,' he recalls. 'My overarching memory of the weekend is just laughing a lot with her. She's uproariously funny and it was hard during the dinner to try and keep the volume down because we were having such a good time.'

As newcomers to the royal workforce soon discover, the mood within the Household will invariably be sunnier, or a difficult decision can be marginally less problematic, when the Queen is around. It is also accepted that if the change of reign has been testing for the King, it has been even more so for the Queen. The Royal Family say so themselves. 'For Queen Camilla, it's been much more difficult in every way, partly not having had the same level of preparation,' says the

Princess Royal. 'But her understanding of her role and how much difference it makes to the King has been absolutely outstanding. And [there is] no doubt that made the difference for him throughout the process. I'm sure lots of people do say to her what a difference she's made, but that is really true. I mean, I've known her a long time off and on and I think she's been incredibly generous and understanding.'[1]

'Obviously for him, it was always going to be,' says Annabel Elliot, Queen Camilla's younger sister. 'But I think she's transitioned beautifully, actually. I mean, I sometimes look at her and I can't really believe it.'

There is still a nervousness within the royal machine as staff and friends of the institution adjust to a different monarch, finding out what the new boss likes and, more importantly, dislikes. 'It's inevitable. It has happened with every new court since time immemorial,' says one old friend of the family. 'With the late Queen, people knew exactly where they stood. If they made a mistake or something went wrong, they knew how it would go down with her and whether it mattered. That inspired confidence. Now, people are worried about upsetting the King. They know he can get very cross about quite minor things and they have yet to find out how he will react in certain situations. At the same time, they know that Queen Camilla is a strong voice of common sense in that regard.'[2]

One trustee of an overseas charity, of which the former Prince of Wales was patron, recalls two very different royal visits. 'He came on his own some years ago and there was so much fuss from him and his staff that everyone was left wondering whether it had been worth the effort,' says the trustee. 'Then he came back a few years later with Camilla. It could not have gone any better. He was a changed man. She's a great asset.'[3]

She has never had any wish to limit his great passions, be it inner-city regeneration or Romanian wildflower meadows. She will gladly wave him off to a night at the Royal Opera House or the Royal Shakespeare Company in Stratford and curl up on the sofa to enjoy a good television drama (she is closer to the late Queen than to her husband in that regard). She is a lover of ballet but, equally, enjoys mainstream pop music like the Rolling Stones (she has been to one of their concerts) and ABBA. Shortly before Christmas 2022, few of those in the audience at London's virtual reality ABBA Voyage show noticed the real Dancing Queen as she and her grandchildren gyrated in the aisles along with everyone else.

It is unlikely that she would ever lure the King there, or even want to. She might, occasionally, try to open his eyes to interests which had failed to grab his attention in the past, horse racing being a case in point. As a couple, they are, however, both very happy to indulge each other's pet habits, such as compulsive window-opening in the case of the King. 'There's a constant battle about it,' says Annabel Elliot. 'He will have opened it. She will creep in behind and shut it. So there's a lot of: "Oh, darling, you shut the window." "Yes, I have, because we're all freezing." So a lot of banter goes on.' If the King usually wins on that front, says his sister-in-law, Queen Camilla 'wins most other things'. She certainly does not follow his example when it comes to eating in the middle of the day. 'She does have a bit of lunch. She'll be furious with me but she is not as disciplined as he is about eating or drinking. She might have that extra glass or that extra biscuit or whatever,' Annabel Elliot reveals.

Queen Camilla's greatest strength, however, is not what she may or may not encourage the King to do or to enjoy. It is the simple fact that she is an intrinsically cheerful character who lifts the mood around her and, more importantly, around him. A happy monarch makes for a happy court.

'She has got a great twinkle and it comes out very readily,' says the Marchioness of Lansdowne, one of her oldest friends. 'It puts people at their ease very quickly. And I think that's a great gift to have. She knows when to wink at a bishop, but when not to – which I think is a rather endearing quality.'[4]

She is not above winking at the regulars of the royal press corps, too, from time to time, especially when she senses that they might need cheering up. 'That was a load of b*******, but that woman is a diamond,' declares one weary Fleet Street tabloid photographer after a shambolic event in the pouring rain during the 2023 state visit to Germany. The press have been waiting for the best part of an hour to see the King and Queen pay their respects at Hamburg's 'Final Parting' monument to the children of the *Kindertransport*.* A combination of bad weather and nervous local officials has meant that the scene is merely a jumble of VIP umbrellas obscuring every face. Queen Camilla soon realizes the problem and gently parts the ways to ensure a clear line of vision between the photographers and the royal couple. It was never going to be a great photograph. Amid the rain and the chaos, it is not going to show the Queen in a particularly flattering light either. However, her actions ensure that the photographers have something to send to their editors (including another shot of the King in his T-Rex/C-Rex tie). All the members of the media 'pack' have similar anecdotes to tell about her; how she will ask after someone who has been taken ill or check if journalists are getting what they need on a challenging tour. There is

---

* The *Kindertransport* network enabled 10,000 Jewish children to escape Nazi Germany for a new life in Britain.

nothing feigned or strategic. She is palpably what one old hand calls 'a good egg'. Journalist Angela Levin was tickled by her upbeat remark to the press at the end of a busy Middle Eastern tour in 2021. 'I'm a lot older now,' said the future Queen, 'but to quote Richard Ingrams [former editor of *Private Eye* and *The Oldie*], I like to think we've still got a "snap in our celery".' It's such a good expression!'[5]

Given some of the treatment which she had to endure from the press in between her two marriages, and especially after the death of Diana, Princess of Wales, she could well be forgiven an icy wariness towards the media in all its forms. Yet, she remains a no-nonsense advocate for a free press, with a track record to prove it. Invited to address Fleet Street editors at the London Press Club awards in 2011, she bowled over her audience with a speech celebrating the 'pivotal' role of journalists in scrutinizing 'all aspects of our society', royalty included. 'I believe freedom of expression, so long as it doesn't contravene the law, or offend others, to be at the heart of our democratic system,' she declared. 'But just one note of caution: in our right to speak freely, please let us not become too politically correct, because, surely, political correctness is as severe a form of censorship as any.' Though welcomed as a neutral plea for calm and common sense at the time, they are words which could probably not be uttered today, at least not without drawing the monarchy into the sort of febrile 'cancel culture' slanging match from which it tries to steer clear. 'Political correctness' has long since been overtaken by much more aggressive terminology on either side of any given debate. Nonetheless, Queen Camilla has her red lines and they will not be crossed.

In February 2023, she invited many of Britain's top authors and publishers to an event to mark the evolution of her fast-growing online book club, The Queen's Reading Room, into a new charity. The timing was exquisite. In the very same week, it had been revealed that the children's classics of Roald Dahl were to be re-edited to remove any inappropriate language which might offend twenty-first-century readers.* Writers from across the political spectrum were appalled that Augustus Gloop, for example, could no longer be described as 'fat' or that Mrs Twit could no longer be 'ugly'. With many of those writers assembled at her Clarence House reception, the Queen delivered a rousing speech of thanks to authors everywhere. 'Please remain true to your calling,' she urged them, 'unimpeded by those who may wish to curb the freedom of your expression or impose limits on your imagination.' To cheers and cries of 'hear, hear', the Queen added with a knowing smile: 'Enough said.' There was no backlash afterwards. She had not mentioned Dahl by name. Yet here was clear recognition that a member of the Royal Family had voiced precisely what the vast majority of the public (and the literary world) felt on the subject – without labouring the point. The following day, the penitent publishers announced that they would, after all, continue to print Dahl in unexpurgated form. Queen Camilla had not been planning to wade in to a live issue. Not for the first or last time, however, a spot of well-aimed common sense had touched a nerve.

During official engagements, the Queen will be one of those keeping an eye on the clock. She will certainly be the only one prodding the King in the small of the back as she did during a tour of Liverpool a few days before the Coronation. The royal couple had come to open the venue for the 2023 Eurovision

---

* Dahl's publishers, Puffin, wanted to make hundreds of amendments to his children's stories to remove 'offensive' words like 'flabby' and 'hag'. The writer Sir Salman Rushdie called it 'absurd censorship'.

Song Contest and the King, as often happens, was running over time as he chatted to the backstage crew. A nudge from a sharp corner of Queen Camilla's handbag provided the requisite prompt to move him on to their next part of this engagement, an interview with a team from the BBC children's programme *Blue Peter*. The show has been running for so long that the royal couple could both recall watching it in their youth. 'They were always making things out of loo rolls,' Queen Camilla recalled, instantly raising a few smiles. At which point, a ten-year-old boy had a question about the upcoming coronation: 'What are you most looking forward to?' The late Duke of Edinburgh always had a quick response to this line of questioning. Asked in April 2002 what he was most looking forward to about the Queen's Golden Jubilee celebrations, planned for June and July, he shot back: 'August.'[6] Though Queen Camilla might have been tempted to say something similar, she instantly had a happier response: 'Seeing the crowds.'

Fiona Lansdowne attributes her easy charm in formal situations to the Queen's parents: 'It was a wonderfully old-fashioned sort of fifties childhood. A very happy, very lovely, stable home. They learned really early on really good manners and how to behave.' Her younger sister, Annabel Elliot, is adamant that their 'wonderful – really wonderful' upbringing underpins the Queen's approach to almost everything: 'We grew up in the fifties and when life was very different, very free. I think we were incredibly lucky. Both our parents were very, very close with no kind of "green baize door" life or anything like that.* No nanny. My mother looked after us.

---

* The green baize door, in well-to-do homes, was the divide between the servants' quarters and the rest of the house (with the baize acting as sound-proofing).

Obviously between three children, there was quite a lot of squabbling or whatever but we were jolly lucky. We were brought up not in a liberal way, but our parents trusted us.'[7]

Other children, says Annabel Elliot, loved the unstuffy atmosphere chez Shand. 'Recently, one of my friends said: "You have absolutely no idea what it was like coming to your house. We always felt that both your parents took such an interest in us and loved you all so much". Because a lot of people grew up in a very different way – with quite distant parents. I do think that when I think back to other houses, that I went to. I wanted to be at home because it was always such fun.' Little wonder that Queen Camilla, when discussing her childhood with Gyles Brandreth, has described it as 'perfect in every way.'[8]

Camilla Shand was born in London on 17 July 1947 and grew up between family homes in East Sussex and London. Her father, Major Bruce Shand, a much-decorated army officer, had a post-war career in the wine trade. Her mother, the Hon. Rosalind Cubitt, the daughter of the 3rd Lord Ashcombe, was closely involved in local charities when not raising Camilla and her younger siblings, Annabel, born in 1949, and Mark, in 1951. Rosalind's charitable work extended far beyond energetic fundraising among the county set. After the use of the pregnancy drug Thalidomide led to the birth of thousands of children with severe deformities in the late fifties and early sixties, she trained as a nurse to help care for those affected.

Camilla and Annabel were always close. 'We were pretty well always together,' Annabel recalls. 'She was a much better rider, better at sport and all that. So I remember being very proud of her, seeing her winning these competitions and whatever. But, you know, we were both quite strong characters and we've always laughed a lot.'[9] Spared boarding school, 'Milla' left her London day school at sixteen, attended a Swiss finishing school and spent six months learning French in Paris. By the late 1960s, she was juggling the debutante party circuit with secretarial work as a receptionist and office assistant. Remembered among her peer group for being popular, pretty, confident and also kind-hearted, she was introduced to the Prince of Wales in 1971. It was not, as is often stated, at a polo match, but at the flat of the Prince's university friend and confidante, Lucia Santa Cruz, the daughter of the Chilean ambassador to London. A short romance later ensued until the Prince was sent away on a long Royal Navy deployment in 1973. Camilla then accepted a proposal of marriage from her previous suitor, Andrew Parker Bowles, a major in the Blues & Royals. They were married later that year with several members of the Royal Family, including the Queen Mother – an old friend of the groom's family – in the congregation.

The Parker Bowleses moved to Wiltshire, where Camilla loved country life and cut a fearless figure with the local hunts. Two children were born, Tom and Laura, while Andrew's military career went from strength to strength. He was decorated for bravery while demobilizing guerilla armies during the countdown to independence in Rhodesia/Zimbabwe in 1980. When the Prince of Wales married Lady Diana Spencer in 1981, Lieutenant Colonel Parker Bowles (he had been promoted the previous year) was the commanding officer of the Household Cavalry escort. A year later, his regiment was the target of one of the IRA's most infamous mainland bombings when the Blues & Royals were blown up as they rode through Hyde Park.* As

---

* The blast killed four soldiers and five horses. Seven bandsmen of the Royal Green Jackets were killed in a separate blast in Regent's Park two hours later. Elizabeth II telephoned Andrew Parker Bowles that evening and told him: 'It's the most ghastly day of my life.'

the colonel's wife, Camilla fully understood the importance of regimental family structures in times of trouble. The 'PBs' were often guests at royal occasions. The marriage would not last, however, and by the early 1990s it was coming to an end. It was, as friends would say, 'one of those things', and it was not a bitter parting. The couple remain on very amicable terms (to this day, they speak to each other several times a week). At the same time, the Prince and Princess of Wales were in the process of separating, too. In 1994, as previously noted, the Prince acknowledged on television that he had resumed his relationship with his former girlfriend of more than twenty years ago, after his marriage had 'irretrievably broken down'. Two years later, Charles and Diana were divorced, too. Multiple factors were in play, as in the collapse of almost any marriage, but many commentators laid the blame squarely at Camilla's door.

Despite the incessant (and, at times, brutal) media interest in their rejuvenated relationship and the barbs of hostile commentators, the Prince and Camilla remained devoted to each other through it all, culminating in their marriage at Windsor in 2005. A civil wedding at Windsor town hall was followed by a service of blessing (officially 'of prayer and dedication') at St George's Chapel. The Queen, who had attended the latter but not the former, later made a warm racing-themed speech of congratulation at the reception, welcoming her son and daughter-in-law to life's 'winners' enclosure'. Though she might now be Princess of Wales, the former Mrs Parker Bowles never used the title and was very happy to be styled as HRH The Duchess of Cornwall. Mindful that a significant minority of his prospective subjects might be unready for a monarch married to a divorcee, the Palace let it be known that, come a change of reign, she would be known as the Princess Consort. At an age when her contemporaries were all winding down, she was entering an entirely new way of life, setting up an extensive portfolio of charitable interests, often in areas with no previous royal patronage, like the campaign against domestic violence towards women. As one member of staff recalls, she was happy to be 'edgy – but not controversial'.[10] She liked to be a hands-on patron, too, regularly standing up in the middle of charity receptions to deliver very much more than a few words of welcome. In February 2022, on the seventieth anniversary of Elizabeth II's accession to the throne, the then monarch stated publicly that it was her 'sincere wish', after her own demise, that 'Camilla will be known as Queen Consort'. By this point, the country had moved on, too. A large majority of people could see that the Prince's second marriage – which had comfortably outlasted his first – was happy and secure. They saw no problem with granting the Queen her 'sincere wish' when the time came.

One reason for the public's ready acceptance was a clear recognition that Queen Camilla had never been terribly interested in titles in the first place. 'She never wants to do anyone down or be on the front page. People sense she wouldn't care what she was called except for the fact it matters a great deal to the King,' says one long-serving ex-courtier.[11]

Family and friends were amused that it took quite some time before the new Queen would even respond to her new status. Passing references or memos or questions to 'Her Majesty' would meet with blank looks until it suddenly dawned that they were referring to her.

It goes back to childhood, her sister notes: 'Obviously, she takes her role very seriously, but we were brought up not to be centre stage and whatever. So I think that is very much part of what makes her what she is.' Humour, self-deprecation and jokes had simply been part of growing up. As children, Camilla and Annabel were not allowed to sit next to each other in church. 'One of us would start to laugh – disastrous,' the younger sister recalls. 'It's gone on all through our lives – though not on Coronation Day.'[12] To this day, Annabel finds it near impossible to follow certain aspects of royal etiquette. 'I find it very hard to curtsey to her,' she says. 'And call her "Your Majesty"? That I can't do.'

Back in the days when it seemed there was no question of the Duchess becoming Queen, her family gave her the nickname 'Lorraine' (as in the French *la reine*). 'She always saw the funny side of that – even if Prince Charles did not,' says a friend.[13]

Her small office, like that of the late Duke of Edinburgh, is regarded as a happy ship, with plenty of laughter and very little turnover of staff. Since becoming Duchess of Cornwall in 2005, she has usually had two private secretaries running the show (one senior and one junior). Yet over nearly two decades, there have been just five in total, and one of those only left because she was emigrating.

However, just as the aura has changed around the King since his accession – as it might do with anyone elevated to prime minister or president – so Queen Camilla is now viewed in a new light. Even her friends have noticed it. One recalls her first post-accession appearance at racing's Cheltenham Festival, a boisterous event which she has always loved. 'She's been coming for years but there was just a very different atmosphere as she walked into the room as Queen,' says one. 'It was more of a respectful hush.' Another admits that, for the first time in her life, she had an unexpected feeling of nervousness before meeting her old friend in her new incarnation for the first time. The same friends were also reminded of an inner toughness that they had seldom seen since the dark days of the 1990s. Since the Sussexes' departure from the United Kingdom, Queen Camilla has found herself cast as the 'dangerous' villain of the piece by Prince Harry.[14] 'With her on the way to being Queen Consort, there was gonna be people or bodies left in the street,' he told the USA's *60 Minutes*.[15] For her part, Queen Camilla was content to let it pass. There was to be no selective briefing on the matter, no 'friends' given the nod to voice sadness or disappointment or set the record straight. After nearly two decades as a member of the Royal Family, she works on the basis that the public have a pretty good idea of what they are getting. Her response to noises off from California would be business as usual – with a smile and without a word.

Those organizations which embraced her (and she them) in the early days of her royal life are now thrilled to be represented by the new Queen, among them her first regiment. She became Royal Colonel of 4th Battalion The Rifles at its creation in 2007. She was in close contact all through the regiment's bloody first tour of duty in Iraq, especially with the families of the bereaved and wounded. She would visit the latter at the military hospital, Headley Court, and discreetly follow their progress. A lasting bond was forged. All those earlier years of marriage to an army officer, through some bleak regimental moments, stood her in good stead. On the battalion's return, just before Christmas, she came to the homecoming parade for the men of 4 Rifles, including a tearful Rifleman Stephen Vause. Severely injured in a mortar attack and unable to speak, he asked his commanding officer to read out a message, thanking her for all her letters, adding: 'One day I will be able to drink the whisky you gave me and toast your good health.'[16] It was the same story when 4 Rifles went on to suffer similar losses in Afghanistan. Captain Harry Parker, who had lost two legs to an IED,[*] met

---

[*] Improvised explosive device

her in hospital and gave her one of his paintings. She, in turn, steered him towards the Royal Drawing School (created by the Prince of Wales). Parker credits his former Royal Colonel with kickstarting his post-military career as both an artist and author.[17]

In 2020, she took part in the Duke of Edinburgh's very last public engagement when she formally succeeded him as overall Colonel-in-Chief of The Rifles. The regiment was delighted when two of her pages at the Coronation were dressed in the regimental livery. The army has been a central part of her life for so long and in so many ways that a trumpet blast can make her misty-eyed. As she told me: 'There's something about buglers . . . military music always makes me cry.'[18]

It is why, a month after the Coronation, she is thrilled to be welcoming a delegation from the Royal Lancers to Clarence House. The late Queen had become Colonel-in-Chief of the 16th/5th Lancers on her twenty-first birthday and had stuck with them through assorted amalgamations until her death. Now, as part of the reshuffle of honorary positions at the start of the new reign, Queen Camilla is taking Elizabeth II's place as the Royal Lancers' new Colonel-in-Chief. This is an especially proud moment as this was her father's regiment. The feeling is mutual, for Major Bruce Shand remains something of a regimental legend himself. 'That whole generation were revered in the regiment,' says Colonel Richard Charrington. 'But for Major Shand to win two MCs – for a relatively junior officer, that is very distinguished.'

Shand won his first Military Cross when his regiment was among those ordered to cover the British retreat to Dunkirk in 1940. Two years later, in the North African desert, he won a bar to his MC (a second MC) after his squadron of armoured cars helped a hundred Indian troops and twenty vehicles escape a surprise enemy advance. Soon afterwards, he was seriously wounded leading his squadron against what turned out to be Rommel's headquarters (the bullet that passed through his cheek killed his radio operator). Shand was captured and spent the rest of the war in captivity, passing much of the time immersed in books.

Today's Royal Lancers are still taught the way in which Bruce Shand kept the enemy at bay across that river on the way to Dunkirk. Lieutenant Colonel Will Richmond tells the Queen that every newly commissioned officer is given a copy of her father's memoir, *Previous Engagements*, as required regimental reading. 'It tells them that the enduring thing is your relationship with your soldiers,' explains Richmond. This is music to the ears of Queen Camilla, since it involves the two things closest to her heart, family and literature. 'We had to force him to write this book,' she says, fondly recalling her father's reticence. 'His first and only book. Wherever he is today, he'd be thrilled that I am taking on this role.'

The rest of the family feel exactly the same. 'It would have meant everything to him. I hope, somewhere, he is looking down and he can see Camilla where she is,' says Annabel Elliot, adding that her sister would 'never have asked' for such an honour but, equally, would have been 'disappointed' had it passed her by.

The Queen has also organized a lively extra event here at Clarence House following on from her meeting with the regiment's top brass. Three days from now, it will be the one hundredth birthday of Michael de Burgh. He served in the Lancers with Queen Camilla's father and has been chosen to receive the Buchan Medal, a special regimental prize for exemplary Lancers. The Queen wants to give him a birthday party, too. De Burgh remembers Major Shand well – 'a great man;

some people just are,' he recalls – since he, too, was seriously wounded in the Second World War. The Clarence House drawing room is filled with his children and grandchildren plus assorted Lancers past and present. 'Can I congratulate you on becoming the mother of the regiment,' says de Burgh, as he starts to stand up unsteadily from his wheelchair. The Queen cannily heads off a potential incident by instantly taking a seat next to him. 'I'm coming down so you don't have to get up,' she assures him, firm and mischievous in equal measure. And with that they just chat away over a glass of champagne, even swapping notes about wounds. De Burgh recalls his 'wretched bullet' and the Queen mentions the one which almost killed her father. She has two surprises in store. The Royal Chef, Mark Flanagan, suddenly appears with a large birthday cake for the guest of honour, who is nervous about cutting such a huge cake. 'We'll do it together,' the Queen reassures him, and they do. Then she hands de Burgh a copy of her father's book. He is genuinely thrilled. 'Oh! I've been asking where I can get a copy of this,' he says. He is even more delighted to see that she has signed it: 'Michael – with best wishes from the proud daughter of the author – Camilla.'

'I was lucky enough to have a father who was a fervent bibliophile and a brilliant storyteller,' she once explained. Annabel Elliot traces this back to their father's wartime experiences. 'He was quiet. My mother was an extrovert. He'd been a prisoner of war and, like so many of that generation, came back from the war wounded in different ways, probably mentally and physically, but he was kind, gentle, quite retiring,' she recalls. 'But he used to read to us from very early days. That's where the great love of reading [came from], certainly in my sister's case.'[19]

The Queen has channelled that inherited love of books and reading into what now makes up a substantial element of her public duties. None of it happened overnight. Rather it is an example of how to build a network of modern royal patronages in depth. It started in 2010. After plenty of homework and preliminary engagements, the then Duchess of Cornwall became patron of the National Literacy Trust, supporting its work to improve literacy at all levels. A year later, she succeeded the Duke of Edinburgh as patron of Book Trust, dedicated to getting children reading. In 2014, she became patron of the Queen's Commonwealth Essay Competition, the oldest international writing prize for schoolchildren, and, the following year, joined BBC Radio 2's Chris Evans to promote the station's annual 500 Words story competition for children. It set a new record in her first year with more than 120,000 entries. In 2018, she took over from the Queen as patron of the Royal Society of Literature. In each case, this was no mere titular involvement but a statement of intent.

By 2020, as Covid transformed every aspect of modern life, she began listing her favourite books on the internet and encouraging others to do the same. It became so popular that an online book club followed. Originally called the Duchess of Cornwall's Reading Room, its focus was very much on connecting books, authors and readers (and very much not on herself). In no time, it had more than 130,000 followers. With the pandemic over, she took on yet another literacy charity previously championed by the bibliophile Duke of Edinburgh. Book Aid International specializes in distributing books to poorer parts of the world, especially those within the Commonwealth. She accepted invitations to attend and even participate in some of Britain's top literary festivals, while directing the spotlight firmly towards the authors, not herself. One month after the Coronation, her book club – now in its new charitable form – organized a literary festival of its own for the first time. Held at Hampton Court Palace, it sold out. Meanwhile, on any regional visit or overseas tour, a strong book-related component will be worked into the programme. It all means that, more than thirteen years on from her initial involvement with the National Literacy Trust, Queen Camilla is now engaged across more aspects of the written word than almost anyone in public life. It is not trumpeted. She wears it lightly, in much the same way that her father liked to tell stories about anyone except himself (even his memoir omits his own heroism). Yet it is a remarkable achievement, one of which her husband is extremely proud. Whenever she holds a reception for one of her literary charities, he will invariably appear unannounced. It also begs the question of when Queen Camilla might follow her father and her husband and write a book herself.

Her long association with the campaign against domestic and sexual violence has followed a similar pattern. As Duchess of Cornwall, she was moved and disturbed by a visit to a Rape Crisis Centre in Croydon in 2010. Here was an issue, she felt, which might benefit from some gentle and judicious royal assistance. 'It wasn't somewhere you'd expect to find royalty but she wanted to do something,' says a staffer from those days.[20] Further meetings followed and the Duchess helped develop a project to ensure that every victim of every assault received a washbag full of toiletries after the trauma of medical examination. 'It was only a crumb of comfort for people at their lowest ebb but that can still make a difference,' says the official.

The Duchess became patron of SafeLives, a charity combatting domestic abuse, inspired by a 2016 meeting with Diana Parkes, whose daughter, Joanna, had been murdered by her ex-husband in 2010. There would be meetings and receptions at Clarence House and a royal appearance on the BBC's

Woman's Hour (with Parkes). Much of the Duchess's involvement in the sector would, self-evidently, be away from the media gaze, but there would be no stepping back following her elevation to Queen. Used sparingly, that spotlight can achieve remarkable results, such as a Buckingham Palace royal reception, in November 2022, dedicated to fighting this 'global pandemic' of abuse. It certainly qualified as 'edgy but not controversial'. Attended by victims of violence and campaigners, it also had an international line-up including three queens, a crown princess and several first ladies. Nor was it any coincidence that Queen Camilla's first solo engagement after the King's accession was to a domestic abuse unit in London.

Another core concern is loneliness among the elderly. If there is a theme running through all of the above, it is the importance of grass-roots volunteers to every cause. Indeed, as president of the Royal Voluntary Service, she helped to identify 500 'Coronation Champion' volunteers, all of whom received an invitation to a Palace garden party or the Coronation concert at Windsor.

Among Queen Camilla's more niche interests, there is yet another which she has inherited from her father. 'He worked in the wine trade, so very early on, unlike most English families, we had wine with our lunch and then some water,' says Annabel Elliot. 'So wine was a big thing in our lives – still is.' In 2011, the then Duchess of Cornwall became president of the UK Vineyards Association (at a time when English and Welsh wines had nothing like the reputation they enjoy now) and has been an enthusiastic promoter of home-grown varieties ever since. Although the Queen's own consumption is modest and the King's more modest still – he prefers a martini before dinner – the couple now have an even greater choice of wines since the monarch has become custodian of the Royal Cellars. 'The wine now is wonderful,' Annabel Elliot confirms. It wasn't too bad before, either.

Charles III

The Queen's late mother, Rosalind, has inspired her in other directions. As Camilla Parker Bowles, her very first charitable role, a full eight years before she was even married to the Prince of Wales, was to become a patron of the National Osteoporosis Society in 1997. She became president in 2001. Both her mother and grandmother had died suffering from this crippling bone disease and her involvement helped a small charity to gather momentum, attention and support. Like Queen Camilla's engagement with literacy, it has been a long and sustained relationship going far beyond public campaigning and fundraising (or even establishing a tie-in with the BBC's *Strictly Come Dancing*). As Duchess, she attended many international conferences on the disease, made numerous speeches and was delighted, in 2019, when the charity was renamed the Royal Osteoporosis Society. As with her other projects, it is a role which might tick along below the media radar for most of the time. She is, though, very conscious that she is part of a unit and that she has a unique platform which, when used sparingly, can give the whole team a lift. So, for example, in 2021, she gave an interview to the BBC's Gloria Hunniford to mark World Osteoporosis Day. Even while discussing the death of her mother and the disease which killed her, she still managed to impart her key message with a lightness of touch and elicit a smile. 'I think we all think we're immortal, don't we, when we're young,' she told Hunniford. 'I'd love to see more young people understanding about it, not just thinking: "poor old bats, we're going to get old and that's what's going to happen to us". But actually understanding what actually happens and how they can prevent it.'

As time goes on, old royal hands are increasingly reminded of another royal stalwart as they watch Queen Camilla in action. Her resolute determination not to be the star of the show but the supporting act, the cheerful adherence to the Churchillian doctrine of KBO,* the ability to inject a remedial note of levity into a stifling situation, the deep love of books and visceral attachment to the armed forces, the default use of plainspeak over jargon – they were all the hallmarks of the consort to the previous monarch.

The Duke of Edinburgh would always fill his diary with the late Queen's engagements before adding his own. Similarly, Queen Camilla will often allude to the King – humorously but also respectfully – as 'The Boss'. Shortly after the death of the Duke of Edinburgh, when still Duchess of Cornwall, she spoke of how much she had enjoyed his company and valued his advice: 'I saw the way he supported the Queen, not in a flashy sort of way but just by doing it quietly. I probably learned from him [that] you're there as, as a support – behind – but occasionally you have to put your oar in and just say: "Look, hang on a minute, I don't think that's quite right." You have to sometimes stick your head above the parapet.'[21]

To Queen Camilla, the Duke remains an exemplar not just to be remembered but followed. On any walkabout, like the Duke before her, she will be punctilious about holding back just enough to ensure that the focus is on the other side of the street. 'He was my father's generation. They were very special,' she has said. 'Some of them went through hell and they never made a fuss about it. They were the epitome of "go on, get on with it, never explain, never complain". I hate that generation going, because the next one is old things like me! They're a very difficult generation to live up to but I'm very proud and very pleased that I knew him.'[22]

Rosalind Shand also bequeathed something else to her daughter. It is a proper passion as well as a favourite form of

* Keep Buggering On

relaxation, and also happens to be something Queen Camilla shares with her husband: gardening. 'To have a King and Queen who really recognize, understand and know a lot about gardening is a great treat for us gardeners – gives us a great lift,' says the broadcaster, author and horticulturalist Alan Titchmarsh. 'If you leave behind your bit of earth better than it was before, then you've paid your rent.'[23] It is 8 June 2023, and Titchmarsh is waiting to greet Queen Camilla at London's Garden Museum where she is marking British Flowers Week, a celebration of all things home-grown. The museum, in a former church next to Lambeth Palace, is a favourite haunt. The King is its royal patron (it owns a delightful Eileen Hogan portrait of Prince Charles working next to a huge vase of flowers) and Titchmarsh is its president. 'It doesn't take much to get me back here,' Queen Camilla jokes as she inhales the scent of a hall bursting with displays of sweet peas, roses, foxtail lily, delphiniums, cat mint and much else.

Also waiting to welcome her is Shane Connolly, the royal florist. He led the team that filled Westminster Abbey with all-British flowers for the Coronation and the Queen wants to pass on her thanks to everyone involved. 'I didn't have a lot of chance to look at them [on the day] but have studied them very carefully since and they were absolutely wonderful,' she tells Connolly. He, in turn, thanks her and the King for being 'perfect, trusting' customers whose only pre-Coronation instructions had been to stick to local flowers, not imports, with no guarantees of what would be in bloom. 'You embraced that uncertainty in the knowledge that they would be beautiful anyway,' says Connolly.

Although she is now a member of the Royal Family, the Queen has retained the Wiltshire home where she moved after her divorce from Andrew Parker Bowles and is especially devoted to her garden there. Ray Mill is a bolthole from public life and a place which her children and grandchildren can treat as home. 'It is my refuge,' she told the writer Monty Don in 2022, 'the one place where I can be completely relaxed on my own terms.'[24] The garden covers twelve acres and includes rhododendrons, azaleas, roses, potted plants from her children's weddings, a large pond, two gnomes and a painted tiger. Shane Connolly describes it as 'utterly enchanting' and 'artless in the best possible way'. It is, he says, 'more relaxed' than Highgrove, not least because Ray Mill, unlike Highgrove, is not designed for large numbers of visitors. Here is an insight into the shared loves but different characters of Charles III and Queen Camilla. The former likes a certain thematic approach to his garden. Though it appears wild and naturalistic in places, one of his gardeners describes it as a 'set piece'. Ray Mill is more a place for family barbecues and children running around in bare feet, a place where Queen Camilla can be mistress of her own domain, as the King is at Highgrove. It is also a place where she can press the pause button on her royal existence for a moment – and where her immediate loved ones can reclaim their mother, grandmother, sister and aunt, as her sister explains: 'For the rest of the family, sometimes it seems totally surreal. But she has, thank goodness, her own downtime. She's a wonderful mother and grandmother. She's very, very hands on. All our children have grown up very much together. It's almost like one family so she's back to being her normal self when she's with all of us. I mean, she wouldn't get away with it otherwise! There's quite a bit of irreverence: "You're not the Queen to us", and so on. There's quite a lot of all that – thank God.'[25]

While older members of the family might have nicknamed her 'Lorraine', the younger ones have a different term of endearment for the Queen. It is one coined by her eldest grandson when he was a toddler: 'Ga-Ga'. 'It's not the most flattering of names but she hasn't tried to change it,' says her sister. 'She's "Ga-Ga" and I'm called "Guy-Guy" – a pair of mad old women! The children just think it's hilarious.'

Her family and friends continue to be impressed by the way she has adapted to her new role while still remaining the same Camilla they knew of old. 'It's obviously been a long journey, and I feel hugely proud of her – just looking back twenty years ago and how she has come through it,' says Annabel Elliot, mindful of a time when cruel headlines and often baseless gossip were a fact of life for her elder sister. 'She's an amazingly stoical, strong person. I'm not sure many people would have been so strong throughout it.' Annabel Elliot's only regret is that the parents and brother, to whom they were both so close, could not see this phase of Camilla's 'long journey.'

'I feel sad that I'm the only one of that age who has seen what happened in the end. You know, there were so many years of difficulties, and then to see this was just extraordinary. Being the Duchess of Cornwall was one thing. But I think suddenly stepping in to Her Late Majesty's shoes is a huge, huge jump and I'm amazed at how well she's adapted to it. I really am. People can see that she's not someone up "there", to be revered. She's an ordinary person who has gone through the same things we all have, and maybe that's reassuring to people in this day and age. She wasn't born and brought up to be Queen.'

There is a reminder of this just a few days before the Coronation. All the key players are assembled in the Buckingham Palace ballroom. A stage has been laid out to mirror the precise layout of the Coronation 'theatre' at the abbey. The Archbishop of Canterbury is rehearsing the moment when he will crown the Queen. Before he can do so, he has to seek a signal of approval from the King, who is, by now, sitting some distance away on the Throne Chair and deep in conversation with someone else. Things are already a little tense. The Archbishop has to interrupt, gently, shouting across the assembled company: 'If you don't nod or indicate, Sir, I can't crown Her Majesty.'

'Don't bother,' the Queen chips in. 'I'm very happy!'

Everyone laughs. Her joke helps to lighten the mood. Nerves are calmed. At the same time, though, no one doubts for a minute that she is also telling the truth.

Chapter Three

London Bridge

King Charles III succeeded to the throne at the wheel. To be more precise, he had just turned off the B976 onto the back drive of the Balmoral estate and was driving through a part of the world as dear and familiar to him as any, when he learned that he was now sovereign of the United Kingdom and fourteen other realms, covering a large part of the Earth's surface.

Schoolchildren are taught that the longest reign in British history began at a Kenyan watering hole; that Princess Elizabeth was watching wildlife from the branches of a giant fig tree when King George VI died in his sleep on 6 February 1952; that his dutiful daughter, having climbed up as a Princess, climbed down as Queen.

History will also record that, seven decades later, on the afternoon of 8 September 2022, her son and heir was on an unmarked Scottish country road, at the wheel of his car, when he was first addressed as 'Your Majesty'. He had been to visit the Queen at Balmoral Castle earlier in the day and had then spent a few hours at his nearby home, Birkhall, before returning to the castle.

In the manner of his late mother, he had climbed into the car as both Prince of Wales and Duke of Rothesay (his title when in Scotland). Twenty minutes later, he would climb out of it as King Charles III – with the new Queen at his side.

* * *

Just two days earlier, the world had seen images of a beaming Elizabeth II waving farewell to one prime minister and appointing a new one. During the long summer months of government inertia since the resignation of Boris Johnson as Conservative leader on 7 July, followed by a drawn-out battle to replace him, the Queen was attuned to the mounting sense that Britain was a rudderless nation. She saw it as her role to make the transfer of power and the resumption of government as swift and smooth as possible. It had even been her plan to travel down in the Royal Train and preside over the resignation of one prime minister and the appointment of another in London. 'She thought it was more appropriate than dragging two busy politicians up to Scotland and back with news helicopters following them all the way,' says a former Palace official.[1]

By late August, she had started to have a change of heart, as had her doctors. 'Although the plan had been for a return to London, she was asking if she might remain in Scotland,' says a senior official.[2] Her private secretary, Sir Edward Young, discussed the situation with the Royal Medical Household, led by Professor Sir Huw Thomas,[*] and also the Cabinet secretary, Simon Case, who, in turn, consulted the prime minister. All agreed that the politicians would have to come to her.

As expected, Liz Truss was declared the winner of the Conservative leadership race on 5 September. By now, plans were already in hand to fly both outgoing and incoming prime ministers to Balmoral the next morning in separate aircraft (a decision agreed in advance between Johnson and all the rival candidates; this was not going to be an easy trip for anyone).

---

[*] Professor of Gastro-Intestinal Genetics at Imperial College London, Sir Huw became Head of the Medical Household and Physician to Elizabeth II in 2014.

The choreography had been carefully mapped out by Sir Edward Young and Simon Case. 'There was a little bit of manoeuvring about what time of day it should be,' recalls one official. 'On the one hand, Boris's camp didn't want to leave London too early as they wanted his farewell speech to be on the morning news. The other candidates didn't want it to be too late as whoever is prime minister wants to hold that first Cabinet meeting the same day.' The action at Balmoral would all happen in the space of an hour at around lunchtime.

Johnson and Truss would each take a plane to Aberdeen and then a helicopter to Balmoral. The Scottish weather had other ideas. 'It was very, very bad weather,' Truss recalls. 'There was some question as to whether we'd be able to land at Aberdeen or not until they found a brief window in the cloud. So the helicopter idea was kiboshed.'[3] The Queen was deter-mined to greet both politicians with equal courtesy and be on her feet while she did so. Boris Johnson was an hour ahead of his successor and spent around fifteen minutes with the monarch. 'Given how ill she obviously was, how amazing it was that she be so bright and focused,' he recalled later.[4] The Queen had found Johnson an intriguing change from his punc-tilious predecessor, Theresa May. Within hours of being appointed prime minister in July 2019, he had let slip to colleagues that her first words to him had been: 'I don't know why anyone would want the job.' If it had been a flagrant breach of the confidentiality rules regarding audiences with the monarch, she was forgiving. When the Covid pandemic locked down the country the following year, the Queen was charac-teristically thoughtful after Johnson himself had ended up in intensive care. She told him he was welcome to use the gardens of Buckingham Palace for walks with his wife, Carrie, and baby son, Wilfred (the monarch herself was shielding at Windsor).

During one such walk, to Johnson's horror, Carrie's Jack Russell, Dilyn, attacked and killed a gosling near the palace pond. He decided that it would be best to say nothing at all, forgetting that nothing went unnoticed by the boss at Buckingham Palace. At their next encounter, the monarch nonchalantly talked about walking in the palace gardens before adding crisply: 'I gather Jack Russells don't go very well with goslings.' That was the end of the matter. Johnson, like all his prime ministerial predecessors going back to Winston Churchill, would learn that no time spent on homework prior to a royal audience was time wasted. At around the time that his government was embroiled in a lobbying scandal involving a healthcare company, Johnson came storming out of an audience with the Queen demanding: 'Why the hell did no one tell me that Randox sponsors the Grand National?'[5] Her views on Johnson's politics would go with her to the grave, but she was never censorious about his chaotic personal life. When he once confided in her that he had been troubled by a dream in which he was late for an audience, she immediately replied: 'Were you naked?'[6] She had heard it all before. 'The Queen had seen enough "yes" men come and go and he wasn't one of those,' says one who saw them both close at hand.

Minutes after the Queen had waved off Johnson for the last time, Liz Truss was ushered in. Once again, the Queen was keen to observe all the formalities. 'She stood up to greet me,' says Truss. 'She was clearly physically not very well but we talked for about twenty minutes. She was alert. I would say she was relieved that the thing had actually happened and that we were now moving things forward.'[7] At the end, the Queen invited the prime minister's husband, Hugh O'Leary, into the room and they exchanged 'pleasantries' about the prospect of family life at Downing Street. Within the hour, however, the new leader was on her way back to Aberdeen, to London and to a podium speech on the doorstep of Number 10. The Queen had one further leadership race to follow that day. Her filly, Love Affairs, was running in the 3.05 at Goodwood.

The Queen's health was already a matter of considerable concern in the upper reaches of government. Liz Truss remembers that, on her first day in Downing Street, one of the very first briefings she received was to talk her through Operation London Bridge, as plans for the Queen's funeral were known.[8] Back at Balmoral, staff recall that the Queen had seemed energized after the day's events, all the more so given that Love Affairs had triumphed at Goodwood. 'She was quite buzzy over pre-dinner drinks and talking about various prime ministers she had known,' says one of the party. 'But then she said she was going upstairs and would have dinner alone.' It was the last time most of her immediate household would ever see her. Even in familiar surroundings, the exertions of this, her most fundamental constitutional duty, had taken a greater toll than anyone had imagined.

The following morning, 7 September, the Queen's health had deteriorated. Fortunately, the Princess Royal, with a diary of engagements in Scotland, was in residence. 'It was purely serendipity that I was there,' she recalls. 'I'd been two days up on the West Coast and I was coming back, stayed the night and was going south.'[9] Also at the castle was the Princess's son, Peter Phillips, the Queen's eldest grandchild. He had come up to host some friends for a shooting party later in the week, though this had now been cancelled. The small houseparty included the duty lady-in-waiting, Susan Rhodes (married to the Queen's cousin, Simon Rhodes), the Queen's equerry, Lieutenant Colonel Tom White of the Royal Marines, and the Queen's senior dresser and confidante, Angela Kelly. Since being widowed the previous year, the Queen had come to appreciate Kelly's companionship and plain-speaking good humour more than ever. When the Queen said that she was planning to remain in bed all day, which was highly unusual even at this stage of her life, the local general practitioner, Dr Douglas Glass, was called.

After his visit, the Queen let it be known that she was still planning to appear, via video link, at the Privy Council meeting scheduled for that evening. Given the change of government, she knew that it would be a large and very important one with several new Cabinet ministers and counsellors to be sworn in. Palace officials made arrangements for an audio-only connection, in case the Queen wished to remain in her bedroom and conduct the meeting from there. George V, after all, had held a Privy Council meeting in his Sandringham bedroom, just hours before his death in 1936. So audio link it would be. Down in London, the connection to Balmoral was up and running with all those Privy Counsellors involved lined up outside the designated COBRA* conference room beneath Downing Street. At which point, with minutes to go, they were told that the Queen would be cancelling 'on medical advice'. 'Everyone had gathered for this Privy Council meeting. It was only cancelled at the time when it was meant to go ahead,' says Liz Truss. 'So people thought: "This isn't good news".'[10] Newly appointed as Lord President of the Council, Penny Mordaunt was preparing to lead her colleagues into the room for the first time. The memory of that evening is an emotional one: 'For me, that was testament to the depth of her devotion to her duty and us: the day before she passed, she was still trying to fulfil her obligations as sovereign, which I find incredible.'[11]

---

* Cabinet Office Briefing Room 'A'

By now, the Princess Royal was already speaking to her elder brother, who was at the opposite end of Scotland holding a series of charitable engagements at Dumfries House in Ayrshire. He had been receiving regular updates, anyway. 'I assume that he knew probably more than we did about our mother's health,' the Princess recalls.[12] A film crew from the American network NBC had just arrived at Dumfries House, led by Jenna Bush Hager,* who was preparing to interview the Duchess about her book club, The Duchess of Cornwall's Reading Room, the following day. Bush Hager remembers enjoying a 'wonderful' and 'joyful' conversation with the Prince over dinner while the Duchess was still trying to return from an engagement at the other end of the UK. She had been attending the filming of *Antiques Roadshow* beneath the great biospheres of St Austell's Eden Project but her scheduled flight up to Glasgow had been delayed into the evening. She was not yet to know it, but, as events would turn out, her engagement in Cornwall would actually be her last as Duchess of Cornwall.

There was no sign that the situation at Balmoral was about to worsen dramatically. Privately, however, Prince Charles needed to make a decision. Should he press on with business as usual or drop everything and head for Balmoral in the morning? It was not a simple choice. The Prince was well aware that the second option would set off alarms across government and the media as well as instantly disrupting the calm of Balmoral. He was mindful that there had been similar lapses in the Queen's health before. One official admits that, at one point, there had been a sudden downturn in her health towards the end of 2021. 'Those closest to her did think she might not see Christmas. When she did, there was then some

---

* Daughter of former US president George W. Bush.

doubt, later, about whether she might ever leave Sandringham,' says one.[13] Whereupon, the Queen was quickly back on her feet, albeit with the 'mobility issues' that were to dog her final year. 'Every family knows that awkward situation when people say their last goodbyes only to see their loved one up and about two weeks later,' adds the member of staff. 'That's very much harder when it's the Queen.' It was harder still with a monarch who was not just determined to keep going but also managing to look the part.

However, on the evening of 7 September, the situation felt different. The Princess Royal and the Prince's private secretary, Sir Clive Alderton, were advising him to be on standby. 'They were both saying to him: "Think how you would feel if you never said goodbye",' says one member of staff. 'Clive said that if it did turn out to be the wrong call, then they could blame it on him.' The following morning, the Princess Royal called again and told him to come at once. A helicopter was already on standby at Dumfries House, waiting to take the Duchess of Cornwall to engagements in other parts of Scotland – a Maggie's cancer support centre in Airdrie and the Great Tapestry of Scotland in Galashiels – before returning for her interview with Jenna Bush Hager. Suddenly, the pilot had a new emergency flight plan, leaving the Duchess's staff with a delicate task: they had to let Airdrie and Galashiels know that she was no longer coming, though they could not say why. The US film crew had just started to set up their equipment when they heard the first sound of rotor blades.

Shortly before 9.30 a.m., the royal couple climbed aboard the helicopter with a small team – Alderton plus the Duchess's deputy private secretary, Belinda Kim, and a protection officer. During the one-hour flight, the Prince immediately began re-reading his briefing papers on the initial phases of 'Operation

London Bridge! The two private secretaries were checking the basics, not least the whereabouts of black ties and mourning clothes (no sooner had Elizabeth II become Queen in Kenya in 1952 than her staff realized that all the requisite mourning clothes had travelled ahead and were already being loaded onto her ship in Mombasa).

As Alderton told staff later, he was dearly hoping that this would be an unnecessary trip and was half-expecting the Prince to land at Balmoral only to be greeted by the Queen on the doorstep, arms crossed, asking: 'What on earth do you think you are doing?' It was not to be.

Other members of the family had woken up to be told that the Queen's condition had not improved overnight. At breakfast time, her equerry, Lieutenant Colonel Tom White, contacted the Duke of Cambridge's private secretary, Jean-Christophe Gray, to say that the Queen had 'had a bad night' and that the Prince of Wales was on his way up to Balmoral. The Prince would be on the phone soon enough himself, suggesting to his sons and siblings that they should do the same. Shortly before 10.30, the Prince and the Duchess of Cornwall (still, formally, the Duke and Duchess of Rothesay in Scottish terms) touched down at Birkhall, their home on the Balmoral estate. Since they had not been expected, the usual cars from the royal car fleet had yet to arrive. They borrowed an elderly Land Rover from a member of staff and the small party set off immediately for Balmoral Castle with the Prince at the wheel.[14] They were greeted at the door by the Princess Royal, who escorted the Prince and Duchess straight to the Queen's bedroom, where they spent an hour at her side. By now, there had been another visit from Dr Glass, who shared the latest situation with Sir Huw Thomas and the medical team. It was clear that this was no false alarm.

At the same time, the Queen seemed stable. According to one of those involved, the consensus was 'a day or two, not an hour or two.' The Queen's private secretary decided that the time had come to prepare a statement since the rumour mills of social media would soon be at work. The Royal Household needed to be on the front foot. Sir Edward Young would not include any clinical details. The mere act of issuing a statement would have a similar impact to the bulletin which Lord Dawson of Penn, doctor to George V, released at 9.25 p.m. on the night of 20 January 1936: 'The King's life is moving peacefully towards its close.' News of the King's death had come just one and a half hours later.

All through the reign of Elizabeth II, the Palace had maintained a strict policy of not commenting on the Queen's health unless she was either undergoing a hospital procedure or missing a public engagement.* It was also well known that the Queen, like the late Duke of Edinburgh, did not like a queue of family well-wishers flocking to her bedside when she was ill. So the combined effect of an enigmatic statement and news that members of the family were heading for Balmoral would be ample confirmation of the gravity of the situation.

At 12.32, a Buckingham Palace bulletin was emailed to every major news organization in Britain. It stated simply: 'Following further evaluation this morning, The Queen's doctors are concerned for Her Majesty's health and have recommended she remain under medical supervision. The Queen remains comfortable and at Balmoral.' Superficially, such a statement could have applied to a dose of flu. Sure enough, though, right across Whitehall, throughout the armed forces and in national newsrooms, the message was clear.

---

* In February 2022, the Palace also confirmed that the Queen had been diagnosed with Covid.

By now, the Prince of Wales had already advised all the immediate family to make plans, with the emphasis on the Queen's two younger children, the Duke of York and the Earl of Wessex, who were still in Berkshire. The Prince of Wales did not want the castle overrun with all the Queen's grandchildren, let alone the great-grandchildren. However, the monarchy observes its own codes, even in the most trying personal situations. Those in the direct line of succession were to be contacted, too. That meant Prince William and Prince Harry. The Prince of Wales called them both.

Prince William's team immediately liaised with the offices of his two royal uncles. By 12.30 p.m., the Royal Air Force had arranged for an Envoy IV to fly them from RAF Northolt to Aberdeen. Take-off would be at 2.30 p.m.[*] Fortuitously, the California-based Duke and Duchess of Sussex also happened to be in Britain for a few days of charity engagements. In his explosive, bestselling memoir, *Spare*, Prince Harry says that he received a call from his father warning him that the Queen's health had 'taken a turn'. 'I immediately texted Willy to ask whether he and Kate were flying up. If so, when? And how? No response,' writes Harry. 'Meg and I looked at flight options.'[15]

Clearly, Prince William did not regard this as the appropriate moment for the intensely difficult conversation he needed to have with his brother. A few weeks earlier, it had been widely reported that Prince Harry was delaying publication of his upcoming memoir until after the Queen's death. There could be little scope for dialogue until its contents were known. The

---

[*] The Envoy IV is one of two Dassault 900LX aircraft now flying with 32 (Royal) Squadron. They have replaced the trusty BAe 146 which carried the Queen and her family for more than thirty-five years.

sense of reckless betrayal following the Sussexes' interview with Oprah Winfrey the year before, and its vague, unanswerable half-claims of institutional racism and hostility towards Meghan, still lingered. 'Some of the family were probably ready to give him a piece of their mind,' says one of those in the midst of this fast-moving turn of events.[16] Friends of the Sussexes have argued that the couple's actions paled before those of the Duke of York; that it was Prince Andrew's self-inflicted downfall, following his association with paedophile financier Jeffrey Epstein and the subsequent court proceedings against the Duke, which had upset the Queen most of all. 'Andrew was the weak one,' says a close family friend. 'She was always protecting him and all that certainly took its toll on her health at the end.' Even so, this was not the moment for such arguments.

This was also precisely the sort of situation when different royal teams talk to one another to get things done. Had the Sussexes been that keen to share a flight, they could have asked their staff to contact Prince William's staff. 'They had all the numbers,' says a senior Kensington Palace aide, who is adamant that there was no call from the Sussexes' camp that morning.

Harry and Meghan had decided to make their own travel arrangements and announced that they would be cancelling their remaining engagements for the day. At which point, Harry writes in his memoir, he received another call from his father to say that he should come on his own. We can easily imagine the dread with which the Prince of Wales approached that call. The Sussexes' capacity for taking offence was well known and everyone was conscious that any conversation could end up in the public domain – as, indeed, this one did three months later. In his book, Harry says his father was 'nonsensical and disrespectful' as he explained that he did not want Meghan coming to Balmoral. 'I wasn't having it. *Don't ever speak about my wife that way,'* is the Duke's record of his response.[17] At which point, his father explained that he simply didn't want lots of people in the house and that the Duchess of Cambridge was not coming, either. 'Then that's all you needed to say,' Harry replied. To which one family friend asks: why, then, did Harry even feel the need to put this in his book? The Prince of Wales had enough to think about without worrying where the Sussexes' next grievance was coming from. By now, Harry had missed all available flights to Aberdeen. He set about chartering his own plane. It was just as well that he did not know the real reason for the Duchess of Cambridge's absence from Balmoral. She had certainly not been asked to stay away. Rather, it was the start of a new term at a new school for all three children. George, Charlotte and Louis had already been for their induction day at Lambrook, their Berkshire preparatory school, the previous morning, 7 September. It was the Duchess who had decided that one parent should be with the children on such an important day. As one royal aide acknowledges: 'It was by luck rather than judgement, but it made it a lot easier to tell Harry he was coming alone.'[18]

It should be remembered that, even at this point, no one knew quite how bad the situation had become. There was serious, mounting alarm, yet there was no panic. 'At that stage, people were still thinking in terms of days rather than hours – let alone an hour or two,' says one member of staff.[19] Hence the fact that the Prince of Wales and the Duchess of Cornwall decided to leave the Queen to rest for a while under the alternating gaze of the Princess Royal and Angela Kelly, while the Rev. Kenneth MacKenzie, long-serving Church of Scotland minister at Crathie church and chaplain to the Queen, read to her from her Bible.

Sir Edward Young set about finishing off some paperwork.

At one point, he even thought about heading back to his digs at Craigowan Lodge for a late bite of lunch. There was no question of Her Majesty being left alone, but nor had the time come for constant medical supervision. Nonetheless, Dr Glass decided not to return to his medical centre at Ballater, eight miles away. Rather, he would base himself for the rest of the day at the small surgery attached to the castle, which he used for appointments with estate workers and their families. It was just as well.

Shortly after 3 p.m., Dr Glass received an urgent call to come upstairs. At the same time, the Princess Royal called Birkhall to summon the Prince immediately. He was out in the grounds of Birkhall, gathering mushrooms – and his thoughts – while the Duchess had gone for a short walk. They both swiftly jumped back into the Land Rover with their team, the Prince of Wales at the wheel once again. He took the South Deeside Road before turning off onto the side road heading into the estate and down the back drive. It was now a question of minutes. By the time Dr Glass had reached the Queen's bedroom, she appeared to have stopped breathing – though only a doctor could say so for sure. Sir Edward Young waited outside. Finally, the doctor emerged to confirm the worst. He agreed a time of death with Sir Edward Young, who recorded the sequence of events in an internal memo for posterity. It is now lodged in the Royal Archives. It reads: 'Dougie [Glass] in at 3.25. Very peaceful. In her sleep. Slipped away. Old age. Death has to be registered in Scotland. Agree 3.10 p.m. She wouldn't have been aware of anything. No pain.'[20]

Sir Edward's first duty was to alert the new monarch before anyone else could do so. He immediately contacted Birkhall, only to be told that the Prince of Wales and the Duchess of Cornwall (as they had now ceased to be) were already on their way back to Balmoral Castle. There was no question of waiting for the car to pull up at Balmoral. 'Imagine if there had been some accident or a hold-up along the way,' explains one senior official.[21] 'It was essential that the new King was told before anyone else.' The Balmoral switchboard worked its way through a list of mobile phone numbers. Signals can be sketchy in rural Aberdeenshire and staff would usually have phones on silent while in attendance. Finally, one of the party felt their phone vibrating, recognized the number, answered and handed the phone to Sir Clive. He had to ask his boss to pull over and stop. Sir Edward Young was now on the other end of the phone. The new monarch knew exactly what was coming next. There, on the side of the road, at the age of seventy-three, he was addressed as 'Your Majesty' for the first time. No further explanation was needed. 'We're nearly there,' the King replied softly. As the Queen and the other occupants of the car immediately voiced their condolences, the King put the Land Rover in gear and drove on.[22] Minutes later, the new King was pulling up in front of the castle, where the Princess Royal was waiting to greet her brother as King. A few moments earlier, she had been visibly distressed. One senior member of staff had felt, on the spur of the moment, that it was simply the natural and polite thing to do to offer her a brief hug. There then followed a wry smile. 'That is the last time that's going to happen,' the Princess said firmly.[23]

At this stage, there was no formal greeting from all the staff. Only the immediate household, led by Sir Edward Young, were fully aware of the situation. He had rushed through the castle to be present at the grand entrance to greet the new King and Queen in person. There is still a time-honoured, constitutional ritual to this moment. As the Queen's most senior official, Sir Edward Young had been scrupulous about being fully prepared. Colleagues recall that, for many months, he had avoided foreign travel or even Tube trains for fear of losing a mobile phone signal and being uncontactable at the gravest moment of his professional life. Having offered his condolences, Sir Edward asked the King the first question which confronts each new monarch: under which name would he reign? Many years before, there had been some speculation that he might honour and emulate his grandfather, George VI (previously 'Bertie'), by choosing 'George'. To no one's surprise, least of all Sir Edward's, he would remain 'Charles'. Sir Edward then proceeded to the second formality. He asked the new King for permission to call the prime minister.

On her third day in charge of the country, Liz Truss had just finished making a statement to the Commons about the impending rise in fuel prices when it was clear that the situation was changing rapidly at Balmoral. 'It was while I was in Parliament doing the energy announcement that Nadhim Zahawi [newly installed as Chancellor of the Duchy of Lancaster] came in with a piece of paper saying that things were bad,' says Truss.[24] From the Commons, she went to join a conference call with other G7 leaders, including the US president, Joe Biden. It was underway when she received a further message from the Cabinet secretary, Simon Case. He had been in contact with Balmoral and things seemed to be deteriorating rapidly. The PM told her fellow G7 leaders that she needed to leave the discussion. 'They all knew what was happening,' she says. Her small team had just adjourned to the flat above Downing Street when Case received Sir Edward's solemn call to inform the new prime minister that the country had a new monarch.

Accompanied by Queen Camilla, the King went straight to his mother's bedside to say his farewells and steel himself for the vast undertaking now before him. Questions would shortly start coming thick and fast; officials would need swift decisions on matters great and small. Sir Edward Young was greatly touched, say colleagues, that the King's first response was to put his arm on his shoulder. As one recalls: 'He told Edward, "I know how much you'll miss her and how loyal you were to her". It should have been the other way round with Edward consoling him but that's the way it is when you are the monarch. Then the King asked him if he would stay on for the time being.'[25]

The first task for Charles III was to break the news personally to the rest of the family who had yet to arrive. It might have been an intensely personal matter but there was still a strict process to be observed, starting with the new heir to the throne. One member of staff recalls the surreal moment as the King picked up the phone to ask the switchboard to put a call through to his elder son. He began by saying: 'Hello, it's . . .' At which point, he paused momentarily. He did not, at that very moment, want to tell the switchboard that he was now King before telling his own son. Besides, if there was no reply to his call, who was to say how quickly word might leak out around the royal network? So, he continued: '. . . it's me.' Fortunately, the switchboard operator recognized the voice.[26]

The King was, thus, able to break the news to Prince William, the Duke of York and the Earl of Wessex as they were driving from Aberdeen airport to the castle. The Queen's beloved niece, Lady Sarah Chatto, who was nearby, arrived in tears. Because the sudden decline and death of the Queen had been so much swifter than anyone had expected, nearly all the members of the Royal Family had been unable to say a formal goodbye. The Duke of Sussex was still in the air and out of contact. In his memoir, *Spare*, he suggests that no one had told him and that he was reduced to learning the news from the BBC website as the plane was landing. Not exactly. A member of the Palace staff says that the King had been urgently trying to make contact with his younger son. 'There were repeated attempts to get through to him but no calls were going through because Harry was airborne,' says the official.[27]

However, some things were already working to the new King's advantage. By chance, both of Sir Edward Young's deputies (the Queen always had three private secretaries) were at Balmoral on that day because of a scheduled staff change-over. All three were staying at nearby Craigowan Lodge on the estate. The King had his core team, led by Sir Clive Alderton, on site, too. It meant that, at this most critical of moments, all the key officials were in the same place. 'Edward and Clive were good friends so it helped to make things work very smoothly right away,' says one member of staff, adding: 'Alderton was always going to take over as principal once his boss became King. But Edward knows about running a head of state machine, which was why one of the first things the King did was to ask him to stay on for the transition.'

'The impressive thing was the way the whole thing just clicked in. All the necessary people were there and, fortunately, there weren't crowds of others who would need to be consoled. Everyone was very calm, taking their lead from the King, who instantly took charge,' says one member of the team. 'I think being at Balmoral made it easier to think. Clive and Edward could just sit down with a cup of tea and go through it all.'[28]

Down in London, staff reacted swiftly. Within minutes of the Queen's death, the Master of the Household, Vice Admiral Sir Tony Johnstone-Burt, had issued the order to suspend all Buckingham Palace refurbishment work. He sent the project managers home and commandeered their open-plan office as the funeral operations room. In France, the Archbishop of Canterbury, Justin Welby, was enjoying the last few days of his holiday in Normandy. Having seen the BBC website carrying news of the Palace's earlier statement, he and his wife had already started making rapid plans to return. 'I was rushing round the house. We guessed that the late Queen was very, very near the end of her life. My head was just spinning with the thought that this is the real thing,' the Archbishop recalls. 'And the phone went. It was my chief of staff. He just said: "London Bridge".'[29] The Welbys packed their car and set off for home overnight, the Archbishop mentally preparing for his first public duty: addressing BBC Radio 4's *Thought for the Day* the following morning.

At Balmoral Castle, Sir Edward Young and Sir Clive Alderton had to conduct the first piece of official business of the new reign. Upon her accession in 1952, the first document requiring the signature of the new twenty-five-year-old monarch concerned a case of buggery in the ranks. Charles III was faced with the pressing need to appoint a new Commissioner of the Metropolitan Police. Sir Mark Rowley was duly approved – and would be sworn in the following week.

As the two sets of private secretaries sat down to start mapping out the days ahead, a footman appeared with a red box. It was the last one that had gone up to the Queen before her death. Like all red boxes, it had just two keys, one for the monarch and the other for her duty private secretary. Over more than seventy years, these boxes had brought her the most sensitive state secrets and Cabinet minutes. They had contained the most exciting and the dreariest correspondence with every sort of document for inspection or approval. The Queen had always gone through it all, whatever the contents, and then sent it back again. Here, then, was the last completed homework of the longest reign in history.

Sir Edward Young and his colleagues were not sure what to expect as he turned the lock. Inside, he found that Elizabeth

II had left a sealed letter to the Prince of Wales and a private letter to himself. We will probably never know what they said. However, it is clear enough that the Queen had known that the end was imminent and had planned accordingly. Were they final instructions or final farewells? Or both? Though this was on an entirely different scale, there were echoes of her mother's final hours. As she lay dying at Royal Lodge in 2002, the Queen Mother had directed her page, Leslie Chappell, to a drawer in a desk. There, he had found a pair of cufflinks for himself and a brooch for her dresser, Jacqui Meakin.[30] Elizabeth II had been completing her own last pieces of unfinished business. There was something else in that red box, too. It was the long-list of candidates to fill vacancies in the ranks of the Order of Merit, together with notes on each one, so that the Queen could approve her own shortlist. Created by Edward VII to honour the most distinguished service in public life across the Commonwealth, the OM had always been in the gift of the monarch, not the government, with membership limited to twenty-four at any one time. Its roll call stretches from Florence Nightingale, J. M. Barrie and Winston Churchill to Nelson Mandela, Margaret Thatcher and Sir David Attenborough. The Queen had always taken it extremely seriously. The paperwork had gone up to her two days before so that she could go through the notes and tick her choices. Here it was, completed and returned for Sir Edward to make the necessary arrangements. It was the last document ever handled by Queen Elizabeth II. Even on her deathbed, there had been work to do.* And she had done it.

---

* The six new members of the Order of Merit, including the Canadian historian Prof Margaret Macmillan, the author and broadcaster Baroness (Floella) Benjamin, and the geneticist Sir Paul Nurse, were formally appointed by the King two months later.

Chapter Four

D-Day

As day turned to evening, the King was still calmly fielding and making calls while responding to a growing list of requests for a decision. One of the most urgent tasks was a simple binary one: when to press the start button for London Bridge? Immediately? Or the following day? In the finest military traditions, thousands of pages of careful planning still needed an official start time, to be known as D or D-Day. Everything else would then fall into place, including the King's first address to the nation (scheduled for D-Day itself) and his Accession Council at St James's Palace (scheduled for 'D+1'). If D-Day was that same day, he would have to return to London instantly. However, the longer the delay in making the formal announcement of the Queen's death, the stronger the case for moving 'D' to the following day. Working side by side, the late Queen's private secretary, Sir Edward Young, and the new King's private secretary, Sir Clive Alderton, calculated that it would make no difference to the date of the funeral. For, if they announced D-Day immediately, the planning grid would put the funeral on a Sunday, and royal funerals are never held on the Sabbath. It would then, in any case, have to be moved to the Monday. So, holding 'D' back by a day would make no difference to the eventual plan. It would still result in the funeral taking place on the same date at the end, but give everyone a little more breathing space at the start. Although most of those who needed to know were already well aware of the situation, the news had yet to be broadcast to the world because there was still a list of family members who had to be informed. Finally, at 6.30 p.m., a statement was issued in the name of 'Royal Communications' (effectively a joint announcement by both the team of the King and that of the late Queen). It said simply: 'The Queen died peacefully at Balmoral this afternoon. The King and The Queen Consort will remain at Balmoral this evening and will return to London tomorrow.' By now, in the words of one official, 'it was too late to head off to the races'.[1] The King had already confirmed the decision that 'D' would wait until morning.

He and his family could also have a night to gather their thoughts. One of the King's first decisions was to ask the Princess Royal to take charge of the houseparty now rapidly expanding at Balmoral Castle. He himself needed time and space to prepare for the unstoppable chain of events which would start to unfold from first light when 'D' commenced. By now, his regular fleet of cars had relocated from Dumfries House and others were on their way up from London. The King also agreed with his sister that she would escort their mother's coffin down to Edinburgh in the days ahead, accompanied by her husband, Sir Tim Laurence. Like Queen Camilla, the Princess Royal would prove indispensable (and indefatigable) over the next few days. She was there when Prince Harry eventually arrived. She greeted him with a hug and escorted him up to the Queen's bedroom, where he was left to pay his respects to his late grandmother. 'I whispered to her that I hoped she was happy, that I hoped she was with Grandpa,' he wrote in his memoir.[2] Harry then joined the family dinner downstairs, noting that, for once, there were no bagpipes at the end of the meal, out of respect for the late Queen. Neither his father nor his brother was there, however.

The King and Queen Camilla had, by now, already returned to Birkhall. There, they were greeted by the first of many sights which would leave them utterly lost for words during those early days of the reign. As their car pulled up, their entire staff were lined up to greet them in full mourning livery.

That evening, the couple would be joined for dinner by the new Prince of Wales, who would also stay at Birkhall. The King needed to have vital but discreet discussions with his elder son. In years gone by, such a moment would automatically have included his younger son, too. But not any more. This was clearly not an occasion for an opening up of hearts and minds with Prince Harry, particularly if he was still taking notes for his forthcoming book. Charles III needed a clear head and no distractions. 'You have to remember, losing a second parent is a big thing, becoming the senior generation is a big thing and there he was, expected to console the whole country,' reflects one of his staff. The following day would set the tone and frame expectations for his whole reign.

Six hundred miles to the south, the postponement of 'D-Day' came as a blessed relief for those preparing one of the most complex ceremonial exercises ever attempted in British history. They now had an extra night to play with before London Bridge would begin in earnest.

A record-breaking monarch of Elizabeth II's global stature was never going to depart this life with one funeral. She would need three. There would be a formal state funeral at Westminster Abbey, drawing the greatest gathering of world leaders ever seen on British soil. This would be followed by the 'service of committal', effectively a second funeral, in front of family friends and loved ones, at St George's Chapel, Windsor, at the end of which the coffin would be lowered into the Royal Vault. After that, there would be a third service, a tiny private burial beneath the King George VI Memorial Chapel alongside the Queen's parents and Prince Philip. This was entirely new territory for the Royal Household. There had been no funeral for a monarch in Westminster Abbey since George II was buried there in 1760. Subsequent monarchs had all elected to have their funerals at St George's. No one had opted for both. They had all predated the jet engine, however. The late Queen had been the first 'world' monarch, travelling further and meeting more people than all her predecessors combined. Now that same world was making plans to come to London, wanting and expecting to pay its respects. By using the abbey as well as Windsor, the organizers could treble the number of mourners.

The man responsible for both the main funeral services was Edward Fitzalan-Howard, 18th Duke of Norfolk. He had been preparing for this moment for twenty years, since automatically becoming hereditary Earl Marshal on the death of his father in 2002. One of the great officers of state, the Earl Marshal is responsible for organizing the three most exalted categories of state occasion: state funerals, state openings of Parliament and coronations. Eddie Norfolk, as he is known to all at Westminster and the Palace, had received a call the day before from Sir Edward Young. 'He had always promised not to call unless it was serious,' recalls the Duke, adding that Sir Edward would say whether it would be a case of days or months. On this occasion, it was the former. 'He said it was definitely not a month. But we didn't know it would be the next day. The Queen had been so brave and must have been in a lot of pain when she met Liz Truss. But she wanted to do the right thing to the end and she went quicker than everyone thought.' His next thought was to call his right-hand man on all things ceremonial, Assistant Comptroller Major Andrew Chatburn, to ensure that he was on standby. 'And I got my white shirts ready.'[3]

Eddie Norfolk had been more attentive to the task in hand than his predecessor, his father, Miles Norfolk. All those who took part in the 1952 state funeral of George VI or the 1953 Coronation of Elizabeth II would recall the imposing figure of Bernard Norfolk. He died in 1975, leaving four daughters but no son, whereupon the dukedom crossed to his second cousin, Miles. A career soldier and veteran of Dunkirk, he was much prouder of his Military Cross for gallantry in Italy than of his rank as England's premier Duke. Miles Norfolk's strategy for regal funeral-planning was to organize it through the heralds at the College of Arms.

'After several years, the best they could come up with for my father was five sides of foolscap, which didn't say much,' says his son and heir, Eddie Norfolk. 'I used to say to my father that we needed better plans. He'd just say: "Look, I organized the Guards' crossing of the Rhine in twenty-four hours in wartime. I can organize a funeral".' A former Palace private secretary also recalls receiving the same 'Rhine crossing' assurances when he gently broached the subject of succession with Miles Norfolk. In the end, the late Duke's talents for amphibious military operations would never be tested on a state funeral. 'My father instinctively knew that, being a lot older than the Queen, this would not happen on his watch,' says his son, adding: 'He would, though, have done a brilliant job if required.' Miles Norfolk's one lasting contribution to the plans for the death of the sovereign was a name. 'There was a debate over what to call it,' says Eddie Norfolk. 'My father happened to see a picture of London Bridge hanging on the wall. So he said:

Charles III

"Let's call it London Bridge."[4]* After succeeding to the dukedom at the age of forty-five, Eddie Norfolk sought the advice of Lieutenant Colonel Anthony Mather, ex-Guards, ex-Palace and something of a ceremonial guru. As a young officer, he had commanded the bearer party at Churchill's funeral in 1965. Andrew Parker Bowles remembers his talents ahead of the funeral of Earl Mountbatten in 1979, when Mather helped him knock the Royal Navy bearer party into shape with just days to go. 'He really knew what he was doing,' says Parker Bowles.[5] Together with Norfolk, Mather worked out that one funeral would not be enough for the Queen. There would need to be a separate service of committal at Windsor. 'Anthony's plan was for two services and lots of processions,' says Norfolk, adding that he cleared the proposals with the Queen and the late Duke of Edinburgh. Finally, in 2015, the two men took their blueprint up to the then Prince of Wales. 'Anthony and I flew up to Birkhall and the Prince kindly gave us two and a half hours in the drawing room,' says Norfolk. 'I said: "Can we sign off now, Sir?" and he said "Yes". Now we had a plan. It would have been awful if all this had happened and he had said, "I don't want to do that".'

Operation London Bridge would draw heavily on the expertise of the Household Division, the five regiments of Foot Guards and two regiments of cavalry who are responsible for royal ceremonial. However, all the armed forces would play a part.

---

* Following the adoption of 'London Bridge', the funeral plans for all senior members of the family were given a 'bridge' designation – 'Forth Bridge' for Prince Philip, 'Tay Bridge' for the Queen Mother and so on. The former Comptroller, Sir Malcolm Ross, also proposed that plans for the funeral of ex-prime minister Margaret Thatcher should be codenamed 'Iron Bridge'. It was vetoed by a very senior police officer who told him: 'Only royals get bridges.'

In total, 5,949 British military personnel would be deployed over those ten days, 4,416 of them from the army. Running the whole show would be Major General Chris Ghika, commanding officer of the Household Division and GOC (General Officer Commanding) London District. Alongside him would be the man sometimes described as the most powerful (or most terrifying) figure in the British Army, the Garrison Sergeant Major London District. At ceremonial events, even royalty and the most senior generals defer to the man known universally as 'Garrison', GSM 'Vern' Stokes. On the morning of 8 September, he was attending a meeting with the BBC at Windsor Castle, to discuss plans for a range of possible ceremonial events. Suddenly, word came through from Balmoral that they should all return to London. Stokes immediately called his commanding officer. 'I was at my desk when I took a call from the Garrison Sergeant Major who said: "Is everything calm at headquarters?"' Ghika recalls.[6] If it had been calm up to that point, it certainly was no longer. London District's 'core group' was immediately summoned to start planning. 'The main thing was that we had a head start,' says Stokes.[7]

By the time that the Palace had formally announced the death of the Queen at 6.30 p.m., Ghika's team were well ahead of events, already poring over computer screens and hefty files of planning notes. They were extremely grateful for the D-Day decision and the extra night's leeway it gave them. The general remembers, very clearly, what was at the top of his list: 'Serial Number One was the death gun salute in Hyde Park by the King's Troop.' Another early priority was tracking down certain key players, not least the bearer party. It was not simply a case of picking eight, strong soldiers to carry the Queen's coffin. The monarch's bearer party is, by long tradition, drawn from Queen's Company, Grenadier Guards, which always maintains a designated team allotted for the task at any given time. But where were they? On patrol with Kurdish trainees in Iraq, it transpired. Where were the state trumpeters? 'There are always supposed to be four state trumpeters in the country at any one time,' says Stokes. 'For some reason, it turned out that all eight of them were on a plane to Canada for a tour with the Household Cavalry Band. We told all of them, including the band, to turn straight round and come back.' The Band of the Irish Guards, meanwhile, were swiftly summoned home from a tour of the Netherlands.

London had been a strange blend of misery and celebration for the first twenty-four hours of the new reign. Outside Buckingham Palace, some stood in tears, while others wanted to raise a toast. A convoy of black taxis stood in silent tribute. Vern Stokes made a swift change to the front of the palace, where the Royal Logistic Corps had been making a guest appearance mounting the Guard. There was nothing wrong with their drill but, at a time like this, the world needed and expected to see red tunics and bearskins outside royal head-quarters. The Royal Logistic Corps marched off and the Coldstream Guards quickly took up their positions.

At moments such as these, the public mood can swing swiftly one way or another, as the Queen had discovered in those febrile days after the death of Diana, Princess of Wales. The King was determined to avoid any similar sort of vacuum. Up at Birkhall, he sat down with Prince William to watch what amounted to a training video prepared by his private secretary, Sir Clive Alderton, for this very moment. Soon after taking over in 2015, Alderton had staged a mock-up of the most complicated feature of the first few days of a reign, the Accession Council, and had it filmed. As the rest of the Royal Family dined solemnly at Balmoral, the new King and new

Prince of Wales were a few miles away viewing Alderton's film on an office computer.[8]

D-Day dawned on 9 September, an eerie calm hanging over the Balmoral estate. Overnight, the Palace's head of ceremonial, Alexander de Montfort, had arrived at the castle to brief all the members of the Royal Family on the details of their roles in the days ahead. At Birkhall, the King and Queen went through the final plans for one of the biggest days of both their lives. Queen Camilla later told a friend that she had found it very hard to sleep, as she contemplated what lay ahead, and had been awake until 4 a.m.[9]

Around the globe, world leaders were delivering their tributes. Among the most stirring was that of President Emmanuel Macron of France. 'Elizabeth II mastered our language, loved our culture and touched our hearts,' he declared, in English, in his address to the people of the United Kingdom. 'To you, she was your Queen. To us, she was *the* Queen.' By late morning, the royal couple were on the way to Aberdeen airport for the flight to RAF Northolt in west London. Usually, their staff would sit alongside them, talking them through whatever would be happening on landing. This time, they moved to the front of the plane to give the pair space to think and read through their hefty briefing packs in private. Both the King's sons were making their own ways back to London – separately – while the rest of the family, still at Balmoral, attended a short service of contemplation and prayer at Crathie church.

The King had two imperatives: to show that he was very much in charge, and to broadcast to the nation. 'When most people have a loss, they get a few days off work. But it's the opposite with a monarch,' observes one of the team who travelled with the couple. Those in the royal party that day still have emotive memories of the reactions as the royal car made its way off the A40 and through central London. 'You had people who weren't waiting to see him but were just going about their business in multicultural London. Usually when they see a royal, people gawp or gasp or nudge each other,' says one of those in the royal entourage. 'This time, they were bowing. The Queen was very touched by the sight of a vicar standing by the side of the road shouting: "God save the King!" One or two saluted. There was a soberness to it; a real feeling that somehow, through the ether, the country was right behind him.'[10] This was all intensely moving for the King and Queen. So too, say those in the royal party, was the simple sight of billboards along the A40 not only showing photographs of the Queen, but also her dates. 'It was the addition of the final year "1926–2022" which suddenly hit you. I'm not a weepy sort of person but that really did hit home,' says a senior member of the Royal Household. 'We were all quite choked.'[11]

At the palace, the crowds were already so substantial that police had created a human one-way system for flower-bearers. The King asked the chauffeur to stop the car outside the gates. The moment that he opened the door, something unexpected happened. As the crowd burst into 'God Save the King', which felt strange enough, the King made straight for a line of tearful onlookers, hand outstretched. However, the first in the line did not want a mere handshake. 'Can I hug you?' she asked. 'Of course,' the King replied. The Queen later told friends of her abiding memories of people spontaneously bursting into the national anthem and of a woman clasping her hands and saying: 'Look after him for us.' 'I will,' the Queen replied, doing her level best to check her emotions. 'I promise.'[12]

As they walked through the palace gates, under the arch and across the quadrangle to the State Entrance, they saw all the

London-based staff lined up in the Grand Hall. As at Birkhall, all were in black ties and black liveries.

Soon afterwards, Sir Clive Alderton summoned the staff together for a briefing. He had been struck by the woman who had given the King a hug. To him, this was a moment that crystallized the change of reign. No one would have asked the late Queen for 'a hug' in a similar situation (and nor would they have received one if they had). If that was a reflection of her age and generation, so this moment summed up the style of Charles III. 'Clive mentioned what had happened with this hug,' recalls one of his team. 'He said: "This reign will have an informal formality to it." That was his phrase. The last reign had been formal, and rightly so, but this one would have "an informal formality". Then Clive lightened the mood, adding: "I wish I could take the credit for him hugging this woman!"'[13]

That evening, Charles III addressed the country with a speech he had been carefully drafting and redrafting throughout the day. His pre-prepared text was largely consigned to the waste-paper basket. He wanted this to be fresh. Queen Camilla was with him, as she had been all day. She positioned herself in a corner of the Blue Drawing Room so that she could see the King, but he could not see her. 'She knew the whole thing would set her off – as indeed it did,' says one who was present. 'But she didn't want to set him off.' He would end up doing the whole thing in one take but it was recorded twice just to be on the safe side.

'Throughout her life, Her Majesty the Queen – my beloved mother – was an inspiration and example to me and to all my family,' he began, 'and we owe her the most heartfelt debt any family can owe to their mother. Queen Elizabeth's was a life well lived; a promise with destiny kept, and she is mourned most deeply in her passing. That promise of lifelong service I renew to you all today.'

In just under ten minutes, he paid tribute to his 'darling wife', announced that the Duke and Duchess of Cambridge would now be Prince and Princess of Wales and spoke of 'my love for Harry and Meghan as they continue to build their lives overseas'. He acknowledged that he could no longer 'give so much of my time and energies to the charities and issues for which I care so deeply'. Coming full circle back to the late Queen, he concluded with a line from his beloved Shakespeare (from *Hamlet*, in fact). It was one which would resonate again and again through the days ahead: 'To my darling mama, as you begin your last great journey to join my dear late papa, I want simply to say this: thank you. Thank you for your love and devotion to our family and to the family of nations you have served so diligently all these years. May "flights of angels sing thee to thy rest".'

Even his most consistent critics had to concede that this had been precisely what the nation had wanted and needed to hear. The King had caught the mood. A YouGov poll conducted two days later revealed that an astonishing 94 per cent of the country thought it had been a 'good' speech while 73 per cent believed that he was providing 'good leadership'.[14] A majority also felt the same about the Queen Consort (as Queen Camilla would be known in those early months of the reign). In the event, it was the first take of the King's address that was broadcast to the world shortly afterwards. It could well be argued that a speech of such clear constitutional significance should have been shown to the prime minister in advance. However, Downing Street officials neither sought a copy nor, interestingly, did it occur to the King's officials to send them one. After more than half a century in public life, the monarch was in no need of ministerial 'advice' at a moment like this, whatever the conventions.

By now, all over the world, members of the armed forces were making tracks. One Life Guards officer had to cut short his honeymoon. Many old soldiers were on the move, too. Brigadier James Stopford, late of the Irish Guards and now a member of the sovereign's ceremonial bodyguard, the Honourable Corps of Gentlemen at Arms, was in Corfu at the wedding of his daughter, Izzie. He was on his feet delivering his father-of-the-bride speech when the incessant vibrations on his mobile phone alerted him to an urgent message: 'You are commanded to return to the United Kingdom immediately to attend to your duties for Her Late Majesty's Funeral.' He concluded his speech with toasts to the bride and groom, to the late Queen and to the King, before taking the next plane home.[15]

That evening, St Paul's Cathedral held the first major service of thanksgiving – and, with it, its first recital (in more than seventy years) of 'God Save the King'. Other congregations were doing the same all over the country. At Malmesbury Abbey in Wiltshire, hundreds had gathered on the afternoon of D-Day for the memorial service in honour of the Earl of Suffolk and Berkshire. The late peer had wanted to conclude with the strains of ABBA. In light of royal events, the family decided that 'God Save the King' would be more appropriate.[16]

Back at Balmoral, Dr Dougie Glass had already signed the death certificate, attributing the death of the Queen to 'old age'. It would be registered by the Princess Royal the following week and published a fortnight later. There had been no such certificate for any previous monarch because English law rules that monarchs are pronounced dead by the Privy Council, not by the medical profession. In 1952, there had been a great panic after the King's local doctor in Norfolk, Dr Ansell, had done what he thought was the correct thing and issued a certificate for George VI at Sandringham. He was immediately ordered to destroy it by both the Queen's private secretary and by the government. Sir Austin Strutt of the Home Office then wrote to senior officials, for future reference, reminding them that it was only Scottish law which required a death certificate for the sovereign. 'I don't think it necessary even to envisage the possibility that many, many, years ahead, The Queen may die North of the Border,' he wrote.[17] A brilliant civil servant in many ways, Strutt could not have been more wrong on this point.

In fact, Charles III and his officials were more than happy to break with tradition and release a formal death notice. 'It meant that we could get it stated, officially, that the Queen had died of "old age",' says one official.[18] 'We wanted it out there. Otherwise, there would have been endless social media speculation about a "cover-up".' The precise cause of death, says a close friend of the family, will never be known simply because the Queen had been suffering from multiple conditions in her final year.* 'She had come to realize that the overall medical prognosis meant she was not going to emulate her mother and reach one hundred, so she had been determined to make the most of that year,' says one friend. 'She made sure she had all the family up over the summer, so that the young ones in particular would always be left with happy memories of her.'[19] The Queen had been giving serious thought as to where she might spend her final days and discussed it within the family. Right to the end, she was endearingly conscious of causing unnecessary inconvenience to others. 'There was a moment when she felt that it would be more difficult if she died at Balmoral,' says the Princess Royal (every

---

* In his biography of the Queen, Gyles Brandreth has suggested that she was suffering from myeloma, a form of bone marrow cancer, a claim rejected by one very senior source. The Palace refuses to comment.

monarch since the creation of Great Britain had died in England).
'And I think we did try and persuade her that it shouldn't be
part of the decision-making process. So I hope she felt that that
was right in the end.'[20]

Former aides remain in awe of the seamlessness with which
she had managed to arrange her affairs. 'How typical of her to
do it so well,' says one, recalling the years of anxiety within the
Royal Household. Serious and detailed thought had been given
to the prospect of a regency, whereby the Prince of Wales might
stand in for the Queen if she was incapacitated. 'With the Queen
Mother going on past her hundredth birthday, of course we
had to think that the Queen would reach the same age. A
regency seemed almost inevitable. That would have been very
difficult. You would still have needed a near-full Queen's household and a near-full Prince's household and it would have been
very hard for the Regent. I always hoped it wouldn't happen
while I was there but I didn't see how we could get out of it,
to be honest. Yet she did manage to get out of it – perfectly.'[21]

The working assumption was that there might be a long,
slow decline in the Queen's health or a sudden public collapse
during an engagement. 'Either way, we would have had growing
voices saying: "It's time for a regency" and that sort of thing,'
says one aide. 'We dreaded something happening in public, so
engagements were kept very tight and very short, with limited
media.'[22] One of the Queen's last duties in public, to open
London's new Elizabeth Line in May 2022, was a case in point.
The event was kept very short with a very small media presence
and no advance notice, just in case. However, all went well and
photographs of a smiling Queen unveiling the £19 billion rail
link still dominated every front page the next day.

From time to time, royal aides would draw up plans for a
variety of regency options. These would include 'regency-light'

(with minimal princely involvement) and 'reversible regency', in the event of short-term incapacitation. Another question, at one point, was the course of action if the Duke of Edinburgh – who would have been on any regency committee prior to his death – had objected to a regency plan. The finest royal brains pored over all the possibilities. At one stage, an ex-private secretary to the Prince of Wales, Sir Stephen Lamport, was brought back from his job in the City to help with a new blueprint. Aides would always find the Prince extremely reluctant to engage on the subject. 'Very correctly he didn't want to be too interested,' says one. 'You could turn up with all the papers and he would say, "Have you been through it all? Are you happy with this?" and that would be that. He didn't want to dwell on the details. He'd much rather discuss something much less important. I think he felt that if you reach out for something, you are tempting fate. He was commendably diffident.'[23]

Towards the end, the Queen had also accepted that it was now time to address certain issues which, until then, had been sitting in what one official calls the 'Too Difficult' folder, forever being 'kicked down the road' because they did not require immediate attention. Top of the list had been that question of the Duchess of Cornwall's title after a change of reign. 'The Queen knew that it had to come from her,' says the official. Her Late Majesty's 'sincere wish' that Camilla should become 'Queen Consort', and not, as previously proposed, 'Princess Consort', had settled the matter, there and then, without so much as a batsqueak of opposition.

It is why, as they look back on what might have been versus what actually happened, courtiers past and present are as one in their amazement at the way the reign of Elizabeth II came to a close. One sums it up in a single word: 'Masterclass.'

Chapter Five

'It's finished'

When Elizabeth II acceded to the throne, much was made of the poignancy of a twenty-five-year-old mother-of-two being guided by the grandest, greatest statesman of the age, Winston Churchill. Now, Britain had a head of state and a head of government neither of whom had been in office for a week. A much-retweeted observation on Twitter noted: 'I have a pint of milk in the fridge which has seen two monarchs and two prime ministers. I can only imagine what the marmalade has witnessed.'

However, the Accession Council showed precisely where the balance of experience resided. This was the meeting of the Privy Council after which the new monarch could formally be proclaimed King around his kingdom. This had never been filmed before, let alone broadcast live on television. No one who had been at the last one, in 1952, was alive now. However, the new King did have some idea of what was coming thanks to the video made by his private secretary.

So many Privy Counsellors had wanted to be at St James's Palace for this moment that tickets had been restricted to the most senior among them, including former prime ministers and archbishops. It gradually dawned on many of those present that there was only one person in the room with more than half a century of frontline public service to his credit. Yet it was the King's grimacing which would generate the headlines. As he sat down to sign the oath to 'preserve' the Church of Scotland, he found that the small desk was cluttered with an inkwell and pen set. His obvious irritation as he hissed at an aide to move it proved a rich source of amusement on social media. 'The pen issue was the one moment he was just a person, not the King,' insists an aide. Running the whole show, less than a week into the job, was Penny Mordaunt, Lord President of the Council. 'Of all the things that could have gone wrong,' she says, 'I think just the pen not working was a good outcome.'[1]

Outside, the most senior herald in the land, Garter King of Arms, climbed onto the balcony of Friary Court, St James's Palace, to be the first to recite a proclamation which would be repeated in the City of London, followed by the devolved capitals and then cities and, ultimately, the smallest towns all over the kingdom. Substantial crowds gathered to witness this throwback to a medieval news bulletin.

This was about much more than pageantry. With so much political upheaval in recent months, there had been very serious government concerns about possible civil disorder. 'We had identified in our integrated review [that] when you transition to a new sovereign, it's a moment of peril for the country,' Mordaunt admits. 'We'd had a lot of political turmoil around the time, and so whilst I was focused on making sure that all of these events were going to work well, in the back of my mind, I was thinking: "How are the public going to respond to this?"'[2]

She received her answer soon enough as she watched the proclamation being announced outside. 'I was behind a pillar watching this with Sir Robert Buckland.* And he was feeling the

---

* Secretary of State for Wales and, previously, Lord Chancellor.

same way too,' recalls Mordaunt. The words of Garter King of Arms were followed by a robust 'three cheers' from the company of Coldstream Guards on duty outside St James's Palace.

'We heard the three cheers,' adds Mordaunt, 'and then, over the palace walls, were hundreds of thousands of people cheering the King. They were all through the parks and down towards Trafalgar Square. And both Robert and I shed a tear at that point because it was such a relief that we knew it was going to be okay.'

The drama of this ancient ritual even upstaged another remarkable scene elsewhere that afternoon. Crowds leaving flowers by Cambridge Gate on Windsor's Long Walk were astonished to see a black Land Rover pull up containing what had once been hailed as 'the Fab Four' – both the Waleses and the Sussexes. Prince William was at the wheel. 'It was very much William's idea. He had organized it in about two hours flat,' says one of his small inner sanctum of advisers. 'He had been giving it a lot of thought and he said: "I know it's awkward but isn't it right in the context of my grandmother's death?" I know he asked a couple of other people, too.'[3]

The two couples then spent the best part of forty minutes meeting crowds and reading the messages among the mounds of bouquets and tributes. They left as they had arrived, in the same car. Both sides would later let it be known that this had been quite an ordeal. The Sussexes allegedly found it 'very difficult,'[4] although, surprisingly, Harry made no mention of it in his memoir. 'I don't think either couple found it easy,' says a member of the Wales team.[5]

Vern Stokes had been mightily relieved that his state trumpeters had returned from Canada just in time for their big moment at St James's Palace. There was rather more work to be done with the bearer party, who would carry the coffin on the day of the funeral. Fresh off the plane from Iraq, says Stokes, they received two immediate orders: 'get a haircut' and 'carry a comb at all times'.[6] Based at Lille Barracks in Aldershot, they immediately began training with a makeshift catafalque and a bedsheet, which served as a replica Royal Standard for draping over their makeshift coffin.

The following day, the eyes of the world shifted from the capital back to the Highlands as the late Queen prepared to leave Balmoral for the last time. The extension of 'D' by twenty-four hours had given the estate staff extra time to pay their respects as the Queen lay 'at rest' in the castle ballroom. On the morning of the departure, led by a piper, the coffin was carried out of the castle to the hearse by a bearer party of six ghillies. These taciturn men of the mountains – the game-keepers whose predecessors had taught the young Princess Elizabeth to love these hills all her life – performed their duty with military precision. It turned out that, like the Queen's Company Grenadier Guards, they had rehearsed this manoeuvre in complete secrecy on an occasional basis over many years – just in case they should be called upon. The only commands were a whispered 'left, right' from the head gamekeeper.

Those lined up outside the castle remember the unroyally raw emotion of the scene. It was a delightful tradition, albeit from another age, that the Queen's annual departure from Balmoral would always be quite an event. First, there would be her customary tea party with the factor (the estate manager), the minister of Crathie church and the local doctor, plus their wives. Every year, the Queen would sigh and tell them: 'I just wish I could stay *one* more week.' Then, the staff would line up in front of the castle and send her on her way waving white handker-chiefs. This time, says one of those present, many people were too busy sobbing into their handkerchiefs to wave. News heli-copters kept a respectful distance. No cameras had been admitted to Balmoral for this part of the proceedings. There was fury among estate staff earlier when one helicopter did venture into view. It turned out to be an overly curious police helicopter, which was swiftly ordered to retreat.

'Many people were in floods,' says one who was there to see the oak coffin draped in the Royal Standard of Scotland and crowned by sprays of sweet pea and white heather, which the Balmoral gardeners had picked that morning. For some, it was the lament played by the Queen's Piper which was the last straw. For others, it was the sudden appearance of the Queen's two surviving corgis looking confused.

'One of the ghillies was in pieces afterwards. And it was a tough moment for the Queen's chauffeur, Andy Fitzgerald,' says one member of staff. 'As he said later, he just had to stare straight ahead and tell himself: "Refocus!"'[7]

The sight of this tiny convoy emerging from the castle gates and meandering through the vastness of the Highlands in bright sunshine remains one of the abiding images of those days. Led by a single outrider, the Queen's hearse was followed by the State Bentley carrying the Princess Royal, along with her husband, Vice Admiral Sir Tim Laurence. The King had been more than happy to let his sister escort the coffin; her long devotion to so many Scottish institutions made her the obvious choice. 'It was a privilege to be part of that, and particularly from the drive from Balmoral down to Edinburgh, where you literally saw people's reactions,' she says. 'As you progressed, you were aware of the trouble people had gone to – lining up the tractors and cleaning them off; literally plaiting the ponies and making sure that they were smartly turned out.'[8] The effort involved in making a tractor or a pony look pristine – particularly in the midst of the annual harvest – was certainly not lost on an ardent countrywoman. Nor was the way in which the tractors dipped their shovels and the ponies bowed their heads in tribute. For those of a certain generation, it was reminiscent of the dockers dipping their cranes in tribute along the banks of the Thames as Sir Winston Churchill's coffin sailed upriver aboard the Thames launch *Havengore* in 1965. 'You just had these snapshots which indicated real respect in a way that nothing else could. It was hugely impressive,' the Princess adds.

Travelling immediately behind the hearse and the State Bentley carrying the Princess was the car carrying Alexander de Montfort, head of ceremonial from the Lord Chamberlain's Office, and the Rev. Kenneth MacKenzie, the minister of Crathie. 'During that first stage, the cortege made its way through countryside she knew well. Many of those people who were lining the route were people that she would have known and recognized,' says MacKenzie. 'We were going so slowly that you would see the same kind of expression – young people, old people, it didn't seem to matter – that this marked the beginning and the end of an era. You could literally see tears welling up in people's eyes. And there was nearly always this involuntary movement of people putting their hand on their heart.'

As the smaller lanes of Deeside gave way to bigger roads, so the numbers grew. MacKenzie and de Montfort, a man with more than two decades spent organizing state occasions, had never seen anything like it. Entire pubs emptied out, their customers raising their glasses among crowds ten deep in the tiniest towns.

Further south, Dundee – a stronghold of Scottish nationalism – was out in force. The crowds were non-stop, all through a journey which took the best part of six hours (with just a brief refuelling stop en route at Brechin Castle, seat of the Earl of Dalhousie). Kenneth MacKenzie remembers that on several stretches of the A90, the cortege was joined by occasional horses and riders galloping alongside through the adjacent countryside, determined to say goodbye in a manner of which the late Queen would surely have approved.

As the journey progressed, the Princess Royal and Sir Tim gradually realized that it was near-impossible to touch the refreshments at their feet in the car, for fear of appearing disrespectful. There was just one window of opportunity. 'We took a couple of bottles of water with us and something to nibble on because it was quite a longish trip,' the Princess recalls. 'But, to be honest, we could only have taken a drink from a bottle while we were going over the Forth Bridge where there weren't any people.'[9]

Kenneth MacKenzie remembers the gradual feeling of the Queen being welcomed into an ever-growing embrace. 'There was a sense in which the Queen was being given by the family to the community, then to the area, and then to the wider area and then the state.'[10] By the time the coffin reached Edinburgh's Royal Mile, the pavements could hold no more. Even the most hard-boiled and cynical observers of Scotland's fractious political landscape began to voice a thought now gathering momentum in private: might that canny Queen have planned it this way all along? After all, she had managed to ensure that all the UK-based grandchildren and great-grandchildren had been with her a few weeks earlier, a scene captured in a delightful photograph by the Duchess of Cambridge (and later released on what would have been the Queen's ninety-seventh birthday). Nor could she have had better timing. 'Scotland was the most ambitious location for ceremonial, but it does look brilliant in September,' says a senior member of the team. 'It also meant that we could plan for a coronation in May, which is ideal. Had the Queen died in July, it would have meant a winter coronation, which would have been miserable. God bless her!'[11]

Having died in Scotland, the late Queen had triggered an

entire subset of the London Bridge masterplan called Operation Unicorn. It also meant that the men of the Royal Company of Archers, the Sovereign's Body Guard in Scotland, would be as busy as at any point in their 200-year history. Made up of both ex-military and civilian volunteers, the Royal Company's 530 members had received an urgent call to arms on the news of the Queen's demise. More than 300 would undertake duties in both Edinburgh and London over the days ahead.

Yet another element of London Bridge had been Operation Spring Tide, the plan for the King and Queen Camilla to visit all the corners of his kingdom within those early days. It had been drawn up by officials in planning meetings over the preceding years. Staff now concede that it was asking a great deal of a bereaved man in his seventies. 'I think had we gone on another year, the programme would have been less intense,' admits one member of his team. 'But the King and Queen never complained, not once. They were just very reflective. It was exhausting but both were carried along by the amazing outpouring of support.'

On 12 September the King addressed both Houses of Parliament at Westminster Hall and then flew to Edinburgh to address the Scottish Parliament too. In between, he marched with his siblings behind the Queen's coffin and up the Royal Mile to attend Scotland's service of thanksgiving for the life of the Queen at St Giles' Cathedral. The new prime minister, accompanying the King on his tour of the home nations, was transfixed as she walked into the cathedral. 'What sticks in my mind, very clearly,' says Liz Truss, 'is that this was the first time I actually came face to face with the coffin. That was a very big moment.'

For many people, including the Princess Royal, this was the first time they had heard – or sung – 'God save our gracious King . . .' 'You have to stop and think about what you're saying.

It's a very obvious note of change,' the Princess recalls fondly. 'I just had to concentrate!'

Later on, all four siblings would stand vigil around the coffin, heads bowed to the floor, an historic image echoing 'The Vigil of the Princes' around the coffin of George V in 1936. A similar vigil had been mounted around the coffin of Queen Elizabeth the Queen Mother by her grandsons in 2002. For the first time, it would now include a Princess. 'I was really grateful that they felt that was appropriate to do,' she remembers. 'Vigils are quite remarkable experiences in a way. You don't see anybody, but you kind of feel it in an interesting way.'[12]

Operation Spring Tide continued at pace with trips to Northern Ireland and Wales. In Belfast, there was the once unthinkable sight of a fervent Irish nationalist addressing a British monarch with words of condolence for the loss of his predecessor. Sinn Féin's Alex Maskey was acting in his capacity as Speaker of the Northern Ireland Assembly and did so with dignity and sincerity. The Queen, he said, had 'demonstrated how individual acts of positive leadership can help break down barriers and encourage reconciliation'. Once again, it was the King's signature which attracted much media coverage. He was clearly furious when his pen began leaking as he signed the visitors' book at Hillsborough Castle. 'Every stinking time . . . !' he muttered. On social media, there was more mirth, although some were now asking more serious questions about the royal temper. After the inkwell incident at St James's Palace and now this moment at Hillsborough, people were going to take a much closer interest in the hitherto banal ritual of the signing of the visitors' book. 'He's had very little sleep. His mother's died. And everyone keeps asking him questions,' said one of his team. 'Now his pen's leaking and he's cross. If that's the worst so far, we'll live with that.'[13]

Charles III

On D+4, the Queen left Scotland for the last time, carried aboard a Royal Air Force Boeing C-17 by a bearer party from the RAF. This colossal cargo plane, capable of carrying a battle tank, flew the tiny coffin from sunny Edinburgh to grey, rainy, rush-hour RAF Northolt in the suburbs of west London. The short flight – the last occasion on which air traffic controllers would use the Queen's personal call-sign, 'Kittyhawk' – also set a record. According to aero-data analysts, it was the most-tracked flight in aviation history.[14]

Yet again, it was the emotional power of the small, impromptu gesture which took the Royal Family and even the most seasoned members of the Royal Household by surprise. All along the west-bound stretch of the A40, heading out of London, departing commuter traffic was simply strewn all over the road as drivers screeched to a halt. They abandoned their vehicles to line the central reservation in the rain and salute the Queen as the hearse made its stately progress in the other direction towards Buckingham Palace. Crowds a dozen deep lined the forecourts of drive-thru takeaways and filling stations. 'There was a moment coming out of Northolt,' recalls one member of staff. 'Cars were just pulling over; and there was this group of teenage lads on a slip road nudging each other. And as we got near, they all started throwing these flowers. And you wondered: why had these seventeen-year-old lads turned out with flowers? What did ninety-six-year-old Elizabeth Windsor mean to them?'[15]

Inside the palace, all the members of the Royal Family were there to welcome the Queen back to royal headquarters for the last time, followed by an informal supper. Afterwards, the Prince and Princess of Wales suggested that the Duke and Duchess of Sussex should attach their car to their police escort for the journey back to Windsor, since they were all going the same way. It was only a small gesture (they would not be sharing a car) and nowhere near any sort of reconciliation. However, the late Queen would have approved.

The Master of the Household, Sir Tony Johnstone-Burt, had prepared the Bow Room for the Queen's last night at Buckingham Palace. As at Balmoral and Holyroodhouse, she would lie at rest so that all her staff could say farewell. If Holyroodhouse had been a simple, low church affair, Buckingham Palace was the opposite: decked out with huge candles, flowers and kneelers for those who wished to pray. 'It was very nicely done but not overdone,' remembers a senior member of the Royal Household.[16] 'You just turned up when you could and no one was hurried through.'

By now, Vern Stokes had prepared his troops for their first major procession, the march from the palace to Westminster Hall, where the Queen would lie in state for five days. He had also been asked to deliver a personal briefing to the King and the other members of the Royal Family. 'I opened it by saying, "Your Majesty, I'm sorry for your loss,"' he says.[17] When he asked for any questions afterwards, there was one from the King himself. 'Garrison, where are you going to be during these processions?' asked the monarch. Stokes explained that he would be keeping a discreet presence nearby. The King had another idea. 'I'd like you to be right in front of me and whatever you do, I'll do,' he told Stokes. Events would later prove that this was the right call.

As the members of the Royal Family lined up to follow the coffin in bright sunshine, Princes William and Harry swapped a knowing glance and, according to one royal source, a wry remark about having been here before. The first time they had walked behind a coffin to Westminster was on the day of their mother's funeral in 1997. They had done so again for the Queen Mother in 2002.

Inside Westminster Hall, the coffin was received by both Houses of Parliament. In symbolic terms, here was the Queen's family surrendering her to the care and safekeeping of the people for five days. The lying-in-state could now begin, offering anyone the chance to pay tribute, as long as they were prepared to endure a very long wait. Initial waiting times of around seven hours would later peak at twenty-four, including a six-mile stop–start shuffle from an entry point in Southwark Park in south-east London. The queue became the dominant strand of the funeral coverage for days. Yuki Tanaka, veteran correspondent for Japan's Fuji TV, was very struck by the depth of feeling after spending nine hours in the line himself. 'You would not get people queuing like that in Japan – maybe three hours at most,' he recalls. 'What was so interesting is that everyone in the queue seemed to have some sort of story or connection – "My granny once met the Queen" – that sort of thing.'[18] Around the clock, day after day, complete strangers swapped Elizabeth II anecdotes gleaned from accumulated decades of awaydays, investitures, ribbon-cuttings, hospital openings, plaque unveilings, jubilee parades and Commonwealth tours. Celebrities, including former footballer David Beckham, were spotted in the mix. An Australian television crew picking out random mourners could hardly believe their luck when they stumbled upon Lieutenant General David Leakey. Having served as Black Rod, the monarch's enforcer at Westminster, until 2018, he had actually drawn up the plans for this lying-in-state ceremony. Now retired, there was no question of him being offered fast-track access. He was having to queue just like everyone else.

The reward for those who had made the effort was a few seconds of pure majesty as they were finally channelled through the precincts of Parliament and out beneath the hammer-beamed splendour of Britain's greatest medieval chamber. With all mobile phones (and thus all selfies) banned, the scene was silent and dignified. Soft lighting bounced off the Imperial State Crown and the Orb, both of them bolted firmly to the lid of the coffin. Lending extra lustre and colour to the grandeur of it all were the uniforms of those units proud to call themselves a 'Body Guard' – the Gentlemen at Arms, the Royal Company of Archers, the Yeomen of the Guard, the Yeomen Warders and all seven regiments of the Household Division. They would take turns to stand vigil day and night in six-hour watches, rotating every twenty minutes. Though a fine sight, they were of limited strategic use. When a disturbed loner lunged at the coffin late on day three, it was regular police who floored him. A brisk tap of sword on stone would be the signal for those guards standing vigil to march off and make way for another detachment. The essential thing was to look down, stay focused and remain utterly still. Charlie McGrath of the Gentlemen at Arms recalled that visibility was limited anyway. 'With an angle of about 45 degrees, the immediate view was just the legs of the mourners as they passed by,' he told the *Guards Magazine*. 'I counted trainers, with bonus points for pink ones, [and] calculated the flow rate per minute.'[19]

The procession to Westminster Hall – the first of four great ceremonial processions in London and Windsor during those final six days – had been faultless. Shortly afterwards, Vern Stokes was briefing all senior officers on the more challenging processions five days hence, notably the long parade through the capital after the funeral service at Westminster Abbey. Stokes liked to use the Guards Chapel, finding that the acoustics were much better than the regimental gymnasium. His main piece of advice for all involved was simple: download a metronome app and practise marching round the house at seventy-five paces per minute. Neither a slow march (sixty-five paces per minute), nor a quick march (116), it is the designated speed for a royal funeral. Later that night, however, Stokes had his worst experience of the entire London Bridge operation.

Charles III

The plans allowed for just one rehearsal for the entire state funeral procession in London. It took place on Thursday 15 September, but in the very early hours, in order to minimize both congestion and unwelcome media attention. It also woke up the new prime minister. 'It was rather disturbing being in Downing Street,' Liz Truss recalls. 'It can be quite a noisy place to live.' There was certainly a fair amount of shouting that evening. 'It was a comedy of errors,' says the Garrison Sergeant Major. 'Everything that could go wrong did go wrong.'[20] He had been annoyed that, at the initial recce, some officers had seemed more interested in catching up with long-lost chums than paying attention. Now, at the very outset, the bagpipes pre-empted his first command, meaning that the whole parade was out of step from the start. More worryingly, an entire band simply went missing because their marshalling officer had managed to lead them to the wrong start-point. At Hyde Park Corner one of the Gentlemen at Arms went the wrong way and was close to being crushed, possibly fatally, between the gun carriage and Wellington Arch. The buses that were supposed to take hundreds of troops on to the committal at Windsor never appeared. Most worrying of all was a basic question of maths. All the parade times had been calculated according to the span of a Guardsman's pace – thirty inches – with all the bass drums beating a time of seventy-five paces per minute. However, according to a tradition dating back to the funeral of Queen Victoria, the coffin would be carried on a gun carriage pulled by Royal Navy ratings. And the average pace of a Royal Navy recruit pulling a two-ton gun carriage turned out to be nearer twenty inches. The result was that the front of the parade ended up parting company with the coffin. It also meant that the coffin would be late reaching the end of the procession route at Hyde Park Corner, from where it would then be driven by road to Windsor. The Earl Marshal, by his own admission, was now a worried man. 'If this ended up going wrong, it would be my responsibility,' he acknowledges.[21]

No one would be going to sleep until after the 0700 debrief. Major General Chris Ghika and Vern Stokes had limited options. 'It was too late to rewrite the plan,' says Stokes. However, he calculated that the organizers had been generous with the time allotted to the drive from London to Windsor. Provided there was no hold-up en route, the hearse would be able to make up the lost time and the final procession at Windsor could still set off on time. It made for a tense few days, however, as the big moment – D+10 – approached.

The King's team had other challenges to deal with. One task was working through a deluge of condolences and trying to work out what had come from whom. It had been the same in 1952 following the death of George VI. 'We were, as usual, confounded by the impossibility of deciding whether some of the signatories were amiable lunatics or foreign relations,' wrote the Queen Mother's treasurer, Sir Arthur Penn. 'How can one tell that the frenzied messages signed "Uncle Poll" reflected the sincere good will of the aged Duke of Brunswick?'[22]

The priority for the King's private secretary was to keep long-laid plans on track and on time. 'Clive was always looking out for the last-minute, so-called "better idea". He was very wary that a better idea could swiftly become a worse idea,' says one official. 'So, in most cases, we would say: "That's charming but we have a plan."'[23] Eleventh-hour calls for changes to the funeral route or guest lists were strongly resisted. One last-minute 'better idea' which was accepted, however, was a suggestion from the new Prince of Wales. As in Edinburgh, the King was due to lead his siblings in another vigil alongside the Queen's coffin in Westminster Hall. Might the Queen's grandchildren not offer the same tribute the following night?

The King agreed. It also had the happy effect of bringing Princes William and Harry back together in public.

The King's staff knew that they had to be sensible with the demands being placed on the monarch. Other members of the family were despatched to different parts of the country. The Prince and Princess of Wales went to Sandringham (where hundreds of people connected to the estate had known the Queen all their lives). The Wessexes headed for Manchester. Even when he had no public engagements, the King had to receive the mandatory calls of condolence from world leaders. As Head of the Commonwealth, he would be expected to make an extra effort with the leaders of its fifty-six member states, even more so with the delegations from his own Commonwealth realms. The smallest decisions still had to be cleared by him. Should the Dukes of Sussex and York be allowed to wear the uniforms which they had forfeited when they gave up royal duties? To agree would risk days of heated debate about the circumstances of their respective departures in the first place. To refuse could seem unduly harsh on two grieving princes who had both served their country in action. The King's compromise passed with almost no complaint from any quarter: they could both wear uniform during their respective vigils at the Queen's lying-in-state.

By now, the greatest gathering of world leaders ever seen on British soil was starting to assemble. Many had been due to visit the United Nations General Assembly but had diverted their aircraft to Britain instead. So many presidential, royal and private jets were entering the UK that the major airports could no longer cope and the Foreign Office were directing them to Farnborough, Biggin Hill and anywhere else with a suitable runway. The Marshal of the Diplomatic Corps, Alistair Harrison, was forced to abandon the usual diplomatic nicety of sending a lord-lieutenant or a lord-in-waiting to greet an incoming prime minister. 'We just did not have enough people to go round. We decided that we could only do official greetings for heads of state,' recalls one of his team.[24]

On the eve of the funeral, 400 representatives from some 170 nations descended on Buckingham Palace for the King's reception. Despite the ongoing building works, almost all the state apartments were pressed into service to entertain the presidents of the USA and France (among many other republics) and the crowned heads of most of the world's monarchies. These included the Emperor of Japan, making his first overseas trip since his accession. Many of those present remember, in particular, a certain aura around Queen Margrethe of Denmark. 'She was looking particularly regal because she is now the world's only Queen Regnant,'[25] says one of those present. 'People were making a point of seeking her out as the world's senior monarch.' On the eve of perhaps the most important day of his life, for the time being at least, the King worked his way methodically through the different drawing rooms and the Picture Gallery. Queen Camilla (still officially referred to as the Queen Consort at this point) and the other working members of the family spread out to do the same. The year before, as foreign secretary, Liz Truss was pleasantly surprised by the number of world leaders who attended the COP26 summit in Glasgow. Now, she found herself co-hosting what she calls a 'once-in-seventy-years event' as prime minister. 'When we did COP26, we thought that was big. But this was, of course, bigger.' Not that anyone was talking shop. 'There was not much business being done,' she says. 'Everyone really was just talking about the Queen.' As one British diplomat recalls: 'It was simply one of those great parties – albeit for all the wrong reasons.'

At 5.30 a.m., well before dawn, on Monday 19 September 2022, Vern Stokes was already on his first walk-through of the entire processional route, dressed in full uniform. He was also checking crowd barriers and looking for any superfluous street furniture. A couple of traffic lights were duly removed from their perches. He repeated the exercise all over again before having breakfast at regimental headquarters. 'It's like being a Formula One driver before the start,' he recalls. 'You are just trying to visualize the whole race and think what could happen.' A keen Formula One fan himself, the Duke of Norfolk was putting on the regalia of the GCVO – Knight Grand Cross of the Royal Victorian Order – for the first time. He had been awarded the GCVO by the late Queen earlier in the year, by way of thanks for organizing the State Opening of Parliament twenty times. Realizing that the Duke needed to be formally invested before he could wear the blue sash and insignia, the King had managed to find a gap in the diary on the day before the funeral to present Eddie Norfolk with his GCVO properly. The Earl Marshal was even more touched to be asked if he would like to bring his five children along to this mini-investiture and presented them to the monarch in what he calls 'von Trapp order'.[26]

By mid-morning, the world leaders were all gathering once again in the Great Hall of the Royal Hospital, Chelsea. This plan, however, would turn into the only serious diplomatic glitch of the day. Given the number of separate delegations, it was clear that they could not all expect to arrive at and leave Westminster Abbey in their own cars. As a member of the Lord Chamberlain's Office explained, 'it would have taken hours each way.' Besides, a queue of hundreds of cars and outriders would hardly reflect well on the King's oft-quoted views on sustainability and climate change. So the leaders would all go by bus.

'Most of them were happy with this, especially since the European monarchs do this sort of thing all the time,' says one senior Foreign Office official. 'However, some of them, including the team around President Macron of France, did not like it at all. They were worried how this would play to their home base, that people might mock them.'[27] French officials were especially miffed that an exception was made for the US president, Joe Biden, whose security team would not countenance him travelling in anything other than his bomb-proof limousine.

The first, and very much the shortest, of the day's three processions began in Parliament with the Grenadier Guards bearer party lifting the coffin from the catafalque where more than 250,000 people[28] had filed past it during 107 hours of lying-in-state. It fell to the Garrison Sergeant Major to begin the final farewell to Elizabeth II. 'Funeral Procession,' he began, at precisely 10.44. 'By the centre, slow march.' At which point everyone, including the 142 Royal Navy ratings pulling the coffin, set off on the first leg from Westminster Hall to Westminster Abbey. There was just one minor error, not that anyone had spotted it except the Garrison Sergeant Major. As the procession marched off from New Palace Yard, the pipes and drums missed a beat, with the result that those behind the coffin were out of step. Knowing the position of the television cameras, Stokes waited until he was out of shot and then shouted an instruction to the King, immediately behind him: 'Your Majesty, we are out of step. Please do what I am going to do.'[29] At which point, the King and everyone else simply changed step.

Precisely eight minutes later, the procession came to a halt at the Great West Door of Westminster Abbey. Now came the greatest and most public challenge yet for the bearer party as they carried the coffin from the gun carriage, up the steps and on through the abbey. Of the eight young Grenadier Guardsmen, at least one was still a teenager. All had been pre-selected by their Company Sergeant Major on the basis of both aptitude and height (all had to be roughly six feet and two inches), together with a team of eight reserves. Their commanding officer, Second Lieutenant Freddie Hobbs, was only twenty-four. Since their return from Iraq, they had been practising day and night in Aldershot. For many television viewers, it was the bearer party – their faultless drill, their youth, their obvious pride in their late commander-in-chief and their regiment – that would prove to be one of the most moving sights of the entire occasion. 'I was 100 per cent confident they were going to be okay,' says Vern Stokes. 'They had rehearsed really well and never let us down.'

The King had carefully chosen the wreath on top of the coffin – roses, hydrangea, sedum and myrtle (from the same specimen that had provided the myrtle for Princess Elizabeth's wedding bouquet in 1947). It had been the late Queen, however, who had chosen all the music. Whenever she was on tour in the royal yacht, she had always loved the Beat Retreat ceremony, especially when the Band of the Royal Marines would blend the Sunset bugle call with the hymn, 'The Day Thou Gavest, Lord, Has Ended'. So, this was to be the first hymn at her funeral. She had also chosen 'Love Divine, All Loves Excelling' and the 'Crimond' variation of Psalm 23 (The Lord's My Shepherd). It was played at her wedding and she had loved it ever since.

The first lesson was read by the Commonwealth secretary-general Baroness Scotland, the second by the prime minister. After an extraordinary first week in office, Liz Truss was now charged with reading from the Book of John, Chapter 14, to an audience of billions. She was, understandably, nervous: 'What I worried about was not the reading itself but "Will I trip up on the step?" or "Which verger am I supposed to follow?" That is what you are thinking during those moments.'

In his sermon, the Archbishop of Canterbury painted a picture of a life lived in service rather than in charge: 'People of loving service are rare in any walk of life. Leaders of loving service are still rarer. But in all cases, those who serve will be loved and remembered when those who cling to power and privileges are forgotten.' Whether he was alluding to the British political contingent, in the North Transept, or the international leaders in the South Transept – or both – was unclear. Much comment would later be devoted to the seating plan. Why, for example, was a key ally like President Joe Biden of the United States seated fourteen rows to the rear of the Royal Family, behind, say, Jair Bolsonaro of Brazil, while Canada's Justin Trudeau was within touching distance of the royal pews? The arbiters of protocol, led by Alexander Scully, deputy comptroller in the Lord Chamberlain's Office, had merely applied some long-established rules of precedence. The Queen's fourteen realms – from Canada to Australia to Tuvalu – came ahead of everyone else, with their governors-general, in turn, ahead of their prime ministers. Next came other heads of state in alphabetical order of country. Hence, Brazil was seated nearer the front than the USA. 'If they had just called it "America", Biden would have been nearer the front,' explains a member of the Palace team, adding that the president had one consolation. 'We actually moved things around to give him an aisle seat for security reasons.'

Biden and his wife had started making travel plans as soon as the Queen's death had been announced. 'Joe and I just decided to attend,' says the first lady, Dr Jill Biden. 'We all grew up with the Queen. She was such a big part of our lives. She was just always there and felt like she always would be – a really beautiful, spectacular, amazing woman.'[30] For the Bidens, a cherished memory would always be tea with the Queen at

Windsor Castle in the year before her death. 'We went up to her apartment. And I loved her sense of independence. She had a big teapot. And Joe said to her: "Here, let me help you."' The Queen had been quite insistent, however. 'No, no, no. You sit,' she told the president. 'I will serve you.' Whereupon she had plenty to discuss with her guests.* 'Here she was with this big teapot pouring tea and we had the best time because she has such a sense of curiosity,' Dr Biden recalls. 'She asked all about American politics and what was going on and [the president's] perceptions of different people and different events.' It was, she reflects fondly, every American's 'picture' of a quintessential British tea party, especially when 'her little dogs came in'. So many similar stories were being swapped throughout the head-of-state zone in the South Transept of the abbey.

British and foreign royalty had their own sections. The most obvious question, as far as the media were concerned, was the whereabouts of the Duke and Duchess of Sussex. Though not in the front row, like the new Prince and Princess of Wales, they were placed immediately behind the King and Queen Consort. If any offence was taken, it was not recorded in the Duke's memoir.

The service managed to overrun by two minutes. The Earl Marshal could cope with that. What worried him was the subsequent marching speed of the Royal Navy versus that of the army. Sure enough, a gap began to open up. The front of the procession, led by the Royal Canadian Mounted Police, would soon be well ahead of the gun carriage, with the coffin to the rear. There was nothing anyone could do. On the other hand, no one seemed to notice anyway. The public, watching on television, simply saw a step-perfect military procession

---

* The Queen met a total of fourteen US presidents, thirteen of them in office and one (Hoover) in retirement.

involving 1,500 marching servicemen and servicewomen and ninety-seven horses, stretching out along the most familiar parts of central London. All eyes were on the family, especially the King, who continued to show great composure and no overt sign of fatigue. 'Everyone could see the sadness on the King's face,' recalls the US first lady, adding that the outpouring of collective grief must have been a great source of comfort. 'You don't forget that people came to acknowledge the person you love and to celebrate her life and what she meant to the world.'

The crowds, though substantial, seemed significantly down on royal events of yesteryear – because they were. The police had been so wary of a crush, a terrorist incident or some sort of disorder that they had installed steel entry gates, even for pedestrians, around the processional area and placed a cap on numbers. The crowds immediately outside the security zone were very much larger, which would be very obvious later.

As the Earl Marshal had feared, the coffin was thirty-two minutes late by the time it reached Wellington Arch at Hyde Park Corner for its rendezvous with the hearse. All those who had been in the procession ahead of the coffin had, by now, formed up around the arch to say farewell. 'Anthony Mather and I had planned it so that everyone in the procession should have the chance to see the coffin with their own eyes and pay their respects,' says Eddie Norfolk. And so the Queen left London for the last time. Even with one more procession to come and the clock very much against him, Garrison Sergeant Major Vern Stokes says he found this scene one of the most emotional sights in the entirety of Operation London Bridge. The moment the hearse set off through Hyde Park, where there was no limit on numbers, the crowds were suddenly very much larger than they had been in the sterile processional zone.

As had been the case in Scotland, it was the Princess Royal who escorted the hearse through the suburbs and down to Windsor at a stately 30 mph. Despite appeals from the police, many members of the public still wanted to throw flowers at the hearse. Some had weighed down their bouquets for added momentum. 'It was a bit like sitting on a firing range as they hit. The protection officer sitting with me was twitching a bit,' says one of those in the cortege. 'I said: "It's alright. They're flowers." It had to look correct so the Queen's chauffeur couldn't stop or use the wipers and just kept to the middle of the road. But there were a couple of sections around Runnymede where there were no TV cameras and so that is when he could use the wipers to push flowers off the windscreen.'[31]

The King and the rest of the family were driven directly at high speed along the M4 motorway to join relatives and friends already waiting at the castle. As host and chief mourner, Charles III would have no time to himself. His convoy of family members was followed by several speeding busloads of Palace officials, heralds and bandsmen plus the Earl Marshal, Vern Stokes and the all-important bearer party. After previous royal funerals, there had been no great urgency once the television cameras had switched off, and the burial could proceed at its own pace. John Dauth, who was then press secretary to Prince Charles, joined the official entourage after the funeral of Lord Mountbatten as the royal train took the mourners from London to Romsey in Hampshire for the burial. The wake began en route as drinks were served. 'I attempted to engage the King of Norway in conversation,' Dauth recalls, 'but he was asleep.'[32]

With Elizabeth II, it was a case of one service completed, another yet to begin. Timings were crucial, as was a sense of decorum. The police had closed the requisite section of the entire M4 motorway for several hours either side of the funeral. Heathrow Airport had stopped all aircraft from taking off or landing, too. Many of the visiting heads of state, having left Westminster Abbey, were now itching to get airborne and make up for lost time at the General Assembly of the United Nations in New York. They would still have to wait.

Down at Windsor, cross words broke out in the marquee where those in the final procession were assembling. The Earl Marshal and his fellow marchers eventually arrived with precisely eleven minutes to go before it was time to begin the last long march. To Eddie Norfolk's consternation, some officials were preparing to inform the King that the funeral would need to be delayed by half an hour because of the late departure from London. 'I was not going to have that. We could not have television satellite feeds to Japan and America running out because Britain could not keep to time. We had to stick to the programme,' says Norfolk. 'There were about 200 people in the marquee and, instead of having fifty minutes for lunch, they had zero minutes. As Earl Marshal, in overall charge, I knew there was a need for me to take command and lead from the front. I felt my father willing me on. I went outside to check with [Major General] Chris Ghika and the army were all ready. So I told everyone to get out of the tent immediately. The heralds were all exhausted and were trying to have lunch. I said, "Get out, we're on parade." Someone said: "We need a pee." I said: "Pee on the lawn." Someone else was complaining about not eating. I said: "Too bad."'

The marchers duly followed the Earl Marshal's orders and lined up on the road – with not a minute to spare. For, at that moment, bang on time, the police outriders suddenly appeared from around the corner, escorting the coffin along the Datchet Road. 'God bless the police – and I told them so,' recalls Norfolk. 'They replied: "We knew what we had to do and so we made up time."'

Just imagine what would have happened if the coffin had arrived and the television cameras showed half the procession in a tent eating lunch.' Only half-joking, he adds: 'I would have been roasted. I would have probably had to emigrate to Australia.'

It was a surreal procession as it was, starting down a quiet, empty country lane before a sharp right turn onto Windsor's Long Walk. There, suddenly, were hundreds of thousands of people lining the one-mile avenue. The late monarch's officials marched ahead of the coffin; the new King's officials marched behind. The Royal Family would only join in once the cavalcade had reached the castle. One of the entourage now admits that it had been a very bad idea to buy new shoes for the occasion. 'I was wondering how much longer I could go on during the London leg. Then, at Windsor, we turned the corner and there was the castle way off in the distance and I thought: "We're never going to get there."' As the hearse drew level with the Royal Mews, there was another of the day's defining moments. Even in her final year, the Queen had still managed to ride her beloved Fell pony, Emma. As she told a family friend: 'Luckily, I have a pony who is like me. She only likes to walk and she is quite close to the ground.'[33] There was the Queen's long-serving stud groom and riding companion, Terry Pendry, holding Emma and doffing his hat. They would say goodbye to the monarch together.*

Much to the disappointment of the Household Cavalry, it was decided late in the day that they should only escort the coffin as far as the castle walls, but not inside. There were simply too

---

* Emma continues to be ridden and exercised by Royal Mews staff at Windsor, under the watchful eye of Terry Pendry, who has since been appointed a Military Knight of Windsor. Before her death, the Queen left instructions that, when the time comes, Emma is to be buried in a corner of the park reserved for her very special horses, including her Canadian mare, Burmese.

many people and movements within to accommodate 102 horses, especially as they would then be heading sharply downhill from the upper ward towards the chapel. As it was, two of them bolted on the final stretch of the Long Walk. 'Horses like to walk, trot or canter, so keeping them at funeral speed is very hard and the troopers did very well,' explains Major General Ghika. Even without the cavalry, it was a tight squeeze getting the hearse and the procession through the castle's George IV Gate. One of those alongside the hearse recalls the 'tink-tink-tink' of an equerry's sword hitting the vehicle's paintwork. During all the processions, the Queen's coffin had been closely flanked on either side by pall bearers. Unlike the bearer party, who actually carried the coffin, the pall bearers were the late monarch's former equerries. As one of them, Major James Patrick, explained later: 'The main challenge was not being caught up in the traces of the gun carriage, being run down by the Naval gun carriage crew or having a foot run over by the Royal Hearse.'[34]

At the top of the castle, in the Quadrangle, the King and the family fell in behind the gun carriage for the last march down to St George's Chapel. If the abbey had been all about grandeur, protocol and world leaders, there was now an atmosphere bordering on informality as the various strands of the Queen's personal life came together. 'All the Queen's racing friends were in one section. It was more like a cocktail party, just as she'd have wanted it,' says one of them. As the service started, however, some found the emotional intensity of it all overwhelming. The Duke of Sussex has often talked of being unable to cry at his mother's funeral. Now, though, the tears came. 'I thought of all the big occasions I'd experienced under that roof. Grandpa's farewell, my wedding. Even the ordinary times,' he wrote. 'Suddenly I was wiping my eyes. Why now? I wondered.'[35]

Perhaps because the sense of finality was now inescapable. There was the breaking of the Lord Chamberlain's wand; the removal of the Sceptre, Orb and Crown from the coffin; the Queen's Piper and his fading lament trailing away down the cloister; Garter King of Arms proclaiming the styles and titles of the late Queen and those of her successor (though, to the poor man's eternal regret, he somehow neglected to recite the crucial last line, writ large in capital letters in the Order of Service: 'GOD SAVE THE KING'). It was the sight of the Imperial State Crown being removed from the coffin which is engraved in the memory of the Princess Royal: 'I rather weirdly felt a sense of relief – that somehow it's finished.'[36]

Finally, the coffin began its almost imperceptible descent to the Royal Vault. Outside, the mourners began to peel away while close family members stayed behind. After a small supper, there would follow the most poignant and intimate element of Operation London Bridge: a strictly family-only affair with no officials, let alone cameras. Ever since his death the year before, the Duke of Edinburgh's coffin had been in the Royal Vault, awaiting this moment. Now both he and the Queen would be reunited in the grave, alongside her parents, beneath the King George VI Memorial Chapel.

It had, by any standards, been the most challenging exercise in royal statecraft and ceremonial since the death of Queen Victoria, if not of all time. Whereas Victoria's funeral had suffered a series of blunders, including runaway horses and a garrulous, mentally ill Boer War veteran gatecrashing her burial, this had been all but faultless, as had the events of the previous ten days. 'It would be unusual to do two comparable events in six months, let alone on one day,' reflects a senior member of the Lord Chamberlain's Office.[37] In the circumstances, it was not surprising that the King was not just moved but greatly uplifted by it all.

By common consent, it had been an assured start to a new reign which was moving at pace. The fact that a coronation date would be fixed just three weeks later was further proof of that. Meanwhile, the unexpected stars of those few days had no time to enjoy any of the adulation. The bearer party of Queen's Company Grenadier Guards were not even allowed a spell of home leave. They were on the next available aircraft to Iraq to complete their deployment. They would not be forgotten, however. All would, in due course, receive the Royal Victorian Medal (plus the MVO* for Freddie Hobbs, now promoted to lieutenant). They would also have a pleasant surprise back in Britain during the summer. The All England Club and Garrison Sergeant Major Vern Stokes had arranged for them all to be guests of honour at the 2023 Wimbledon tennis championships.

---

* Member of the Royal Victorian Order

Entering Buckingham Palace for the first time as King and Queen on 9 September 2022, the day after the death of Elizabeth II.

The King greets the prime minister, Liz Truss, at Buckingham Palace on 9 September 2022. She has been in office for three days, he for one.

The Accession Council at St James's Palace, 10 September 2022. The King
signs the oath to 'maintain and preserve' the Church of Scotland.

United front, 10 September 2022. The new Prince and Princess of Wales and the Duke
and Duchess of Sussex meet mourners who have brought flowers to Windsor Castle.

Saluted by crowds from the moment the hearse left Balmoral six hours earlier, Elizabeth II travels down Edinburgh's Royal Mile to the Palace of Holyroodhouse on 11 September 2022.

The King and his siblings stand vigil during the four-day lying-in-state of Queen Elizabeth II at Westminster Hall. More than 250,000 people queued for up to twenty-four hours to pay their respects.

The state funeral of Elizabeth II on 19 September 2022. Charles III leads the Royal Family out of Westminster Abbey behind the coffin. The Imperial State Crown, the Orb and the Sceptre rest on top, along with a wreath including roses, sedum and myrtle chosen by the King.

The final journey. The funeral procession nears the end of Windsor Castle's Long Walk ahead of the Service of Committal at St George's Chapel and the burial.

Following the collapse of the Truss administration after forty-nine days, the King appoints Rishi Sunak as his second prime minister at Buckingham Palace on 25 October 2022.

Two months into his reign, the King assumes the role of Ranger of Windsor Great Park, succeeding his father, the Duke of Edinburgh. The park contains some of the oldest oak trees in the land, including this one.

The first state visitor of the reign is President Cyril Ramaphosa of South Africa on 22 November 2022. Buckingham Palace had not staged a state banquet for more than three years.

Christmas Day 2022 at Sandringham.

The King and Queen are welcomed by members of East London's Bangladeshi community during a visit to Brick Lane on 8 February 2023.

The head of the armed forces is greeted by Ukrainian troops as they undergo training from NATO forces in Wiltshire.

Six months into the new reign, the King and Queen leave the UK for the first time. Their state visit to Germany in March 2023 includes the King's visit to the cheese production line of an organic farm near Brandenburg.

Literacy and literature have long been core parts of the Queen's work. The German state visit includes a trip to a Hamburg school with the German-born illustrator of *The Gruffalo*. Everyone is invited to have a go.

Chapter Six

Transition

In the days after the late Queen's funeral, the King and Queen retreated to Scotland. It was a chance to decompress but also to start making plans. The King had always loved Birkhall, the Queen Mother's former home on the Balmoral estate, with its tartan-lined walls, its collections of Spy cartoons and grandfather clocks and its steep, terraced garden, full of roses and fruit trees, sloping down to the River Muick over which he has built a new suspension bridge for walkers. 'It's lovely to bounce on,' says Queen Camilla, adding that all visiting children make a beeline for it and 'bounce about on the bridge for hours'.[1] The fact that Palace staff would allude to Birkhall as 'the marital home' – a phrase which, tellingly, was not applied to the King's Gloucestershire home, Highgrove – denoted its place in the residential pecking order. Following his accession, he now had the run of more residences than any monarch in modern times, with five in Scotland alone – Balmoral Castle, the Palace of Holyroodhouse, Dumfries House and the Castle of Mey, in addition to Birkhall. He was also master of the monarch's main English residences: Buckingham Palace, Windsor Castle and Sandringham, in addition to his existing homes at Clarence House and Highgrove. He still retained a Romanian farmhouse in Viscri, Transylvania, which he operates through a charitable

121

foundation preserving Saxon culture (and a nod to his own Transylvanian heritage through Queen Mary's grandmother, Claudine, Countess Rhédey). He had also bought a Welsh farm, Llwynywermod, in 2007, ostensibly for use while in Wales but also to promote local Welsh crafts and culture. Like Highgrove, it had been a Duchy of Cornwall purchase and so custody of it now passed to his elder son, as the new Duke of Cornwall. However, both are still very much seen as 'Charles' rather than 'William' properties. The King was aware that being painted as a man with a dozen homes was not a good look at a time of national economic difficulty and began to draw up reforms to the broader royal property portfolio. In addition to all of the above, the new Queen would retain her old home in Wiltshire, Ray Mill, her sanctuary from pre-royal days. Some of the King's staff expected the question of royal residences to become an early 'problem' issue in the media, yet it did not. Perhaps there was just too much else going on on the royal front. Perhaps, among the general public, there was an understanding that after seventy years of one monarch, it would take her successor a while to adjust.

Nor were there loud calls for an overhaul of the royal finances, as some officials privately thought there might be. Having depended on the Duchy of Cornwall throughout his adult life, the King would now hand that on to Prince William and inherit the same system which had financed the previous monarch. Private costs and the rest of the family would continue to be paid for through the Privy Purse, chiefly via the Duchy of Lancaster (which generates around £20 million annually). All official expenditure as head of state is paid for by the annual Sovereign Grant which is pegged to the profits of the Crown Estate, the vast government-run property portfolio. In 2012, the grant was fixed at 15 per cent of profits with a further

10 per cent later added to fund the £369 million cost of refurbishing Buckingham Palace. Shortly after the King's accession, however, the Crown Estate saw a huge spike in projected income thanks to offshore wind licences. Pre-empting headlines about a bumper 'pay rise' during an economic downturn, the King directed that any corresponding rise in royal income should go back to the public purse. Royal officials and the Treasury then agreed to cut the overall funding formula from 25 to 12 per cent, thus keeping the 2024–25 grant the same as before at £86.3 million. For the time being, at least, rows over royal finances would not cloud the start of the new reign.

There was much else to be resolved first, not least the merger of the former household of the Prince of Wales with that of the late Queen. As previously discussed, one of the King's first actions on arriving at Balmoral Castle as King was to ask Sir Edward Young to stay on. He would be called 'Joint Private Secretary to His Majesty The King' and work alongside the King's right-hand man for the previous seven years, Sir Clive Alderton. However, Alderton would now become 'Principal Private Secretary to Their Majesties The King and The Queen Consort'. The title 'Queen Camilla', though entirely correct, would not start to enter official use until the Coronation. Alderton would also move into Sir Edward's former office at Buckingham Palace with its special safe for state documents. Sir Edward would stay on for the transition and then move on after the Coronation.[*]

Sir Clive Alderton's deputy would continue to be Chris Fitzgerald, formerly of the Diplomatic Service. Previously

---

[*] Sir Edward went on to be ennobled as Lord Young of Old Windsor, to be elevated to Knight Grand Cross of the Royal Victorian Order (GCVO) and the Order of the Bath (GCB), and to be appointed to the honorary role of Lord in Waiting to the King.

based at the British mission in Brussels, he was a Foreign Office high-flyer, having followed a similar path to the one that had originally led Alderton to the Palace. These two would be supported by a pair of assistant private secretaries. One would be a senior diplomat on secondment from a Commonwealth nation. New Zealand's Nathan Ross now occupies a post previously filled by a Canadian who had succeeded an Indian. The other joint number three was Dr John Sorabji, an expert in constitutional law who served all through the period of transition and then returned to academe after completing a review of royal patronages. He has since been replaced by Muna Shamsuddin, a former head of department at the Foreign Office. As Prince of Wales, the King had also created the entirely new role of director of community engagement to ensure that his work reached parts of society which might not normally have much time for (or contact with) royalty, especially among minority communities. He had appointed Dr Eva Omaghomi, formerly of the Prince's Trust International, and he wanted her performing the same role for him as monarch. In other words, the cadre of senior officials around the King might, perhaps, suggest a leaning towards diplomats and internationalists. No one, though, could complain that he was surrounding himself with old-school courtiers drawn from the smarter regiments or the aristocracy.

There would also be a great deal more work for what had previously been the office of the Duchess of Cornwall. Led by her private secretary, Sophie Densham, this small team was now running the first full-time consort operation since the retirement of the Duke of Edinburgh in 2017. Nor had there been a Queen Consort for seventy years.

By chance, a major reshuffle had already started within the royal media operation during the days before the Queen's death.

The Court Circular will record that Elizabeth II's last official engagement – shortly after appointing Liz Truss as prime minister – was to invest her outgoing press chief, Donal McCabe, as a Lieutenant of the Royal Victorian Order (LVO). At the same time, the Prince of Wales had just appointed a new head of his media operations. He had, by way of a change, turned to the top echelons of Fleet Street rather than the world of public relations or government communications. His choice was Tobyn Andreae, deputy editor of the *Daily Mail*, Britain's bestselling newspaper. Andreae's expertise in navigating a fast-changing news landscape would prove invaluable even as he was still preparing to take up his new position. On the morning of 8 September, he set off for a planning meeting as the incoming communications secretary to the Prince of Wales and the Duchess of Cornwall. By the time he returned home on his first day, the job specification had changed already. His new bosses were now Their Majesties The King and The Queen Consort.

Where possible, offices would merge, though some job cuts would be inevitable, especially in the former princely operation at Clarence House. Everyone accepted that things would have to change under a new monarch. Many staff felt that the process should have been handled rather more sensitively, especially when they received what amounted to a redundancy notice in the middle of the first service of thanksgiving for the Queen at St Giles' Cathedral, Edinburgh. In a general letter to Clarence House staff, leaked to *The Guardian*, Sir Clive Alderton wrote that staff 'supporting the former Prince of Wales's personal interests, former activities and household operations . . . will no longer be needed.' He added: 'I appreciate that this is unsettling news and I wanted to let you know of the support that is available at this point.'[2] One insider concedes that while the timing was 'dreadful', Palace personnel were worried they should actually have issued the notice much sooner. Given that employers are obliged to inform employees immediately of any change in circumstance which might cause more than twenty redundancies, a sharp-eyed lawyer could have argued that the missive ought to have been sent on the day of the Queen's death.

The new monarch also asked the late Queen's Master of the Household, Vice Admiral Sir Tony Johnstone-Burt, to remain in post. The Falklands War veteran and specialist in helicopter warfare had started the job nine years earlier, taking charge of around 250 staff spanning 'F' branch (food), 'H' branch (housekeeping) and 'G' branch (general). He had been the architect of the protective cocoon around the Queen and Prince Philip during the Covid pandemic, a system which he nicknamed 'HMS Bubble', because of the similarities with life at sea.

Long before the new reign, the Master of the Household had been working to ensure that his staff were ready for the inevitable change of pace that would accompany it. That might mean a few tweaks to the kitchen routines. For example, the new King refuses to serve foie gras, has a fondness for egg dishes, hates lunch (as previously noted), likes an old-fashioned tea and prefers menus in English rather than French. However, he also arrived with an overall vision for the way he wanted to use Buckingham Palace for entertaining. 'The King was clear about having four priorities for himself and the Queen Consort: communities, Commonwealth, climate and biodiversity, and culture and the arts. So the "Four C's", as we call them, are the North Star we follow,' says one of Johnstone-Burt's team. 'These are our instructions. The King will say: "Lip service is not good enough, I want to make a difference." We have got to be ready to do this on roller skates if necessary. We've got to be flexible.'[3]

There would, though, be no tinkering with the most wide-ranging department of all. The Lord Chamberlain's Office handles protocol, ceremonial, the presentation of honours, royal clergy, the Royal Medical Household (the royal doctors) and even the monarch's swans. In the office of any other head of state this would probably be called the Protocol Department, but no other head of state has to appoint Poet Laureates or deal with bargemasters, watermen and the Honourable Corps of Gentlemen at Arms. To confuse things further it is not actually run by the Lord Chamberlain but by an ex-military figure called the Comptroller and his team. 'It was once mooted that we should be called "the Protocol Office",' explains a senior member of this small, polymathic unit. 'But the late Queen said – and I say this in staff meetings – "We don't do protocol. We do manners here." If people are feeling uncomfortable because we stick rigidly to things, then it's not good manners.'[4]

One immediate and very obvious effect of the change of reign was a drop in temperature. When Edward VIII became King in 1936, he famously went round Sandringham ordering all the clocks to be switched back to real time instead of 'Sandringham Time'.* There was an echo of that when the King walked into Balmoral for the first time as King. 'It was quite hot and one of the first things he said was: "Let's get some windows open",' says one member of staff.[5] The King's dislike of stuffy rooms is well known to those who have worked with him over the years. The Conservative politician Jeremy Hunt remembers meetings with the then Prince of Wales at Clarence House during Hunt's days as health secretary: 'He never turns the heating on in the winter months, to avoid climate change,

---

* Introduced by Edward VII, Sandringham Time or 'ST' involved forwarding the clocks by half an hour in winter to extend the day's shooting.

and it gets pretty chilly in there.'[6] Buckingham Palace staff can now tell the King's whereabouts simply by looking at the windows. If the net curtains are flapping, a window is open and he cannot be far away. Queen Camilla has always been entirely happy for him to have his fresh air and an icy breeze blowing through most parts of the house, as long as she can keep her own study, in the words of one member of staff, 'like a sauna'. The one downside of this extra ventilation, however, can be an increase in noise from outside. Six months into the reign, officers of the Household Division received a polite request from the King's equerry asking if soldiers might lower the decibels when barking orders outside St James's Palace. 'Full marks for vigour,' he wrote, 'but please could you pass down to those on guard that some volume control would be very much appreciated.'[7]

The palace was still some way off being a suitable place of work, let alone a home, for the royal couple during those early days. Even the monarch's study was still a building site as the ten-year refurbishment programme continued to move from one wing to the next. It was well known that the King and Queen Consort had no great wish to swap Clarence House for royal headquarters. Elizabeth II and Prince Philip had felt the same in 1952. Back then, the prime minister, Winston Churchill, had been very clear that monarchs should live 'above the shop' and it was akin to formal ministerial advice. It had been a tearful move, according to Prince Philip's equerry, Mike Parker.[8] There was no prospect of Liz Truss or her successor as prime minister, Rishi Sunak, presuming to dictate where monarchs should live. However, the King immediately accepted that the business of monarchy needed to be conducted from the palace.

In those early days, he set up a study in the newly refurbished

Belgian Suite, the ground-floor apartment, next to the swimming pool, where visiting heads of state usually stay. He has since moved his workplace upstairs into the late Queen's study, the desk now marginally less cluttered with photographs but the view out over the garden unchanged.

He has also given plenty of thought to what happens to the palace after the refurbishment work is completed. As the headquarters of the head of state, with hundreds of staff based there, it cannot simply become a regular seven-day tourist attraction, as some have suggested. On the other hand, the King wants to widen public access well beyond the current summer opening times laid down by the late Queen when she was away at Balmoral. His preferred solution is to follow the business model for Windsor Castle. That is open on most days of the year, raising funds to maintain the treasures of the Royal Collection Trust (RCT), although there are some days when certain state apartments are off-limits because they are needed for an investiture or a royal reception. 'The aim is for what we call "maximum-flexi",' says one official. 'When this work finishes in 2027 we will be judged on the amount of public access. This is going to be "the people's palace" and the aim is to open it as much as possible throughout the year. It may not be on the scale of summer opening but we can do weekends, we can do private tours. It's all down to the set-up. So, you might have a big reception for the King one evening but you want that room open to the public the next day.'[9]

With greater access, however, come financial concerns. At present, the RCT opens up the palace to the public during the summer months. The RCT can then recruit temporary staff and set fixed budgets. Increasing footfall and ticket sales does not always equal more income for the trust, though. Trying to open throughout the year, on a variable basis depending on royal events and state occasions, could prove costly. As a charity, the RCT cannot knowingly set out to make a loss. It can generate funds by making full use of a part-time workforce. Making partial use of a full-time workforce could soon lose money. 'We did look at the RCT projections,' says one official. 'It's very hard to make it work.'

At the time of the Queen's death, the private parts of the palace were undergoing a complete overhaul for staff and guests alike, notably in the east wing, which most people think of as the front. The top floor has always been staff accommodation. The northern half used to be known as 'Finches' Floor', with all-women bedrooms and a shared bathroom block. The other half was 'Pages' Floor' for men. After the refurbishment, every third bedroom will have been divided into two bathrooms, providing en-suite, unisex accommodation across the floor. The next floor down, the Chamber Floor, will revert to office space for members of the Royal Family. Below that, the Principal Floor contains the grander guest suites, in between conference rooms like the Chinese Drawing Room. These suites, which are usually allocated to the senior members of a visiting entourage, are being modernized to include showers and office space in place of elderly bathrooms and sitting rooms. The aim is to be able to switch easily from offices to bedrooms and back again, in keeping with the 'maximum-flexi' mantra.

Squeezed between the Principal Floor and the ground-floor offices are the tiny windows of the Mezzanine Floor. These low-ceilinged rooms had long been used as offices until the architects discovered that they were actually too small to meet the minimum oxygen requirements for shared office space, but could be used as bedrooms. When the late Queen was informed, says one staffer, she was unsurprised. 'Well, of course,' she replied. 'They always used to be bedrooms in the past.' So these rooms are now being converted back into small bedrooms for overnight staff accommodation. If a Gentleman Usher needs a berth for a night, he will be put here. 'The whole objective is to have this place fit for the twenty-first century and still working properly for King George VII in 2077,' says one of Sir Tony Johnstone-Burt's team. Mindful of the 'climate change' element of the King's 'four C's', Johnstone-Burt's project managers are also working on next-generation solar panels, heat exchange units beneath the palace lake, and 'slinky' heat pipes.

Two weeks after the Queen's funeral, the new King and Queen Consort began regular public duties, still firmly based in Scotland. There was a visit to confer city status on the ancient abbey town of Dunfermline. The diary included engagements with the Scottish Seafood Association and Glasgow's Burrell Collection. Closer to their Birkhall home, the Queen Consort visited the Braemar Literary Festival and the couple went to thank the neighbours in Ballater for their support following the Queen's death. Even when there were important engagements in London, such as a Privy Council meeting or a visit from the King of Malaysia, the King returned to Scotland soon afterwards.

In part, it was because he loves the place and, as monarch, has a greater say in deciding what he can do, where and when. In part, there remains that perennial, unspoken royal angst about the future of the 'U' in United Kingdom. 'It's something all the Royal Family think about all the time, especially in Scotland. It's not just about shortbread, pipers and kilts, and the family need to reflect that,' says a former adviser to the late Queen, adding that the first constitutional drama of her own reign involved Scotland. There were many complaints and even legal action when it was confirmed that the new monarch would be Elizabeth II of Scotland, regardless of the fact that there had never been an Elizabeth I north of the border. There was also an outbreak of vandalism against Scottish pillar boxes bearing the 'EIIR' cypher. The Queen and her ministers had simply been following established royal precedent. She was Queen Elizabeth II of Australia, New Zealand and umpteen other places which had never known Elizabeth I either. Moreover, she had been proclaimed Elizabeth II by the Privy Council at her accession. However, Winston Churchill was sufficiently alarmed by this early challenge to the Queen's authority that he made two concessions. The Post Office in Scotland would use the Scottish Crown rather than 'EIIR' on its pillar boxes and postal vans. Churchill also adopted a new policy on regnal names (though its legality remains unclear). He announced that monarchs would 'adopt, in future, whichever numeral in the English or Scottish line were higher.'[10] The starting point for English names would be the Norman conquest of 1066 and, for Scottish names, 1306 (the coronation of Robert the Bruce). So, a future King Edward, for example, would still be Edward IX. A future King James would, though, be James VIII in all corners of the kingdom and not James III. That is because England might have known James I and II, but Scotland has had seven of them. Elizabeth II and her officials remained nervous to the point of paranoia about inciting any fresh nationalist sentiment. Soon after her Coronation in June 1953, the Queen had been due to attend a service of dedication at St Giles' Cathedral in Edinburgh. The organizers wanted her to hold the Scottish sceptre during the service. The very suggestion prompted her private secretary, Sir Alan 'Tommy' Lascelles, to raise it with the prime minister, who, in turn, sought legal advice from the Lord Chancellor, Lord Simonds. Back came stern words of warning. 'Anything that would suggest the service was in the nature of a second Coronation would be undesirable,' wrote the Lord Chancellor's advisers, adding that 'this symbolism might be regarded as implying that Her Majesty recognized Scotland as a separate Kingdom.' The ministerial advice was clear: 'The Lord Chancellor therefore thinks that it would not be proper for Her Majesty to hold the Scottish sceptre on that occasion.'[11] She duly inspected it instead. Charles III would do exactly the same when he came to receive the Honours of Scotland at St Giles' Cathedral in Edinburgh in July 2023. However, he went to great lengths to give his event a more pronounced Scottish flavour than the service for his mother in 1953. Scottish traditionalists had been upset that Elizabeth II had arrived in day dress. Charles III wore the robes and insignia of the Order of the Thistle. He also commissioned several new works from Scottish composers for a service which was widely acclaimed for the calibre of its music.

Writing a joint paper for three major think-tanks in the first weeks of the reign of Charles III, Professor Robert Hazell, founder of the Constitution Unit at University College London, identified two dominant issues for the new King: Scotland and the realms. 'The main challenge to the monarchy lies in the threat to the union. If Scotland votes to become independent, that will damage the monarchy's standing, even though responsibility will lie with the politicians,' he concluded. Republicanism overseas, on the other hand, was a lesser threat: 'If some of the fourteen other realms where Charles is now head of state decide to become republics, the monarchy may privately be relieved. It would reduce the workload, and the risk of reputational damage.'[12] As will be discussed elsewhere, that risk of reputational damage – primarily from campaigns for historical justice and reparations – is not something the King either can or wishes to ignore.

However, there is little Charles III can do with regard to the monarchy's future in these realms, beyond listening to his governors-general and endorsing the democratic process, as he has always done. In assessing the King's options regarding the Union, however, Hazell affirmed that this would be trickier: 'It will be hard to stand idly by, but a greater risk to the monarchy would be to allow itself to be co-opted by unionist politicians, as Liz Truss attempted to do when she sought to join Charles's inaugural tour of the nations.' Truss's presence at the King's side in the capitals of the home nations during those days immediately after the Queen's death did indeed lead several commentators to suggest that she was somehow trying to politicize the moment or burnish her prime ministerial credentials in her first week in office. She emphatically denies this. Her presence alongside the new King, she says, was part of the pre-agreed plan for Operation London Bridge and would always have applied to whomever happened to be prime minister of the day: 'I was simply invited to go along and I thought it was the right thing. One of the first things we decided when we came in to office was that we were not going to be changing any of the [funeral] plans.'[13]

The new King and his first prime minister barely had time to establish any sort of rapport. They met on several occasions in the days after the Queen's death. However, once the funeral was over, there were only two of the regular weekly audiences which are the cornerstone of the King's constitutional role. After the first one, there was much hilarity on social media when the King was filmed greeting Truss with the words: 'Back again . . . Dear oh dear.' The Twitter commentariat instantly interpreted this as an unguarded royal dig at Truss. It was nothing of the sort but, rather, a typically Charles-ish sympathetic remark because Truss had already been at the Palace earlier for a Privy Council meeting. 'He was simply saying "I'm sorry you've had to make another trip". That's all,' says an aide. Truss says she was unaware of the jokes doing the rounds on Twitter and elsewhere. 'By this stage, I was not reading any media, I was so frustrated with it.'[14] She says she enjoyed her encounters with the King and always found him fully briefed, as he had been years earlier when she met him as Prince of Wales in her days as environment secretary. 'He's humorous, friendly, very engaged on the issues,' she says. 'At the time, there was a lot of Vladimir Putin sabre-rattling going on and we talked a lot about Russia.'

She adds that she had always enjoyed the company of Queen Camilla when both were in their previous roles. Both attended the state reception at that COP26 summit in Glasgow in 2021. As foreign secretary, Truss was deputed to escort the then Duchess of Cornwall around the formal welcome party at the Kelvingrove Art Gallery. 'I was her chaperone and I was meant to be taking her to meet the Alpine leaders – Austria and Switzerland and so on,' she says. 'But she's such an engaging character. It was very hard to get her across this room, especially past Angela Merkel, who was demob happy and very keen to talk to the Duchess. I got her there in the end.'[15]

On 19 October, the King received Liz Truss for only her second weekly audience at Buckingham Palace. The following day, he received her telephone call to say that she was going to resign. His reign had barely begun; it was only hours earlier that he had held his first 'credentials' ceremonies to welcome new heads of mission to the UK (the new ambassador for Ukraine and the new high commissioner for Pakistan). Now, he was about to welcome a new prime minister. Truss's first attempt at a radical 'mini-budget' had spooked the markets and sent the pound crashing to an all-time low against the dollar. She had lost the confidence of her party. On a personal level, says a friend, the King felt sympathy for a woman destined to go down in the history books for the shortest premiership in British politics. He himself had already exceeded the country's shortest reign (Lady Jane Grey) and would surpass that of Edward V a month later. When Truss came to resign formally five days later, she brought her husband and also her children to meet the King. 'He was very sympathetic to the situation. I remember him talking to my daughters about what they wanted to do and what they liked doing at school,' she recalls. 'I saw him again at Remembrance Sunday and he said: "Your daughters are terribly good at maths", which was nice of him.'[16]

No sooner had Truss and her family left the room than the King prepared for his first appointment of a prime minister. Rishi Sunak had been the runner-up during the long summer battle for the Conservative leadership which had eventually yielded Liz Truss. The last thing the British electorate had wanted was another protracted bout of navel-gazing by the Tory Party. It was spared. The vacancy left by Truss had been filled in four days. A half-hearted bid from previous leadership hopeful Penny Mordaunt had fizzled out and a much-hyped return by Boris Johnson never materialized. Less than two months after succeeding to the throne, the King was already starting to look like a veteran at the helm of a meandering ship of state.

Soon afterwards, he was presiding over one of the most demanding but spectacular set-pieces in the royal repertoire. A state visit requires the full involvement of every department within the Royal Household – from the chefs in the kitchens and the grooms in the Royal Mews right up to the Lord Chamberlain. The King had been keen to press ahead with the autumn state visit of the president of South Africa, which was already at the early planning stage before the death of the Queen. After her accession, Elizabeth II had waited more than two years before welcoming her first state visitors, the King and Queen of Sweden (the latter was Prince Philip's aunt). Charles III waited two months. Since the builders had now finished work on Buckingham Palace's main state apartments, the ballroom could accommodate a state banquet once again. It had been more than three years since Britain had last organized a state visit. Donald Trump, who arrived in June 2019 ahead of the seventy-fifth anniversary of D-Day, has the distinction of being the last state visitor of the Queen's reign. That was followed by the Covid pandemic, the death of Prince Philip and the declining health of the Queen. Now, as the new Head of the Commonwealth, the King was keen to organize his first incoming state visit in honour of one of the most important Commonwealth nations. It would also be the first major post-accession, post-Covid, post-refurbishment test for the Master of the Household and his team. Except that much of the rest of the palace was still in the process of being refurbished. The building team were not happy. 'Our rather serious French project manager has said this is like conducting open heart surgery on someone running a marathon,' admitted one of the Master of the Household's team, going about his rounds on the morning of the banquet. Most of the Royal Household team, however, were delighted to be dusting off the gold plate and the Royal Minton dinner service once again. Here and there were nods to the new reign. The flower displays around and on top of the state banquet table were all in autumnal colours and sourced locally, with plenty of berries and crab apples from Windsor. For the previous state visit by a South African president, that of President Jacob Zuma in 2010, the ballroom had been a riot of colour, just as the Queen wished it to be. That meant plenty of imported flowers, including gerberas from South Africa and orchids flown in from Singapore. The King wanted the decorations to be more sustainable from now on, even if that meant a more sober look to the ballroom. In other regards, the King had followed tradition. Despite his aversion to eating in the middle of the working day, there would, nonetheless, be the customary welcome lunch for the state visitor (all of it local and seasonal produce, including a cold poached egg with the langoustine starter). The menus, for this visit at least, would also be in French, as the late Queen preferred.

There were a few teething troubles, notably the official welcome on Horse Guards. The usual pavilion had been erected. The usual line-up of the prime minister, senior ministers and the chiefs from the services waited to be presented by the monarch. However, no sooner had Cyril Ramaphosa completed the ritual inspection of the Guard of Honour than the King invited him to board the Irish State Coach for the carriage procession. The VIPs had been ignored and returned to their offices without so much as a handshake. It was an easy oversight for a monarch hosting his first state welcome but some old hands wondered why there had been no one there to nudge him. 'It looked poor. It's not as if the prime minister had nothing better to do,' was the verdict of one ex-Palace official.

Following lunch, the King and Queen Consort, along with the Prince and Princess of Wales, led the South African entourage through to the special exhibition laid out in the Picture Gallery, just as the late Queen liked to do. The Royal Collection would always find appropriate treasures and documents linking the monarchy and the honoured guest, after some careful, diplomatic pruning of the low points in the bilateral relationship (of which there are usually many, given Britain's naval, military and imperial past). So, this exhibition skipped swiftly from photos of the first royal visit to South Africa, by Prince Alfred in 1860, to the Queen's first visit in 1947 and then on to memories of the reciprocal visits by the Queen and Nelson Mandela. 'This lovely picture,' remarked Mr Ramaphosa, observing a shot of those two post-war giants. 'You were lucky to have known them both,' the King replied. Also in the display was the magnificent chess set which Mandela had given the Duke of Edinburgh.

Later in the day, the King was keen to check on the banqueting arrangements. Elizabeth II always did this on her own. The King was very clear he wanted to do this jointly with Queen Camilla, so the two of them inspected all the arrangements together, talking to the florists and table-layers. Flowers aside, the palace ballroom looked exactly as it would have done for the late Queen. The state banquet is the one occasion when exuberant opulence is the order of the day and George IV's gold-plated extravagance is laid out, unapologetically, for all to see. There was, though, one very subtle difference this time – a less feminine ambiance. This was not just because it was the first banquet in more than seven decades hosted by a King. It was also because Ramaphosa had come without his wife, who was undergoing an operation at home. So the royal procession into dinner was led by two men, albeit closely followed by Queen Camilla and the Princess of Wales in evening gowns (both careful not to wear diplomatically difficult off-cuts from the Cullinan Diamond).* Before the (locally sourced) dinner of brill, Windsor pheasant and vanilla parfait with seasonal berries, the King greeted his guest with the words for 'welcome' in all of the six main dialects of South Africa. 'President Ramaphosa,' he began. '*Avuxeni, Dumela, Sawubona, Molo, Molweny, Ndaa.* My wife and I are delighted to welcome you to Buckingham Palace this evening.' It was an oratorical flourish

---

* Extracted from South Africa's Cullinan mine in 1905, it was the largest gem-grade diamond ever found, given to Edward VII in 1907 and cut into smaller pieces. In recent years, there have been unofficial demands for its repatriation.

which the late Queen would not have tried, though she did famously preface her 2011 state banquet speech in Dublin with a few words of Gaelic.

The state visit was also a reminder of the reduction in front-line 'working' royalty. The Waleses and the Wessexes were present but the Princess Royal and her husband, Sir Tim Laurence, were on an official tour of the Falkland Islands. The royal guests included those regular stalwarts, the Duke and Duchess of Gloucester, aged seventy-eight and seventy-six, and the eighty-seven-year-old Duke of Kent. However, here was the Royal Family as 'slimmed down' as it had been in years. It had been no great surprise, just days earlier, when the King had announced two small but significant changes to the rules governing the list of counsellors of state. These are the handful of royal names permitted to stand in for an absent monarch. Previously limited to the monarch's consort plus the four adults closest in line to the throne, this meant that the Dukes of Sussex and York could, in theory, be called upon to sign legislation in certain circumstances. Rather than take the more aggressive step of deleting Sussex and York from the list, the King simply extended it. He stated that he would be 'most content' if Parliament saw fit to include the Princess Royal and the Earl of Wessex (both of whom had previously been counsellors of state in years gone by anyway, until Princes William and Harry had come of age). Nor were there any objections, four months later, when the King declared that the Earl of Wessex was to become the Duke of Edinburgh. Indeed, since that had been the clearly expressed wish of the late Queen and Prince Philip on the Earl's wedding day in 1999, some had started to wonder why the King was taking so long. It transpired that he had waited until the Earl's birthday to make the announcement.

Chapter Seven

'Headwinds'

If the King could have been said to have had a 'honeymoon period' – as the media likes to define the first phase of any new administration – then it was not a long one. A change in the weather occurred just a month after the Queen's funeral, on 20 October to be precise. That was the day on which the first trailer appeared to promote the new series of *The Crown*, the lavishly produced Netflix dramatization of the late Queen's life.

Now embarking on its fifth season, the plot had reached the nadir of her reign, focusing on the mid-1990s and, in particular, the collapsing marriage of the Prince and Princess of Wales. The trailer made much of the misery of a tearful Diana beneath the strapline 'The Beginning of the End.' As the pre-publicity inevitably triggered articles revisiting old scandals and reopening old wounds, the Palace did not engage. Like many of the family, the new King had never watched the drama. One of his aides had called the previous series 'trolling on a Hollywood budget.' There had been particular irritation after Prince Harry had said it was 'loosely based on truth', not long after initial reports that the Sussexes had struck their own deal with Netflix.[1] 'Would Harry have spoken if he didn't have a contract with the broadcaster?' asked one former staffer. 'It stinks.'

Charles III

The first inkling of the Sussexes' Netflix project would be revealed soon enough: a six-part fly-on-the-wall confessional, *Harry & Meghan*. Even that was only going to be a prelude, a mere hors d'oeuvre, ahead of something bigger still. For, on 27 October, just one week after that trailer for *The Crown*, Prince Harry's publishers announced that his long-awaited memoir* was finally close to completion and would be published around the world in early January. Promising 'raw, unflinching honesty', it would be variously titled *Spare* (in English language editions), *The Minor* (Italy), *Reserve* (Germany), *The Other One* (Poland), and so on. It was not hard to detect an overarching underdog theme.

The announcement all but eclipsed the news, on the same day, that the Royal Mint had struck the first coins featuring the face of the King. The 50p coin would be in circulation by December with the King following tradition and facing to the left (in the opposite direction to his predecessor). After the Queen acceded to the throne, it had been seven months before she was invited to approve the first coin – a penny – featuring her image. Here was another example of that monarch in a hurry, keen to maximize 'the remaining time God grants me'.

Asked about the King's feelings on all this imminent incoming fire from the Sussexes and their associates, one Palace staffer talked of 'headwinds that we face from across the Atlantic'.[2] That was one way of describing an extraordinary twelve-week run of non-stop disobliging headlines and combative allegations, all of them entirely beyond the control of the King and his staff. Storm-force gales might have been a better metaphor.

Even back in the dark and dismal 1990s, when royal fortunes were at a generational low, the Royal Family would not endure

---

* Prince Harry and his publishers, Penguin Random House, had first announced he was writing an 'intimate' memoir in June 2021.

quite such a concentrated series of painful revelations in such a short time. That this should all be unfolding in the first phase of a new reign might once have been considered disastrous. However, there were two unexpected aspects to these 'headwinds' which would work in Charles III's favour. First, this constant diet of extraneous negativity, though awkward and at times embarrassing, made very little impact on public attitudes towards the monarchy. Surveys and opinion polls show that any subsequent small dip in support corrected itself soon afterwards. Second, it appeared to have no discernible impact on the King himself. Like his mother before him, he was clearly enjoying being monarch.

The new series of *The Crown* finally landed on 9 November, four days before the King was due to lead the nation in honouring Britain's war dead at the Cenotaph on Remembrance Sunday. During the previous two seasons of *The Crown*, Prince Charles had been played by Josh O'Connor as a hunched, brooding self-doubter. Now, with Dominic West taking over the role, he had acquired a more aggressive, alpha persona. The makers of the series and its many fans like to say 'it's only a drama'. The Palace fear that, following its global success, it is gradually becoming a settled narrative of the modern royal story, accepted broadly as fact by many millions of people around the world. With reported production budgets of £10 million per episode, *The Crown's* sumptuous locations, costumes and casts lend extra credence to plotlines which, in some cases, are a wilful distortion of the truth, if not pure fantasy.

Prince Philip was deeply hurt to be informed that an early episode blamed him for the death of his sister and her family in a plane crash.* A subsequent series included the Queen

---

* The death of Princess Cecilie and her young family in 1937 was an accident that had nothing to do with sixteen-year-old Prince Philip.

purportedly conspiring with her staff to undermine Mrs Thatcher's government.[*] Now, two months into the new reign, the latest series began by showing the Queen ordering Prime Minister John Major to replace the royal yacht. Major was shown to be under parallel pressure from a scheming Prince of Wales, desperate for his turn on the throne. The real Sir John Major swiftly issued a statement dismissing this as 'a barrel-load of malicious nonsense'. It had reached the point where eminent figures from the world of the arts, such as Dame Judi Dench, publicly called for the series to carry a health warning. Eventually, the producers added a disclaimer to the trailer, conceding that it was 'fictional dramatization', though the series itself went ahead without one.

Those 'headwinds' then started blowing from within, following the first of a bold new style of Buckingham Palace event. On 29 November, the Queen Consort took over the state apartments to host a reception honouring the international campaign against violence to women and girls. Like her campaigning to promote literacy, this is a key strand to Queen Camilla's public work. As noted earlier, there was a remarkable guest list, including the first ladies of seven nations alongside many victims of abuse. It was the first time that guests at an ostensibly traditional reception in the palace's Picture Gallery had paused midway to hear their royal host deliver a powerful, gritty speech on a subject like this. The Queen Consort listed the names of some of the women killed in the past year alone, victims of a 'global pandemic of violence'. Survivors, representatives of charities large and small and celebrity campaigners were delighted and honoured to be recognized in this way. It was an event that

---

[*] *The Crown* reimagined events after the 1986 *Sunday Times* report that the Queen found Mrs Thatcher 'uncaring'. In reality, a royal aide had voiced his own opinions, then denied it and later resigned.

would never have happened under the late monarch, not that anyone was objecting to it taking place under the new one. It was, however, definitely a noteworthy moment for those caring to chronicle the transition.

The following day, however, social media exploded for different reasons. One guest had alleged that a lady-in-waiting had been much too direct in her line of questioning. Ngozi Fulani, representing Sistah Space, a London-based charity for women of African and Caribbean heritage, posted her version of the conversation on Twitter. She later said that she had felt 'interrogated' and 'violated' after a woman she identified as 'Lady SH' had repeatedly asked 'where are you from?' and 'where do you really come from?' Hours later, a mortified Lady Susan Hussey had unhesitatingly apologized and offered her resignation from her honorary, unpaid position. It was one she had occupied since 1960, when she first became a lady-in-waiting to Elizabeth II. The widowed eighty-three-year-old was also godmother to Prince William. The previous year, it had been Lady Susan who had accompanied the Queen to the funeral of Prince Philip. She was among the most trusted of the trusted. A public debate raged on, with both her and Fulani subjected to vitriolic online abuse.

Just hours after Fulani's original message on Twitter, the Palace had issued a statement saying that it had 'investigated immediately' and that 'unacceptable and deeply regrettable comments' had been made. It added: 'We have reached out to Ngozi Fulani on this matter, and we are inviting her to discuss all elements of her experience in person if she wishes.' Without naming Lady Susan, it went on: 'The individual concerned would like to express her profound apologies for the hurt caused and has stepped aside from her honorary role with immediate effect. All members of the Household are being reminded of the diversity and inclusivity policies which they are required to uphold at all times.'

Charles III

There was no recording and, thus, no transcript, but Ngozi Fulani's version had been endorsed by two witnesses and was not challenged by the Palace. The Prince and Princess of Wales were, at that very moment, about to board a plane to the USA for the announcement of the former's 2022 Earthshot Prize. Their staff were frantically calling Buckingham Palace for further details before take-off. Given the months of preparation for this event, and the fact that it was their first visit to the USA since the Sussexes had set up their rival court in California, they had visions of the whole mission being derailed by a 'royal race storm'. Did they let the Palace's statement stand or should they issue words of their own, too? With the aeroplane about to start its engines at Heathrow, the Prince put out a statement of his own: 'I was really disappointed to hear about the experiences of a guest at Buckingham Palace. Racism has no place in our society, these comments were unacceptable and it is right that the individual concerned has stepped down.'

Some within the royal orbit felt that the Prince's intervention was 'overkill', especially given that Lady Susan was his godmother. The messaging was clear, though: any unforced errors which might bring the institution into disrepute could not be tolerated. Just as she'd always done for more than sixty years, Sue Hussey had been trying to strike up conversation with nervous guests at a daunting reception. It had been a well-intentioned attempt to seek some sort of common ground. One of those guests, however, had clearly felt marginalized and unwelcome as a result. The monarchy had already been stung by the Sussexes' allegations of institutional racism during their television interview with Oprah Winfrey the previous year. Meghan had said that, during her first pregnancy, there had been 'concerns and conversations' within the Royal Family about the likely colour of the baby's skin. The Waleses were

146

still smarting from their Caribbean tour earlier in the year which had been attacked for 'colonial' overtones. Given the possibility of similar claims – or worse – from multiple Sussex platforms in the coming weeks, the King could not afford any charges of double standards. With a speed that astonished the Palace's regular critics, a case which had landed out of nowhere on social media at 7.25 a.m. had been heard, judged and closed by teatime. Twitter was barely getting into its stride when its target had already stepped aside. Some of Sue Hussey's legion of loyal friends were perplexed, however. This had been a noisy, crowded, international gathering (with many people in various forms of national dress). Given that guests and representatives from so many countries were present, there was plenty of 'where are you from?'-style interaction. With more than six decades of royal receptions all over the world behind her, would the lady-in-waiting have spoken precisely those words attributed to her? Fulani herself had said that she did not want Lady Susan to lose her job (the unpaid honorary position was never a 'job', as such). A few weeks later, Prince Harry would voice sympathy, saying 'Meghan and I love Susan Hussey' as he blamed the whole sorry saga on 'the British press'. So, was Lady Susan really to be dispensed with just like that? Yes and no.

The Palace had to act fast and be seen to do so, too. The King's main concern, thereafter, was that the two women should be reconciled. His director of community engagement, Dr Eva Omaghomi, set to work along with the Bishop of Dover, Rose Hudson-Wilkin, honorary chaplain to the King (and formerly to the Speaker of the Commons) and the Church of England's first black female bishop. Two weeks later, they organized a reunion in the more intimate setting of the Regency Room. Overlooking the garden, this quiet green and gold drawing room is where the late Queen would often record her broadcasts. It was, according to one of those present, a warm and very emotional gathering over several cups of tea: 'There were plenty of tears all round. Lady Susan apologized unequivocally and Ngozi had even brought her a gift. The main thing was that they should part as friends – which they did.'[3] It is an indication of how gravely the Royal Household regarded the matter that the details of a private meeting were released through a Buckingham Palace statement. 'Lady Susan has pledged to deepen her awareness of the sensitivities involved,' it added. 'Ms Fulani, who has unfairly received the most appalling torrent of abuse on social media and elsewhere, has accepted this apology and appreciates that no malice was intended.' The Palace also pledged to 'focus on inclusion and diversity, with an enhanced programme of work which will extend knowledge and training programmes.'

The experience had shaken both women profoundly. Neither would continue in their respective public roles. Fulani would step back from her position within her charity soon afterwards. Meanwhile, the Palace was already phasing out the centuries-old lady-in-waiting role which Sue Hussey, together with Dame Mary Morrison, had performed for as long as anyone in the history of the Court. The Queen Consort wanted a less formal pool of her own friends who could be called upon on an ad hoc basis. They would be known as 'Queen's companions' (as it happens, they would include Lady Susan's daughter, Katharine). The King's personal affection for a loyal family friend who had been at the side of the late Queen through most of her reign remained undimmed. He also liked to be able to talk to Lady Susan as a great repository of royal knowledge and would continue to do so. With the exception of himself and his sister, there are few people inside the palace whose experience of state occasions and royal engagements could rival Lady Susan Hussey's. Thousands (perhaps tens of thousands) of people will have received one of the letters she would write on behalf of the late Queen, be it a reply to a picture sent by a child or a thank-you letter for a gift during a walkabout. Those decades of service are reflected in her continued presence at private events inside the palace and at Royal Family gatherings.

Another reason for the Palace's instant response to the incident was that it drew attention to a shortcoming of which it was acutely aware: the institution needed to be more diverse and inclusive. The 2023 Sovereign Grant annual report showed that 12.2 per cent of senior Royal Household roles were filled by staff from an ethnic minority (versus a civil service average of 10 per cent).[4] The Lord Chamberlain's Committee (providing 'leadership to the Royal Household') also had double the FTSE 100 target[5] for major companies of at least one main board director from an ethnic minority. However, across the royal workforce, the staff average of 9.7 per cent remained well below the target (and the overall civil service average) of 14 per cent. There had been dismay a few months earlier when two promising candidates for an internal Palace research post, both from minority backgrounds, had pulled out of the running at the last minute without explanation.[6] In his detailed study of modern courtiers and court politics, Valentine Low shows that the Royal Household had been well aware of its deficiencies in this regard for a generation. It had been identified in the nineties when the internal 'Way Ahead Group' was addressing key issues such as this. As one official of that period told Low: 'The question is, "Why didn't it go faster?"'[7] With the 'headwinds' now gathering strength across the Atlantic, this issue was only likely to be amplified. For on the very same day that Ngozi Fulani's original tweet detonated on social media, the sound of fresh ticking could be heard beneath the throne.

* * *

Charles III

On 1 December 2022, the inaugural trailer appeared for the Sussexes' upcoming six-part Netflix documentary about their new life in California. The first of several teasers, it opened with Harry warning gravely that 'I had to do everything I could to protect my family'. It also promised 'the full truth'. The Royal Family and their staff were, therefore, steeling themselves for a reprise of the Sussexes' March 2021 interview with Oprah Winfrey. Also presented as 'the truth', that programme had been the most astonishing unburdening of family secrets since the late Princess of Wales had sat down with the BBC's Martin Bashir in 1995. In addition to Meghan's allegations of royal 'conversations' about skin colour, she had said that she received no Palace support when she was feeling suicidal. Later in the same film, Harry had claimed that he had been 'cut off' financially and was no longer speaking to his father. Although the Sussexes' principal target was the media and although there were several inconsistencies – the couple had claimed, for example, that the Archbishop of Canterbury had secretly married them before their wedding (not true, said the Archbishop) – the film had been excruciating for the family. It had also prompted the late Queen to issue one of the most-quoted lines of her long life: 'recollections may vary'. However, that Oprah Winfrey exchange had lasted eighty-five minutes. This new iteration of the Sussexes' 'truth' would last the best part of six hours. With little indication of what might be in store this time – except that it was unlikely to be good news – the Royal Family simply had to press on with their engagements.

On 7 December 2022, the King could feel a particular sense of pride, plus a few pangs of sadness, as he cut the first slice of a huge cake on the stage of Central Hall, Westminster. He had come to mark the fortieth anniversary of Business in the Community (BITC), a favourite charity. He had been its founding patron since a meeting in 1982 with black community leaders campaigning for better job opportunities in many parts of inner-city Britain.[8]

Over the years, he had helped to cajole leaders of some of Britain's best-known companies into adopting more socially responsible and inclusive recruitment policies. At least 1,000 companies representing more than six million employees had now signed BITC's Race at Work Charter. Indeed, it had almost become a rite of passage for the new CEO of any large British company to be invited to join the then Prince of Wales on one of his 'Seeing is Believing' bus tours of a struggling corner of a British city. Few declined.

Once he became King, though, he was always going to have to wind down his active involvement in organizations like this. So, the Central Hall gathering was both a celebration and a parting of the ways. 'Keep it going for God's sake,' he told the 350 party guests, adding: 'We are only as good as the marvellous people we help. That's the point.' On this occasion, there would be no earnest call to action, as there might have been before his accession. It was another reminder of the transition from Prince to sovereign. However, the event barely made the news, let alone the headlines, because the media were focused entirely on a celebration of another royal patronage elsewhere.

The Duke and Duchess of Sussex were in New York on the same day to receive a 'Ripple of Hope Award' from the Robert F. Kennedy Human Rights Foundation 'in recognition of their work on racial justice, mental health, and other social impact initiatives.' The foundation's president, Kerry Kennedy, saluted them for being 'incredibly brave' in speaking out on such issues. After receiving the award, which also praised their 'lifelong commitment to building strong and equitable communities' through their Archewell Foundation, the Sussexes issued a joint statement: 'Together we know that a ripple of hope can turn into a wave of change.'

Back in Britain, staff who had watched the King bring about his own 'wave of change' over many decades, through his Prince's Trust, Business in the Community and multiple other organizations, could either laugh or cry. Even the Sussexes' most fervent admirers would acknowledge that, in its two-year infancy, Archewell had yet to demonstrate a 'lifelong commitment'. That, though, was of no great concern at the Palace. What alarmed the King's team was what was coming next, just two days later: the first three episodes of *Harry & Meghan*, that six-part documentary which the couple had been busy making when not 'building equitable communities'. In return, so it was reported, they would receive a substantial but undisclosed sum. The next three episodes would air a week later.

Though the main villains of the piece were once again the British press, the first salvo opened with many withering remarks about the Royal Family and the monarchy. Harry talked of 'the pain and suffering of women marrying into this institution', reliving the misery his mother had endured for so many years. He was determined that history would not repeat itself. He also claimed that, for male members of the family, 'there can be a temptation or an urge to marry someone who would fit the mould – as opposed to somebody who you perhaps are destined to be with'. The clear inference that he was talking about his elder brother astonished friends of the family. 'On top of all the other breaches of trust, here was Harry making a blatant attack on Catherine. For William, this was the lowest of the low,' says one.[9] Opinions were divided as to whether this really was a calculated slight against the new Princess of Wales or whether it was a case of 'Harry shooting his mouth off' with yet another round of scattergun assertions and thoughtless allegations. Elsewhere in the show, Harry accused his family of 'a huge level of unconscious bias', while Meghan dismissed the couple's original engagement interview with Mishal Husain of the BBC as 'rehearsed' and 'an orchestrated reality show'. This came as something of a surprise to the BBC, not least Husain herself. As one of its most experienced and highly regarded journalists, she felt that she had conducted a thoroughly professional interview. She coolly restricted her response to the words of the late Queen: 'recollections may vary'. What would have dismayed the late monarch most, perhaps, was the historically befuddled section in which a commentator sympathetic to the couple described the Commonwealth – of which the Sussexes had so recently been such passionate advocates – as 'a privileged club' and 'Empire 2.0' which had been 'created' by Britain in a way that 'protected its commercial and capitalist interest'.[10] If so, it was odd that it had just held its latest summit in a nation (Rwanda) which had never been part of the British Empire while its membership had reached a record high six months earlier with the addition of two new member nations previously colonized by France.* Nor was the modern Commonwealth 'created' by Britain. It was started by the eight 'free and equal' nations which signed the London Declaration of 1949.

Four days later, the trailer for the second tranche of the *Harry & Meghan* series landed with more of the same. 'I wasn't being thrown to the wolves; I was being fed to the wolves,' said Meghan. 'They were happy to lie to protect my brother,' said Harry. The last three episodes duly explored more incidents of 'heartbreaking' Palace collusion with the hated media –

---

* Gabon and Togo, both French-speaking, were admitted to the Commonwealth in June 2022.

conducted primarily, so the couple said, to promote William's reputation.

This formed the haunting backdrop to the Sussexes' relocation to California, although this was depicted as an audacious escape to 'freedom' by friends and allies. Overall, this was not so much a documentary series as a curated self-portrait. Hence the prominent credit in the title sequence for the couple's own production company, Archewell. Stylishly filmed and with bumper audiences, it was highly watchable and clearly a success from Netflix's point of view. But for the couple? It merely seemed to go over the same old ground and the same old resentments which had already polarized opinions on both sides of the Atlantic. The Sussexes' fans hugged them closer still. Their critics groaned all the more. The neutrals remained neutral. In the words of one non-partisan television critic, it was 'six hours of first-world whingeing'.[11] One of the most contentious moments, among British viewers at least, was when a smirking Meghan performed a comic repeat of her first curtsey to the Queen. The queasy look of discomfort on Harry's face was that of a man all too aware of the consequences yet unable to do anything about it. Social media lit up once again while criticism was not confined to the usual suspects. Yet the King and the family said nothing.

Despite media demands for a response, the Palace strategy was one of 'show not tell'. So, on the same day that Netflix first aired *Harry & Meghan* around the world, the King was with religious charities in north London. 'I know this looks like a carefully scripted response to the Sussexes but he really has had all this in the diary for a long time,' remarked one Palace staffer as the King visited a cafe for refugees and asylum seekers before joining the Archbishop of Canterbury to celebrate Advent at the Ethiopian Christian Fellowship Church. Many more viewers would watch Harry in the Californian sunshine airing his grievances with his family – 'I'm probably never going to get a genuine apology' and so on – than would view news clips of the King going about his worthy, unexciting rounds in wintry London. What was abundantly clear, however, was which of them looked more contented with life.

In between the first and second tranches of the *Harry & Meghan* show, Charles III went to record a programme of his own. For the first Christmas broadcast of his reign, he chose St George's Chapel, Windsor, as his location. The sight of the words 'HM The King' at 3 p.m. on 25 December was always going to be one of those moments when the nation (like any bereaved family) had a collective gulp. Elizabeth II, for so many millions, had been a Christmas Day staple as enduring as crackers and 'Jingle Bells'. Hers had been that increasingly rare commodity: a television broadcast that families watched together. The King had elected to speak a few yards from the spot where she had been laid to rest just three months earlier. His subliminal message was one of continuity and, thus, re-assurance, though he had made a few tweaks of his own. The late Queen would not have insisted on 'sustainable decorations' for the Christmas tree. By speaking in the chapel, he also side-stepped the old Fleet Street parlour game of deciphering the photos on the Queen's desk to determine who might be in or out of favour. There would be no photos in St George's Chapel.

The King pointedly began with a tribute to his parents and an acknowledgement of the way in which Christmas can amplify loss. Interestingly, he made no reference to the Platinum Jubilee celebrations for the Queen earlier in the year. That had been a momentous and joyful national high point of 2022, but one which the King felt would jar with the tone. Following her example during the last twenty years of her life, when the late Queen's Christmas broadcast had become overtly spiritual, so he now did the same, dwelling on the inspirational power of 'everlasting light' in a dark world: 'My mother's belief in the power of that light was an essential part of her faith in God, but also her faith in people – and it is one which I share with my whole heart. It is a belief in the extraordinary ability of each person to touch, with goodness and compassion, the lives of others.' The same belief, he went on, was to be found right across the faith spectrum in 'churches, synagogues, mosques, temples and gurdwaras.' Here was a not-so-subtle nod to the 'Defender of Faith' role he feels duty-bound to observe if not always to declare. The King recorded it all in one take but still had to do it twice more thanks to passing air traffic from Heathrow Airport. 'I must have a word with the chief executive,' he joked to the technicians on the way out.

Because of the Covid pandemic, this was the first full family Christmas at Sandringham in three years, with an emphasis on togetherness. Though the Sussexes were clearly not expected, the Duke of York was invited to join the rest of his family for the traditional walk to and from church. There was little respite from those trans-Atlantic winds, however. Not only was publication of *Spare* fast approaching but, ahead of it, came all the promotion. Prince Harry had agreed to do two set-piece television interviews for the book and those two networks were determined to maximize attention during the January lull. First, on New Year's Day, came the trailer for Harry's confessional with Anderson Cooper for CBS in America. The clip seemed almost like a Netflix rerun as Harry lobbed the same charge of media/Palace collusion into the mix: 'Silence is betrayal.' A day later, aiming at a British audience, ITV's Tom Bradby tried a different tack with his trailer for the tell-all interview which would be broadcast in the UK two days prior to publication. It struck a more original, even positive note: 'I would like to get my father back, my brother back . . .' Three days later, there was a further whiff of rapprochement as ITV released another trailer. Asked if Harry would attend the King's Coronation, he teased: 'The door is always open. The ball is in their court.' Goaded time and again, the Royal Family still said nothing.

And then perhaps the most carefully and expensively choreographed public relations operation in modern publishing history went careering off the tracks. First, a US-based *Guardian* journalist obtained a chunk of the text on the morning of 5 January – a full five days ahead of the rigidly enforced global publication date. Hours later, a regional bookseller in Spain thoughtfully decided to put a few copies of *Spare* on sale early so that regular customers could buy them as Epiphany gifts. Suddenly, the Sussexes' sworn enemies, the British tabloid press, who might gladly have paid a seven-figure sum for an exclusive glimpse even a day before publication, were holding a copy of the whole book for just a few euros. As teams of Spanish translators worked against the clock to despatch one chapter after another to ecstatic editors around the globe, the contents of *Spare* were distilled for the whole world. And there were still five days to go until publication of the most candid and caustic royal memoir ever written. Among the most sensational claims were that Prince William had physically attacked his younger brother during an argument about Meghan's behaviour towards staff, 'ripping my necklace' and pushing Harry on to a dog bowl (which cracked); that their father had pleaded with them after Prince Philip's funeral: 'Please, boys. Don't make my final years a misery'; that Harry's infamously ill-judged decision to wear a Nazi uniform to a party was not all his fault; that he had killed twenty-five Taliban insurgents in Afghanistan; that he had taken copious quantities of drugs since his schooldays . . .

There were also intimate revelations about the loss of his virginity and about a frostbitten penis on an Arctic expedition. In among it all were moments of great tenderness and sadness as he explored the breakdown of his parents' marriage. None could be unmoved by his account of his mother's death and his part in her funeral procession. Given Prince William's pathological determination to protect his family's privacy, he was, say friends, mortified by Harry's casual betrayal of so many fraternal secrets. Yet, the overall depiction was not an unsympathetic one. As the *Times* reviewer noted: 'It's probably of great credit to William and Kate that, even in this hostile account, they come across as sweet and well-meaning people.' Ditto Harry's father: 'Prince Charles comes across as a sweet, dufferish, rather vain old man . . . padding off to the bathroom at Balmoral in his slippers so he can have a soak and listen to an audiobook.'[12]

No one could have been dreading the book more than Queen Camilla. Early on, Harry recalled his fears ahead of their first meeting: 'I recall wondering, right before the tea, if she'd be mean to me. If she'd be like all the wicked stepmothers in storybooks. But she wasn't. Like Willy, I did feel real gratitude for that.' However, he repeatedly accused his stepmother of conducting her own public relations campaign at the expense of the young princes. 'Stories began to appear everywhere, in all the papers, about her private conversation with Willy,' Harry wrote. 'They could only have been leaked by the one other person present.'[13] He resurrected this accusation when describing his feelings at his father's second wedding. Indeed, this specific leaked conversation with Prince William would serve as a prime piece of evidence – Exhibit A – in Prince

Harry's central claim of collusion between the Palace and the press. *Spare*, however, omitted to explain what actually happened, twenty-five years earlier, although it was fully documented at the time. Prince William was, indeed, introduced to his future stepmother in July 1998. News of the encounter did, indeed, surface in *The Sun* soon afterwards. The then Camilla Parker Bowles was as mortified as everyone else and an internal investigation was launched. The one person whom she had told was her own personal assistant, Amanda MacManus, keeper of her diary. MacManus had confided in her husband, James, a newspaper executive, who, over a game of tennis, confided in an ex-colleague who told a friend on *The Sun*. The full facts emerged when Amanda MacManus issued a public apology and immediately resigned.* Through presented as a conspiracy in *Spare*, the true sequence of events was, rather, pure cock-up. A quarter of a century later, the new Queen and her staff made no comment. Naturally, the world wanted to hear Prince William's thoughts. His staff remain adamant that he and the Princess refused to open a book which has caused so much pain. 'Neither of them read it,' says one of their senior advisers. 'He is a grown-up forty-year-old with the BBC app on his phone so he knows what it says. But he has people like me to tell him what else he needs to know. We gave him the key points.'[14] It had been the same with the Netflix series, too. While much of the commentariat urged Prince William to respond to some of the more incendiary Sussex charges, whether on screen or in Harry's book, he decided to remain silent.

---

* Camilla Parker Bowles felt desperately sorry for her assistant, never held her personally responsible and soon reappointed her. MacManus then remained at her side for another twenty-three years and became her private secretary. She retired in 2021 but is still involved with some of Queen Camilla's charities.

Looking back, one of Prince William's team reflects: 'My boss would say: "Whatever the rights and wrongs, I hope that people feel I behaved properly in keeping my counsel." You can imagine what he feels about this, especially regarding what has been said about his wife. But he is being admirably grown-up.'[15]

Throughout the book, Harry was keen to stress his devotion to the Queen and Prince Philip. Reflecting on his grandmother after her death, he wrote: 'Special relationship, that's what they said about us, and now I couldn't stop thinking about the specialness that would no longer be.'[16] He did not, however, hold back when attacking some of her staff. They would not respond, though they were interested in what had been omitted from the book. One privately recalled that the Queen had been 'as angry as I'd ever seen her' in 2021 after the Sussexes announced that she had given them her blessing to call their baby daughter 'Lilibet', the Queen's childhood nickname. The couple then fired off warnings of legal action against anyone who dared to suggest otherwise, as the BBC had done. However, when the Sussexes tried to co-opt the Palace into propping up their version of events, they were rebuffed. Once again, it was a case of 'recollections may vary' as far as the Queen was concerned. Those noisy threats of legal action evaporated and the libel action against the BBC never materialized.

Most worrying for the Palace was the relative lack of detail about recent notable events. It did not go unnoticed that Harry and Meghan's wedding, their married life and their eventual departure from the royal world amounted to a small part – less than a fifth – of Harry's book. This suggested either a sequel or, perhaps, a memoir by Meghan in due course.

For days afterwards, further revelations were unpicked, along with various errors. Writing in tandem with a well-known ghost-writer, J. R. Moehringer, Harry had painted a forlorn picture of a lonely Eton schoolboy being told, by a lackey, of the death of his adored great-grandmother: 'I took the call. I wish I could remember whose voice was at the other end: a courtier's, I believe. I recall that it was just before Easter, the weather bright and warm, light slanting through my window, filled with vivid colours. "Your Royal Highness, the Queen Mother has died."'[17] Harry was actually in Switzerland, skiing with his father and brother, when all three received the news. The book also recounted his fury with an impertinent interviewer during a trip to Africa, an encounter which so upset him that he resorted to a binge of drug-taking. The interviewer had, in fact, been Tom Bradby. Overall, the book was rich in delicious details, candid and certainly 'raw and unflinching'. According to the publishers, Penguin Random House, it broke all previous sales records. Those early leaks, while undoubtedly infuriating, had caused no damage. Yet, the overall message felt wearily familiar, namely that the evil press, the hapless Royal Family and their scheming advisers are all locked in a downward spiral of doom and misery. As with Oprah Winfrey, as with their Netflix series, as with all the promotional interviews, here was another retelling of the same reverse fairy tale about the Prince and Princess who lived happily ever after by not being royal any more.

By now, those much-hyped promotional shows with Bradby and Cooper felt, to most viewers, like one course too many at the end of a long banquet. They garnered decent ratings, of course, but yielded nothing new. The *Times*'s television reviewer was one of many who felt underwhelmed: 'Petty, pious, paranoid, delusional, with an ego both monstrous and fragile, the nation's formerly favourite cheeky chappie has turned into a rather pathetic middle-aged man.'[18] Even the most assiduous royal-watchers, even the most combative belligerents in the Sussex/Cambridge/Windsor culture wars were in need of a break.

Charles III

The King resumed public duties two days later – yet again in Scotland – with a trip to meet charity workers at the Aboyne and District Men's Shed. It was now exactly twelve weeks since the first trailer for the new series of *The Crown* had kickstarted that almost ceaseless run of bad news beyond his control. The headwinds would return, no doubt, but, for now, they had blown themselves out. Nor had they had any discernible impact on the King. Indeed, friends and family noticed that, for all the burdens and brickbats, he was as happy as they had ever seen him. 'I'm ready for it,' he said of being King to an old friend during those difficult months.[19] He also added that he had never wanted his late mother to emulate her regal contemporaries and abdicate in his favour.* 'I am just glad it happened now and that it didn't happen a moment before it did,' the King added. 'Twenty years ago would have been too soon.'[20] When he was heir to the throne, his closest officials and friends knew to expect periodic bouts of gloom, self-pity and anguished table-thumping in times of crisis. Now they noticed a new confidence, what one friend calls a 'serenity' about him, adding: 'He says he loves not having people always telling him something is too difficult.'[21]

The opinion polls, sure enough, showed barely any variation in the King's approval ratings from the start of these 'headwinds' to the end. They remained a few points down on his post-accession high but still firmly around the 60 per cent mark (with a quarter in the 'don't know' camp and less than 15 per cent against).[22] And he had yet to say a single word on the subject. As the Queen herself liked to say in times of adversity: 'This, too, shall pass.'[23] And so it had.

---

* In the last decade of the Queen's life, she saw the Kings of Spain and Belgium, the Queen of Holland and the Emperor of Japan all retire from their thrones.

Chapter Eight

Doing the Same – Differently

Once again, there appears to be some subtle messaging in the royal neckwear. It is lunchtime on 9 March 2023 (as usual, there is no sign of lunch) and Charles III is wearing another pink tie with a humorous motif. However, this one is not covered in a 'T-Rex' design but in little blue owls. Looking around the palace ballroom, it is not hard to understand why. Many of the greatest universities in the land are represented here today, their most senior staff in a variety of robes. In among the chancellors, vice-chancellors and professors there are representatives from the highest echelons of science and culture, including the Royal Society and the Royal Academy of Arts. Here, too, are some of Britain's most distinguished religious foundations and a handful of local authorities with a strong royal connection. What they all have in common is that they have the ear of the monarch – whether he wants to listen or not. For, together, these twenty-seven illustrious institutions are called 'the Privileged Bodies'. And their privilege, enjoyed by historic right or by a grant from the Crown, is that they are all entitled to present a loyal address to the sovereign in person.

Today, they have come to do exactly that, following a tradition which occurs after every change of reign and also when a monarch marks a major anniversary like a jubilee. Their addresses all follow a similar pattern. There are expressions of condolence for the loss of the late Queen followed by pledges of loyalty and goodwill for the new King. They have also been given a few polite guidelines from the Lord Chamberlain's Office, not least a request to keep each speech to roughly a minute. The first speaker, the Archbishop of Canterbury, has clearly not received the memo. His loyal address on behalf of the General Synod of the Church of England goes on for a good three minutes. It could be a long afternoon if others follow suit. Fortunately, everyone else sticks to the rules. Oxford goes ahead of Cambridge because it is fractionally older but the vice-chancellor of Cambridge pulls rank by reminding everyone that the King himself is an alumnus, that his late father was chancellor and that eight of the university's professors bear the title 'Regius'. The Dean of Windsor observes that St George's Chapel is celebrating the 675th anniversary of the Most Noble Order of the Garter.

It is not all about past glories. The chancellor of Glasgow University, former Olympic rowing champion Dame Katherine Grainger, talks of her colleagues' work on everything from climate change to dementia in ex-footballers. The Religious Society of Friends are represented by Leasa Lambert, who talks of the Quakers' support for 'trans people', Ukraine and the pursuit of reparations for the slave trade.

One of the most striking addresses is from the Lord Mayor of the City of Westminster, Labour councillor Hamza Taouzzale, who is by some margin the youngest speaker at the age of twenty-four. He praises the King for his environmental work and for 'the obvious honesty of your emotions and the transparency of your intentions'. He adds: 'You are the Monarch to us all but, particularly, I feel, for your younger subjects, the generation of the Carolean age.'

Doing the Same – Differently

It later transpires that it is not the first time Taouzzale has been here. His grandfather, Mokhtar, came to Britain from Morocco in 1971, was employed as a Palace porter and took young Hamza inside royal headquarters for a look when he was a boy. Now, the porter's grandson is here addressing the sovereign on behalf of the people of Westminster.

The King listens to all twenty-seven institutions and then thanks them collectively: 'You remind us of an essential truth: that a nation's wealth and strength can be found, beyond the size of its economy or its place in the geopolitical landscape, in the values that it embodies.' He also notes how much has changed since the last time the Privileged Bodies had gathered before the monarch – during the late Queen's Diamond Jubilee celebrations in 2012. 'Beyond our shores, war has returned to Europe,' he reflects. 'And globally, the challenge of climate change and biodiversity loss is more urgent than ever before.'

The 300 guests then move through to the Picture Gallery for a reception. In many ways, the occasion is exactly the same as all the gatherings which these Privileged Bodies enjoyed with the late Queen (on five occasions in total). This is an event where Charles III is simply stepping straight into those immense shoes.

Yet it also bears a few tiny pointers to the new reign, too, for those who care to look. There is the reference to climate and biodiversity, of course. That is not something Elizabeth II would have added. Several guests notice the chill in the air (because, as ever, the King wants the windows open in the adjacent state apartments). The guests are all mingling, too, moving around the state apartments, glass in hand, spotting old friends. The late Queen liked to have a receiving line at her events so that she could be sure of meeting and shaking the hand of every guest. For big receptions, she also liked guests to be put in pre-arranged clusters depending on the nature of the gathering – so, for example, she might move from a group of dentists to a group of teachers to a group of people from a particular city or regiment or company. It helped make each conversation easier if each cluster had something in common. The King does not do it this way. 'The Queen liked to do things in a formal way,' says one of his senior team. 'She liked people in groups, she'd shake hands and then she'd move on and everyone else would stay put. The King says: "People want to see me, which is nice, but they want to see each other". So if you want friendships renewed and networks made, you need to let them move around. He doesn't mind if it's all a bit random. But the overall aim is the same.'[1]

It is certainly the case that the King genuinely enjoys his new role, just as the Queen enjoyed it too. He is clearly planning to carry on doing all the things that Elizabeth II used to do. They may not be undertaken in exactly the same way, but they won't feel that different either. Many commentators, for example, had predicted that flat racing's royal days were numbered once Elizabeth II had died. The Prince of Wales had never been much of a fan, they observed, and that would soon be reflected once he was King. In fact, Charles III has not only maintained the tradition of the Royal Ascot houseparty and carriage processions, but has taken a much keener interest in the late Queen's racing operation, especially after enjoying his first win with Desert Hero, on the third day of the 2023 royal meeting at Ascot.

Among those in the royal party that day were Lord and Lady Lloyd Webber. 'The trainer and [racing manager] John Warren*

---

* Formerly racing manager to Elizabeth II, Warren became bloodstock and racing adviser to Charles III.

had told us that Desert Hero had "stomach ulcers" which was not promising,' recalls Madeleine Lloyd Webber, a former international three-day-eventer and herself the owner of two major studs. 'So we couldn't believe it when we saw the horse coming up the straight. I thought: "Oh my God, he's going to come second." And then he won. The Royal Box went completely mad. It was wonderful. I remember the Queen had tears streaming down her face and the King was ecstatic. Maybe this was the moment he really connected with racing.'[2]

In the course of a visit to Dumfries House – during which one of the King's mares gave birth to a foal sired by the Lloyd Webber stallion Too Darn Hot – both the Lloyd Webbers were impressed by the King's eagerness to learn more. 'He was asking very good questions about stallions and so on. He'd been up at Sandringham and he went round all his yearlings and then made time to see all the foals, too,' says Lady Lloyd Webber. 'I think he really enjoys the breeding and the farming side of it all.' Her husband points out that he himself came to racing via a similar route: 'I don't follow it all but I do find it really exciting when one of our home-breds is in action.'

For this new-found interest, as with much else, the King can thank Queen Camilla. While she has always loved the sport, the King had tended to regard it as mother/grandmother territory, best left to others (Prince Philip felt the same). However, by encouraging him simply to appreciate the racing interests he has now inherited from his mother, the new Queen has ensured that the King enjoys it much more. He may never be as knowledgeable and may never fully catch the racing bug, given all his other interests. Yet when Queen Camilla urged him to watch a live video link showing one of their mares giving birth, he was gripped. In March 2023, it was announced that all the horses that the King had inherited from his mother were to be registered in the joint name of Charles III and Queen Camilla. John Warren likes to recall a conversation from the days when the King was still a prince: 'He said [racing] was like a garden - until you had your own, you didn't think much about it. When you do, you tend it, develop it and enhance it.' As Warren told *Horse & Hound*: 'His Majesty is being true to his word.'[3]

The same applies to Windsor Castle itself. For a man who had seldom spent much time at Windsor since his youth, he has quickly reconnected with the ancestral seat, to a degree that has surprised even those who know him very well. Some had assumed that he would be put off by the incessant air traffic in and out of neighbouring Heathrow Airport. Some imagined that his heart and soul would always be wedded to Highgrove, the Gloucestershire home which he recreated in his own image. Before and after the Queen's death, some experts had even confidently predicted that the new King would be happy to let his elder son have the run of Windsor.

Rather, it seems that a dormant childhood love of the castle and its contents has been reignited. As he told one old friend: 'I used to pedal my car down these corridors past all these paintings and I loved them.' It was Windsor that instilled in him an early love of the Venetian scenes of Canaletto, so much so that when he finally visited Venice for the first time in 1981, it reminded him of Windsor. 'I'd love to have gone to Venice when I was young but my family didn't do that sort of thing,' he told his friend.[4] Aside from the Queen Mother, no one encouraged this strong artistic streak in the young Charles. It was, he lamented, a similar story with the arts in general. While he developed an early love of classical music, 'the family were more interested in George Formby.'

Doing the Same – Differently

As King, he can now enjoy all the treasures of Windsor and, in his words, 'feel it without being ridiculed for feeling it.' Another friend found him in the private wing of the castle, lovingly rearranging pictures and furniture. 'It was certainly less cluttered. The dog bowls had gone and he was asking for suggestions on what should hang where.'[5]

A senior official points out that the monarch is also driven by a sense of obligation: 'The King often talks about the need for a living tradition, that this is a proper house. Windsor is not Versailles. It needs to be lived in and the living tradition informs everything.'

Unlike the other royal residences, Windsor is much less affected by the presence of the monarch due to its size. In other words, it doesn't matter much whether the monarch is there or not. The royal residential section, in one corner of the world's largest inhabited castle, comprises only a fraction of the floorspace. During their stay in 1982, Ronald and Nancy Reagan were amazed that they had to walk through the Queen's bedroom to join her for breakfast on the private terrace. With or without the King in residence, the state apartments can remain open to the public while the resident population of some 300 curatorial and administrative staff, clergy and their respective families can go about their lives regardless. 'The Royal Family basically have a glorified flat there and the rest runs itself,' says one former official.[6]

A new pattern has evolved where the King often spends Thursday and Friday at Windsor before a weekend at Highgrove (with or without Queen Camilla, who much enjoys the chance to retreat to her garden and grandchildren at her own home in Wiltshire). The King often returns on a Sunday afternoon, not least to see his grandchildren at Adelaide Cottage. The

Prince and Princess of Wales are said to be 'extremely happy' in this relatively ordinary home in the grounds. 'They are there as a family with total privacy and without lots of staff,' says one official. The idea that they are itching to replace the Duke of York at Royal Lodge (with its pool and children's toy cottage) is said to be 'overpriced'. 'It might happen but it's not planned,' is the verdict. Just as George V was insistent on raising his family in York Cottage, Sandringham, it seems that those who are predestined to live in large palaces and castles often cherish a spell in something very much smaller. The future William V and his future Queen seem to think so too.

Elizabeth II might also have had her own mixed feelings about Windsor Castle when she came to the throne. This was, after all, where she was effectively incarcerated for much of the Second World War.* Yet, after her accession, while Buckingham Palace was always the office, she came to love Windsor as 'home'. Charles III, it seems, may now do the same.

Indeed, the Windsor connection has now gone one step further. One key appointment has been that decision to make himself Ranger of Windsor Great Park. That was a role which the late Queen had conferred on the Duke of Edinburgh soon after her accession and was no mere honorary position. There is a full-time Deputy Ranger, employed by the Crown Estate, which runs the park. However, the Ranger can direct the strategy and priorities. In 1952, the Queen had more than enough to take on as sovereign. She asked the Duke to take charge of the private royal estates and also gave him the Ranger role. In part, she knew that he would be very well suited for

---

* Princess Margaret later told the BBC's *Desert Island Discs*: 'The feeble barbed wire wouldn't have kept anybody out, but it kept us in.'

the task, but she was also conscious that he needed a domain of which he could be master. In any case, as the Duke would sometimes remind patronizing courtiers, both his mother and grandmother had been born at Windsor, in the presence of Queen Victoria, so he was not a complete outsider. The Duke went on to be the longest-serving Ranger in the park's thousand-year history. Indeed, it was one of a handful of positions which he chose not to relinquish when he retired from public life in 2017, remaining Ranger up to his death in 2021. It mattered that much to him.

There was mild surprise when Charles III put himself in the post so quickly. Some had wondered whether he might appoint the Windsor-based Earl of Wessex (soon to be Duke of Edinburgh). There was even speculation that this might be a useful role for the otherwise redundant Duke of York, since this was not a public-facing position and he had been living on the Windsor estate longer than anyone else in the family. While the King's grandfather, George VI, had also made himself Ranger on becoming King, he too had also lived on the estate prior to his accession. Charles III, however, came to the throne with homes and estates as far afield as Highgrove and Dumfries House, on top of the private royal estates which he automatically inherited, namely Balmoral and Sandringham. He had a great deal of property to think about without Windsor Great Park as well.

'I suppose it's a bit like getting a new train set,' observed one friend of the family. 'You've been playing with the same old train set for years. Then, suddenly you have a new one and you want to play with everything at the same time.'

Given the King's unquenchable passion – bordering on obsession – for trees and tree-planting, it was perhaps inevitable that he would want to assume custody of an estate which can boast Europe's largest collection of veteran and ancient oak and beech trees. These include the 900-year-old Signing Oak and another specimen, Offa's Oak, which is so old that scientists estimate its age at somewhere between 1,300 and 1,500 years. Either way, it predates the Normans.

A bitingly cold winter gale is blowing across the park and doing nothing to dim the King's enthusiasm during one of his early tours of inspection with Deputy Ranger Paul Sedgwick. It is three months into his rangership and there is much to learn about this 5,000-acre estate, but the King, being a serial tree-planter, is particularly interested in the tree side of things. 'The sycamore is such a special tree, particularly in the landscape as they make such special shapes,' he shouts above the wind as the two men walk past the famous equestrian statue of George III, known to all as the 'Copper Horse'. Forever haunted by the spectre of Dutch elm disease, the King wants to know about the state of his elms. 'I hope we've got the resistant ones,' he says above the wind. Sedgwick tells him that it is the field maple which is proving especially durable as the estate staff plant new avenues to commemorate the late Queen's Platinum Jubilee.

They move on to watch two Crown Estate apprentices learning how to cut back some of the branches on a wonderfully gnarled 600-year-old oak known locally as the 'Elephant Tree'. The apprentices explain that they both always wanted outdoor jobs and are six months into their training. 'You haven't lost a finger yet?' the King jokes.

The tour meanders on all day through different parts of the estate. The King stops to meet a team of hedge-layers from the Bracknell area. They explain that they are a group of volunteers, all retired, who meet every week or so to plant or replant hedges all over Berkshire – for the fun of it. The King has stumbled across a gang of kindred spirits. This is music to his ears. He has long been a fanatical hedge-layer. 'I'm so glad it keeps you going,' he tells them excitedly. 'It keeps you sane!'

The area in which 'transition', as the Palace calls it, has been smooth to the point of seamlessness is in the monarchy's dealings with the armed forces. As the commander-in-chief, to whom new recruits must swear their oath of allegiance, the King is every bit as wedded to the military as his late mother. This is something for which no training is required. The Windsors are the quintessential forces family. The late Queen was a Royal Navy daughter, wife and mother. From the earliest age, there were few days in her life when she did not encounter someone in uniform. Her grandfather, George V, was so wedded to naval routines that he liked to run his household like a ship.

Every year, the United Kingdom celebrates the official birthday of the head of state not with a cake but with the Birthday Parade, otherwise known as Trooping the Colour, a vast exercise in precision military ceremonial followed by a gathering of the Royal Family on the Buckingham Palace balcony. Since the UK is one of only two countries in the world without a national day,* many British embassies and high commissions around the world designate this occasion as that date. Here are the armed forces, monarch and nationhood all wrapped up in a single celebration.

The importance of the Birthday Parade was stamped in the King's mind from the earliest age. 'I remember so well when I was small, I was always looking up at people with wonderful uniforms on and breastplates and always wanting to pull [their] swords out,' he once told me. 'There was a wonderful

---

* The home nations have their own national days, but the UK, as a whole, does not. The only other country without a national day is Denmark.

man, the Earl of Athlone, the Colonel of the Life Guards, a wonderful figure with a white moustache. It's so funny looking back on those people.'[7]

At the first Birthday Parade of his reign, he even revived the tradition of the monarch on horseback. The Queen rode every year at the Trooping the Colour until 1986, when her horse, the ever-reliable Burmese, was retired. Elizabeth II decided to retire with her and always travelled in a carriage thereafter. It meant that she ceased riding in public at the age of sixty. Yet here was the new King, at the age of seventy-four, keen to remain in the saddle, just as he had been since becoming Colonel of the Welsh Guards in 1975. It meant that the King had actually been riding at this event for considerably longer than his late mother ever did. His decision suddenly looked a little unwise on the day of that first Birthday Parade as sovereign. The King appeared on a new horse, a mare called Noble, which had been a gift from the Royal Canadian Mounted Police. Noble, it transpired, had vaulted the fence and twice escaped her Windsor paddock in the week before the parade. 'He always used to ride this wonderful old horse, George, who would just go to sleep,' says a former Palace aide. 'That's not what happened this time. He was on a very feisty horse.' The fact that he managed to keep Noble under control for the best part of two hours was testimony to those equestrian skills learned in his youth.

The King has always been grateful for his own experience in uniform. 'I think it's vital that those of us who find ourselves in this extraordinary position understand something of what our armed forces are expected to do,' he told me. 'It is a remarkably good form of training for all sorts of other things in life.'[8]

The heir to the throne's early years in the Royal Navy were not plain sailing. When Prince Charles failed in his first attempt to acquire the bridge watch certificate necessary for moving up the promotional ladder, he had to resit the exam just like anyone else. 'Poor Charles,' the Queen remarked to a dinner guest at that time. 'Hopeless at maths and they made him a navigation officer!'[9]

Yet, he was always popular with his men – a 'natural'[10] commander, said one – though always happier at the helm of an aircraft than a ship. 'The fun was flying helicopters – which I enjoyed enormously,' he said. 'The Fleet Air Arm was the most enjoyable time I had.'[11]

Long before joining the Royal Navy, Prince Charles had learned to fly while at Cambridge University, mastering the basics of a Chipmunk under RAF Squadron Leader Philip Pinney. By the time the Prince arrived at the Royal Navy's officer training academy at Dartmouth, he had already progressed to jet aircraft. Naval flying, therefore, seemed a natural fit, and the Prince was very good at it, winning the 'Double Diamond' trophy as best helicopter pilot with 707 Naval Air Squadron. During his days flying a Wessex helicopter from HMS *Hermes*, his superiors found that the Royal Marines all wanted to fly with the Prince. It was not just down to his aviation skills. Rather, as Admiral Lord West, former First Sea Lord, pointed out, it was because there was 'no doubt whatsoever it was absolutely better maintained than any other helicopter on board.'[12]

The Prince finished his naval career in command of the minesweeper *Bronington*. There was a near-disaster during an exercise off Holyhead when the ship's anchor started to pull up the main UK/Irish telephone cable. Mistake swiftly rectified, the incident never made it into the papers.

Always fit and seemingly undaunted by any physical challenge, the Prince would routinely attract 'Action Man' headlines. Not only had he undergone the Royal Marines' famously arduous commando training regime at Lympstone, but he also went ice diving beneath the Canadian Arctic. A year after leaving the Royal Navy, he became Colonel of the Parachute Regiment whereupon he insisted on undertaking the regimental parachute course. The Prince argued that he could hardly look the Paras in the eye, let alone wear the famous beret, if he did not.[13] Strictly speaking, there was no need since he had already undertaken a parachute jump with the RAF in 1971 (landing in a dangerous tangle of cords in the waters of Studland Bay). However, he felt that duty demanded it.

Throughout his years as Prince of Wales, he relished his associations with all his regiments and units, sometimes holding military investitures at his own home. He was adamant that both his sons should have proper military careers, too. That they should both end up as professional helicopter pilots, like both their father and their uncle, the Duke of York, was ironic given that it was the Queen's least favourite mode of transport. She always viewed rotary aircraft as suspect, following the death of the Captain of the Queen's Flight, Air Commodore John Blount, in a helicopter crash in 1967. She refused to fly in one until 1977, when a Silver Jubilee trip to Northern Ireland left her with no choice. Her successor, however, remains a great fan. 'There's nothing like hanging around in a force ten gale, you know, dangling the rope underneath,' he once explained to me. 'Very good for the soul!' The new Prince of Wales would agree. This may explain why Prince William has two helicopter pilots on his staff, in addition to himself. Both his equerry, Commander Rob Dixon, and his Head of the Private Household, ex-equerry Lieutenant Commander James Benbow, are qualified Royal Navy helicopter pilots. 'Kensington Palace could probably mount an invasion of a small country,' remarks one member of the Royal Household.

Doing the Same – Differently

The King's elevation to the throne has forced a reshuffle of many honorary positions, not least within the Household Division. The new Prince of Wales has replaced him as Colonel of the Welsh Guards (with the new Princess of Wales taking Prince William's old position as Colonel of the Irish Guards). Becoming King would inevitably mean stepping back from close contact with some units with which, as Prince Charles, he had forged a close, personal bond. He would also, with heavy heart, appoint his elder son to be Colonel-in-Chief of the Army Air Corps, after more than three decades of proudly wearing its blue beret. The long-running saga of what to do about the Grenadier Guards would be resolved even sooner. The late Queen had appointed the Duke of York as Colonel in 2017, after the retirement of the Duke of Edinburgh. She then reappointed herself to the role in place of Prince Andrew after his links to the convicted paedophile Jeffrey Epstein forced his withdrawal from public life. The new King, knowing that the Grenadiers could not go on without a fully functioning Colonel indefinitely, appointed Queen Camilla to the post.

After the death of the Queen Mother, Prince Charles was extremely proud to succeed her as president of the Victoria Cross and George Cross Association. Over more than twenty years, he has come to know all the holders of the two highest gallantry awards personally, not to mention the deeds which earned them membership of the most exclusive club in the world. In short, all these appointments add up to an uncomplicated, unbreakable bond with those who now serve King and country.

On an overcast February morning, faceless soldiers in balaclavas and camouflage paint are crawling across a field in Wiltshire under fire from enemy machine guns and mortars. The rounds are blank but the sound is real enough. The most sobering aspect of this exercise is that these troops are being taught how both to attack and defend a trench. It is more than a century since the end of the First World War. Only the night before, the grim but acclaimed re-enactment of its horrors, *All Quiet on the Western Front,* picked up seven BAFTA screen awards. Yet here are real troops preparing to use the same battle tactics resurrected from that bygone hell-scape in a twenty-first-century conflict. These are Ukrainian civilian volunteers receiving fast-track basic training from British, Commonwealth and NATO forces before they return to fight the Russian invasion of their homeland. The course had originally been just three weeks in length but, at the request of the Ukrainians, has been extended to five. It is a fraction of the nine months of basic training required to produce an infantry soldier in the UK. What's more, these men will be going straight from here to a war zone. Into the midst of this sombre exercise, steps the King.

'Are they accommodating you somewhere decent?' he asks the Ukrainian colonel. 'Aldershot,' comes the smart reply. The King smiles knowingly, all too familiar with the Hampshire garrison town (a place not known for its beauty) since it used to be home to his Parachute Regiment. What really interests him, however, is how today's fighting forces are coping with the return of trench warfare.

'You're having to dig trenches?' he asks one group of recruits. Conversation, through interpreters, is stilted, but the King persists, asking them how they cope with flooding. 'Do they start to fill up? Do they get up to here?' he says, pointing at his waist. He has specifically asked for the small media contingent to hold back. He wants to look the recruits in the face and that means they need to remove their balaclavas. Many do not want to be on camera, for fear of Russian reprisals against their families at home. The King, however, always likes to talk to people face to face (he has often remarked how frustrating he finds public walkabouts if he is greeted by a wall of mobile telephones).

Meeting a group of eight Ukrainian paratroopers, proudly wearing red berets as part of a new leadership course, he enjoys swapping parachuting banter. 'Have you jumped out of a balloon?' he says. 'Not too many injuries, I hope?' Through the interpreter, one replies: 'We're hardy folk.'

'I know you are,' says the King warmly. 'I am full of admiration and can only wish you well.' The soldiers have been told to speak only when spoken to. As the King moves on, one of them breaks ranks and addresses him in faltering English. 'I want to say: "Thank you".'

Also in the party is the head of the army, General Sir Patrick Sanders. He explains that the King has been embedded in military life since before the Falklands War. 'He's got that extraordinary longevity and he engages at a personal level. You can't meet him without feeling that.'

During his tour of inspection, the monarch meets the international training contingent who share his dismay at the return of trench warfare to European soil. 'It's old school, sir. It's crazy. It's the same as World War One,' a Dutch lieutenant tells him.

'Trenches are not something we train for much at home – but bullets haven't changed in a hundred years and nor has artillery,' says Major Tony Harris of 1st Battalion, Royal New Zealand Infantry Regiment.

The King bids the Ukrainians farewell. 'You are amazing. I don't know how you do it,' he tells Lieutenant Colonel Sergei Shutenko. 'We will hold this day in our memories,' a visibly emotional Shutenko says afterwards. 'I will be telling my children and grandchildren that we have met the premier monarch of the world. Songs will be sung.'

* * *

Charles III

No previous monarch saw as much of the world as Elizabeth II. When it comes to distance travelled, however, her successor has almost certainly trumped her already. From his university days, Prince Charles was routinely despatched to represent the Queen overseas at events which the monarch could not undertake herself. For many decades, the Prince would therefore be the regular royal face at state funerals overseas or at independence ceremonies for former colonies like Fiji, the Bahamas and Zimbabwe. He would often be a royal pathfinder, making the first official royal tours to places like Ukraine or Turkmenistan. He would be sent to test the waters before the Queen made a full state visit to countries like Russia and Poland. And, towards the end of the Queen's life, once she had curtailed long-haul flying and, finally, all overseas travel, it was the Prince who undertook the big trips for her. A royal tour can include visits to any number of countries by any member of the family. It is not the same as a state visit, which, by definition, involves an invitation from one head of state to another. So, King Charles III's first state visit was always going to be a big deal. However, even before his accession to the throne, he had already met more world leaders than almost any head of state on today's international stage. It is yet another area where King Charles III is both a new boy and a veteran, once again stepping into the late Queen's shoes with a minimum of difficulty.

The only obvious outward change, as the King takes his first steps overseas as monarch, is the State Bentley waiting at the end of the red carpet. On his previous trips abroad, he would be climbing into the British ambassador's car. Built for the late Queen to mark her Golden Jubilee, the bomb-proof claret-coloured variation on the Bentley Arnage is unique and reserved for the monarch. For this occasion, the manufacturers have driven it from Britain halfway across Europe. This may be at odds with the King's environmental messaging but, as the standard bearer for all things British, his visit is also an excellent promotional opportunity for the UK car industry. Compromises must be made.

In any case, this, the first state visit of the reign, is to an automotive superpower – Germany. Back in the UK, there could be a public outcry if the King and Queen Camilla were seen travelling everywhere in a Mercedes. Besides, considerably more carbon emissions will have been incurred by the two German Eurofighters which the host nation generously despatched to escort the King's RAF Voyager into German airspace. It is another clear indicator of the importance attached to the visit.

After being driven into the centre of the capital, the royal couple are greeted at Berlin's Brandenburg Gate by President Frank-Walter Steinmeier and his wife, Elke Büdenbender. It is the first time a state visitor has been welcomed here on the cobbles of Pariser Platz, beneath the winged statue of Victory which once divided West from East until the fall of the Berlin Wall in 1989. Previously, official welcome ceremonies would take place in the sedate surrounds of the presidential residence, the Schloss Bellevue. However, state ceremonial is still a work in progress in post-reunification Germany and this powerful symbol of reconciliation is much more impressive. Looking down on the scene from tinted windows on the north side of Pariser Platz are glum-looking diplomats at the French embassy. The King's visit to Europe was originally going to involve two back-to-back state visits, starting with France. However, the threat of civil disorder and violent protests against proposed pension reforms by President Emmanuel Macron forced a last-minute cancellation. The honour of hosting the first state visit of the reign, therefore, has fallen to Germany. Given that

Germany was also the destination of the Queen's last full state visit of her reign, the hosts are thrilled by the diplomatic symmetry. The French, on the other hand, remain deeply disappointed.

From the start, it is clear that the King's officials have been tweaking the schedule to squeeze some of his own interests into the regimented formalities of a state visit.

Since the British and German governments are both as one with him on issues like climate change and green energy, the King's team have been pushing at an open door. The first engagement of the entire trip is a 'sustainability reception' full of academics, energy lobbyists and environmental groups. It is certainly not the sort of event that the Queen would have enjoyed. She began her last state visit to Germany with a boat trip.

The King hears President Steinmeier praise his long-held advocacy of environmental issues, declaring: 'We are all benefiting today from Your Majesty's convictions.'

Later on, during the official speeches before a state banquet of pickled carp and chicken, the president raises the issue which now hangs forebodingly over every royal tour of Europe: Brexit. Mr Steinmeier points out that it is six years to the very day when the British government informed the European Union of its plans for a post-EU future.

'Let me say, in all honesty, that, for me personally, this was a sad day,' he goes on. 'Back then many feared that Brexit could make the Germans and the British drift apart. However, this did not happen. Too strong are the ties between our countries.'

One of those ties, he reflects, is the monarchy. He presents the King with a photograph of a thirteen-year-old Prince Charles arriving in Germany, with his father in 1961, en route to visiting some of the Duke of Edinburgh's relations. All the Duke's sisters married German aristocrats and some of their descendants are here tonight, including Princess Xenia von Hohenlohe-Langenburg and Bernhard, Hereditary Prince of Baden. So, too, is former chancellor Angela Merkel. Since leaving office in 2021, she has kept a low public profile. Ex-chancellors, as a rule, do not attend state banquets. Often described, in her day, as 'the most powerful woman in Europe', Mrs Merkel was a very great admirer of the late Queen and is very happy to re-emerge into the spotlight for this event. She is even happier to discover that she is seated next to the King.

Bilateral ties are much in evidence the following day during the centrepiece of the whole visit. No previous British monarch has addressed the national parliament, the Bundestag, and no previous state visitor has done so speaking German. It means a near-full house in the seat of German democracy as the King launches into a celebration of what unites the two nations. On the serious side, he talks at length of their shared leadership in supporting Ukraine against Russian aggression and also, as everyone expects, talks of shared endeavours 'in combating the existential challenge of climate change and global warming which confronts us all'. However, he devotes much of his fifteen-minute address to cross-cultural themes, from sporting rivalries to the German love of Monty Python and Shakespeare. He celebrates the fact that the most sacred part of his upcoming coronation will be enriched by 'the astonishing music of Georg Friedrich Handel – who was born a German and died British'. The King is tickled that a 1962 British comedy skit, 'Dinner for One', has long been a New Year's Eve tradition on German television and the fact that 'for the last fifty years we have laughed together, both at each other and with each other.' There is genuine laughter from the politicians as he crams Brahms and Byron into the same sentence as the Beatles and Kraftwerk.

No one can quite believe the King has ever listened to a single song by the pioneers of electronic 'krautrock' pop music, but the Kraftwerk reference is picked up right across the German press and social media later. So, too, is his solemn expression of sadness for the German civilian victims of Allied bombing during the Second World War and his appeal for the 'restless pursuit of a better tomorrow'. He does not mention Brexit once and he receives a standing ovation. The only German legislators not here are a few representatives of the far-left party, Die Linke, who have staged a boycott in opposition to the idea of a hereditary monarchy linked to empire and military conquest. They may or may not be amused to learn that their empty seats have been allocated to members of the royal entourage, including the King's equerry, Lieutenant Colonel Johnny Thompson, in full military uniform.

The King's speech sets the tone for the media coverage of the rest of the tour. He is not seen through the prism of the Diana years, as would often have been the case before. Nor do commentators make much mention of the Netflix royal saga, *The Crown*, which has been very popular in Germany. There is only passing comment on the sideshow of *Harry und Meghan*. Rather, the new King Charles is viewed as a different entity to the old Prince Charles. 'He came, he spoke, he inspired,' ran the front-page headline in Germany's (and Europe's) bestselling newspaper, *Bild*.

The state visit continues on familiar lines with a series of engagements reflecting deeper underlying themes, like a visit to a new UK–German military unit and a meeting with Ukrainian refugees. Just like the late Duke of Edinburgh, so Queen Camilla ensures that on any walkabouts she is the support act, not the star turn. She takes the opposite side of the street to the main media circus and keeps an eye on the clock. However, she also has her own separate programme of engagements to extend the bilateral messaging to other areas, notably some of her own core interests such as children's literacy. At one school, she joins up with Axel Scheffler, the German-born, British-based illustrator of many famous children's books, including *The Gruffalo*. Together with the president's wife, Elke, they read *Gruffalo* extracts in both German and English. The atmosphere is upbeat and lively. Queen Camilla turns her own hand to drawing a Gruffalo (signing it 'Camilla R') and cheerfully submits to a grilling from the children. What about pets? 'I love dogs. Dogs are my favourite animal. I have two pet dogs, they are Jack Russell Terriers – Beth and Bluebell – and I rescued them. They were left by the side of the road to die.'

On hobbies, she tells the class that her favourites are gardening, reading and swimming in the sea. 'I used to have horses but sadly I don't ride any longer. I'm too old,' she explains, adding: 'Last night I watched on my screen one of the foals being born which was very exciting.' Everyone is delighted. The children have met a Queen. The British and German officials have two happy first ladies. Queen Camilla has flown the flag for children's literacy. And the press have their photographs (including the royal visitor's artistic handiwork) plus a story about the Queen and horses. As an exercise in diplomatic soft power, it has been an hour well spent.

Personal passions continue to feature in the King's itinerary, not least his visit to an organic dairy farm outside Brandenburg. There he inspects livestock and is soon happily up to his elbows in curds and whey in a cheese-making facility. He has brought along his cousin, Prince Bernhard of Baden, to take a look since the Badens have their own award-winning organic farm in

Germany. 'I was just following the example of Highgrove,' cousin Bernhard says modestly. There is a flash of the old Charles at a reception in the farm shop where he meets members of Germany's oldest conservation organization, NABU. They are promoting a new project to restore degraded peatland across central Europe. He is among like-minded souls here, especially when the project's finance director, Dr Frank Woesthoff, starts complaining bitterly about the international market in permits for carbon emissions. 'We hate them. We are the enemies of carbon credits. We don't believe in them,' he says. The King nods vigorously as the conversation continues. He cannot quite stop himself: 'The worst thing is these subsidies for fossil fuels,' he begins. 'It so annoys me . . .' Then he remembers that he is a head of state, these days, not a Prince. Carbon trading in the UK is a matter of government policy. His views are hardly surprising and there are no ripples on this occasion but, even in an ostensibly private conversation like this, such remarks are not kingly. He quickly reverts to listening mode.

As ever on a state visit, the monarch is accompanied by the (then) foreign secretary. Six months into his job, this is as much of a first for James Cleverly as it is for the King. He is enjoying the way in which diplomacy operates when you are alongside a monarch. 'The fundamental difference is that I've got more time to think,' he explains. 'And it gives me a lot of time to have conversations in the margins of his meetings. When you're in [the King's] slipstream, that time is amplified and that is hugely useful.'[14]

Nor has Cleverly been required to do much work on the King's speeches, like the one to the Bundestag. As ever with these things, it was a collaborative affair, delivered on 'ministerial advice' with help from the embassy. The late Queen and her private secretary would often work from a preliminary Foreign Office draft which would then make several return journeys between the

Palace and the Foreign Office before delivery. The new King observes all these conventions but he likes to be more hands-on in the early stages. 'He always hated people writing his speeches,' says one who worked for him back in Prince of Wales days.[15] Asked if he has had to provide much input to the Bundestag address, Cleverly admits he has not: 'The short answer is no. His first draft was where it needed to be.' The foreign secretary points to the King's language in the Bundestag speech: 'His turn of phrase – with things like the fact that we can have a smile at each other's expense – that does a lot of pitch-rolling for the sort of conversations I have which may be a bit more gritty and granular.'

Offering advice on world affairs to a monarch who knew Churchill and de Gaulle as a boy, Nixon and Reagan as a young man, or Havel, Mandela and the Dalai Lama in middle age might be something of a challenge for a minister who was a student when the Berlin Wall came down. James Cleverly is well aware of the constitutional rules: 'If I found myself having to put forward strongly worded advice, that would be awkward.' He admits, however, that this would be highly unlikely. 'The King has been an observer of world events for so long and he reads the room very well.'

As in the previous reign, a state visit invariably involves a trip to another part of the host nation. On their final day, the King and Queen Camilla travel by train to Hamburg to underline some of the messages of the visit. The city is not only at the forefront of applying green technology to the marine industry but it also suffered some of the heaviest Allied bombing in the Second World War. There is a river cruise to inspect the former and a tour of a bombed-out church to remember the latter. Of greater interest to the media is the King's visit to the Rathaus, or town hall, where a balcony appearance is planned. It's the middle of the working week and it is pouring with rain. Might the numbers be disappointing? The square in front of the Rathaus, it turns out, is completely packed and the welcome is exuberant. Even old hands at the British embassy and the German foreign ministry are surprised, and try to pinpoint the last such welcome for a foreign visitor. Some go back to a previous visit by the Prince of Wales more than twenty-five years earlier, if not that of the late Queen in 1965. 'You've seen the exuberance,' remarks Cleverly, adding that Hamburgers are famed for being 'calm, quiet and stoical.' But not today.

Before flying home, the King and Queen host the traditional state visit 'return' event, a combination of thanks to the hosts and a celebration with the British expatriate community. For much of her reign, the late Queen would hold a return banquet to thank her hosts. Latterly, she would hold a reception or embassy party, as she did on her last state visit to Germany in 2015. This time, the British embassy has taken over a huge warehouse on a Hamburg industrial estate and transformed it into an indoor music festival, draped with giant banners promoting 'GREAT Britain.' The King and Queen Camilla are heralded with a full fanfare from the Band of the Royal Marines before a sea shanty band and a Beatles tribute act takes over (paying homage to the city's place in early Beatles folklore). There are stalls handing out British food and drink. At one point, the King is introduced to the 2023 German entry to the Eurovision Song Contest, the heavy metal band Lord of the Lost. The monarch, in a dark blue suit, chats to the rockers, in full, skin-tight, goth/zombie costumes, without batting an eyelid, much as if he were at a garden party, which this most certainly is not.

The first state visit of the new reign has been very much in keeping with all those previous state visits – more than 120 of them – undertaken by Elizabeth II. The aim has been identical, in seeking to celebrate and strengthen bilateral relations. Yet, the tone and style have been entirely different, as everyone knew they would (and should) be.

'King Charles III and wife Camilla are not as glamorous as William and Kate. And they don't have Hollywood glitz like Harry and Meghan either,' writes the left-of-centre *Stern* magazine, summing up the week. 'But in Germany, the couple showed something that is perhaps even more important in the end: they are likeable, funny and approachable. This bodes well for the future of the British monarchy.'[16]

The *Frankfurter Allgemeine Zeitung* goes further: 'It is important to defend peace and freedom in Europe,' it notes. 'Who could do that better as a symbol than the highest representative of one of the oldest democracies? Charles has weight, as a person and as a monarch. In this respect, he is also our king.'[17]

In this respect, furthermore, he has also filled those formidable shoes. Other areas, however, will prove more challenging.

Chapter Nine

Operation Patek

The main challenge for Charles III and the organizers of his Coronation was the one before. Seventy years on from the magnetic drama of 2 June 1953, every retrospective article or documentary about the coronation of Elizabeth II would still focus on that sense of national renewal, of a post-imperial British resurgence, of an uncomplicated post-war optimism framed around a beautiful young Queen. How could Coronation 2.0 – codename: Operation Golden Orb – possibly compete? It could not. That is why the King and his advisers knew that they had to do things differently. What 1953 did provide, however, was a template for Golden Orb. The most famous aspects of 1953 – from the rain to the advent of television – have been repeated so many times that they have become part of royal mythology. Unpublished documents and accounts in the Royal Archives, however, show that precisely the same issues which were keeping Palace staff awake at night ahead of 6 May 2023 had been causing similar anxieties in 1953: whom to invite? Where to put them all? What to wear? And so on.

One principal difference in 2023, however, was the close personal involvement of the monarch. Charles III was seventy-four at the time of his Coronation and had been able to give it much thought over many years. Aged twenty-five at the time of her succession, with two young children and taken entirely by surprise by the sudden death of her father, Elizabeth II was happy to delegate most of the planning. She was certainly attentive to the personal details, be it official prayers for the family (Prince Philip, she decided, was to be prayed for ahead of Prince Charles[1]) or the choice of candleshade for her Coronation banquets (she wanted 'fully decorated'[2]) or the offer of souvenir items from Paragon China of Stoke-on-Trent ('Dudley, I don't want any of the Paragon mugs at all, thank you,' she informed deputy treasurer Dudley Colles'[3]). However, she was content to leave major decisions to a triumvirate of the Duke of Edinburgh, Prime Minister Winston Churchill and the Earl Marshal. Charles III would take a very much closer personal interest. The King wanted to be consulted on everything. Though only a small boy in 1953, he had been raised on tales of that day. He had also seen it with his own eyes. Every other person involved in the planning of Golden Orb had not. They would need to refresh themselves with the events of one of the great days in Britain's post-war history.

Long before dawn rose, cold and wet, on 2 June 1953, Britain had already enjoyed its first electrifying thrill of the day. News that a British-led expedition had been the first to conquer Mount Everest had broken in the morning papers. Though it would later transpire that news of this feat had been held back for optimum effect, the sense of pride and astonishment was universal. The Union flag had been planted on top of the world, no less. As Prince Philip later told a Canadian interviewer: 'If I ever had the misfortune to get on one of those radio programmes where I would be asked to name my most unforgettable experience, I would reply, in all honesty: "When I heard of the ascent of Everest on the day of the Coronation."'[4] Ronald Beaty of Wakefield was trying and failing to get to sleep on the side of the road near Hyde Park Corner, having bagged a prime spot to watch the procession the next day. His account, written in a letter to his younger sister, Joan, and her young family, then living in Bombay, was later deposited in the Royal Archives. 'It was during the silent watches of the night that the news boys came round with the glad tidings that Everest had been conquered,' wrote thirty-eight-year-old Beaty. 'What excitement this caused all round and what a Coronation present for the Queen.'[5]

By first light, many of those with invitations to Westminster Abbey were already on the streets of London. The largest contingent would be the peers and peeresses, almost a thousand of them in total. In years gone by, it had been customary for noble families to attend a coronation in the family's horse-drawn coach. The Earl Marshal, however, had expressed a clear view (supported by the police) that peers should not do so on this occasion due to the volume of traffic, the risk of things going wrong and a sense that post-war Britain might have a limited appetite for aristocratic showing off. Instead, they were all urged to come by car or the London Underground. Most families had long since sold their ancestral carriages or else put them on public display. A few, however, were determined to have one last grand outing, notably the Marquess of Bath. As the Duke of Windsor later noted with amusement, it was only fifty years before that a peer had been mocked for arriving at Edward VII's coronation in a motor car. Now, aristocrats were in trouble for using a horse-drawn carriage.[6] This prompted a quarrel with the Earl Marshal, which eventually reached the Cabinet table. Tickled by this attempt at old-world glamour, Churchill sided with the Marquess of Bath, asking that 'further consideration be given to the suggestion that Peers who still possessed coaches should be allowed to drive to the abbey in them.'[7] The question had been a subject of surreal debate in upper-class circles, according to Henry 'Chips' Channon, the Tory MP and diarist. 'People's conversation has taken a Gilbert and Sullivan quality,' he wrote shortly before the Coronation. 'Winnie Portarlington announced at luncheon that she has harnesses but no coach; Edie Londonderry has a coach but no horses; Mollie Buccleuch has no postillions – but five tiaras.'[8]

The future Duke of Devonshire, the then nine-year-old Marquess of Hartington, later recalled the drama of travelling in the ducal coach from the family's London home in Mayfair. The coach had been transported from Chatsworth, the ancestral seat in Derbyshire, together with two large grey horses from the local brewery. The family had clambered aboard at around 6 a.m., allowing plenty of time, but the coachman lost his way near Victoria. Hartington's father, the eleventh Duke, was reduced to leaning out of the window, in full robes and ermine, in order to shout directions up to the driving seat, 'to the huge amusement of the gathering crowds'. The family eventually arrived at the abbey 'not late but definitely not calm'.[9] Things proved even more stressful for the Earl of Shrewsbury. As his carriage approached Whitehall, the horses (also borrowed from a brewery) were spooked by the size of the crowd and refused to budge. Eventually, a car had to be summoned and the Earl only just made it to the abbey in time.[10]

In the event, the public preferred the horse-drawn spectacle anyway. Ronald Beaty was captivated by Lord Bath in his pomp. 'Well, this fine old equipage, complete with coachman and footman in liveries of a bygone age, went by us in slow and lovely state to the loud cheers of the crowd, while the sleek transport of our day went shooting by scornfully!'

Inside the abbey, the peers and peeresses ended up in opposite grandstands, the peers seated in the South Transept, above and behind the Royal Family, and the peeresses in the North Transept. Lady Bagot's account of the day, which now sits in the Royal Archives, records how 'everything seemed to be gold' – including the carpet. 'The Peeresses sparkling with the most wonderful jewellery I have ever seen, and all wearing long white gloves, were an enchanting sight,' observed Nancy Bagot. 'I wished I was a Peer and could look at them instead of the Peers.'[11] Instead, she stared across at a row of bald heads where her husband, Caryl, the 6th Lord Bagot, was sitting. 'Husband-spotting seemed to be one of the main amusements,' she noted. Many peers had fortified themselves against up to eight hours in the abbey by concealing sandwiches in their coronets. These had to remain in their laps or under their chairs. Space was so tight that there was nowhere to put anything. Coats were banned. Lord Bagot had gone as far as having a special secret pocket sewn into his coronation robes and had filled it with Horlicks Malted Milk tablets. However, the pocket proved so secret and the seating so cramped that he was unable to relocate his tablets until he got home. All the peers and peeresses were seated by rank and by precedence; Lady Bagot found that she was number 245 and placed immediately next to the wives of those whose peerages were created at around the same time (1780 in the case of the Bagots).

Many peeresses would recall the cold, the perils of needing the loo and the royal arrivals. Lady Bagot was entranced by the elegance of both Princess Margaret and the Queen Mother, in contrast to Queen Victoria's eighty-year-old granddaughter. 'Poor Princess Marie-Louise became very flurried, snatched her train from the train-bearers before the latter had time to fold it and, bundling it over her arm, started up the stairs to the Royal Gallery train dragging behind.'

The first public glimpse of the Queen came shortly after the Gold State Coach moved off from the palace at 10.26. Standing on the Mall, onlooker Denise Boyle was struck by a new and different demeanour. 'We have seen her looking radiantly happy on other occasions – but she did not look so now,' she wrote in a letter to her family. 'One was just struck with her peaceful serenity – she was almost motionless.'[12] Most of the crowds who had been up all night waiting for a glimpse would have to wait many hours more. The Queen would only make a relatively short trip to the abbey and a much longer procession back, taking in five miles of central London. Loudspeakers relayed the entire service across the capital.

Inside the abbey, there was one false start which caused great amusement. Sensing the royal party was now on its way, the entire congregation stood up. 'All the processions were lined up and all the guests had been installed,' recalls Sir John Aird, then a page to his uncle, the Earl of Ancaster, bearer of St Edward's Staff. 'Then these ladies descended in green uniforms with green carpet sweepers and started cleaning the carpet. Suddenly the organist started playing Greensleeves and everyone laughed. It certainly lightened the mood.'[13]

By now, 18 million people were clustered around 3.2 million television sets (according to BBC estimates), of which nearly 2.5 million had been sold in the months before the Coronation. A fleet of military jets would soon be carrying the first reels of film across the Atlantic for retransmission on North American television later the same day. Most of the Commonwealth had to await cinema versions. The actress Dame Joanna Lumley, then a seven-year-old 'army brat' in Kuala Lumpur, would finally see it in a packed school hall, 'twice in black and white and once in glorious colour . . . a coronation medal on a ribbon pinned to my chest.'[14]

The sequence of events which followed is now enshrined in national folklore; the Queen's composure as she turned to her

maids of honour and said, 'Ready, girls?'; the soaring excitement as Parry's 'I Was Glad' welcomed the monarch. Nancy
Bagot was transfixed as the Queen came into view, the eagerly
anticipated Norman Hartnell gown finally revealed: 'When she
did appear, one noticed no one else. Sometimes, she moved
very slowly, seeming to float, so lightly does she walk. The full
skirt of the beautifully embroidered Coronation dress fell in
shining stiff folds which swayed slightly . . . Her pale skin
seemed to glow.'

The service began with the Recognition, as the Archbishop
presented the sovereign to the North, South, East and West and
the first cries of 'God Save The Queen' rang out. Next, she took
the oath to 'govern the Peoples' of all her realms and territories
'according to their respective laws and customs'– the pledge
she would honour until her dying day. Whenever, in later years,
royal commentators would raise the idea of the Queen abdi-
cating, this moment was the riposte. At this point, four-year-old
Prince Charles was ushered into the abbey. Whereupon the
television cameras suddenly turned away ahead of the
anointing, the most intimate part of the ceremony. This was
the first of the pre-agreed 'no-go' zones for the BBC. As the
Queen moved forward to King Edward's Chair to receive the
anointing oil on her hands, chest and head, she was followed
by four Knights of the Garter, clumsily shuffling alongside with
the canopy to cover her. Chips Channon was among many who
noticed that it sagged awkwardly. 'We were just behind one of
these old chaps holding the canopy, Viscount Allendale. He
had quite advanced Parkinson's,' explains Lady Rosemary Muir,
the senior maid of honour. 'So the whole thing was shaking.'[15]

The Abbey rose as one for the great dramatic set-piece
coming next. As the Archbishop placed St Edward's Crown on
the Queen's head, all put on their coronets in unison to cry:

'God Save The Queen'. Many likened the sight of the arms of the white-gloved peeresses to the necks of a flock of swans. The nation looked at their television sets agog. Even those who could not see it were spellbound. 'A mighty hush descended upon everything and everybody,' wrote Ronald Beaty, as he and a million others followed the service via the loudspeakers lining the route. 'Then the trumpets blared forth, the guns thundered from Hyde Park and the Tower and the people every-where, even on the route outside, rose to their feet and shouted "God Save The Queen". It was a magnificent moment, a moment when all the world knew that Elizabeth was indeed Crowned.' At which point, the heavens responded. 'Strangely enough, at the very moment of the crowning, the rain came down in torrents and I <u>mean</u> torrents.'

Starting with the Archbishop and the Duke of Edinburgh, the ritual of the homage descended through the aristocratic pecking order, tier by tier. After the royal dukes came the non-royal dukes, marquesses, earls, viscounts and finally barons, all repre-sented by the senior peer of that particular rank. When each one knelt before the Queen, the rest of his ilk, watching from their section of the abbey, would kneel and remove their cor-onets. Thus the 25th Lord Mowbray, the premier baron of England, brought up the rear on behalf of the barons, much to the amusement of his fellow peers, who would later recall the mothballs cascading from his robes.

The cameras averted their gaze for the Holy Communion which followed, leaving viewers staring at an altar cloth for three minutes before the Queen retired to St Edward's Chapel to change crowns. After a brief interlude, she emerged again to process back through the abbey, this time wearing the Imperial State Crown. In the purpose-built annexe at the far end of the abbey, there was a moment for everyone to take stock. It had now been three hours since the Queen had arrived. The service had been conducted without mishap, and the ceremonial element was at an end. Time for a glass of champagne, a sandwich and a huge sigh of relief before the carriage procession home.

If the Queen was relieved, the Archbishop of Canterbury was elated, busily congratulating everyone like a West End producer after a sensational first night. As he worked his way through all the main players, he was a little over-enthusiastic shaking hands with the maids, each of whom had a small ampule of smelling salts sewn into a glove. 'The Archbishop came in saying "You've all done so well",' says Lady Rosemary Muir. 'He shook my hand so hard the ampule broke. The Queen said: "What's that smell?" And everyone laughed. Then we all went off in the procession.'

Out in the streets, most of the crowds had yet to catch a glimpse of the Queen. Ronald Beaty and the throng around him at Hyde Park Corner were amused by the tiniest things, like watching the troops lining the street being marched off for a lavatory break, odd numbers first, even behind. Finally, the first elements of the 16,000-strong procession began to appear. 'The Gurkhas were superb and received an extra loud cheer and the Women's contingents from the three Services marched by like Guardsmen, very conscious of the great honour that was theirs,' wrote Beaty. The rain had taken its toll. 'The Pakistanis were very smart, though their beautifully starched turbans hung dismally down by the time they reached us. The Naval contingents, too, were perfect even tho' the sailors' faces were white with Blanco running off their white caps.' Security was minimal if non-existent. The only precaution against any sort of public disorder was to be found outside Parliament. The authorities had decided to put a protective box around Oliver Cromwell. Just in case.

Like everyone else, Beaty was charmed by the sight of Queen Salote of Tonga riding in her carriage with the hood down, open to the elements and cheerfully getting drenched. She had been unmissable in the abbey earlier. 'Eyes alight with interest and excitement,' wrote Nancy Bagot. 'She wore a rose-pink robe and a headdress looking rather like two tall knitting needles with a pink feather between; it made her appear to be about 10ft tall.' Few recognized the tiny man sitting opposite her, the Sultan of Kelantan.* It later emerged that he had been very keen to pull the protective hood over the carriage. Queen Salote had craftily pretended not to understand him.

For Princess Marie-Louise, who had been in such a temper before the service, the day did not get much better. In his fine study of the Coronation, Hugo Vickers records that, as she left the abbey, the elderly Princess was so thirsty that she poured herself the nearest glass of water and drank it in one. It was neat gin. On the way back to the palace, she almost fell out of the carriage while her tiara slipped off her head.[16]

As the prime ministers' procession came by, Ronald Beaty was struck by the contrast between India's Jawaharlal Nehru – 'very serious of aspect' – and Pakistan's Khawaja Nazimuddin, who 'sent such cute little "Ta-ta!" waves from the window of his coach'. The crowds were delighted to see so many heroes of the Second World War, like Viscount Montgomery. 'I looked up and there was Monty,' recalled Beaty, 'looking straight down at us with the rain dripping off the end of his nose. Wild shouts of "Monty" went up and he smiled and shrugged as if to say "No use looking at me, I can't help the rain".'

* A well-worn Coronation myth is that Noël Coward, when asked who was riding with Queen Salote, replied: 'her lunch'. He later told *The Times* that he had never said it but that story had stuck and had even prevented him from visiting Tonga.

The procession also included the two most senior maids of honour, Lady Rosemary, the daughter of a duke (Marlborough), and Lady Jane Vane-Tempest-Stewart, the daughter of a marquess (Londonderry). They rode in the carriage of Lord Tryon, Keeper of the Privy Purse. The other maids, as daughters of mere earls, went back to the palace by car. 'Lord Tryon had all these sweets – very good sweets – in his Privy Purse,' Lady Rosemary recalls. 'I remember going up Hay Hill and out came the Mars Bars.'

Finally, at around 4 p.m., Ronald Beaty's section of the crowd saw what they had been awaiting for the best part of a day and night in grim, uncomfortable conditions: 'The Queen's quite fabulous fairy-tale golden coach bearing Her Majesty, looking a little tired, I thought, but none the less beautiful. Now the crowd really went to town with a full-throated roar of cheering. It was a wonderful sight to see a solid mass of people sort of brace themselves and surge forward like a mighty wave while a sea of little flags and periscopes waved gaily in the air above their heads.'

Six hours after leaving the palace, the Queen finally made it back there. There was a momentary respite, during which two maids of honour had to stop Prince Charles from running off with the Imperial State Crown. The weary but elated Queen had removed it and placed it on a table in order to rest her neck. She would soon need to place it back on her head, however. For the balcony beckoned . . .

It is 16 March 2023 and that little boy is now a seventy-four-year-old man. Yet he is still captivated as he is reunited with the Coronation regalia. 'It's incredible,' murmurs King Charles III. 'My grandfather must have had a very small head,' he adds. For while the Crown Jewels may be hereditary, the dimensions of each monarch are not.

Charles III

No one beyond the door to this unremarkable, backstreet office building in London's West End has been informed of this particular royal engagement. The press have not been invited and it will certainly not be going in the Court Circular. Today is thoroughly private. Some of the most precious and famous treasures in the world have been brought here (in their elderly and suitably anonymous travelling cases) for refurbishment and alteration ahead of the Coronation. Internally, this four-month exercise is referred to only as 'Operation Patek'. It involves three crowns, each with a wristwatch-themed codename. 'Patek' refers to the most important of the lot, St Edward's Crown. This is the 5lb centrepiece with which the Archbishop of Canterbury will crown the King at the climax of the ceremony, and which will not be worn again until the next coronation. 'Rolex' is the Imperial State Crown, which the King will wear when he leaves the abbey. More familiar to the general public, it is a little lighter and has more regular use since it is the crown which the monarch wears to open Parliament. Finally, there is 'Cartier', the crown which will be worn by the Queen Consort both during and after the service. Whereas the rules are clear enough in terms of what sovereigns wear at coronations, they are more flexible for queens consort. Over two centuries, successive consorts had commissioned a new crown for each coronation, the last being Queen Elizabeth in 1937 (Prince Philip, as a male consort, did not have one in 1953 and wore his ducal coronet instead). Queen Camilla will not be following suit, at her own insistence. Since the accession of Charles III, his general policy with royal paraphernalia, as with much else in life, has been to recycle. He even issued an early edict that he wanted no new day-to-day uniforms, equipment or even stationery decorated with his 'CIIIR' cypher until all the old supplies branded with 'EIIR' had been used up. That meant no new crowns, either, 'in the interests of sustainability and efficiency', according to a Palace statement.[17]

So his Queen will wear an old one. Much as the King would have loved her to wear his grandmother's circlet, the Queen Mother's Crown would have either needed serious surgery, which he was reluctant to authorize, or else it would have triggered a major diplomatic incident. For the Queen Mother's Crown is set with the egg-shaped Koh-i-Noor diamond, the 105-carat 'Mountain of Light'. As discussed elsewhere, it is now the subject of repatriation demands from several nations, including India, who claim that the stone was effectively stolen by the East India Company in 1849. The Koh-i-Noor, like the Elgin Marbles from the Parthenon in Athens, has also become emblematic of the wider debate about what some like to call museum artefacts and others call British imperial loot. Were the new Queen Consort to wear the stone to Westminster Abbey on Coronation Day, it could prompt some Commonwealth nations to ask whether the new Head of the Commonwealth was the right man for the job, after all. The Queen Mother's Crown will, therefore, remain untouched in the Tower of London while the fate of its most famous component part remains, ultimately, a decision for the British government. The Queen Consort has come up with an uncontroversial alternative. She will wear Queen Mary's Crown, instead.

All three crowns, though, have required some serious work following very careful measurements of the heads of the King and Queen Camilla. The man in overall charge of this is Mark Appleby, the head of the jewellery workshop at Mappin & Webb (which boasts royal warrants from both the late Queen and the former Prince of Wales). For the previous six years, he has also had the title of Crown Jeweller. As such, he is not just responsible for crowns and sceptres but everything from the gold dishes which come out for the Royal Maundy ceremony to the silver gilt Lily Font used at royal christenings. He is the only person, apart from the monarch, authorized to touch everything. One of his duties is the annual cleaning of all the Crown Jewels, conducted after dark and under armed guard inside the Jewel House of the Tower of London. Now fifty-nine, Appleby started in the trade at sixteen and previously worked for the former Crown Jewellers, Garrard. He was one of the very last people to officiate in the funeral of Elizabeth II, unscrewing the brackets and removing the Orb, Sceptre and Imperial State Crown from the coffin in St George's Chapel just before it descended to the Royal Vault. There is nothing quite like a coronation for what Appleby calls 'clearing out the Tower'.

He is also the first Crown Jeweller on record who has had the daunting task of sawing St Edward's Crown into pieces. Just as human beings have grown in size over the generations, the same applies to monarchs. The crown has had to expand very slightly to fit the head of Charles III. This has entailed making four strips of yellow gold, each seven millimetres wide, before sawing up the crown, inserting each strip and then welding it – imperceptibly – to fill the gaps. Appleby's team have also produced eight new 18-carat gold beads to sit across the extra strips. He works closely with his Mappin & Webb colleague Martin Swift, who held the title of Crown Jeweller before him. Swift has made every strip and every bead at his workbench. This in itself is a monument to the jeweller's craft over the centuries. He sits at what is rather like a desk with the all-important bench 'skin' above his lap to catch the tiniest fragments of gold or anything else that falls off. There are rows of ancient instruments like scorpers (a form of fine chisel) and a triblet, a long steel cone for measuring ring diameters. Stripped of its purple velvet cap, its arches, its jewels, its monde (the orb and cross at the top), St Edward's

Crown looks much like a child's toy. Yet even this outer frame, or circlet, tells a story. Swift points to a dent on the inside rim, a legacy from the day in 1671 when Colonel Blood attempted to steal the Crown Jewels from the Tower and flattened the crown with a mallet so that he could stuff it inside his trousers.[*] What impresses Swift and Appleby most of all are the tiny gold screws which hold all the jewels in place. They would be hard enough to make today, yet their predecessor, royal goldsmith Robert Vyner, made them 400 years ago. The two jewellers point to another little-known fact. 'People think crowns are round,' says Swift. 'They're not. They are oval.'

Similar work has been needed on the Imperial State Crown, aka 'Rolex'. It was altered ahead of the previous coronation because Elizabeth II felt the arches (or 'crosses pattées') were too tall and she wanted them lowered. Charles III is happy with the height but, as with St Edward's Crown, needs this one to be a fraction broader. So, all the jewels, including the Black Prince's Ruby – with its tiny hole for the royal feather which Henry V wore at the Battle of Agincourt – and the Stuart Sapphire, have been removed while two new strips are inserted.

'Cartier', or Queen Mary's Crown, fits the Queen Consort but she wants a simpler look, so the eight arches have been reduced to four. It will also be reset with three pieces from the Cullinan Diamond. Mined in South Africa in 1908, as noted earlier, this was the largest gem-quality diamond ever found. It was so large that it was cut into several smaller pieces, each of which still ranks among the finest diamonds in the world. Cullinan I, otherwise known as the Star of Africa, sits in the Sceptre with Cross and Cullinan II resides in the Imperial State Crown. Numbers III and IV, which were often worn as brooches by the

---

[*]   Blood was captured but later pardoned by Charles II.

late Queen (who called them 'Granny's chips'), and Cullinan V will be mounted in Queen Mary's reconfigured crown for the Queen Consort.

These are historic alterations to some of the most famous royal treasures of all, which is why the King and Queen Consort have asked to see Mark Appleby's team in action. The royal visitors are transfixed by all the earnest activity throughout this workshop. For the crowns are not the only pieces receiving expert attention. Other jewellers are working on bracelets, earrings, necklaces and much else for Mappin & Webb customers who will have no idea that a loose setting in an engagement ring is actually being repaired alongside the Crown Jewels. At one bench, someone is completing a new Plowden Medal, a major conservation award. On a shelf stands a new piece of silverware, almost as well known as the Imperial State Crown, awaiting collection. It is this year's Footballer of the Year trophy for the Professional Footballers' Association.

The King loves seeing the most intricate tasks performed in the traditional way – by hand. 'So you look forward to coming to the office?' he asks diamond-setter Chris Kendall, who, after twenty-two years here, does indeed. Mark Appleby takes the royal visitors into a sideroom and shows them a video of work on St Edward's Crown. 'What a task to have to start chopping that,' says the Queen Consort, acknowledging the burden of responsibility on anyone charged with sawing up four centuries of royal history. The royal couple are in awe of the craftsmanship of the seventeenth-century goldsmiths who made these works of art in cramped, candlelit conditions (in the aftermath of Cromwell's sale or destruction of the original Crown Jewels). 'Without specs,' notes Queen Camilla. 'And the plague and goodness knows what,' adds the King. They inspect the Imperial State Crown and its jewels, including the Black Prince's Ruby with its tiny hole. The King knows its history well. 'I have a feeling that a plume went in it,' he says. Martin Swift explains the process of dismantling something as minutely detailed as Queen Mary's Crown. The Queen feels vindicated in her decision to reduce the number of arches from the original eight: 'I think it looks better with four.' She is fascinated by some of the rock crystal imitation diamonds which have just been removed from Queen Mary's Crown, including a gleaming replica of the Koh-i-Noor (which Queen Mary wore at the 1937 Coronation of George VI when the real thing was in Queen Elizabeth's crown). 'You wouldn't know this is a copy,' Queen Camilla notes admiringly. In years to come, if the Indian government has its wish, that may be just as well.

The royal couple move through to another room to meet the royal hatter, Philip Treacy. He has been asked to produce the only perishable part of each crown, the soft inner lining known as the cap of maintenance. 'It plays a huge part,' explains Mark Appleby afterwards. 'You can't wear a crown without a cap. It would leave a terrible mark on your forehead and it might cut you too as it is a sharp piece of gold.' Treacy points out that it is only the cap which stops a crown 'becoming a necklace'. He was the obvious choice since he was making hats for the then Camilla Parker Bowles well before her marriage to the then Prince of Wales. The milliner began by making a cross-section of the royal heads and then creating wooden templates. From these, he has made adjustable inner caps, like the inside of a helmet or a construction worker's hard hat. The purple outer layer is then puffed up with a horsehair mesh which stops it imploding like a collapsed soufflé. 'We are trying to make these crowns, that are not light, light,' says Treacy later. He was particularly concerned about St Edward's Crown, given its weight.

'It is extremely heavy and complicated to fit,' he adds. 'Now I understand when I watch that footage of Queen Elizabeth II at her Coronation, concentrating. She is doing that because she is concentrating on keeping her crown on.'

He is still bowled over by the thought that his handiwork will not just be on television at the Coronation but on public display for years to come in the Jewel House of the Tower of London. 'I'm just a kid from the west of Ireland. This is the greatest honour of my career,' he says. 'Fairy tales come from these crowns. When you look at a crown and you see that hole drilled for Henry V's feather at the Battle of Agincourt – it's beyond a dream. We've never fitted a crown before. So that little string holding the lining in place is the most important bit of ribbon in the world.'

There is one essential piece of Coronation regalia which will not be recycled. In 1953, there was alarm bordering on panic when it transpired that no one could find the bottle of anointing oil. This had originally been made by Squire & Sons for the coronation of Edward VII in 1902 and there was still plenty left after the coronation of George VI in 1937. However, a bomb, which landed on the Deanery of Westminster Abbey during the Second World War, had destroyed it. By the time of the coronation of Elizabeth II, Squire & Sons had been taken over by another company and the apothecary who had made the last batch had died. A memo in the Royal Archives, however, reveals that one of his descendants, a Mrs Marrogodato, 'née Squire', had unearthed the family recipe for 'a mixture of sesame and olive oil perfumed with roses, orange flowers, jasmine, cinnamon, flowers of Benzoin, Musk, Civet and ambergris.'[18] The handwritten notes go on to give precise measures and instructions, starting with civet and musk rubbed into sesame oil which should then be left to 'digest for a few days'. Other ingredients come later while the ambergris (extracted from the stomach of a sperm whale) is among the last. The memo notes that this formula for 'compound oil' goes back to the coronation of King Charles I, making it older than most of the Crown Jewels.

King Charles III has decided to go back in time further still. While the current royal chemists still retain a small sample of that 1953 oil, the new King could perhaps foresee the inevitable headlines and endless complaints from animal-lovers if he were to be anointed by oil made from the entrails of a musk deer, the glands of a civet cat and the bowels of a whale. Even if all the other ingredients were thoroughly wholesome and organic, it might be an unwelcome distraction. Following a suggestion from the Archbishop of Canterbury, the King has hatched a more original plan, based on the Old Testament. According to Chapter 30 of the Book of Exodus, the earliest anointing oil was made from olive oil mixed with cinnamon and myrrh. Biblical kings such as Solomon and David had been anointed in this way. Furthermore, the King's maternal grand-mother, Princess Alice (the Duke of Edinburgh's mother), is buried on Jerusalem's Mount of Olives, at the Russian Orthodox Church of St Mary Magdalene.* It had been her dying wish to have her remains buried there, alongside her aunt, Grand Duchess Ella, a nun who was murdered by the Bolsheviks in 1918 and is now a saint in the Russian and Greek Orthodox Churches. It was Ella who had inspired Princess Alice to set up her own order of nuns in later life. The church also sits next to the Garden of Gethsemane, where Jesus Christ would come to pray shortly before his crucifixion. So why not source the

---

* Princess Alice of Battenberg married Prince Andrew of Greece in 1903. They had four daughters before Prince Philip was born in 1921.

oil from there? Rather than entrusting the task to a white-coated pharmacist in a British lab, here was an opportunity to connect the King and the Anglican Church to the Eastern Orthodox Church, the King's paternal family, King Solomon and Jesus Christ himself. So, in March 2023, the Anglican Archbishop in Jerusalem and the Orthodox Patriarch of Jerusalem arranged to have olives harvested from two groves next to the church. These were then pressed before being mixed and scented locally with 'essential oils', including sesame, rose, jasmine, cinnamon and orange blossom. Lambeth Palace researchers had established the historical or scriptural provenance of each ingredient. Having met the King on a number of occasions, Patriarch Theophilus III regarded it as the highest honour to play a role in the coronation of a monarch who had, in the past, made several contemplative visits to Orthodox monasteries in Greece. 'I felt him [to be] a very humble person,' he said. 'This is a very good quality for a king – humility.'[19] The two Christian leaders then consecrated the oil at Jerusalem's Church of the Holy Sepulchre before despatching it in a silver flask to the Dean of Westminster, Dr David Hoyle, for safe keeping.

Some weeks later, the Archbishop of Canterbury, Justin Welby, arrives at Westminster Abbey to inspect the results, since he will be the one conducting the anointing. 'Goodness, me. Isn't it extraordinary,' says Welby as he takes a sniff and tries to describe it. 'Lavender,' he suggests. 'With something muskier underneath,' says the Dean, adding that it will be a great improvement on the coronation of Elizabeth I. She complained that her anointing oil was 'grease' and 'smelt ill'. The Archbishop is determined to use it sparingly. 'You don't have to pour very much?' he asks. 'You really don't,' says the Dean, assuring him that the days of Old Testament oil running down the King's beard are long gone.

Chapter Ten

No Plus-One

Seeing his mother being crowned in 1953 was certainly not Charles III's only exposure to the business of becoming sovereign. Over the years, he had represented Elizabeth II at the enthronements of Emperor Akihito of Japan and King Willem-Alexander of the Netherlands, among others. These, though, had been inaugurations rather than crowning moments. In matrimonial terms, they were the equivalent of a civic ceremony in a register office, whereas the British model is closer to a full-fat church wedding with bridesmaids, lace, confetti and cake.

While Britain is the only northern hemisphere nation which still crowns its new head of state, it is not the only country in the world to do so. In 1997, the then Prince of Wales travelled to Lesotho for the coronation of the British-educated King Letsie III. It was a considerably larger affair than his own would be twenty-six years later since it was held outdoors. The government of Lesotho opted for the national football stadium in the capital, Maseru, resulting in a capacity crowd of 25,000. The Prince joined the South African president, Nelson Mandela, in the royal box for what was, surely, the first coronation to carry advertising hoardings ('Lewis Furniture Wishes To Congratulate His Majesty On His Coronation'[1]). However, the drama and magic of the occasion was undimmed as the thirty-four-year-old King Letsie rose from his throne, wearing his calfskin feathered crown, his robe and his royal cloak, to receive the acclamation of his people. The Prince of Wales, dressed in his white naval uniform (which would today trigger a Twitter-fuelled social media storm about colonial privilege but at the time upset no one at all), greatly enjoyed it. He seemed genuinely touched by the warmth of the welcome as he made a short speech on behalf of the Queen. The monarchy was still feeling bruised following the death of Diana, Princess of Wales two months earlier. Noting that King Letsie's ceremony had lasted more than four hours (as a result of which, some people had suffered dehydration and sunstroke), the Prince was concerned for the press corps. 'Were you all right in that heat?' he asked them during the onward flight to Pretoria. One reporter expressed the hope that the next British coronation might be a little speedier. 'Don't worry,' the Prince replied. 'I'll keep it short.' A quarter of a century later, he would be true to his word.

What the planning for the 2023 Coronation illustrates clearly is that recurring sense of a King wanting to get on with it. It was only four weeks after the death of Elizabeth II that the Palace fixed the coronation of Charles III for 6 May, leaving just seven months to organize things. In 1952, the Palace and the government took twice as long to decide the date and then still had well over a year to play with. Indeed, some of those organizing the 2023 event would say that Elizabeth's advisers had far too much time on their hands. It meant that everyone had the luxury of dithering or turning a small issue into a protracted debate.

So it was with the choice of date back then. Among the many obstacles to finding a day in 1953 was a likely general election in South Africa, then still one of the monarch's realms, and the need to avoid local election campaigns in England in May. The government was also reluctant to hold a coronation on a Friday. 'The superstitious, who are numerous, would be upset,' Churchill's private secretary, Jock Colville, wrote to his boss.[2] Any time after mid-June was discouraged because the trees would be in full leaf and would thus obscure many views of the route. Choosing a bank holiday would cause trouble with company pay rolls. And so on. However, the main concern was the racing calendar. The Coronation, Colville warned, should not be allowed to clash with either the Derby or Royal Ascot or the 2000 Guineas at Newmarket.[3] It was not until 10 April 1952 that the Queen's private secretary, Alan Lascelles, told Churchill that she had 'definitely decided' on 2 June 1953. Seventy years later, King Charles III moved at double the speed. His chosen date would clash with both local election week and the 2000 Guineas, as it happened. So be it. There were no complaints.

As well as being in a hurry, the King was determined to shape this event in his own image. All minor as well as major decisions would have to clear his desk, creating decision-making logjams when he was preoccupied elsewhere. One participant in the royal procession became increasingly worried when his long-expected involvement had still yet to be confirmed less than three weeks before the day itself. Nothing could be done, he was told, until it had been signed off by the King. Eventually it was, but it had been a nervous and rather awkward wait.[4]

In 1953, it was the hereditary Earl Marshal, the 16th Duke of Norfolk, who was expected to be in command of everything. The accession of Elizabeth II meant a second coronation for Bernard Norfolk, who had also organized the 1937 crowning of George VI. He was Earl Marshal for longer than anyone.

In office for more than half a century, he organized the state funerals of George V and George VI, buried Sir Winston Churchill and arranged the investiture of the Prince of Wales in 1969. There was one man who could trump his authority in 1953, however. The Queen had appointed Prince Philip as chairman of the Coronation Commission, with the Earl Marshal as his deputy chairman. The commission also included the prime minister, Winston Churchill, most of his Cabinet, plus the prime ministers of all other realms. They would have oversight of everything. At their very first meeting, however, Prince Philip proposed the creation of two committees which would make the decisions and get on with the job. The Coronation Joint Committee would include all the other Commonwealth realms. The Coronation Executive Committee would take decisions on purely British issues. The Duke of Norfolk would chair them both. And, with that, the Coronation Commission adjourned. It would only hold one other meeting. In the meantime, Prince Philip and Winston Churchill were happy to leave everything to Bernard Norfolk.

By 2023, the office of Earl Marshal had been inherited by Eddie Norfolk, 18th Duke. As previously noted, he had been the chief architect of Operation London Bridge, the funeral plan for Elizabeth II, revising and updating it at regular intervals over twenty years. 'It was like constantly revising for a Physics A-Level, but never knowing when the exam was going to be,' he reflects.[5] By common consent, the farewell to the late Queen could be said to have earned him a top grade. Operation Golden Orb, however, was very different. A funeral had to happen fast. A coronation did not. Some years before, the Duke had drawn up some basic coronation ideas in consultation with the previous Archbishop of Canterbury, Dr Rowan Williams. This established certain core principles for Golden Orb, whenever it might happen.

'We agreed that we wouldn't build extra seating in the abbey, that we would get the length of the service closer to an hour and a half . . . and that we couldn't have all the hereditary peers,' says Norfolk. However, some firmer ground rules had been established in 2015 following the arrival of a new private secretary to the Prince of Wales. Previously British ambassador to Morocco, Clive Alderton had been seconded to the Prince's office earlier in his diplomatic career. He therefore knew the ways of the Palace and, in the words of one colleague, 'did not want to be caught napping'. So, on a December evening, he invited his opposite number from the Archbishop's staff at Lambeth Palace to Clarence House to view the entire footage of the 1953 Coronation. 'It was freezing – typical Clarence House – but Clive lightened the mood by serving Coronation chicken,' recalls a senior source. 'They reached several conclusions. The ceremony should be an hour and forty-five minutes. And they agreed an important principle for the Coronation. The most important thing was not *who* was at it – which had been the big deal last time – but *what* they did. It had to be rooted in a thousand years of history and also speak to modern Britain. The content was key.'[6]

Now that the time had come, Alderton knew that the King and Queen would want to be across all the details of the Coronation. He also knew that Whitehall had changed beyond all recognition since 1953 and the days of an omnipotent Bernard Norfolk. 'No one person could do it,' says the source, 'and the government was footing the bill'. The public side was down to the Department for Culture, Media and Sport while the Cabinet Office handled the constitutional side. As one royal staffer puts it, the DCMS were 'putting on the show' and the Cabinet Office 'made us legal'. The Earl Marshal would still, officially, serve as ringmaster. Invitations would go out in Eddie Norfolk's name 'by command of The King'.

In the event, it would be Alderton running the show on the monarch's behalf, in tandem with the deputy prime minister, Oliver Dowden. 'Clive Alderton chaired the main weekly Coronation Organizing Committee, which had this huge cast of Whitehall, the military and so on,' says one of the Palace team. 'Below that, on one side, you had the "Senior Sponsors group" – with very senior government and Palace people. On the other were various sub-committees. Then Alderton and Dowden would have lunch to go through it.'

There was a separate committee specifically on the order of service, also chaired by Alderton, alongside the Archbishop of Canterbury and Dean of Westminster. Then there was the 'Earl Marshal's Group', drawn from within the Royal Household, which focused on ceremonial, heraldry and dress codes. Eddie Norfolk was also keen to push plans for a Coronation concert at Windsor Castle, one which would extend the sense of celebration across the country and also 'showcase' British values to the wider world. There was no power struggle. A successful entrepreneur and businessman, Norfolk was quite content to let things take their course, providing he could be confident it was all going to work. 'He knew which battles to fight and which not,' says a member of his committee. 'He was also well aware, from the outset, that if it did not work, it was all in his name and the final responsibility would rest on his shoulders.'

Eddie Norfolk would also be a lightning rod, however unfairly, for one of the most frequent sources of complaint: the guest list. Although the crowning of Charles III would have the largest worldwide audience of any coronation in British history, it would also have one of the smallest congregations. The decision not to cram Westminster Abbey with scaffolding and tiers of temporary seating was, in part, a question of health and safety. Modern regulations would not allow 8,000 people from floor to rafters inside a thousand-year-old church. It was also a question of aesthetics. Why diminish the drama, the spectacle and the beauty of the abbey for millions looking on via television in order to squeeze in a few extra VIPs? The result was a congregation one quarter of the size of that in 1953. It would also be by far the most socially, ethnically and politically diverse in coronation history.

Arguments over seating allocations had been very heated seven decades before, however. Bernard Norfolk's Coronation Joint Committee began by studying the seating for the 1937 coronation, starting with the aristocracy. Peers and peeresses had been allocated no less than 1,300 tickets. A special sub-committee on seat allocation initially decided that the same number should be set aside in 1953 'to be on the safe side'.[7] That way of thinking would not prevail for long. It was soon clear that the nobility would have to take a large cut to make space for all the delegations from the Commonwealth. This had grown substantially in both size and expectations since 1937, following autonomy for India, Pakistan and Ceylon. Increasingly independent-minded dominions like Australia and Canada also expected a greater ticket allocation for the crowning of *their* Queen. Eventually, the organizers would settle on a ration of 910 seats for the House of Lords (455 peers plus peeresses) and 650 for the House of Commons (325 MPs plus spouses). To twenty-first-century minds, it might seem extraordinary that post-war Britain was still ready to allocate more seats to its unelected aristocracy than to the elected representatives of the people. However, there was little pushback at the time. The House of Lords, made up entirely of hereditary peers in those days, commanded seniority. A memo from the senior herald at the College of Arms, Garter King of Arms, to the Duke of Norfolk in October 1952 shows the prevailing

Establishment view. The peers had a formal role, wrote Sir George Bellew, because they were there to pay homage to the monarch. Lowly members of the Commons, on the other hand, had 'a watching brief', nothing more. 'I think the purpose of their presence is to witness the deed,' Bellew wrote of the MPs, arguing that the role of the peers went back to Saxon times.[8] 'As a sort of living manifestation of England's history, they add absolutely incomparable and irreplaceable lustre,' he went on. 'In the absence of their personal dignity and of their robes and coronets, the Coronation would lose much of its importance as an occasion of occasions in the eyes of the world.'

There were plenty of people pushing in the opposite direction, arguing that this was a modern coronation and that it should acknowledge the role of parliamentary democracy. Should not elected representatives play a part? Even the Duke of Edinburgh took an interest in that idea. Less than four months before the Coronation, he attended a meeting of the Coronation Committee of the Privy Council which was responsible for examining the constitutional elements of the ceremony. There, the Labour leader, Clement Attlee, and the Liberal leader, Clement Davies, both suggested that it should not just be the aristocracy who paid homage to the Queen. They proposed that the Speaker of the House of Commons should do the same on behalf of the Members of Parliament since MPs had, after all, been elected. At which point, the Duke of Edinburgh asked if all the MPs present might, at that moment, kneel in homage, too. The Archbishop of Canterbury, Dr Geoffrey Fisher, thought this was a very bad idea. The homage, he argued, was 'a purely feudal ceremony'. He warned 'that if the nation as a whole were to be represented then school teachers, artisans and so forth should be included in the homage.'[9] Others argued that if the Speaker of the British Parliament was included, then the speakers of all the other Commonwealth parliaments would want to take part. Bernard Norfolk felt that he had more than enough problems simply marshalling his 910 peers and peeresses to do homage in the correct order. He had no wish to have other ranks, such as MPs or teachers, cluttering up the abbey with their own walk-on parts. So he had a clever idea. He proposed a sub-committee to explore the possibility of including the Speaker in the ceremony, safe in the knowledge that it would agree nothing. Sure enough, by the time it had convened and deliberated, the general view was that there simply wasn't enough time to start tinkering with the ceremony, especially as the printing and binding of 9,000 orders of service was about to start. On 24 February 1953, the sub-committee formally agreed to order an enquiry to examine 'what changes in the Homage might be introduced at a later Coronation and to frame recommendations'.[10] In other words, they were not going to give the Commons a central role on this occasion. They would leave it to the future Charles III to reconsider an enhanced role for MPs. Fast-forward to 2023, and nothing much had changed. There would, however, be one MP who would cause quite a stir.

The major change was the decision to omit all but a handful of the aristocracy. As Eddie Norfolk and Rowan Williams had agreed years before, and as Sir Clive Alderton would remind people, the constitutional landscape had changed the moment the hereditary peers left the House of Lords in 1999. As well as freeing up hundreds of seats, their omission from the Coronation would also reduce the length of the processions and save time. That is because, in the days when hereditary peers had all the main roles in the ceremony, each needed someone to carry his coronet. So they each came with a page. Some brought two. In total, it meant another fifty people, albeit schoolboys, processing in and out of the 'theatre'.

Each page had to be a boy aged between twelve and fourteen, although a special exemption was made for nine-year-old Lord Hartington, future Duke of Devonshire. His grandmother was the Queen's Mistress of the Robes and no one was going to quarrel with her. Peers would usually appoint a son or grandson if one of them met the requirements. If not, they might cast around for a distant cousin or a friend's son who could fit into a pageboy uniform. Andrew Parker Bowles was at prep school when he was informed that he was to be the page to Lord Simonds, the seventy-one-year-old Lord Chancellor. 'Bernard Norfolk was a friend of my mother. It was he who suggested me to Lord Simonds,' he recalls.* 'He was the nicest man alive and gave me a set of cufflinks as a present.'[11] Julian James, meanwhile, was in his first year at Charterhouse when he was summoned to have tea with an illustrious Royal Navy contemporary of his grandfather. Admiral of the Fleet Viscount Cunningham of Hyndhope had been appointed Lord High Steward, one of the highest offices at the Coronation. It involved carrying St Edward's Crown and earned him the right to appoint two pages. However, the great war hero had no children. 'A dozen of us were invited to tea with him so he could check who was up to the mark,' recalls James, who made the grade.[12]

In 2023 pages would be largely redundant, except for those attending to the King and Queen. Even the handful of the old aristocracy who were to play a part would not require coronets because the Earl Marshal had banned them anyway. One or two, like the Duke of Wellington (bearer of the Queen's Crown), wanted to bring his family coronet, and would thus have

---

* Gavin Simonds, later Viscount Simonds, had no grandchildren. He and his wife, Mary, had lost one son in infancy, a second at Arnhem and their third on active service in East Africa.

needed a page, too. The Earl Marshal, however, stood firm, arguing that the sight of a tiny handful of guests crowning themselves amid 2,000 commoners would be divisive and look ridiculous.

Aside from the defenestration of the nobility, the other very noticeable change in ticket allocations at the coronation of Charles III was a new general rule which, though practical, would upset many: with a few exceptions, there would be no spouse or 'plus one'. If the church capacity was to be reduced by three quarters, so the thinking went, then there would have to be tough decisions. After much discussion among the sub-committees, it was decided that the Lords and Commons would have a ration of fifty tickets each. They would – in theory, at least – be chosen by ballot and there would be no room for spouses. A small number of additional peers and MPs (such as Cabinet ministers or friends of the King) would receive tickets via different allocations. Those who failed to get a seat in the abbey could apply for another ballot to stand on the pavement outside Parliament – with a companion. All those hereditary peers (in other words, the large majority) who had no seat in the Lords would just have to watch it on television like everyone else. Traditionalists and constitutional experts might be appalled to see the number of parliamentarians slashed from more than 1,500 in 1953 to a mere one hundred. Such was the public's disenchantment with the political class that there was barely a ripple beyond Westminster.

Instead, the largest single group present in the abbey would be 400 holders of the BEM, the British Empire Medal, the entry-level decoration in the honours system. If the Coronation were to identify a public-spirited cohort of 'ordinary' people, then the BEM would be as good a filter as any. There was no application process. The Cabinet Office simply sifted through previous honours lists to identify 400 thrilled, if slightly baffled, nominees. 'They are all people who have come to attention at a community level,' explained a member of the Lord Chamberlain's Office. 'The honours lists gave the Cabinet Office the ability to be equitable in terms of geography and gender.'[13] The 400 lucky BEM-holders would be the very first to receive the formal invitation, decorated with British trees and flowers on recycled card with gold foil. It was designed by heraldic artist Andrew Jamieson on the theme of the 'green man', the symbol of spring, rebirth and, thus, a new reign. In 1953, a prized position for the families and staff of peers and MPs was in the stands next to the abbey. This time, 400 young people with links to royal charities would be invited to watch the procession outside the abbey and then watch the service on big screens in the adjacent church of St Margaret's Westminster, followed by a Lambeth Palace lunch hosted by the Archbishop of Canterbury.

Back in 1953, the arguments about seating went on for months. When there were still not enough seats for the Commonwealth delegations, things took a more brutal turn. Sir Alan 'Tommy' Lascelles, private secretary to the Queen, spotted some low-hanging fruit during a meeting of the Coronation Joint Committee in July 1952. Supported by the Archbishop of Canterbury, he suggested that 'the Baronets* might be entirely removed from the list.'[14] The high sheriffs of the counties had been there in 1937. Now, they, too, would be chopped, freeing up ninety-four seats in an instant. An especially delicate cut was the removal of widows of peers. Bernard Norfolk wrote to Lascelles warning him to prepare the Queen for an ambush if

---

* A baronetcy is the lowest-ranking hereditary title (effectively a hereditary knighthood). It is not a peerage and confers no seat in Parliament.

dowagers were to be axed. 'One would not be surprised if a move was not made direct to Her Majesty to get it altered,' wrote the Earl Marshal.[15] He was not wrong. There was shock in high places. 'This is scandalous,' declared Chips Channon on hearing that two elderly dowager Duchesses, who had served Queen Mary and Queen Alexandra, were not to be invited.[16]

Winston Churchill turned out to be particularly annoyed by the meagre ration of seats for the trade union movement. They might not be on his side politically but he was dismayed to see that their allocation had been almost halved from the thirty-seven seats they had received at George VI's coronation. 'Why should there be less than in 1937?' he asked Jock Colville, who took the matter to the Coronation Joint Committee.[17] The trade unionists had Churchill to thank when their ration was eventually upped to sixty.

Smaller, shorter and denuded of tiaras, coronets or nobility it might be, but the coronation of Charles III also spared the Palace and the Foreign Office from having to act as travel agents. Ahead of the crowning of Elizabeth II, on the other hand, it was the hosts who were expected to accommodate all the international VIPs heading for London. Bernard Norfolk's sub-committee on overseas guests divided them into four categories. There were 'Royal Guests', namely prime ministers and senior representatives from all the Commonwealth countries, plus their wives. Into this category were added seven royal rulers of British protectorates, including Queen Salote of Tonga.[18]

Next came 'Official Guests', representatives of all foreign countries sending 'special missions' to the Coronation, including the USA, France and Germany. These were followed by 'Distinguished Visitors', notably 'African Chiefs', including the Paramount Chief of Swaziland and the Kabaka of Buganda and, finally, 'Colonial Territories'. There were ninety-one representatives from all Britain's colonial possessions, nominated at local level. As well as seats within the abbey, they would all need places to stay. The two most senior categories would be paid for by the British taxpayer. The two lowlier tiers would have to pay their own way. At which point, Royal Household staff began block-booking hotels all over London, subject to clear guidelines from the Lord Chamberlain's Office entitled: 'Coronation accommodation for Foreign representatives in hotels'. Among the stipulations were that 'Iron Curtain countries should not be housed in the same hotels as other countries', 'Israelis not with Arabs', 'France not with Lebanon', 'Libya and Ethiopia not with Italy', 'Greece not with Italy', 'Germans not with the French or any other countries that they occupied', 'Japan not with any other Asiatics [sic]' and 'Spain not with Central and South American republics'.[19]

The same report, now in the Royal Archives, records some of the issues relayed by the management of certain hotels. One complained about the visit of a foreign potentate who 'was so sacred in his own country that he could not be approached erect'. As a result, the hotel reported, there was 'a caterpillar of the Faithful crawling along the passage on their stomachs from the lift to the door of his suite, to the great inconvenience of other guests'. Each delegation was assigned two ex-members of the armed forces, known as 'attached officers'. They were supposed to act as a host-cum-guide on behalf of the Queen and pick up any incidental expenses, although this would turn into a costly business for one or two of them. Commander David Maitland-Makgill-Crichton, an heroic figure at Dunkirk, spent £12 (£270 today) taking the prime minister of Finland to the Stork Night Club and tried to recoup the cost. 'I realize that this is not really an admissible claim but it was nevertheless the right thing done at the right time,' he pleaded. The claim was struck out.[20]

Back in 1953, the Royal Household was not only expected to pay for hotel accommodation for VIP Coronation guests – which came to £15,268[21] (or around £350,000 today) – but it even had to pick up some travel bills. Delegations from across Europe, arriving at Dover, were met by a special Pullman train costing £1,059, including £147 for 190 lunches and £42 for 'liqueurs and coffee'. As if the Queen did not have enough to think about, she was also hosting a full royal houseparty. All of Prince Philip's sisters were invited to stay at the palace with their husbands (making up for the lack of a royal wedding invitation five years earlier, when their German war service was still deemed unacceptable to the British public). The house guests also included the Crown Princes of both Norway and Denmark, plus wives.

Every cost was meticulously logged by the Privy Purse Office, right down to the hire of an extra car for one of the Gulf leaders. 'The Ruler of Qatar had an inordinate amount of luggage which could not all be got on to the car,' says a note in the accounts. 'He insisted that one of the tribal slaves should remain with the luggage and travel with it.'[22] Everything was double-checked, even a 17-shilling bill for taking seven members of the Bahraini delegation to London Zoo (accepted) and a £4 claim for morning coat hire by the officer escorting the Turkish delegation (rejected).[23]

Many of the overseas leaders were keen to be taken to other events during their stay, not least the Derby. All would expect an invitation to a state banquet. Given that the palace could not accommodate them all at a single sitting, there would have to be two banquets (costing £1,314 each). Wartime sensitivities still lingered. The first state banquet, on the evening after

Coronation Day, was principally for wartime allies, including General George Marshall, leader of the US delegation. The following evening, the guests included the Japanese Crown Prince and the German vice-chancellor, Franz Blücher.

None of this would be an issue in 2023. Ahead of the coronation of Charles III, the Palace was certainly not expected to pay for other people's travel arrangements. There would be no royal houseparty, not least because much of Buckingham Palace was a building site, and no state banquets, either. Charles III would host a large reception on the eve of the Coronation. The really significant difference this time round was in the status of the delegations. It had always been the rule that monarchs (even former ones) and other heads of state past and present did not attend coronations for the simple reason that they would outrank the new monarch being crowned. By longstanding diplomatic convention, precedence is based on the length of time in office. Self-evidently, a new monarch is therefore junior to every other head of state in the room. Ahead of the coronation of Elizabeth II, Winston Churchill reminded the Duke of Windsor of this rule when the ex-monarch started dropping hints that he might turn up for his niece's crowning. 'It would not be in accordance with constitutional usage (or precedent) for the Coronation of a King or Queen of England to be attended by the sovereign or former sovereign,' the prime minister explained.[24]

Charles III and his advisers regarded this as one Coronation tradition that could be eliminated. 'When it is the start of your reign, why would you not want as many other world leaders present as possible?' explained one official. 'The monarchy is there to deliver soft power for the UK and for the Commonwealth, too. The King wanted to maximize that.'[25] If the Queen's state funeral had attracted the largest gathering of world leaders ever seen on British soil, the King's Coronation would exceed that. In total, there were acceptances from ninety-nine heads of state – including the president of France and the King of Spain – plus senior representatives of another one hundred countries and territories, including the first lady of the United States. However, they would not be allowed extended delegations, as they had been in 1953. The rule would be a simple one: two seats per nation. If a president wished to be accompanied by a spouse, a child, a prime minister, an ambassador or a bodyguard, that was up to them. They would, though, only have a single seat next to them.

Foreign Office officials had learned one important lesson from the Queen's funeral, however. Putting heads of state on a shuttle bus had gone down extremely badly with some. The French president, Emmanuel Macron, had been among those unhappy about being herded onto a coach with other leaders, but he was not as miffed as some. 'Macron was peeved but some of the Gulf leaders really were furious,' says one diplomatic source, 'so we ditched it for the Coronation.'[26] It would not be eco-friendly – or, to use the King's preferred phrase, 'sustainable' – but there would be no avoiding a cavalcade of limousines filling the streets around the abbey from first light.

Chapter Eleven

The Henry V Test

People always want to play a part in the Coronation. In 1953, young officers from the Forces shamelessly used family connections to secure an appointment as one of the 400 'Gold Staff officers' who acted as ushers at the abbey. The top jobs, by long medieval tradition, would be decided by the Court of Claims. This august body would include the highest judges in the land – plus, inevitably, the Duke of Norfolk – under the chairmanship of the Lord Chancellor, the head of the judiciary. The greatest legal brains would apply themselves to all requests for an official role in the ceremony. Some of these were from ancient families who had always performed the same role over the centuries. So, in 1953, the respective claims by Lord Hastings and Lord Churston to carry a golden spur at the coronation of Elizabeth II were upheld. This was because the family could should show an identical role at the coronations of George VI, George V, Edward VII and so on back down the centuries.

Some very grand applicants, however, were to be disappointed. Since Norman times, the Lord of the Manor of Worksop had been able to claim the right to present successive monarchs with a glove to 'protect' their anointed right hand as they held the sceptre. For many generations, the lordship of Worksop had belonged to the Dukes of Newcastle, who had claimed this right at successive coronations. However, not long before the 1953 Coronation, the 9th Duke had transferred the manorial rights to a business, the London and Fort George Land Company Ltd. He saw no reason why this should preclude him from parading with his glove. He sent his lawyer before the court to argue that, since the new company remained in family hands, this ancient privilege should follow suit. The court refused, sniffily pointing out that 'the service claimed is one which, by its nature, cannot be performed by a limited company'.[1]

The Duke of Somerset, meanwhile, submitted a claim to carry either the Orb or the Sceptre with Cross, on the basis that his family had processed with one or the other on 'a very substantial number of occasions since the coronation of James II'. The Lord Chancellor, Lord Simonds, concluded that Somerset's claim was just as flimsy as Newcastle's. In his similarly dismissive judgement, he told the Duke's lawyer: 'If you wish to establish it as a prescriptive right, you have to go back a very much longer way than James II.'

With every coronation, there would be applications from a few endearingly eccentric no-hopers, and Elizabeth II's was no exception. Mrs Mary Long submitted a claim 'to carry the Queen's towel by virtue of the tenure of Heydon Hall in Norfolk'. H. R. Boorman MBE sought to present her with 'three maple cups' on the basis that he lived at Nether Bilsington Manor in Kent. Neither would receive a summons to the abbey.

Ahead of the coronation of Charles III, it was clear that all this was a tradition too far. With the legal system still struggling to cope with a backlog of cases from the Covid pandemic, the public would never tolerate an emergency court of senior judges convening to decide who should or should not be entitled to give the monarch a glove. Instead, the task was handed over to a team of Cabinet Office civil servants who established the 'Coronation Claims Office'. In 1953, the Court of Claims had been required to assess a total of twenty-one claims.[2] In 2023, however, there were more than 400.

'The great number have been claims from people who don't have a proper claim at all but just want to come,' said one of the Cabinet Office's advisers. 'We've had children from Canada asking for invitations. We've had someone saying "my grandfather was a guardsman on parade in 1953" and so on. The claims may be tenuous but good for them for writing in. It's been an entirely positive process.' In total, thirteen claimants were accepted on the grounds that they could prove the historic involvement of a direct descendant or predecessor. They included the Earl of Erroll, who had applied to bear a silver staff as Lord High Constable of Scotland, while the Earl of Dundee was granted the honour of carrying the 'Quartering of the Standard (Scotland)'. One of Whitehall's most senior civil servants was also on the list. As permanent secretary at the Ministry of Justice, Antonia Romeo also held the ancient title of Clerk of the Crown in Chancery. In this capacity, she had invoked historic precedent and lodged a claim 'to record the proceedings and have five yards of cloth'. The Claims Office granted her the right to record the event (with pen and paper in a plum seat in the front row of the North Transept), but there would be no cloth on this occasion. One or two legitimate claimants were acknowledged and then rejected. Since the fifteenth century, the Earl of Shrewsbury (who also ranks as the premier earl of England and Ireland) had been entitled to process at every coronation carrying his white wand as Lord High Steward of Ireland. The 21st Earl had done so in 1953 (as has been noted, travelling to the abbey in the family coach). His son, the 22nd Earl, wrote to the Claims Office offering the family's traditional services once again in 2023, though there would be no prospect of travelling in the coach (that had long since been donated to a museum near the family's Staffordshire home).

With UK–Irish diplomatic relations still at a post-Brexit low, the chances of an English aristocrat being invited to parade as 'Lord High Steward of Ireland' in front of the Irish president were always going to be zero. 'Your claim is an established claim,' the office finally informed Lord Shrewsbury. 'It has been decided, however, that on the occasion of His Majesty's Coronation, the Lord High Steward of Ireland will not form part of the procession. Therefore you will not be required to attend as Lord High Steward of Ireland and to carry the white wand.' Lord Shrewsbury was not surprised by the decision. 'We are very proud of our family traditions but we know that hereditaries like us are over,' he reflects. He was, however, a little disappointed by the decline in standards. 'I have the file for 1953 and every letter to my father was signed by the Earl Marshal. This letter has arrived by email and no one has had the courtesy to sign it.'[3] Rather amusingly, the unnamed civil servant added that this decision would not prevent the earl or his successors from making the same claim 'in respect of future Coronations'. Until then, says Charles Shrewsbury, the white wand of office will stay safely where it is – 'in the gun room'.

As for the famous glove, its historic connection with the Manor of Worksop is no more. In 1953, after the Duke of Newcastle had lost his case at the Court of Claims, the Queen let it be known that she wanted the tradition of the glove to continue. So the honour was given to Lord Woolton, Chancellor of the Duchy of Lancaster. He had been supposed to carry the Sword of State as Lord President of the Council but was too unwell to stand up for long, let alone hold a heavy sword. Having resigned through ill health, he was then given the less onerous job of Chancellor of the Duchy and the role of glove-bearer by way of thanks for his long years of service during the war. Seventy years later, the honour of bearing the glove was given to Lord Singh of Wimbledon, broadcaster, crossbench peer and a leading voice of Britain's Sikh community.

At Elizabeth II's coronation in 1953, the only non-Anglican participant in the ceremony had been the Moderator of the General Assembly of the Church of Scotland, who was invited to present the new Queen with the Bible. Charles III was going to do something very different indeed. Though constitution and law meant that this would remain a steadfastly Anglican service, it would also be the first coronation ceremony to feature representatives of all the main faiths. Just as Lord Singh would present the glove, thus incorporating the Sikh community into the ceremony, so Lord Patel, eminent Scottish scientist and the first Hindu to be made a Knight of the Thistle, was invited to carry the sovereign's ring. Lord Kamall, a British-born Muslim academic, was asked to carry the armills (bracelets) and Baroness Merron, chief executive of the Board of Deputies of British Jews, would present the Robe Royal.

These decisions were just a handful of the twenty-first-century amendments to the 1953 running order. They were, though, every bit as significant as the items of regalia themselves. For they underlined the King's oft-quoted remark about the monarch's hereditary role as 'Defender of the Faith'. Speaking in 1994, he had declared: 'I personally would rather see it as Defender of Faith, not *the* faith, because it means just one particular interpretation of the faith, which I think is sometimes something that causes a problem.'[4]

For the best part of a decade, the government had been gently lobbying the then Prince of Wales's office to come up with an accession and coronation plan, according to an official of that period. Despite the recurring sub-plot in the Netflix drama *The Crown*, which depicts a power-hungry Prince of Wales, the real one had actually been very resistant to the idea. 'He had no wish to give any indication that he was itching for promotion,' says one who knows him very well. 'He has a strong faith and his view was that every day his mother drew breath, he would give thanks to the Almighty.'[5] Within the Palace, it was well known that any private secretary trying to engage with the Prince on any change-of-reign planning would need to approach the subject very sparingly – 'no more than an hour at a time,' says one official.[6] Anything that could give the impression of an impatient Prince getting ahead of himself was subjected to what one senior adviser would call 'the Henry V test'. Would this smack of young Prince Hal trying to oust old King Henry IV? The Prince and his staff concluded that creating a committee and discussing coronation plans with Whitehall officials would indeed fail that test. However, giving some discreet thought to the tone and structure of the next coronation service seemed sensible enough by the time that Elizabeth II was approaching her ninetieth birthday.

That was the thinking which lay behind Clive Alderton's 2015 invitation to his Lambeth Palace counterpart to come for that evening of binge-watching the footage of 1953 over a Clarence House supper of Coronation chicken. Following that meeting, a new draft of Operation Golden Orb began to take shape. 'Of course, they had a template going right back to the Liber Regalis.* And remaining faithful to that ancient text would

---

* Written in the late fourteenth century and stored in the Westminster Abbey library, the Liber Regalis is regarded as the earliest instruction manual for English coronations, although the first record of an English coronation is that of King Edgar in Bath in 973.

counter the inevitable "it's all too modern" critics,' says one of the team. 'But if they had simply decided to repeat what happened in 1953, the public would soon have lost interest.' The running order would be cut back considerably, just as Prince Charles had promised in Lesotho more than twenty-five years earlier. Hence the target time of one hour and forty-five minutes. The Earl Marshal had been saying the same, arguing that the running time of a Formula One Grand Prix (his favourite sport) or a football match (including half-time) was a useful indicator. The omission of hereditaries from the homage would certainly lose some time. Another early decision was to change some of the readings. Out went the fiery epistle from the Book of Peter, with talk of 'punishment of evildoers.' In came the Book of Colossians: 'By him were all things created . . . whether they be thrones, or dominions, or principalities.' However, this draft still avoided any attempt to address the 'Defender of Faith' issue. That would certainly have failed the 'Henry V test.'

Nothing more would be done until the conclusion of the funeral for Elizabeth II. At which point, planning began in earnest and at speed. The King had very clear thoughts about music from the start. As well as being the first coronation to involve female composers, he wanted this to be the first to feature gospel singers. The eight-strong Ascension Choir would perform two pieces written by Debbie Wiseman. This would be the first coronation to feature a piece entirely in the Welsh language, with Sir Bryn Terfel singing Paul Mealor's 'Coronation Kyrie.' It would also include a lesser-known 1924 brass fanfare by Richard Strauss, simply because the King had heard it during a visit to the Royal College of Music some years earlier, had liked it enormously and had made a mental note to remember it for this very occasion. His pick of the outstanding composers and conductors of the day would include Lord Lloyd Webber, Sir John Eliot Gardiner, Sir Antonio Pappano, Sir Karl Jenkins and Judith Weir, the first woman to hold the office of Master of the King's (or Queen's) Music. While the funeral of a monarch is the responsibility of the church in which it takes place, tradition dictates that it is always the Archbishop of Canterbury who writes the liturgy for coronations. A liturgy steering committee took shape under the Archbishop's 'Coronation Planning Director', Danny Johnson. The members then passed their proposals to the Archbishop, who took them to the order of service committee and thence to the King. 'What was very clear very early on was just how much had changed in the few years since the previous review,' says a member of Johnson's steering group. There were two observations in particular. They agreed that the need for both a stronger multifaith element and for a greater female presence no longer seemed especially bold or progressive. It just seemed the obvious thing to do. 'It was so important to get the other faiths involved but it all had to be worked out in the context of a strongly Anglican service. It was very sensitive, too, of course and was the last piece of the jigsaw. In fact, it was only signed off with days to go.'[7]

Every piece of Coronation regalia had to be scrutinized for its inner meaning, especially if it was to be carried by a non-Anglican. 'These are instruments of state, not royal heirlooms,' explains the Lambeth Palace staffer. 'It is in effect the state presenting them to the King and asking him to perform certain tasks with them. But you had to understand the full meaning before asking someone from outside the church to present them.'

When Prince Charles had first voiced his 'Defender of Faith' aspiration in 1994, some Anglican commentators had thrown their hands up in horror, even though he was very clear he would still be Defender of *the* Faith. In fact, the sentiment was really no different from that later expressed by Queen Elizabeth II in 2012. At the very start of her Diamond Jubilee year, she told a multifaith gathering that 'the Church has a duty to protect the free practice of all faiths in this country.'[8] However, if the Coronation were to involve tinkering with ancient oaths and titles, then the King might not only upset strong traditionalists. There could even be a legal challenge. Yet there was a way round this, for the Archbishop could always add some extra words of his own. He would talk of 'an environment in which people of all faiths and beliefs may live freely', before asking the King: 'Are you willing to take the Oath?' Sir Clive Alderton's committee had a further idea. At previous coronations, monarchs had said little more than 'I will' or 'I do'. Legally, there could be no tinkering with the Coronation Oath itself. But after saying 'All this, I promise to do', the King would bolt on a short prayer, with an overt multifaith element: 'Grant that I may be a blessing to all thy children, of every faith and belief . . .' In other words, Charles III would defend all while formally remaining 'Defender of *the* Faith' too.

Though radically different, it would be scarcely noticed at all. Similarly, before the entry of the King, the service would open with a procession of all the main faith groups, from Buddhists to Zoroastrians. The fact that the Coronation was happening on a Saturday presented a problem for the Chief Rabbi, Sir Ephraim Mirvis, since Jewish religious law precludes motorized transport on the Sabbath. So the King offered Mirvis a room for the night at St James's Palace, within walking distance of the abbey. Palace staff arranged a kosher caterer to prepare Friday night dinner for Mirvis and his wife, Valerie (with kosher Coronation chicken on the menu).

The Chief Rabbi was also in the group of religious leaders who would take part in another new addition to the ritual.

Though they might not want (or be allowed) to participate in certain explicitly Christian rites during the central section of the service, those rules did not apply before or after the King's role in the 'theatre' of the abbey. So, at the very end, before processing out of the Great West Door, he would be 'greeted' by a row of leaders from the main religions. In unison, they would declare themselves 'neighbours in faith' and profess 'the value of public service'. This was not exactly a prayer, nor a blessing. Even arch-traditionalists would struggle to find fault.

So much has been written about the King's interest in other faiths over the years that his own has often been overlooked. While the late Queen would routinely be photographed heading to or from church most Sundays, her son and heir would not, often leading to speculation that he lacked her dedication to the Church of England. This is strongly denied by those who have discussed it with him privately. 'He is a deeply faithful, practising Christian with a profound life of prayer and reflection and retreat,' says the Archbishop of Canterbury firmly. 'It's expressed differently but, in terms of the depth of his faith, there is no difference between him and the late Queen, and, for that matter, the late King George.'[9] Aside from religious high days and holidays, the King has preferred to worship privately, often at the Chapel Royal in St James's Palace. He also had his own 'sanctuary' built in the garden at Highgrove and made of natural cob (clay and straw). 'The great thing is that it is somewhere where nobody can get at me,' the Prince told me in 2008. 'Anywhere in the house, there is always a telephone or somebody can always come. It is very important to have somewhere just to allow a moment.'[10] The retreat was consecrated by his old friend from Cambridge days, Richard (now Lord) Chartres, the former Bishop of London. 'It is a wonderful space, one of the last redoubts of wattle and daub,' says Chartres, who has celebrated Holy Communion there, and describes the King as 'a traditional, devout communicant with an accent on the mystical.'

Chartres points to the monarch's passion for the Book of Common Prayer as an example of his traditionalism. The King, he adds, is deeply interested in all things spiritual, from, say, Sufism to 'the holiness in everything that lives'. It was the King himself, says Chartres, who recently sent him a film about the Greek Orthodox monk and saint, Joseph the Hesychast. 'He doesn't see other faiths as local editions of his own and he is very clear that you can't engage with other faiths from a superior position,' says Chartres. 'It is why he has a tremendous appreciation of the contribution all faiths make to civic society.' That should not, however, be mistaken for some vague, insipid embrace of anything and everything from across the multifaith spectrum. As Chartres puts it: 'You have to combine an openness to others with the fact that you have to follow your own way. You can't be promiscuously benign.'

Richard Chartres has been studying coronations for many years. He would even be invited to process in this one, carrying the Queen's ring. On the sixtieth anniversary of the crowning of Elizabeth II, he was invited to deliver Westminster Abbey's 'Coronation Lecture'. He has traced the evolution of the modern British rite from the Old Testament, through Western culture via the Frankish kings, Pepin the Short, Charlemagne and Charles the Bald, to England's King Edgar and thence to Westminster Abbey. Some elements, like the anointing and the investiture with crown and sceptre, he says, have barely changed. Other aspects are entirely modern, like the idea that the Church of England has some historic obligation to defend other faiths. 'History shows that to be complete rubbish,' he says. 'Look at the discrimination against Jews, Catholics, dissenters and so on.'

Equally modern, says Chartres, is that immodest British claim, at every major royal occasion, that 'no one does this sort of thing as well as we do.' That, too, goes back no further than the twentieth century. 'Up until the Victorians, we weren't very good at pageantry at all. The Hapsburgs and the Papacy were much better,' he says, pointing to the shambolic catalogue of errors at Queen Victoria's unrehearsed coronation (during which the Archbishop nearly broke a bone ramming the ring on her wrong finger). Royal ceremonial, in Victoria's view, was something to be endured – and privately. 'Then there was what I call a heraldic arms race,' Chartres explains. 'There is a precise equation between the dwindling power of monarchy and the increasing complexity of royal ceremonial. By the end of Victoria's reign, people wanted royal events to capture the romance and the popular mood.' As the British Empire reached its zenith under Edward VII and George V, so the monarchy became a focus for boastful, imperial exceptionalism, egged on by a new popular press. The Mall was laid out as a grand ceremonial thoroughfare, to match those on the continent, with the new Admiralty Arch at one end and the Queen Victoria Memorial at the other. Composers like Parry and Elgar produced great imperial anthems which, in addition to Handel's Zadok the Priest, would ring out at future coronations. The crowning of Elizabeth II would be the last in that tradition, the last in which the monarch was enthroned with the command to 'hold fast from henceforth the seat and state of royal and imperial dignity'. Charles III would delete the word 'imperial' from his order of service.

Yet another major change to the order of service was the overarching theme of the Coronation itself. As the Archbishop points out, the modern coronation is entirely different from the Stuart or Georgian model, however much the framework may be similar. 'For a long time coronations were all about: "Kings are sent by God. Don't mess with Kings",' he says. 'That's understandable. But things have changed. What we are saying, this time, is that his job is to serve the people.'[11] Elizabeth II had said the same, of course, but this time it would be more explicit for the benefit of a twenty-first-century audience.

The Archbishop also decided that he wanted to insert a sermon, on the basis that this had been a feature of most coronations over a thousand years, albeit not the previous two. It would, he insisted, be 'a short sermon'. This was going to add on a few minutes, so Alderton's clock-watching liturgy committee continued to seek other ways of clawing back time without jettisoning moments of key symbolic importance. Sensible amendments would include performing some of the magnificent new musical compositions before the start. And did the King really need to put on certain pieces of regalia like the ring or the armills? Could he not simply touch them? Indeed, he could.

It is immutable royal law that every major royal occasion has to be preceded by an unexpected glitch which escalates into a drama. Ahead of Prince Harry's wedding, it was the eleventh-hour non-appearance of the bride's father. For Prince William's wedding, it was the absence of invitations for two former Labour prime ministers (Tony Blair and Gordon Brown) while the guests did include the ambassador from Syria at the very moment that the al-Assad regime was committing fresh human-rights atrocities. Before the Prince of Wales's wedding to Lady Diana Spencer in 1981, the Spanish royal family announced a boycott because the honeymoon was due to start in Gibraltar. Before his wedding to Camilla Parker Bowles in 2005, a proposed civil ceremony inside Windsor Castle had to be re-located to the town hall following an error over the licensing arrangements, whereupon the event had to be postponed for twenty-four hours following the death of the Pope.

Coronations, inevitably, stir up even greater problems. In 1953, the great debate had been about television. The authorities took as their starting point the previous coronation in 1937. This been recorded by black-and-white film cameras but the material had all been edited afterwards by the Archbishop of Canterbury, in order to remove 'any unsuitable parts'. In July 1952, the Duke of Norfolk informed the Coronation Joint Committee that the Queen favoured the same arrangements with film cameras for her own coronation, albeit in colour this time. However, when the Duke broached the subject of television by reading out a letter from the BBC requesting live access, the committee was greatly perturbed.[12] According to the minutes: 'Sir Alan Lascelles and Mr Torrance [the deputy high commissioner for South Africa] referred to the great heat and blinding light which those on television often have to endure.' Since Lascelles was the Queen's private secretary, everyone could safely assume that was her view, too. The Dean of Westminster felt that 'it would add enormously to the strain on The Queen if Her Majesty knew that she was being closely watched by so great a number of persons'. The Archbishop argued that 'it was unfair to expose The Queen and others to this searching method of photography'. There was, no doubt, an element of self-interest here since accounts of previous coronations usually highlight the errors not of monarchs but of Archbishops of Canterbury. Sir Albert Napier, permanent secretary to the Lord Chancellor, argued that many viewers would consider television coverage as 'uncalled for'. The high commissioner of New Zealand was even more robust according to the minutes of the meeting: 'Mr Doidge said he considered that television produced caricatures on occasion. It was an immature art.' This was an interesting contribution since tele-vision did not actually exist in New Zealand and would not do so until 1960. Herein lay the problem. No one had any idea what they were talking about. The committee eventually concluded that the TV cameras might be allowed to film the procession in and out but nothing of the ceremony itself.

There was no doubt that the Queen agreed with the committee. Churchill's private secretary, Jock Colville, who had previously been her private secretary, spoke to all the senior courtiers at the Palace and reported her hostility back to the prime minister.[13] Three days later, Churchill raised the matter with the Cabinet. Its members sided with the committee and the Queen. The public would have to settle for an edited programme later in the day, instead.[14] So much for all that talk of egalitarian post-war technological innovation which had inspired the previous (Labour) government's Festival of Britain just a year before.

The archives reveal the BBC's tactical game. Through the summer of 1952, executives patiently briefed the press and civil servants on advances in technology. The head of outside broad-casting, Seymour de Lotbiniere, wrote to Churchill's press secretary, Thomas Fife Clark, explaining that television lighting was much less intrusive than cinema photography, adding: 'We have always avoided "close ups".'[15]* Fife Clark began to see merit in the idea, warning ministers: 'It does seem to be neces-sary to be very careful on these points, since television is developing at so great a speed that what seems revolutionary in July 1952 may be a commonplace in June 1953.'[16] It was a prescient point.

---

*   Seymour de Lotbiniere, an extremely tall Old Etonian, was also a pioneer of modern sports commentary.

When, in October 1952, the Earl Marshal announced the decision to exclude television from the ceremony, the public response was instant and hostile. Nor was it confined to the popular press. The radio correspondent of the *Daily Telegraph* reported that 'the sense of regret and frustration at Broadcasting House is deeper and more general than any I can remember over any previous issue.'[17] Even the normally staid *Church of England Newspaper* urged the Archbishop and his colleagues to think again: 'Why not let everybody see it who can? The Monarchy in this country is not an underground movement.' In the House of Commons, the Labour MP Lieutenant Colonel Marcus Lipton warned Churchill that the 'ban on television has caused bitter disappointment' and risked tarnishing the entire coronation with 'a wide-spread sense of grievance.'[18]

At which point, the Royal and National Archives reveal a series of frantic handbrake turns. Thomas Fife Clark proposed 'a line of orderly retreat for the Earl Marshal, the Commission, the government and all concerned if a new decision were reached.'[19] All these eminent public figures were suddenly worried that they were seriously out of step with public opinion. Worse still, they feared that all this criticism might rebound on the Queen herself. Winston Churchill talked to the Earl Marshal, the Archbishop and the Queen's private secretary. They concluded that, 'subject to The Queen's approval', they were happy for television to go ahead, provided that it omitted the anointing and Holy Communion.[20] A month later, at the second and final meeting of the Coronation Commission, the Duke of Edinburgh insisted on one caveat: no 'close-up' photography.[21] Here was a near-total Establishment surrender and a victory for the BBC. It would be the coming of age of television in Britain, the first time more people had watched a national event than listened to it on the radio. Even the staunchest opponents would later see the error of their ways. Writing to the BBC's director of television, George Barnes, shortly after the event, the Archbishop of Canterbury was contrite. 'You know that I am no great supporter of TV, regarding it as an extravagance, and a supreme time waster,' he began. But not on this occasion. In short: 'It was grand.'[22]

The big glitch in 2023, however, was not an attempt to keep the people out. Rather, it was a plan to include them even more. Not that anyone saw it coming. The authorities had been focusing on an entirely different potential flashpoint. Within both the Palace and the government, there were fears of protests and considerable media noise surrounding the presence of the Stone of Destiny at the abbey. Originally the seat upon which Scottish kings sat for their enthronement, it had been captured by Edward I in 1296 and brought to England. There it had been built into St Edward's Chair, becoming an integral part of the Coronation furniture. In 1950, it was removed in an audacious Christmas raid by four Scottish nationalists, triggering a huge police operation (for the first time in centuries, the border was even, briefly, closed). The stone suddenly reappeared, deposited on the high altar of Arbroath Abbey, albeit with some damage done. It was eventually returned to Westminster Abbey ahead of the Queen's coronation, though Winston Churchill was determined not to appear remotely triumphal. He wanted zero publicity and urged that the operation be conducted 'without public fuss.'[23] In 1996, Prime Minister John Major decided that the stone should go back to Scotland, with the proviso that it was returned for future coronations. It was placed in a display case in Edinburgh Castle, alongside the Scottish Crown and Sceptre, and the tourists duly queued to look at this 125kg block of pinkish sandstone. Ahead of the coronation of Charles III, however, prominent nationalists, including former Scottish National Party leader Alex Salmond, professed outrage at the prospect of 'stolen property' heading south once more. He declared that the Scottish government should stand firm, and urged the first minister, Humza Yousaf, a self-proclaimed republican, not to be a royal 'poodle.'

The issue failed to ignite in Scotland, however, and Yousaf was among the officials present for a small, solemn ceremony to send the stone on its way. On 29 April, as the abbey held a short service to welcome it to Westminster, there was a sense of a crisis averted. Too soon. On the very same weekend that the stone came south, the Archbishop's office gleefully announced an amendment to the order of service in the form of a new addition to the homage. After the Prince of Wales had pledged his loyalty as the King's 'liege man of life and limb', there would be the homage of 'the people'. This would not just happen throughout the abbey. It could take place in parks, pubs or the privacy of the home. 'I call upon all persons of goodwill,' the Archbishop would declare, 'to make their homage, in heart and voice, to their undoubted King, defender of all.' The public were expected to respond: 'I swear that I will pay true allegiance to Your Majesty and to your heirs and successors according to law. So help me God.' The Archbishop would then say: 'God save the King.' To which the public would be asked to respond: 'God save King Charles. Long live King Charles. May the King live for ever.'

The idea was born of perfectly good intentions – to allow ordinary people to play a part previously reserved for earls and viscounts. It would, instead, underline the old adage that no good deed goes unpunished. In short, it bombed. The problem was one of tone and presentation. To most regular churchgoers, here was an optional form of words in an order of service, not

unlike saying 'I renounce evil' at a baptism. Here were senti-
ments, after all, no different to those expressed in the national
anthem. To others, though, especially non-churchgoers, it
smacked of a direct command to swear allegiance. It would
undoubtedly have been welcomed by the public in 1953.
Seventy years on, Britain is a secular country where only a tiny
percentage of people go to church. Far more are likely to
channel their beliefs through social media and the press, as
they did in this case. 'Asking us to chant our allegiance does
seem an odd request when so many of us think that the
monarchy is an outdated institution that needs drastic reform,'
Baroness Jones of the Green Party told *The Times*.[24] Even a
staunch royal ally like Jonathan Dimbleby, former official biographer, said that the King would find the idea 'abhorrent',
telling the BBC: 'He's never wanted to be revered'.[25] Anti-royal
campaigners piled on the confected outrage. The pressure
group Republic accused the Archbishop of holding the people
'in contempt'.

With this genteel rebellion gathering momentum and the
order of service about to go to the printers, there was a swift
about-turn. The organizers had been stunned by the reaction.
The Archbishop would no longer 'call upon' the public to do
anything. Rather, a muddled compromise was hastily added
to the liturgy. The Archbishop would, instead, say the following:
'I now invite those who wish to offer their support to do so,
with a moment of private reflection, by joining in saying "God
save King Charles" at the end, or, for those with the words
before them, to recite them in full.' Here was a vintage piece
of Establishment fudge. In the words of one old courtier: 'How
very Church of England.' Looking back, the Archbishop is
stoical. 'I knew there would be something in the service that
people would jump on and that was it,' he reflects, adding that

many people have subsequently said to him: 'Oh, I did homage in my front room'. The words, he says, were 'shouted' by the 400 young charity workers watching in St Margaret's, Westminster. Ever the optimist, he adds: 'What would this country be if we didn't find something to argue about? That's part of who we are.'

Chapter Twelve

'Jam it on'

As the coronation of Charles III drew closer, a predictable source of public anger would be the cost. Neither Whitehall nor the Palace would comment as media estimates kept on climbing, unchallenged, from £100 million (13 April, *The Sun*) to £150 million (4 May, *The Sun*) to £250 million (7 May, *The Guardian*). Less than two weeks later, the Treasury released official figures for Queen Elizabeth II's funeral. The overall cost to the public purse had amounted to £162 million, with almost half (£73.68 million) billed by the Home Office and, therefore, covering security.[1] The second highest bill (£57.4 million) came from the Department of Culture, covering public access and stewarding. The military element, including all the parades and personnel, amounted to just £2.89 million. These figures would serve as a benchmark for May 2023, although they covered ten days of national mourning, including five days of lying-in-state, versus one weekend for the Coronation. The final cost of crowning the King would, inevitably, be many times the £1.5 million budget for 1953.[2]

At that time, the government faced little external pressure to cut costs. It was only the natural parsimonious instincts of the Whitehall civil servant that was helping to drive down the bill. Neither the press nor the Opposition was looking to make trouble on this point. Following a meeting with the Duke of Norfolk, Jock Colville reported back to Winston Churchill: 'The Duke said that a number of Labour peers and other supporters of the Opposition had come to him and had said that they hoped, above all things, that there would be no attempt at an austerity Coronation.'[3] The Ministry of Works would recoup around a third of the bill through sales of grandstand seats and also by offering Abbey guests the chance to buy the 'EIIR' chairs on which they had sat. The latter were billed at £7 and 10 shillings each. They would prove a safe investment. In 2012, Christie's sold a pair of 1953 Coronation chairs for £7,500 and they continue to come onto the market. Having missed the chance to buy one as a page boy, Andrew Parker Bowles later bid at auction for the two chairs bought in 1953 by the Captain of the Queen's Flight, Air Vice-Marshal Sir Edward 'Mouse' Fielden. They continue to serve as a happy reminder of a great day. The coronation of Charles III would involve a limited edition of just one hundred chairs produced by six graduates from the Prince's Foundation. All made of British oak and covered with blue velvet embroidered with the cyphers of the King and Queen, they would be auctioned for charity at a later date.

What the bill for Elizabeth II's funeral reveals is that the largest expense to the public purse, by far, was the process of making the event safe and accessible for the public. It would be the same with the Coronation. While it would be some time before a final figure was released, government sources were clear that the cost of policing and public access would dwarf the cost of actually putting on the show. Spectacular though it was, the 2023 Coronation was very much a scaled-back, low-budget affair compared to that of 1953. Back then, there had been such a shortage of horse-drawn coaches for the various carriage processions that the Royal Mews ended up borrowing extra vehicles from the studios of film producer Alexander Korda. That, in turn, led to a shortage of both manpower and horsepower. Colonel Arthur Main of the Coaching Club came to the rescue with an extra twenty trained horses plus a team of amateur volunteers to drive them.[4]

As well as bringing in extra transport, the Royal Household had to update some of its own. The famously uncomfortable Georgian-era Gold State Coach would become marginally less bumpy for Elizabeth II and Prince Philip in 1953 after the addition of a post-Georgian invention – the tyre. Four new rubber rims were attached to the wheels, along with a new braking system, for the sum of £1,928.[5] Even so, it remained a surprisingly rocky ride.

In 2023, the man in charge of the Royal Mews, Crown Equerry, Colonel Toby Browne, would require no outside help with horse-drawn transport. Only a handful of carriages would be needed. The King and Queen would travel to the abbey in the nearly new Diamond Jubilee State Coach. They would return in the Gold State Coach and that needed no fresh work, either. In 2011, it had undergone an overhaul which solved the riddle of why it was always quite so uncomfortable. The hefty leather straps which acted as the suspension system were actually of unequal lengths. It was because of this that the whole carriage did not swing evenly but, rather, in a figure of eight. It is now much improved.[6]

The King's 'recycling' mantra has been closely observed in the Mews. The state liveries worn by the coachmen (several of them women) are always handed down from one generation to the next anyway. As noted earlier, the King has said that anything with the late Queen's 'EIIR' cypher should remain in use until replacements are required and that would apply to overalls, aprons, wheelbarrows and horse blankets. The only exception would be for equipment on public display at big occasions – like the Coronation – when the public would expect to see 'CIIIR'. Even then, the King's sustainability edict was still in force. For example, all the blue Coronation dressings for the Windsor greys pulling the Coronation coaches would be made from recycled plastic.

In 1953, the main royal expenditure had been in the wardrobe department. The Privy Purse accounts for the period show that the largest single item of expense was the Ede & Ravenscroft bill for 'Supplying purple Coronation Robe for The Queen'. It was not unusual to commission a new Robe of Estate (the purple robe worn at the end of the ceremony) for each coronation, and her late father's would have been too long for Elizabeth II. This was charged at £2,612 plus £1,469 purchase tax.[7] The robe, therefore, cost more than the Royal Household expenditure on champagne for the entire Coronation year: £3,443 for 250 cases (non-vintage). The Duke of Edinburgh had been almost parsimonious. When choosing his coronation robe, he had opted for Ede & Ravenscroft's 'pattern B' velvet at £485, which he 'thought would be sufficiently good'. He (or perhaps the Queen) then had a change of heart. It was decided that the Duke really should have the superior 'pattern A' after all. However, it would cost an extra £232. Rather than submit a further bill to the Treasury, the Duke paid it himself.[8]

Seventy years later, the recycling rule applied to robes, too. The King's crimson Robe of State (the mantle worn in the early, pre-crowning stages of a coronation and at the State Opening of Parliament), would be an heirloom, used by his grandfather, King George VI, and his great-grandfather, George V. It was the same with his purple Robe of Estate (the long mantle worn post-crowning and on departure). For the first part of the service, the Queen Consort would wear the crimson Robe of State made for Elizabeth II in 1953. The only new robe ordered in 2023 would be her purple Robe of Estate. This was made by Ede & Ravenscroft, but the gold embroidery would be added by the Royal School of Needlework at Hampton Court.

'Darling, come and look at it from this end,' the Queen Consort tells the King as the couple inspect work in progress. It is 21 March 2023 and the royal couple are in Hampton Court's Albemarle Suite where half a dozen expert embroiderers are all working simultaneously on her Robe of Estate. As patron of the Royal School of Needlework, Queen Camilla knows the staff well. Between them, they have settled on a floral theme for this robe, reflecting her love of gardens. The detail is exquisite. Sewn into the velvet is lily of the valley (her birth flower), as well as the King's favourite flower (a delphinium). There is even a scabiosa, otherwise known as the 'pin cushion flower'. 'It's a heraldic joke,' explains manager Gemma Murray later. 'The pin cushion is a reference to the fact that the Queen is our patron.'[9] The robe also includes the flowers of all the home nations. Norman Hartnell ran into trouble when he did the same with Elizabeth II's Coronation gown in 1953. He wanted to include daffodils for Wales but was told firmly by the heralds at the College of Arms that Wales could only be depicted by the leek. So the leek it was. The heralds have been overruled this time and the Queen Consort will have daffodils. Both she and the King prefer them. She has been closely following progress on the robe via photographs.

'It's never the same as seeing it in real life,' she says. 'I think you're absolute stars to do anything quite so beautiful. The sad thing is this isn't to be worn the whole time.'

Charles III

'We each have a favourite bit,' jokes the King. 'The little tiny details are fantastic.' As patron of QEST (the Queen Elizabeth Scholarship Trust, founded by his grandmother to champion excellence in traditional crafts), this is right up his street.

He is enchanted by the embroidered image of a dandelion with its seeds in flight, as if blown by an invisible gust or passer-by. 'You have to finish it by a certain date?' he jokes. The head of the studio, Anne Butcher, assures him that everyone is acutely conscious of the ticking clock.

Next door, the King inspects another new creation, the Stole Royal, the band of gold and coloured silk worn around the monarch's neck after the anointing. He would gladly have worn the same one made for his mother in 1953, except for the fact that it names Ceylon, South Africa and Pakistan as realms. They are all now republics (and Ceylon is no more). Another Stole Royal is therefore needed. The most visible piece of new embroidery is the three-sided screen which will be erected around the King at the moment of anointing, offering him the only privacy he will enjoy during the entire ceremony. This will replace the wobbling canopy, carried by those four senior Knights of the Garter, which caused such mockery in 1953. The screen is a substantial piece of kit, in three parts, which must be held upright throughout. It will, therefore, be entrusted not to four elderly knights but to a team of fit, non-commissioned officers from the Household Division. The King and Queen are transfixed by the detail. The names of all fifty-six Commonwealth nations are being sewn with gold thread onto the branches of the tree which spreads across the rear section of the screen (the part which will face the congregation). The King inspects the poles that hold it upright. 'Limed oak?' he asks. It is, indeed, limed oak – from Windsor, of course.

'Jam it on'

Every account of every coronation reveals the perennial concern for non-royal guests: what to wear? There were long lists of instructions in 1953 for those not in uniform. For women it was evening dress with tiaras or head covering 'in the form of a veil' but which 'should not cover the face'. The rules for men went from various forms of court dress (with 'black beaver' hat) to evening dress, Highland dress and then the bare minimum – morning dress or lounge suit. For peers, the rule was simple. They would wear coronation robes and coronets. For their wives, the Earl Marshal's instructions were rather more complicated: 'Sleeves should be about nine inches long and each have two narrow bands of miniver pure and a like edging which may be scalloped'. He added: 'Tiaras should be worn if possible'.[10] In 2023, these instructions have been turned upside down. It is to be morning coat or lounge suits for men, day dress for women (with optional hat or fascinator) and uniform or 'celebratory national dress' for both. And definitely no tiaras. 'This is not going to be a tiara competition,' one member of the Royal Household says firmly.[11] As previously discussed, the Earl Marshal was determined that those remnants of the hereditary peerage who were invited to the abbey should not try to upstage other guests by appearing to flaunt ancestral regalia. That not only meant no coronets but no coronation robes either. As one of them recalls: 'Eddie Norfolk was very keen not to make life any more difficult for the tiny surviving band of ninety-two hereditary peers still sitting in the Lords by stirring up any ill feeling.' So the rule was that peers could wear their parliamentary robes, standard scarlet uniform for the State Opening of Parliament, but not the more elaborate crimson coronation robes traditionally worn by peers on Coronation Day alone. What confused matters further was the fact that hereditary peers without a seat in Parliament were not entitled to wear coronation or parliamentary robes. Where did that leave people like the Duke of Devonshire or the Duke of Northumberland, who had received invitations as friends of the King and Queen but had no seat in Parliament? The Duke of Norfolk's advice was to wear morning dress like everyone else. One or two hereditaries were still not happy and sought to bend the ear of the King. When word reached him, he overruled the Duke of Norfolk and let it be known that anyone wanting to wear old family robes should be allowed to, providing the material was in a presentable state and not too moth-eaten. So inherited kit was granted a reprieve, to the delight of the tiny cohort of those in possession of both an invitation and a coronation robe. However, that was as far as it went. When one senior peer started agitating to be allowed to empty the entire aristocratic toy box – coronet, page and horse-drawn coach as well as robes – he was told very firmly that he would do no such thing.

The King's U-turn on coronation robes echoed an identical decision at the time of the previous coronation in 1953. Back then, there had been an argument over military uniforms. The secretary of state for war, Anthony Head,* had issued orders for all members of the armed forces to wear the new standard-issue No. 1 Dress. The prime minister, Winston Churchill, was worried that this would make the Coronation look dull. His private secretary, Jock Colville, had warned him that the occasion was succumbing to 'morning dress drabness'.[12] The eternal romantic, Churchill wanted to see everyone in the grandest, oldest Full Dress uniforms at their disposal, 'as this may well be the last great ceremony which can be held with even a

---

* Head served in the Life Guards, won the Military Cross in 1940, was an MP and diplomat and became Viscount Head. He died in 1983.

semblance of the old magnificence.'[13] Head was worried about old soldiers trying to wear ill-fitting family heirlooms, noting that 'a red tunic, above all items of clothing, looks almost comical unless it fits really well.' Unconvinced, Churchill and Colville decided to take the matter all the way to the Queen. As Colville put it to her private secretary, the prime minister 'dislikes the principle of compulsory levelling down to the lowest common standard.' Their strategy worked. The Queen informed the Earl Marshal that every officer inside the abbey should 'wear the maximum full Dress which he can produce and to which he is entitled.'[14]

At last, the moment has come. The Archbishop of Canterbury, Justin Welby, stands solemnly before the King, arms aloft, preparing for the climactic moment when St Edward's Crown is placed on the royal head. His hands start to descend. At which point, the King offers some practical advice: 'You have to jam it on.' He points a gloved hand to his eyebrows. 'It has to come down to here first – and then push down. Because otherwise, if it's at the back, it's fatal.' The Archbishop explains that he is worried about hurting his monarch. 'I don't want to break your neck, sir. It might ruin the service!' The King gives him a reassuring smile. 'It won't,' he assures Welby. 'But it's so huge. It's got to be on right and I can't do anything about it.' The last thing anyone wants is a wobbly crown.

There is, in fact, no crown at this point. It is 21 April 2023 – nine days before the Coronation. This is yet another rehearsal and the Archbishop is doing his best to improvise, with an invisible crown between his hands. He duly follows the advice of the King and gives the imaginary five-pound circlet of bejewelled gold and velvet a good shove. Here is another instance of the gently shifting balance between 1953 and 2023. Seventy years ago, a young Queen was deferring to an elderly archbishop four decades her senior. Now, the oldest candidate for crowning in British history is giving a few tips to an archbishop who, unlike himself, has never seen a coronation before. Welby is more than happy to take lessons. As he explains afterwards, there is really only one way to ensure a faultless ceremony: 'Repetition, repetition, repetition.'

For the final few weeks before the ceremony, the ballroom of Buckingham Palace has been transformed into a rehearsal studio. It now houses a full-scale replica of the business end of Westminster Abbey, otherwise known as the Coronation 'theatre'. Not only is there a temporary raised floor, just as there will be in the abbey, but the Royal Household workers have installed identical blue and gold carpet. Even the throne itself appears identical to the one in the abbey. On closer inspection, it is not actually the very ancient St Edward's Chair but its twin. When the abbey held the joint coronation of William and Mary in April 1689, they built a second throne for Mary and this is it. The only obvious difference is that it does not have a space for the Scottish Stone of Destiny built in beneath the seat. So, Mary's Chair will serve as the throne during these rehearsals. Day after day in the lead-up to the Coronation, different players have been in here going through their parts, with various stand-ins. They include the first female bishops in history to participate in a coronation, Rose Hudson-Wilkin of Dover and Guli Francis-Dehqani of Chelmsford. With ten days to go, they will be joined by the King and Queen Consort. Earlier this afternoon, the King's valet, Lee Dobson, was here standing in for his boss and wearing a replica of the colobium sindonis and the other vestments. That way, the Bishops of Durham and of Bath and Wells could practise getting the King in and out of his various chairs without twisting his robes. By the time the King and Queen arrive for this rehearsal, two dozen people are going through their paces. The appearance of the royal couple causes a brief stiffening, but it is clear the pair are more relaxed than anyone else. The mood actually lightens. The King produces a pair of glasses to read his draft order of service and reminds his team that he needs cue cards with large lettering on the day. (An autocue monitor is out of the question.) The King can't be fiddling with spectacles when he is trying to grasp his sceptres and orb. 'There is one moment where he has to try to hold three things in two hands,' the Archbishop recalls later. 'I said that was a bit Monty Python and he roared with laughter.' With so many carefully choreographed movements, Justin Welby likens the whole exercise to a musical. 'You really are moving in rhythmic and detailed ways,' he explains.[15]

Others find themselves transported back to the days of the school play. After all, Justin Welby keeps talking about 'the cast', coronations take place in the 'theatre' of the abbey and the King was a keen actor in his youth. 'We often remark upon how grateful we are that our schools did a lot of drama and both of us spent time on stage,' the Princess Royal reflects. 'It's really good training. Apart from the fact it gives you a bit of confidence, it teaches you about learning lines and making sure you do the rehearsals so you get it absolutely right.'[16]

Queen Camilla's two 'companions' for the Coronation, her sister, Annabel Elliot, and her old friend, the Marchioness of Lansdowne, have very similar thoughts. 'It was more like a pantomime, actually, because there were so many bishops and nobody quite knowing what they were doing,' Fiona Lansdowne jokes later.[17] All are conscious that this is a particularly challenging moment for Annabel Elliot. Just the day before, she buried her husband, Simon, who died the previous month after a long illness. And now she is trying to learn her moves as her sister prepares to be crowned Queen. It's all the more impressive given that today should have been the Elliots' wedding anniversary.

There will also be two teams of page boys. Queen Camilla will be assisted by three grandsons and a great-nephew, who will wear uniforms based on two of her regiments, the Rifles and the Grenadier Guards. The King will have four pages, too, including Prince George, plus sons of family friends, all of them in scarlet court dress.

In 1953, Elizabeth II had no pages and no companions. She chose six 'Maids of Honour' to carry her train. For a few weeks, ahead of the big day, they were international celebrities. All were of similar height, titled, good-looking and unmarried, although Lady Rosemary Spencer-Churchill, daughter of the Duke of Marlborough, was just a few weeks away from her wedding. The maids were not close friends of the Queen (Lady Rosemary was a much better friend of Princess Margaret), but all received a fashionably modern diamond 'EIIR' brooch handmade by the Goldsmiths and Silversmiths Company to the Queen's own design,[18] along with a handwritten letter. A cousin of Winston Churchill, Lady Rosemary had grown up at the family seat, Blenheim Palace, during the war. Then, one day, she was suddenly told that she had been picked for this starring role. 'I was just off to America when this letter came from the Earl Marshal,' she says. 'It's funny. I don't want to sound blasé, but after growing up at Blenheim, that just seemed a normal sort of thing to do.' Lady Anne Coke, daughter of the Earl and Countess of Leicester, also received her invitation out of the blue. She had known the Royal Family since childhood, as near neighbours in Norfolk, and her mother was a lady-in-waiting. However, she was touring the USA working as a pottery sales rep when she received the summons.

'Jam it on'

The maids recall their own Coronation rehearsals as nerve-wracking occasions. Their training included ninety-four different diagrams of who was supposed to be where at any given point.[19] 'Whenever we had a rehearsal, the Duke of Norfolk would say: "Maids! I'm afraid we'll have to do that again",' says Lady Rosemary. Yet, they would all look back on the experience with great respect and affection for their commanding officer. 'Bernard Norfolk was wonderful,' recalls Lady Rosemary, adding that the Earl Marshal's main problems were with the more senior participants in the processions. 'You had all these generals who had just fought and won the war and they didn't want to be told what to do. They were quite difficult.'

No one is being difficult at Buckingham Palace today, however. Everyone defers to the Rev. Mark Birch, who is reading out the precise running order from a big folder. His title, Minor Canon and Precentor of Westminster Abbey, is deceptive. There is nothing minor about it. He has been working with the Lambeth Palace team on the rubric – effectively the stage directions – for months. If this really was a musical, as the Archbishop calls it, he would be the stage director.

For Queen Camilla, all along, the main anxiety has been the anointing. Just like monarchs, queen consorts are also anointed at coronations, though to a lesser extent. Having a clergyman who is neither a hairdresser nor a milliner placing a heavy crown on one's immaculate hairstyle is challenging enough. Having oil smeared on one's face is of rather greater concern. 'Just a tiny bit of oil, I promise,' the Dean of Westminster, Dr David Hoyle, assures her. 'It is the merest dab,' the Archbishop insists, as he imitates the short sign of the cross he will make on her forehead.

261

Charles III

For the King, the anointing of the Queen is a slightly nerve-wracking moment, too. Before she is crowned, the Archbishop has to seek the affirmation of the monarch who must 'nod' his approval from the Throne Chair. Except, as every monarch knows, nodding while wearing a crown is extremely risky. For, if you lower your head, the whole thing can topple forwards and fall off. That would be a disastrous portent at the start of a reign. It is why the late Queen always asked for the Imperial State Crown to be delivered the day before the State Opening of Parliament. That way, she could wear it around the house and get used to it. When reading the Queen's speech, as she revealed to the broadcaster Alastair Bruce, she would always hold the words up to her face. Lowering one's gaze was much too dangerous. 'If you did, your neck would break,' she explained.[20] The Archbishop is sympathetic and also aware of the dangers of asking the King to bow his head with five pounds of gold perched on top of it. He has a solution: 'Just give me a look that says you mean it!'

In another part of the ballroom, the soldiers from the Household Division are rehearsing their moves with the Anointing Screen. The three panels must slot together to shield the King from the world as the Archbishop administers the oil. Mark Birch will never forget the first time the King saw this new arrangement. 'I remember the expression on the King's face sitting in the chair, as the screens came around, and it was a look of really intense focus, a sense of the significance of what this would mean on the day. This meant everything.'

For all the dense ceremonial and the polished splendour of what the Archbishop calls 'the bling', the simple message that the King and his clergy want conveyed is that he is being installed as servant, not master. The result will be an opening exchange which Justin Welby describes as 'a mic-drop moment.'

'Jam it on'

Every previous coronation has started with the words of the Archbishop. This one will begin with a young boy welcoming the monarch to the abbey. To which the King will reply: 'I come not to be served but to serve.' The boy in question, Samuel Strachan, is a fourteen-year-old member of the choir of the Chapel Royal, hand-picked by Sir Clive Alderton's committee. Everyone at the Palace rehearsal is quietly wondering how Samuel will cope with the pressure of opening the entire event before the watching world. Young Samuel does not flinch. Unlike all the adults here, who are following scripts and printed service sheets, he calmly marches up to the King and recites his twenty words perfectly – and entirely from memory: 'Your Majesty, as children of the kingdom of God we welcome you in the name of the King of kings.'

The Archbishop has been practising for several weeks now. Back in the spring, his Coronation planner, Danny Johnson, and his team put sticky tape down on the floor of the Guard Room at Lambeth Palace to replicate the dimensions of the Coronation space. Fake crowns were procured from a theatrical hire shop in Canterbury. Time and again, the titles of all the key players were then thrown into a basket, to be drawn out by lot. The only person who always played the same role was the Archbishop himself. He remembers the first day that he rehearsed the anointing. Handel's Zadok the Priest was playing on the iPad and Lambeth Palace's head gardener was playing the King. Even in these makeshift circumstances, the experience had been so emotional that the gardener had tears running down her cheeks. 'I had chills running up and down the spine, too,' the Archbishop recalls. 'You suddenly thought: "This is a moment".'

He is also haunted by tales of coronations past when archbishops muddled up the regalia. Swords have often been a source of confusion since five of them are involved at various points of each coronation. Another problem is that St Edward's Crown looks very similar from all angles. In 1937, Welby's predecessor, Cosmo Gordon Lang, had draped a piece of red thread over the front of it to show him which way round to place it on the head of George VI. An over-zealous cleaner had tidied away the thread with the result that a baffled Lang had no idea if he had the thing back to front and so ended up guessing. Justin Welby will not be relying on thread in 2023. He has learned that the crown is decorated with two emerald-coloured gems, a square one at the front and an oval one at the back. 'So I wander around my kitchen going: "Square – front; oval – back; square – front; oval – back . . ."'

Six days later – and with just three to go before the Coronation itself – the rehearsals move to Westminster Abbey. Everyone is now acutely conscious that they will soon be doing this for real in front of a global audience of billions. For Annabel Elliot, the only way to cope is to keep focusing on childhood productions. 'It was completely mind-blowing,' she recalls later. 'I mean, you do think: "This is a play". I remember when we were at school, doing plays – both of us. I think it was easier to think like that. Otherwise it could have been overwhelming.' This entire process has also made her feel even more protective of her elder sister. 'She's quite a bit smaller and I thought: "Is she going to be alright? Is something wrong? Is the crown going to fall off her head?" I think I had that nervousness all the time.'[21]

She and Fiona Lansdowne are here, above all, to keep spirits up, not to look after royal regalia. 'Familiarity is very important,' says Elliot later. 'I think it was a great help to have Fiona and I; to have the odd laugh or conversation; just being there and making sure the boys didn't go off on some tangent.'

As the Queen's only surviving close relative, Elliot is, once again, conscious that her parents and her younger brother

Mark Shand (who died following an accidental fall in 2014) would have been so proud to see Camilla's crowning moment. 'I felt terribly sad about my family,' she later admits. 'And then I went on to pinch myself. I'm still pinching myself now! I mean, it still seems absolutely extraordinary.'[22]

The 'cast' has suddenly expanded at this rehearsal. A cluster of earnest-looking functionaries are standing in the nave looking up at the pulpit. They are all from Downing Street and have come to watch the prime minister, Rishi Sunak, rehearse his reading from the Book of Colossians. Further up the aisle, the choir are in their stalls running through one of the twelve new pieces of music which the King has commissioned for this ceremony. They are still getting to know one another since the regular abbey choir has been supplemented by reinforcements, from Truro Cathedral School and Belfast's Methodist College. For the first time, female choristers will take part in a coronation. Suddenly, there is a frisson of excitement as a royal visitor arrives through a side door. It is the Princess Royal. She does not actually have a role to play in the service but, like the three-day event champion she once was, she has come to walk the course ahead of the main event. She will be taking part in the King's carriage procession, riding home from the abbey immediately behind the King in her Household Cavalry capacity as Gold Stick. She wants to ensure she can make a swift exit if she is to be in the saddle ahead of the monarch.

There is a strong smell of fresh carpet. Newly laid rolls of blue and gold pile will give rise to online speculation that the abbey is sending a subliminal message of support to Ukraine. In fact, these are just the colours of Coronation. The abbey staff are determined to ensure that the carpet remains pristine. All those involved in the rehearsal (royalty aside) have been told to put blue plastic covers over their shoes or else take them off.

Charles III

Both Archbishops – Canterbury and York – plus the Dean of Westminster and his team are here. So, too, are those bishops who will attend to the monarch. By a thousand-year-old tradition these are Bath & Wells, representing the south, and Durham, from the north. Another pair – Norwich and Hereford – have been appointed as 'Bishops Assistant' to look after the Queen Consort. The sight of the highest churchmen in the land padding around the altar in blue plastic bags or just their socks lends a welcome note of the absurd to these otherwise grave proceedings. Mark Birch is, once again, going through the script line by line to ensure everyone is in the right spot. There has already been a vigorous debate over whether the clergy should wear gloves while handling the priceless regalia. 'It was decided that probably we were in more danger of dropping things if we were wearing gloves than without them,' says Birch. 'So no gloves.' A significant problem has been identified before all the treasures have even appeared in the abbey. All those carrying the regalia – many of them in robes – have to walk up some steps and through a small cloister door. That did not happen in 1953 because there was the huge temporary royal annexe where people would collect their sword or sceptre. In 2023, there is no annexe, so it is the cloisters which serve as backstage and there are trip hazards galore. There have also been tweaks to the running order to account for the fact that the King and Queen Consort are also the first people ever to be enthroned beyond the age of seventy. Both are in good health but if there is the odd moment when they could be sitting rather than standing, especially when fully robed, it is to be welcomed. 'It was important that we actually worked out a moment when we could take the first train off the Queen's shoulders,' says Fiona Lansdowne, 'because it was very heavy.'

At the Great West Door, the page boys have arrived for their first trial run with the two trains. The King's equerry, Lieutenant Colonel Johnny Thompson, and Prince William's former private secretary, Jamie Lowther-Pinkerton (who is also Prince George's godfather), are here to marshal these young attendants. 'Herding cats,' whispers Lowther-Pinkerton. In fact, the pages are on their best behaviour. One of them, Gus Lopes, thirteen-year-old son of the Queen Consort's daughter, Laura, has his right hand in a plaster cast, following a recent cycling accident. He will soldier on regardless, holding his grandmother's train with his uninjured left hand.

The patience of these boys is exemplary compared to that of the pages at the Coronation rehearsal in 1953. Gus's grandfather, Andrew Parker Bowles, has memories of his first practice at the abbey dragging on and on. 'We all had little swords, which is, of course, very exciting for a boy of thirteen. So, when we got bored, we all unsheathed our swords and started to have a sword fight,' he remembers fondly. 'At which point, these Gold Staff officers were sent to sort us out – which they did very firmly.'[23] Another perk of being a page, he says, was the supply of barley-sugar sweets to boost energy levels. However his fellow page and prep school contemporary, Duncan Davidson, a grandson of the Duke of Norfolk, had hoarded so many sweets by various means that he was sick at the rehearsal.

There are no such problems today. Everyone is obediently awaiting instructions. The Lord President of the Council, Penny Mordaunt, is here to process with a sword which will be held upright for long stretches of the service. She must arrive with the heavy Sword of State and leave with the much lighter, diamond-studded Jewelled Sword of Offering. She has also been doing a good deal of homework on what to wear. She has looked up the role of her predecessor in 1953, the fifty-nine-year-old Marquess of Salisbury, who wore court dress with breeches.

Charles III

As the first female Great Officer of State to take part in a coronation, Mordaunt has decided that something else is required for this landmark moment. After consulting the experts in Savile Row and talking to the Palace, she has bought a crepe cape dress in 'Poseidon' blue (reflecting her service in the Royal Naval Reserve and her naval constituency of Portsmouth North) and has had it embroidered with a fern motif, the symbol of the Privy Council. It will be worn with a matching hat by Jane Taylor, a favourite of the late Princess of Wales. The ensemble is supposed to be understated. As she puts it later: 'My role was to show the regalia. It was to be in the background, almost like a blank canvas.'[24] It would not turn out quite that way.

The Prince and Princess of Wales arrive with all the children. The Princess takes the younger two, Charlotte and Louis, for a look round the abbey while George learns the ropes and their father goes through his main role – the homage – with the Archbishop. Justin Welby offers him one piece of advice. 'If you ever get lost in this, Sir, just look confident and bow and that will carry you through everything.' Prince William chuckles, with the conspiratorial look of one who knows this already.

Finally, the King and Queen Consort arrive, appearing relaxed, even amused by the scene before them. Suddenly, the occasion feels less formal as grandchildren come up for a kiss on the cheek and everyone enjoys a spot of catching up. It really is starting to feel like a rehearsal for a family wedding. Mark Birch gently gets the show back on the road while the Archbishop speeds things along. 'And . . . pray, pray, pray and then tee-dum-tee-dum-tee-dum and pray, pray, pray,' he says, rattling through the order of service to reach the parts which require more careful choreography. At one point, as the King moves from St Edward's Chair to his Throne Chair, the bishops fail to lower him onto the seat and he sits down sharply. 'You've enthroned yourself like Napoleon,' the Archbishop observes. 'It's a long way down,' the King replies stiffly. The chair will need to be raised a few inches before the day. The homage starts solemnly enough as, for the first time, the Prince of Wales kneels before his father and recites his oath of loyalty. At the end, he leans forward to give him a kiss. There follows a debate about which side he should be kissing. The Prince then tickles the King under the chin and jokes: 'Your left cheek is better!' Everyone laughs – and anxiety levels move down another notch.

Soon afterwards, the Archbishop has another trial run at crowning the Queen but cannot attract the attention of the King. 'Darling,' she shouts, 'we need a nod!' More laughter. The King is concentrating on holding two sceptres at the correct angle at the same time. 'It's top heavy,' he concludes, nodding at the upper end of the Rod with the Dove. The King's two bishops practise steering him through his turns without him getting twisted in his own robes. The pages are told that they must learn not to crash into Penny Mordaunt. She is training herself to 'look expressionless' and 'not fall over' while holding her sword upright and averting her gaze from intimate moments like the anointing. The Rev. Mark Birch tells the pages that they are to regard Mordaunt as 'an immovable object'. 'I've been called worse,' she replies.

The pages take it all in. Annabel Elliot later reveals that there is a certain rivalry between the two sets of pages: 'A lot of ragging went on about "the Queen's team" and "the King's team" – very competitive.'[25] It all helps to ease the tension. It is the same when the Archbishop botches the blessing. 'And the blessing of God Almighty,' he begins, 'be amongst you and remain with you.' At which point, he forgets his lines, dries

269

up and looks lost. 'Always?' the Archbishop of York chips in helpfully, adding cheekily: 'You must have said this before!' The King, along with everyone else, bursts out laughing. As Justin Welby later admits, his memory is no better than that of the family spaniel – 'in other words, zero.' Finally, all line up to rehearse the procession at the end. The King wants to do the whole thing in real time in his robes and with the Orb and sceptre in his hands. He now realizes just how heavy the Orb is and wants to work out the best way of holding it securely while walking in a straight line extremely slowly for the best part of five minutes, escorted by his bishops. The King is conscious that his attendants have been rehearsing all week. 'Are you staying in a hotel?' he asks Durham as the procession shuffles along at glacial speed. The bishop explains that he is quartered at the Lambeth Novotel with his wife. The King asks if she will be coming to the Coronation, too. 'No, she's going to watch it on television,' the bishop replies, politely circumventing the fact that even the main players have been restricted to a single ticket. The King offers his sympathies: 'It's so frustrating we can't fit in all the other halves.'

Watching over it all is the Earl Marshal. He has learned from Operation London Bridge, and especially from that close shave with the timings of the Queen's funeral procession, that moving parts can work at different speeds. There are just three days to go with a dress rehearsal still to come (it will not go well). Eddie Norfolk has been taking copious notes. As with the funeral, if things don't go to plan, it is still his name on all the invitations.

At least today's rehearsal in Westminster Abbey has been more successful than another one when an old friend of the Queen, Sarah Keswick, steps in to take her place. 'Sarah Keswick was the stand-in for the Archbishop to crown her but they made this crown absolutely enormous,' Annabel Elliot recalls. 'It just slipped straight down to her shoulders. That was a very funny moment. Everyone was in hysterics – no head, just the crown!'[26]

At the Great West Door, the rehearsal is finally at a close and, for a few minutes, it really is a family party as the King and Queen chat to their grandchildren about the big day ahead. Like his father, Prince William is struck by the weight of the Orb and jokes that his father will struggle to hold it in the palm of his hand for so long. 'You'll need to go to the gym,' he jokes. 'I do my pull-ups!' the King replies.

He betrays no signs of nervousness, perhaps because there isn't much time to dwell on anything anyway. The prime minister of New Zealand is about to arrive at the palace and guests are already appearing for the pre-Coronation garden party. There will be 8,000 people for tea. Almost every waking hour between now and the morning of 6 May has been mapped out with duties for the King. In 1953, international guests at the Coronation were in London for days – in some cases weeks – and Elizabeth II's staff were able to spread out the requisite invitations and handshakes either side of the main event. Seventy years on, the number of delegations will be up three-fold (since the world now has more than three times the number of nation states) and most of them will be in London for one night – if that. The King has a clear list of priorities, in ascending order. As previously noted, there is neither the time nor the space to invite everyone to a state banquet. So the King will entertain them all at a Buckingham Palace reception on Coronation eve. Prior to that, he will have a meeting, a reception and a photograph with all the heads of all the Commonwealth delegations at Marlborough House. Those who will receive the maximum royal facetime, however, are the governors-general (the sovereign's alter egos) and the prime ministers of all the King's realms. These nations are here to see the crowning of their head of state, too. The King has invited them all to a rather intimate lunch less than twenty-four hours before the big show. Despite his innate aversion to eating at this time of day, he will entertain them to ballotine of Norfolk chicken followed by seasonal fruit savarin in mint and lime with Chantilly, all served on arguably the prettiest china in the Royal Collection. The 'Coronation Service' – commissioned from Yorkshire's Rockingham Works by William IV and first used at the coronation of Victoria – is only brought out for coronations.

All the frontline 'working royals' are here, except for Queen Camilla. She is pacing herself before the trip to the abbey. There is no 'top table' and the Royal Family are scattered among round tables of ten. The King sits between the governor-general of New Zealand, Dame Cindy Kiro, and Philip Davis, prime minister of the Bahamas. The Princess of Wales is at another table, in between the Canadian governor-general, Mary Simon, and Ralph Gonsalves, the avowedly republican prime minister of St Vincent and the Grenadines. A friend of the late Fidel Castro, 'Comrade Ralph' is the only premier present who has organized a referendum on abolishing the monarchy (held in 2009, it came down squarely in favour of retaining the Crown). The atmosphere is lively and extremely warm. Most of this lot know each other anyway. Sir Rodney Williams, from Antigua and Barbuda, has created a WhatsApp group for all his fellow governors-general and they are regularly swapping vice-regal notes. An eminent doctor who remains in general practice when not at his desk in Government House in St John's, Sir Rodney is a trusted adviser on Caribbean affairs to the King. 'He's a very charming person – very warm and very friendly,' he says. 'I admire the way he interacts with people. That, to me, speaks to the measure of our King.'

'Jam it on'

There is a strong personal element to many of these relationships. Governors-general like Sir Rodney Williams have known the King for years, chewing over matters great and small on the telephone or in person. When the governor-general's wife, Lady [Sandra] Williams, was organizing a fundraiser for her Halo Foundation, supporting charities across Antigua, she approached the future King. He gave her a lithograph of one of his paintings, raising a handsome five-figure sum. Many Antiguans will have little or no interest in the distant crowning of their distant head of state, but Sir Rodney has been keen to ensure that the public understand the context. He has organized a three-month programme of educational 'conversations' and civic events all over his country either side of the Coronation. While he is processing through Westminster Abbey, there will be a military and youth parade through the capital, St John's, followed by the lighting of a giant coronation cake at nightfall.

In the United Kingdom, parties large and small are being planned for the weekend. Whereas celebrations for the last coronation were confined to a single day, this one is a weekend affair with an extra bank holiday bolted on to make it a three-day event. The Palace has issued its themes for each day but, given the reaction to the 'people's homage', no one will be urged to do anything. Those who wish to go to the beach or the pub are most welcome to do so. Otherwise, it is Saturday for the Coronation, Sunday for street parties or community 'big lunches', and Monday for 'the big help-out' – a nationwide festival of voluntary work. Party organizers are looking nervously at the weather forecasts. Though the day of the Coronation will be wet, it looks as though the skies will be clear for the main day of national partying on Sunday.

While there has been nothing quite like the appetite for souvenirs and gifts which was a memorable feature of 1953, staff at the Royal Collection Trust have been pleasantly surprised by the reaction to their range of official royal souvenirs. Five days after launching their fine bone china mugs and tankards plus a Coronation biscuit tin, they sold out. *The Washington Post* reports that a limited edition of £1,475 'Garden of Kings' lidded Coronation pots by the Moorcroft Pottery have all gone, while John Lewis is rationing sales of its Coronation teddy bears to two per household.[27] In 1953, the Palace had also been inundated with unexpected gifts from all over the world, despite a formal policy of rejecting them. As a result, the Chester H. Roth Company of New York received a distinctly sniffy response to its offer of a 'Lifetime gift of Nylon Hosiery'. The Privy Purse office replied it was 'contrary to the Queen's rules to accept gifts from commercial firms as opposed to private individuals that are personally known to her'.[28] There was a similar response when Air India called to say that they had a basket of mangoes for delivery to the Queen. These were refused until they turned out to be from the Indian prime minster, at which point Sir Alan Lascelles immediately despatched profuse thanks to the Indian high commissioner.[29]

One gift that no one will miss is the traditional offering from the High Sheriff of Gloucestershire. In 1953, he informed the Palace that he wished to present the Queen with a lamprey pie, following a tradition dating back to King John, the first monarch to be presented with a coronation eel platter. Lascelles checked the provenance of the claim with Sir Austin Strutt at the Home Office and was not best pleased to learn that it was valid. So, the Queen agreed to accept her eel pie.[30] Seventy years on, the current High Sheriff, Henry Robinson, has inadvertently let the tradition slip. 'Had I known of this ancient right I should have immediately started baking,' he says, 'but ignorance is bliss, at least for the Palace.'[31]

Chapter Thirteen

'A decent-sized hat'

For a religious, deep-thinking traditionalist like Charles III, this is the day that completes an apprenticeship of seventy-four years. He has already been the sovereign for eight months and could remain so legally and indefinitely without a coronation. Today, however, is an inauguration, a swearing-in ceremony and a passing-out parade rolled into one. Biblical in its origins, it is a religious affirmation before the Almighty, the King's subjects and the world. Unlike his mother, his grandfather and his great-grandfather, whose paths to the throne were indirect, Charles III really was born for this moment. For a man of such strong emotions – 'he can cry at a sunset, that one', says a close friend – this ceremony will be as trying as it should be triumphal. It will be the grandest moment of his life but, in many ways, the humblest, as he is stripped to his shirt and then invested with all the symbols of those virtues and duties it is now his obligation to uphold. As his old university chum and spiritual sounding board Richard Chartres writes in a special Coronation edition of *The Spectator*: 'Simply invoking abstract universal concepts such as justice and tolerance does not generate the energy necessary to bind people together in a common cause. It is when the abstractions are embodied in a story, a community memory . . . or in symbolic representative figures, that they are invested with power.'[1]

Charles III

For the King and his inner circle, the greatest challenge has been to reflect the complexion of modern Britain while also keeping the traditionalists happy. 'In 1953, no one was remotely surprised that Britain was crowning a God-fearing Protestant,' says a member of Sir Clive Alderton's liturgy committee. 'Now we have a King who has made his life's work about inclusivity. But he must also go back to 1953, to Charlemagne and to the Book of Solomon.'

Few might now remember the scenes and excitement of 1953, but most of Britain could still recall the last time that Westminster Abbey had felt such pent-up excitement, joy and nerves. That was twelve years earlier for the wedding of Prince William to Catherine Middleton. Some of the same guests are among those arriving at the bewilderingly earlier start time of 7.30. The early birds are the wise ones. Aside from members of the Royal Family, senior representatives of the realms and world leaders, no one else has reserved seats. Guests will be steered to a specific section of the abbey according to the colour of their ticket. One Duchess, having assumed that she would have an allocated seat near the front, arrives at the last minute and, to her dismay, is steered to the back row.

It was an even earlier start in 1953. Some of the troops were up at 2 a.m. and the first lights were seen to go on in Buckingham Palace at 5.00 a.m., though the Queen did not want too much noise. The Ministry of Works had proposed playing early morning tunes through loudspeakers to amuse the crowds, starting with 'Oranges and Lemons' and 'Over the Rainbow.' Back came a firm edict from the Master of the Household: 'The Queen does not wish music to be rediffused in front of the Palace between 5.30 and 7.30 a.m.'[2]

Seventy years on, the crowds, like the processional route, are smaller this time. This is not a church-going, Anglican nation feeling a thrilling sense of post-war rejuvenation through the prism of an impossibly glamorous young Queen. This is a rancorous, largely secular land divided down many lines and uncertain about its future. For the most part, however, it is happy to enjoy the sense of permanence encapsulated in the most spectacular state occasion in the royal repertoire with the nation's most familiar septuagenarian at its heart.

Hundreds of royalists have been camping out for days on the Mall in order to ensure a prime view while tens of thousands more are turning up from first light to line the streets. There would be many more but the government and the police have erected steel fences and gates around the entire processional route, as they did for the Queen's funeral. They will close them as soon as they have admitted a comfortable, controllable crowd which looks respectable enough on camera. They do not want those 1953 scenes of a delirious public, fifty deep, held back only by rope, national servicemen and self-restraint. Fearful of protest groups, today's 'gold commanders' will err on the side of caution, citing the unarguable grounds of health and safety. Latecomers will be steered to jumbo video screens in neighbouring parks. The government's priority is that it should look good on television around the world, as indeed it will, even if much of the route feels a little sterile. The international media towers next to Canada Gate have been in action around the clock for days. Here, Australian and American networks simultaneously address their respective breakfast and evening audiences. They all know this set-up very well. After the Platinum Jubilee eleven months earlier, followed by the great farewell to Elizabeth II three months later, some overseas networks initially felt that yet another royal spectacular on the Mall might not warrant quite the same outlay. For all his merits, some initially took a hard-nosed business view that 'Charles is not as big a deal as his mum.'

As the day drew nearer, however, newsroom executives around the world reverted to full royal wedding mode. They cleared the schedules and flew their top presenters to London.

It has been an early start for the attendants. Annabel Elliot, Queen Camilla's sister, her fellow-companion, the Marchioness of Lansdowne, and the pages have all been collected from their homes by a bus at around 6.00 a.m. and brought to Buckingham Palace under police escort. Once again, it brings back memories of school plays. 'It was like being in a play because literally we walked in and there was make-up, hair, costume,' says Elliot.

King Charles III and the Queen Consort have awoken in the relative calm of Clarence House, still spared any obligation to sleep in Buckingham Palace due to the ongoing building work. From today, she will be known as 'Queen Camilla' or, simply, 'The Queen'. Both titles were correct before, just like 'Queen Consort', and she was not bothered either way. The use of 'consort' was a means of avoiding any confusion with the late Queen while there was an unspoken sense among some Palace officials that it also obviated any debate about her title. It was only the previous year that the late Queen had used the seventieth anniversary of her accession to state her 'sincere wish' that 'when that time comes, Camilla will be known as Queen Consort as she continues her own loyal service.' That 'sincere wish' was duly observed. The Coronation, however, was the natural point to move on; to acknowledge that every queen of every king in history has been called either 'Queen' and then her first name or simply 'The Queen'. The Coronation invitations had referred to her as 'Queen Camilla'. The Court Circular, which had continued to call her 'Queen Consort' right up to her last pre-Coronation mention on 3 May, will switch to 'The Queen' from now onwards. Today's order of service does the same. The word 'Consort' does not appear at all.

'A decent-sized hat'

By the time the King and Queen are driven over to the palace to put on their robes, most of the guests are already inside in the abbey. As in 1953, some have come armed with furtive snacks since they will be in their seats until at least 1.30 p.m. One friend of the family, sitting in the North Transept, has come with a banana as an emergency ration in his inside pocket. It then dawns on him that he cannot possibly peel the thing, let alone eat it, in case he is caught by a television camera at that precise moment. Besides, what do you do with the peel in the middle of a coronation? The banana will therefore return home, with its owner, untouched, if a little squashed.

The final version of the seating plan is a closely guarded document, subdivided into dozens of different categories in no particular order.[3] So, the '09' list, for example, covers the entire political spectrum, in no particular order of seniority. It starts with '09B' (there is no '09A'), which consists of the leaders of the Northern Irish, Scottish and Welsh parliaments, followed by '09C' covering the prime minister and all British Cabinet ministers. It then jumps to '09E' for ten members of the Opposition, including the Labour leader, Sir Keir Starmer. The fifty members of the House of Lords, reportedly chosen by ballot, comprise '09F'. They include former Labour Cabinet ministers Lord Mandelson, Baroness Hoey and Lord Boateng, plus the Tory peer Baroness Rock and the cross-bench peer and former Paralympic champion Baroness Grey-Thompson. Another 'ballot' has produced the names of fifty members of the House of Commons. Listed as '09G', they include Conservatives John Penrose, Joy Morrissey and Alok Sharma plus Labour veterans such as Harriet Harman and Barry Sheerman. It is only when the list gets to '09H' that we find all seven former British prime ministers. Along with the first ministers of the devolved parliaments, prime ministers past and present are the only politicians allowed to bring a spouse or partner.

A dozen names are listed under '09J', representing the Privy Council. It's a spread of eminent senior former politicians and civil servants, among them the former deputy prime minister Sir Nick Clegg, the former chancellor of the Exchequer Lord [Alistair] Darling and the former Cabinet secretary Lord [Robin] Butler. Senior civil servants from the devolved governments of Northern Ireland, Scotland and Wales make up '09K', '09L' and, finally, '09M' (the latter including someone familiar to the King: Manon Antoniazzi, now chief executive of the Welsh Senedd, who used to run the Welsh section of his office when he was Prince of Wales). The most striking contingent of all, however, is '09I'. It is the allocation for 'Hereditary Peers'. In 1953, as noted earlier, they were granted 910 seats (including spouses). Today, they have been given just four – one for each rank of the aristocracy below a duke (there are several dukes on other lists). So, the seventy-nine-year-old Marquess of Huntly (the oldest marquessate in Scotland) is here to represent all the marquesses while the Earl of Derby (one of the oldest earldoms) is here for the earls. Viscount Hereford (an auctioneer at Bonhams and holder of England's senior viscountcy) represents the viscounts. Finally, Lord Mowbray, Segrave and Stourton, a thirty-one-year-old commodities analyst and holder of the country's oldest barony, is here for the barons. Unlike his great-grandfather in 1953, he will not be scattering mothballs around the abbey.

Other categories include '10' for those in the procession, including, for example, the Lord Chamberlain, Lord Parker, and the Earl of Caledon (who is carrying one of the royal standards); '14' for clergy and 'faith communities', '15' for the judiciary (just eight of them, versus the dozens who attended in 1953) and '18' for the emergency services. Section '19' is loosely defined as 'Public Service' and spans forty luminaries such as the broadcaster Loyd Grossman, the former boss of the Heritage Lottery Fund, Carole Souter, and the arts administrator Sir Nicholas Serota. All Britain's main media organizations have a single ticket under section '47' while '48' has just two seats allocated for winners of the Nobel Prize, represented by the physicist Sir Roger Penrose and the medical scientist Sir Peter Ratcliffe.

All receive the same joining instructions. The chief topic of conversation is the paragraph concerning the 'facilities'. 'Guests are advised that there are very limited toilet facilities in Westminster Abbey which will be available between 7.30 a.m. and 10.00 a.m.,' it warns. These will then close for the duration of the service and only reopen at 1.30 p.m. Dark tales circulate of the queue for a solitary loo in 1953, although this was a myth. There were actually 152 Elsan chemical toilets concealed beneath the interior grandstands then (according to James Wilkinson, abbey historian and a member of the choir that day). The guests in 2023 are taking no chances. Television star Adam Hills, who is part of a delegation of 'outstanding Australians' selected by his country, has revealed that he has been in training already: 'I've been doing literal dry runs where I've tried to take in as little amount of fluid as possible and space out the caffeine consumption.'[4] Those still smarting from the absence of an invitation can console themselves, as they watch television, that they can drink as much morning coffee as they like. Several hereditary peers have formed themselves into a very jolly WhatsApp group for uninvited aristocrats and will spend the morning sending one another photos of themselves in their ancestral robes and coronets. Inside the palace, the page boys are being kept occupied. A room has been set aside with video games to keep them amused. Jamie Lowther-Pinkerton also has a cricket ball for a spot of catching practice. Anything to take their minds off what is about to unfold.

Like any good wedding, all eyes are on what people are wearing. Most guests are dressed for a wedding anyway. The majority of men are in morning coats and most women are in day dress and hats (though the dress code insists that these are optional). Here and there, peers of the realm stand out in their scarlet parliamentary robes, enlivening that 'morning coat drabness' Jock Colville was lamenting in 1953. One baroness is spotted extracting a hip flask for some early fortification ahead of the royal arrivals. A handful are indeed proudly sporting crimson family coronation robes, following that royal U-turn on the dress code for hereditaries. The Earl of Derby has gone one better. An Honorary Captain in the Royal Naval Reserve in Merseyside, he asked the King if the family's ancient office of Vice Admiral of Lancashire might be revived for the day. The King agreed and Lord Derby is dressed as a vice admiral beneath his coronation robes. Equally conspicuous is the ex-Tory Cabinet minister Rory Stewart, a one-time tutor to Princes William and Harry and former chief executive of one of the King's charities. Today, Stewart is in a pre-war Privy Councillor's Levee Dress uniform (including striped trousers with 'gold oakleaf lace – 2½ inches' and black cocked hat with 'ostrich feather border', as laid down in 'Dress and Insignia At His Majesty's Court, 1921'). He will certainly stand out afterwards when he adjourns from the abbey for lunch at the local Pizza Express.

Of equal interest is who is sitting with whom, given that this is a service where most people have received a solo invitation. The Duke of Norfolk has a ready response to anyone complaining that a spouse has not been invited: he is on his own, too. His wife, Chica (he remarried in 2022), is not on the list. Similarly, US pop star Lionel Ritchie may be the star turn at the Coronation concert at Windsor the following evening, but he has a single ticket. He arrives later than most, looking for an allocated seat in the nave, and discovers that he does not have one. He spots his friend Sir Lloyd Dorfman, philanthropist and former chairman of Prince's Trust International, who points him towards an empty space. They are among those listed in category '05' – 'Main Guests of Their Majesties'. Others include Dame Julia Cleverdon (former chief executive of Business in the Community), the fashion designer Ozwald Boateng, *Vogue* editor Edward Enninful, environmentalist Tony Juniper, broadcasters Ant McPartlin and Declan Donnelly (better known as Ant & Dec), equality campaigner Lord Woolley, biographers Gyles Brandreth and Jonathan Dimbleby, and Amelia Fawcett, banker and chair of the Royal Botanic Gardens at Kew.

To widespread surprise, the solo rule has even extended to some of those in the 'royal box' in the South Transept. It is smaller than it has ever been for a coronation. The King's siblings have been permitted to bring both spouses and children, as have his first cousins, the Earl of Snowdon and Lady Sarah Chatto. The same rule applies to the first cousins of the late Queen, the Dukes of Gloucester and Kent, Prince Michael of Kent and Princess Alexandra. Their children, however, have all been invited on their own. So, the Earl of Ulster, son and heir of the Duke of Gloucester, is without the rest of his immediate family. Likewise, the Earl of St Andrews, son of the Duke of Kent. The days when extended lines of distant royal cousins would stretch back through the South Transept would seem to be over. The royal turnout is below fifty today and goes no further back than row seven, which has been allocated to the non-Windsor side of the family. The Mountbatten clan, who are the King's cousins through the late Prince Philip, would traditionally take up several rows at a big royal gathering. Today, there is just one of them,

Countess Mountbatten, representing the lot. There has been much media comment that Lady Pamela Hicks, the daughter of the King's beloved uncle, Lord Mountbatten, has not been asked. She had also been a bridesmaid and former lady-in-waiting to the late Queen. Palace officials respond that these have all been 'hard choices'. Lady Pamela, however, has let it be known she thinks the scaled-back guest list is 'very sensible', that she understands the constraints on space and that she will be very happy watching on television, where she will see her daughter, India, who is part of the BBC commentary team. The late Queen Mother's family have just two representatives: Sir Simon and Lady [Caroline] Bowes Lyon. In the same row, there are Michael, Carole, Pippa and James Middleton – the parents, sister and brother of the Princess of Wales. That has been a direct request from the Prince of Wales himself. 'Having them all there was very important to him,' says one of his team. 'He was absolutely insistent that his wife's family should be properly included.' Ahead of the previous coronation, Winston Churchill had been so alarmed by Lord Mountbatten's claims that 'the House of Mountbatten now reigns' that he had formally advised the Queen to reaffirm the family name as 'the House of Windsor'. Such are the shifting sands that, seventy years on, the Middletons outnumber the Mountbattens four to one.

There is one royal guest who could have brought his wife and children had he wished, but he is still on his own. The question of whether the Duke and Duchess of Sussex would attend – and how – had been lingering long after the initial deadline for a reply, 3 April, had passed. Nine days later, the Palace issued a statement confirming that the Duke would attend but 'the Duchess of Sussex will remain in California with Prince Archie and Princess Lilibet'. It was what had been expected. The Sussexes' favoured media outlets were informed that Meghan's non-appearance was because of a coronation clash with Archie's fourth birthday. Cynics have suggested that she might also be fearful of a negative reaction from the British public as she emerged from her car. The police restrictions on public access to the area around the abbey entrance, however, are such that no one would have been within booing range today anyway. As with the late Queen's jubilee and funeral, the Duke keeps to the script and makes no attempt to upstage the main parade. Normally, members of the family arrive at these events according to their place in the line of succession, with those furthest from the throne arriving first. Today, Prince Harry arrives well before those, like the Gloucesters, who are a long way behind him in the pecking order. They, however, are 'working' members of the family and he is not. It's another subtle distinction of the way protocol and precedence are being tweaked under the new regime. The same applies to the Duke of York, who must arrive well before the younger siblings whom he used to outrank. At least the King has allowed him to wear his Garter robes today, a gesture which will mean a great deal to the Duke.* Harry is the only royal Prince in ordinary morning dress (he left royal life before the time had come to be made a Knight of the Garter). He looks cheerful and waves to a few familiar faces as he walks up the aisle, especially a row of Victoria Cross holders. He is seated in the third row of the royal section, alongside the York contingent (the Duke, his daughters and their husbands) plus Princess Alexandra. Harry is immediately behind the Princess Royal, in her robe and striking red-plumed bicorn hat which remains on her head throughout. Social media snipers instantly conclude that Harry has been deliberately placed behind his aunt's tall hat to obscure his view. It is nonsense. Not only do

---

* The Duke of York was created a Royal Knight of the Garter in 2006, along with his younger brother, the Earl of Wessex.

the Lord Chamberlain's Office not think like that, but the Princess Royal has only switched to that seat following her request for a speedy exit. 'The hat was an interesting question,' the Princess recalled later. 'I said: "Are you sure you want me to keep the hat on? Because it's quite a decent sized-hat." And the answer was yes. There you go. Not my choice.'*[5] Just behind the royal party sit the world leaders and representatives, including the first lady of the United States, Dr Jill Biden, representing President Joe Biden, accompanied by her granddaughter, Finnegan. 'The excitement was palpable. Everybody knew that this was a moment in history,' she says later, recollecting her slightly nervous walk up the aisle and the friendly face at the other end. 'Everybody was curious – you know: "Who's coming in?" – and then we walked to the very end and then turned right. We were seated alphabetically by country. So, of course, United States of America – we were at the end right next to Ukraine! So I was next to my friend Olena Zelenska, and it was just great to see her there. As it was, my granddaughter and I were dressed in blue and yellow, the colours of Ukraine. And so Olena said: "Thank you so much for your support".'

Being towards the back, the first lady is in a position to take in the full global reach of this event, as she explains later: 'Right in front of me, there were all the world leaders. I had to reflect on this moment in history. Joe always says that all politics is personal and that really is true. I thought of all of Joe's relation-ships with all the leaders in front of me and how important it was.' She, too, is also struck by some of the headwear: 'All the women had beautiful hats.'

---

* A Palace official later explained that the Princess was expected to keep her hat on because royal ladies do not remove hats in church, even if in uniform.

'A decent-sized hat'

There is some awkwardness in the North Transept where the light blue tickets for one area look very like the light green ones for another. Some people have, therefore, been steered to the wrong block of seats. They are very unhappy when ushers try to dislodge them from a good seat and send them to a worse one. No such trouble for two old friends of the King – and of each other – who have grabbed adjacent seats. Lord [Nicholas] Soames, former MP and grandson of Churchill, and Lady [Susan] Hussey, stalwart lady-in-waiting to the late Queen, had sat next to each other at the investiture of Prince Charles as Prince of Wales in 1969. And here they are side by side today, completing a circle of sorts. It is also recognition that Lady Susan's lifetime's service to the late Queen remains beyond reproach. Alongside them both are US senator John Kerry, an old eco-ally of the King, and Lady [Anne] Glenconner. In 1953, she had been among the maids of honour to the Queen and still recalls being saved from fainting by the speedy intervention of Black Rod, Sir Brian Horrocks. Today, she can actually enjoy the show.

This part of the abbey is reserved for category '04' of the guest list – 'Friends'. Unlike other parts of the crowd, they include many couples for the simple reason that both halves know the King and Queen equally well. Among them are the royal biographer William Shawcross and his hotelier wife Olga, the historian Simon Sebag-Montefiore and his novelist wife Santa, plus her parents, Charles and Patty Palmer-Tomkinson, the King's old skiing companions. Sir Francis Brooke, chairman of the Ascot Authority and his wife, Katharine, one of Queen Camilla's new ladies-in-waiting or 'companions' (and daughter of Lady Susan Hussey) are here, too, along with Lord and Lady Bamford (Gloucestershire neighbours of the King). Others include Tiggy Pettifer (former nanny to Princes William and

Harry) plus her husband, Charles, philanthropists Hans and Julia Rausing and the war photographer Sir Don McCullin and his wife, Catherine.

Among the acting contingent, Edward Fox and his wife, Joanna David, are in shouting distance of Dame Joanna Lumley, who is here with her husband, the conductor Stephen Barlow.

Westminster Abbey is packed with all those conductors, composers and musicians hand-picked by the King himself. Arguably the most musical monarch since George III, he has been keenly involved in all twelve new pieces for his Coronation. Several will be played before he arrives including the spellbinding 'Sacred Fire' by Sarah Class and Dr Grahame Davies and sung by South African soprano Pretty Yende (her daffodil-like yellow gown will be one of the stand-out images of the day). The order of service omits Davies's dual role. A Welsh poet, he was deputy private secretary to the King prior to the accession, handling Prince Charles's Welsh portfolio. Lord [Andrew] Lloyd Webber is sitting in the Choir with his wife Madeleine (they have a dual invitation since both are friends of the King and Queen). This is a day to evoke so many memories for the composer. As a Queen's Scholar at Westminster School, he spent much of his youth in and around the abbey. Not long after the death of Elizabeth II, the couple were invited to dinner with the King and Queen Camilla, during which the monarch gently asked if the most successful composer on the planet might consider composing an anthem for his Coronation. 'I was very honoured – he knows more about the English choral tradition than I do,' Lloyd Webber says later. The King initially wanted something from the Book of Solomon but the two men agreed that this was a little 'heavy' and they eventually settled on words from Psalm 98 – 'Make a joyful noise'. 'Once I had the words, I wrote it in a day,'[6] says the peer (who was born in the same year as the King). He set the piece, which was to follow the crowning of Queen Camilla, in the key of C. Mindful of his own days as a choirboy, he wanted it to be an enjoyable rather than a challenging exercise. He knew that by this stage in the ceremony the choir would already have been singing for the best part of an hour and a half. 'What the King liked about "Make a Joyful Noise" was that it was making a joyful noise unto the Lord,' Lord Lloyd Webber adds. 'He was saying: "This is not about me. I answer to a higher King."' There was one other royal request. 'The King said: "I want a trumpet fanfare at the beginning and the end."' There would be no shortage of fanfares – or trumpeters to play them.

Many guests will long remember the flowers. Royal florist Shane Connolly has filled the abbey with 120 different home-grown varieties. He is particularly thrilled that no sooner had he installed the small meadow of wild grasses, cowslips, prim-roses and violets by the Great West Door than it was buzzing with bees.

At Buckingham Palace, the King and Queen appear in the Marble Corridor, ready for the 10.20 departure in the Diamond Jubilee State Coach. It is the first time the King has seen Queen Camilla in her full Coronation gown. 'She looked absolutely wonderful,' Annabel Elliot recalls later. 'When he saw her – you could see his face lit up. He was very proud of her.' The Queen's immediate family, as well as her attendants and all the pages, are here to wave the couple off before jumping into cars which will speed through the back streets to the abbey. Watching her elder sister step into the carriage is an emotional moment for Elliot: 'It makes tears come to my eyes thinking about the whole day. I felt she looked very vulnerable. And she was obviously incredibly nervous. She doesn't show it a lot and said: "No, no, I'm not at all nervous". But of course, she was. I mean, this is just the most extraordinary moment in your life.' The King, on the other hand, still manages to retain an almost transcendental calmness, 'as if it was just another day at the office,' according to Annabel Elliot.

There is a strict Palace ban on mobile telephones yet, somehow, most of the royal party seem to have one in their hand at this precise moment. 'They weren't supposed to have phones but everyone took this shot of them going off and getting into the carriage,' the Queen's sister admits. Once again, she finds herself close to tears as she thinks back to two little girls watching the 1953 Coronation on a tiny black and white television. And now, seventy years later, it has come to this. 'There goes this golden coach with my sister. I can't explain the feeling, but it's so surreal. This cannot be happening . . .'

Major General Chris Ghika, commanding officer of the Household Division, and his staff officers have set off ten minutes ahead of the Diamond Jubilee State Coach to 'prove the route.' There are six Windsor greys pulling the royal couple in their three-ton carriage, the only one in the Royal Mews with hydraulic stabilizers. The first cheers are heard from the 3,800-seat grandstand erected by the Queen Victoria Memorial and filled with an invited mixture of veterans, National Health Service staff and charity workers. The rain has started and most have already put on their plastic ponchos. This parade, 'The King's Procession,' is very much smaller than the 'Coronation Procession' to come. It is restricted to an escort of around 200 men and horses from the Household Cavalry plus a single, mounted band (there will be nineteen bands on the return). The idea is to reflect humility on the way to the abbey and celebration on the way back. Though this is officially classified as 'a walk,' it is a brisk one. Indeed, it is so brisk that a procession which was supposed to take thirty-three minutes actually takes twenty-six. The King and Queen are, therefore, early for their own coronation, even arriving ahead of the pages. Unbeknown to them, the Prince and Princess of Wales and their two younger children are running a minute and a half late. The Waleses are supposed to be there eight minutes ahead of the King and Queen. Yet they will now arrive after them. Although the congregation inside the abbey don't know it, there is an awkward scene unfolding outside as the King and Queen remain in their coach. It is an added layer of stress that the couple really do not want or need on a day like this. A Sky News camera captures the monarch's frustration, the words translated by a lipreader: 'We can never be on time . . . There's always something . . . This is boring.' As with his irksome pen in the days after his mother's death, it's a snapshot of a man under extreme pressure in the full gaze of the world's media. There will be plenty of post-mortems once this is over. Conflicting sources will suggest that the Waleses' decision to make a Coronation Day video has added precious seconds to their schedule and made them late. Kensington Palace staff working for the Waleses say that because the King was early, the car carrying William and Catherine was caught behind his procession when it should have been ahead. The Prince of Wales's equerry, Commander Rob Dixon, will take a fair amount of flak, nonetheless. It is unusual for the two most important arrivals at such a significant event, and over such a well-trodden route, to be so unpunctual. The result is some frantic rewriting of the running order. There isn't time for the Waleses and their two younger children to enter ahead of the King and Queen. They must now follow behind and bring up the rear.

One factor, unspoken, may have been nervousness about street protests. More than 11,500 police have been drafted in from all over the country, making this the largest police operation ever mounted in London.

It had been expected that there would be some sort of small but vocal demonstration by the anti-monarchy campaign group Republic with their new slogan of 'Not My King'. They are not regarded as a security threat, however, unlike certain other groups with different agendas. According to the Metropolitan Police Commissioner, Sir Mark Rowley, credible intelligence reports have already revealed a number of threats to the event. Rumoured tactics include a plan to throw paint at the procession, a plan to throw rape alarms (for scaring horses) and a plan to 'lock on', whereby protestors handcuff themselves to part of the parade route.[7] In total, sixty-two arrests will be made during the day, among them six people arrested at 6.40 a.m. on 'suspicion of going equipped for locking-on'. The main perceived threat is from extremist environmental protest movements like Just Stop Oil, whose recent 'lock on' tactics have brought motorways and cities to a halt for hours. For the Coronation to be halted even for a few minutes, before the eyes of the world, would be hugely damaging for the international standing of both King and country. While acknowledging the right to demonstrate peacefully, the Met has already warned of a 'low' tolerance 'for any disruption, whether through protest or otherwise'.[8] Some sort of stunt on the homeward leg would be bad enough but manageable. Disruption before the main event has even started would be very much worse.

Shortly before 11 a.m., however, the Coronation is back on schedule as a different procession finally begins its solemn, stately progress on foot, through the abbey. There are 144 participants, all of them representing or carrying some important facet of royal honour, patronage or authority. They include a rugby star (Richie McCaw representing the Order of New Zealand), an Olympian (Lord [Sebastian] Coe for the Companions of Honour) and the only living Vietnam War VC

(Australia's Keith Payne, representing the holders of the Victoria Cross). Once again, the King's private secretary, Sir Clive Alderton, and his committee have sought an appropriate balance of ancient and modern. So, some are here in the footsteps of their ancestors. Former actor Delaval Astley, who played Cameron Fraser in the BBC radio drama *The Archers*, is processing in his capacity as the 23rd Baron Hastings and hereditary bearer of The Spur. The Royal Standard is carried by Francis Dymoke, the Hereditary King's Champion. His forebears have participated in every coronation since that of William the Conqueror, who gave them the manor of Scrivelsby in Lincolnshire as well as the office of champion. Should anyone seek to challenge the King to a duel today, it will be Mr Dymoke, a sixty-eight-year-old farmer and retired accountant, who must step forward to take up the challenge. He has long been a champion of the King in other ways, not least as a former chairman of the Lincolnshire branch of the Prince's Trust. Unlike most of his predecessors at these ceremonies, he is not wearing a suit of armour or entering on a horse.

In the early days of planning this coronation, there had been a novel suggestion to invite the great environmentalist Sir David Attenborough to carry the Orb ('it's a symbol of the world and so, in a way, is he,' said one member of the Earl Marshal's team).[9] It was felt, however, that this would be placing undue pressure on a national treasure two days shy of his ninety-seventh birthday. So his fellow member of the Order of Merit, nursing pioneer Dame Elizabeth Anionwu, will carry the Orb instead.

Beyond the gaze of the television cameras, all these key players begin this procession outside in the Great Cloister where they must first collect their allotted treasure off a table. 'There was an extraordinary scene,' Mark Birch recalls later. 'Lots of police were making sure everything was properly protected.

We lined people up all the way around the cloisters. Then the regalia was brought out and people from the Tower and the Crown Jewellers put these things into people's hands.'

Among those in the queue is Penny Mordaunt, Lord President of the Council. She is struck by the sight of so many VIPs in their finery and by the scent of all the flowers. Just before it is time for her to process into the abbey, she receives a short lecture from the King's Armourer. He tells her to look straight into his face, to remember it and to ensure that she hands her sword back to him and nobody else afterwards. She is also preparing herself for a long morning of standing to attention with eight pounds of upturned steel. 'I didn't lift the sword or put my heels on until the last minute,' she recalls later. Many people, including General Sir Gordon Messenger – Constable of the Tower, Lord High Steward and bearer of St Edward's Crown – remain seated until it is time to leave. No one wants to go down in history like Lord Rolle, who fell down the steps at Queen Victoria's coronation and had to receive a helping hand from the monarch herself.[10]

Chapter Fourteen

'I was glad'

The King and Queen enter the abbey to a piece of music that he has loved since boyhood – Parry's 'I Was Glad'. Up in the triforium, the scholars of Westminster School make their traditional cry in unison. 'Vivat Regina Camilla!' they shout. 'Vivat Rex Carolus!' No monarch has been as devoted to Sir Hubert Parry as this one. In 2011, Prince Charles even presented a BBC documentary, *The Prince and the Composer*, exploring Parry's life and works. The thunderous strains of his great coronation anthem, written for Edward VII, has brought a serene smile to the King's face as he processes slowly through the nave, catching the eye of old friends from charities like the Prince's Trust and a cluster of former staff from Clarence House. The frustrations caused by the botched arrivals at the Great West Door have swiftly evaporated. He spots two great family friends and allies, the Earl and Countess of Airlie. Ginny Airlie served as a lady-in-waiting to Elizabeth II for half a century. A pivotal Lord Chamberlain through the most testing times of the late Queen's reign, David Airlie was her exact contemporary and childhood friend, to the extent that she would occasionally refer to him as her 'twin'. Though unwell of late, he has been absolutely determined to make it to Westminster Abbey and to rise from his wheelchair to bow to his sovereign. He is the only person present today who was also at the coronation of George VI in 1937, when serving as a page to his father.*

The Queen and her companions are equally caught up in the moment. 'It is an extraordinary feeling going into Westminster Abbey,' her sister, Annabel Elliot, recalls later. 'You could feel the tension, but – it's a cliché – you could also feel the love. Everybody felt so happy about this, you know, the day had come. And I remember thinking that as we had to walk very slowly up the aisle.' At the same time, she is still inwardly incredulous: 'I can't believe it. This simply cannot be. This must be some terrible joke – that my sister is Queen!'[1]

At this point, Fiona Lansdowne is just focusing on getting to the other end of the abbey. 'I was quite busy concentrating on walking very slowly and not tripping up,' she says later. 'But just walking behind [the Queen] and knowing that she felt confident was a great thing.'[2]

The King and Queen reach their Chairs of State and wait for the last notes of Sir Hubert Parry to subside. At which point Samuel Strachan steps forward and, as clear and composed as ever, recites his welcome from 'the children of the kingdom of God'. Having scoured all past Coronation liturgy for those sections of the service not strictly governed by constitutional or religious law, Alderton's committee has made a purposefully inclusive change to the very first part of the ceremony. Through history, it has always been the Archbishop who conducts the Recognition, presenting 'your undoubted King' to the East, South, West and North. Today, he is joined by former politician and diplomat Baroness Amos, the first black member of the

---

* Lord Airlie only missed the coronation of Elizabeth II because he was serving overseas with the Scots Guards. Less than two months after the coronation of Charles III, his family announced his death, on 26 June 2023.

Order of the Garter, Lady Elish Angiolini, the first female Lord Advocate of Scotland, and Christopher Finney GC, chairman of the Victoria Cross and George Cross Association. Each takes a point of the compass.

In the time-honoured way, the liturgy moves to the Coronation Oath whereby the monarch swears to govern according to 'respective laws and customs'. Not only is it prefaced by the Archbishop's line about 'people of all faiths and beliefs', but it omits the names of all the other countries where the King is head of state. The oath sworn by Elizabeth II named them all, from Australia and Ceylon to South Africa. This one alludes only to the 'Realms of your Possession', a tacit acceptance that the republican debate is a live issue in some of the remaining realms and today is not a day to poke it. The King works his way through his responses methodically. He is deep in the constitutional smallprint here and it is better to be workmanlike than theatrical. There is also the Accession Declaration Oath, whereby the King promises to be 'a faithful Protestant'. Both must be signed. The King's equerry, Lieutenant Colonel Johnny Thompson, steps forward with desk and pen. For one day only Thompson has been renamed 'The Groom of the Robes' and is much in evidence throughout. For a ghastly moment, it looks as if there is a problem with this pen, too, but after a second go at the 'C' of 'Charles', the ink begins to flow.

By now, social media has clocked a constant presence in the corner. Penny Mordaunt's unflinching posture with the Sword of State and her outfit have won broad approval online. Even her opponents think so. 'Got to say it,' Labour frontbencher Emily Thornberry tells Twitter, 'the sword bearer steals the show.' Mordaunt will receive hundreds of letters in the weeks ahead, including – to her delight – many from young girls who have drawn pictures of her. So much for being a 'blank canvas'.

She is totally unaware of this at the time. 'I was concentrating on being expressionless,' she recalled later, 'and trying not to fall over.'[3] Mordaunt is proving more sturdy than some of the heralds. During the disastrous dress rehearsal two days earlier, the Duke of Norfolk had been concerned that some of them were starting to flag and has since issued orders that they should rotate at regular intervals during the service.

The prime minister's epistle and Justin Welby's sermon – short, as promised, and restating the theme of 'a King to serve' – are precursors to the most sacred moment. It is the one which requires the most choreography. The King must be divested of his Robe of State and all his finery before moving to St Edward's Chair for the anointing, or what the Palace team have been calling 'the Solomon moment', since the Old Testament king is the template. It has to be done at a certain pace, too, in order to hit the thunderous entry of the choir during Handel's Zadok the Priest. During the chaotic dress rehearsal, the bishops were still fiddling with the robes when 'Zadok' burst forth. This prompted an ugly moment when Mark Birch asked the director of music if he would play Zadok a little slower next time (he would not). It is all exactly on time today, however. The television cameras briefly capture the King in his shirt as the Anointing Screen is marched into position by the screen-bearers from the Household Division. The opening bars of Zadok the Priest ordain what is coming next. Equerry-turned-Groom of the Robes Johnny Thompson takes charge, undoes the last hooks of the kingly vestments and waits for the stupendous chorus to crash in before nodding to the two bishops to remove the robes.

The shirt-sleeved monarch then disappears. Aside from the King and clergy, Penny Mordaunt is the only other figure at the business end of proceedings. Even the Queen and the rest

of the family cannot see what is happening. 'It was very carefully staged to ensure that it was only those people who were
involved in the anointing that could peer in,' Mordaunt recalls
later. 'And I actually lowered my eyes because it was just this
incredibly important central moment of the whole service.'[4]

It transpires that there was originally some debate within
the Palace as to whether this moment should be made public.
'It felt extraordinarily intimate,' the Archbishop of Canterbury
explains later. 'Yes, there's a billion people watching, but this
was a moment where it felt we were almost alone. There was
a sense of the presence of God that was utterly indescribable.'
Alderton and his committee had been under strong pressure
from the BBC to let them film 'the Solomon moment' but had
stood firm. Alderton argued that some things should remain
unknowable. 'The mystery of monarchy had to be preserved,'
insists one of his team. 'The King needed a few seconds out
of the public gaze to make his own pact with his Maker. The
BBC got very cross.'[5]

The King is now gradually reclothed in the gold Supertunica,
the Imperial Mantle and all the other symbolic finery. 'I could
see directly to where the King was stripped down to that linen
shirt and then, slowly, layer upon layer of "kingliness" being
put upon him – those extraordinary gold precious robes,' the
Marchioness of Lansdowne recalls. 'Spiritually it meant a huge
amount to him.' Fiona Lansdowne has taken the bold decision
not to wear her glasses today. 'I couldn't actually read the
service sheet but I have got a memory for music and I knew
my cues from the music. We knew that when a hymn started,
we were supposed to walk here or do this.'

Outside, the rain is bucketing down but there are still large
numbers around the country who want to congregate en masse,
even in the wet, rather than watch this at home. At the

Charles III

Badminton Horse Trials in Gloucestershire, one of the sporting events of the year, the crowds are entirely untroubled by the rain and flock to the big open-air screens as the dressage competition is put on hold for the duration of the service. In London's Hyde Park, there are similar scenes. When Lord Singh comes up to present the glove, a huge cheer breaks out among a large Sikh contingent. A nearby Hindu family do the same as Lord Patel appears.

The King is working his way through the regalia laid before him, almost ticking it off piece by piece, as he steels himself for the crowning. There is total silence as the Dean, dressed in a cope which was worn at the coronation of Charles II, transfers St Edward's Crown from the altar to the Archbishop. 'I had to go down three steps and I couldn't see the steps because I had the crown in front of me,' the Dean admits later. 'I knew the one thing I really mustn't do is fall down. That was absolutely not acceptable.' However tempting, the King does his best to resist looking up. The majesty of perhaps the most extraordinary moment of his life lies in his complete powerlessness. He, quite literally, cannot move. Effectively trapped by his robes, his bishops, his regalia and the burden of history, he is no longer so much a servant as a slave to destiny. Justin Welby slowly lowers the crown as the King has advised him to, front first and then back. Except he is not entirely sure of his first attempt. He lifts it slightly and has a second go before crouching down to double-check the level of the ermine, like a mason having one last squint at his brickwork. It is not the most elegant performance but the King gives him a look which bespeaks forgiveness and relief. He has a sceptre in each hand. They may be conferring great power upon him but the monarch can do nothing at all to adjust what is on his head as his hands are full. He looks almost endearingly helpless. Even the Royal

Family are awestruck by this moment. 'The actual crowning really is the moment that makes the difference,' the Princess Royal reflects later, recalling that 'sense of relief' eight months earlier as the crown was lifted from her mother's coffin. 'When the Crown goes on, you see that responsibility being moved on.'[6]

Around the abbey – and beyond – the cry goes up: 'God save the King!' 'That was amazing to see – the moment that the crown was put on the King's head,' Dr Jill Biden says later. Even fifteen rows from the front, the first lady has a good view of the proceedings, with a little help from some of the abbey staff. 'We were alphabetically seated, but the ushers were so kind and they said: "Come here . . . lean over this way a little bit more". So I had the perfect view of when the crown was put on his head. For me and for my granddaughter and for the people of the world – I mean, it was such an important moment.'[7]

Equally important is the fact that the Archbishop has secured a tight fit for the crown and (though the King has no idea), it is the right way round. 'I'm afraid that is going down in history,' Justin Welby says later, reflecting on his double-crowning at the key moment. 'You have to get it level or it wobbles. And the symbolism of a wobbly crown is not a good one. I just completely without thinking, ducked down to check the line of it.'[8]

The much-truncated homage is something of a relief for everyone. The Prince of Wales pledges his loyalty and then gives his father that kiss on the cheek, eliciting a contented smile from the King. In 1953, it had been a peck on the cheek from Prince Philip which made Elizabeth II smile, finally lowering her guard, just for a second or two. It's a moment when the human touch breaks through the ritual.

On the basis of what she has just seen, the new Queen may have her doubts about Justin Welby's crown-handling skills as her turn approaches. Following the Archbishop's modest 'dab' of oil, the Dean of Westminster lifts Queen Mary's Crown from the altar and marches down to present it with surprising speed. This coronation is certainly being conducted at a brisk pace.

The Archbishop is gentler this time and does not 'jam' on the Queen's crown, though she still needs to rearrange a few hairs. Unlike the King, she has both hands free at this juncture. For Annabel Elliot, thinking back to those unable to witness this moment – her late husband, her parents and her brother – this is the most challenging moment of the day. 'Obviously, the image that stays with me personally the strongest is when the Archbishop puts the crown on her,' she reflects later. 'I had to hold back the tears then.'[9]

The Queen and her companions turn to the King and curtsey. 'We were so lucky, Annabel and I, to be able to do that with her,' Fiona Lansdowne recalls, adding: 'and not fall over.'

It is the cue for Andrew Lloyd Webber's anthem. 'Make a Joyful Noise' does precisely what it says. The King has previously told the composer he had 'tears and goosebumps' when he heard it for the first time merely as a studio recording. Who can tell what he is feeling now? The Fanfare Trumpeters of the Royal Air Force give the piece a terrific lift-off before the choir launches in. The Queen is now looking palpably relieved. The most hazardous part of the ceremony is over. 'To start with, I thought she seemed very nervous,' Annabel Elliot remembers. 'But as the service progressed, I felt her get stronger and stronger. And by the end, I think she was flying.'[10] Across the aisle, Queen Camilla's son, Tom, and daughter, Laura, are watching with obvious pride, alongside their father. A page at the last coronation, a grandfather of three pages at this one, Brigadier Andrew Parker Bowles occupies his unique place in coronation history with good-humoured dignity throughout.

'I was glad'

The King and Queen briefly retire to St Edward's Chapel, behind the altar. It serves as a glorified vestry where they can remove their crowns and readjust before returning for Holy Communion. In 1953, this was one of those moments deemed too intimate for public consumption. Seventy years on, the television cameras still keep a respectful 1950s-style distance as the King and Queen receive the bread and wine. Television viewers can vaguely make out what is happening in the corner of a screen viewed from the other end of the Choir. The one lay person with a proper close-up view, as ever, is Penny Mordaunt.

Finally, the royal couple retire once more to the makeshift changing room in St Edward's Chapel. Robes and crowns must be prepared for departure while the congregation belt out 'Praise My Soul, the King of Heaven'. 'We went into the vestry and then it became a bit of a party,' says Annabel Elliot. 'We were there for about fifteen minutes and it did feel like a wedding. Everyone felt so happy.' She recalls the light-hearted reminders about who was supposed to wear what for the final procession: 'You know: "This is my crown. That's your crown!" It was terrific.'

For some, like one very old friend of the Queen, today has been an intensely emotional experience: 'When I think back to those days when Camilla was getting so much grief in the press and how she soldiered on without complaining out of loyalty and love and then you look at today – well I was in floods. This felt like proper closure.'[11]

An extended fanfare heralds the reappearance of the King, now in his Robe of Estate and the Imperial State Crown, the one which he will wear at state occasions for the rest of his reign. He is holding the Orb in his left hand and his sceptre in the right – very much undoubted, anointed, crowned and enthroned. The Queen retains Queen Mary's Crown, but now, at last, she is wearing her new Robe of Estate. The world can finally see all that magnificent embroidery by the Royal School of Needlework (and will make a closer inspection when the robe enjoys pride of place in the summer exhibition at Buckingham Palace). As the national anthem reaches the end of the first verse, the King is alongside the royal pews where the Princess of Wales and the Duchess of Edinburgh, both in the front row, plunge into floor-scraping curtseys. All the men bow, including the Duke of Sussex in row three. Indeed, tellingly, he drops his head for longer than most. Prince Louis, who has spent some of the service in a side room with his nanny, is back with his sister and parents for this moment. He has also very clearly memorized the words to the national anthem.

Led by the Earl Marshal and then by Penny Mordaunt, who has now swapped her hefty Sword of State for the lighter and more user-friendly Jewelled Sword of Offering, the procession moves slowly to the other end of the abbey. There is a sense of repressed elation that the whole thing has unfolded with only minimal and eminently forgivable glitches. The King teases the Archbishop about nearly forgetting to seek his approval before crowning the Queen. 'I hope we're not going to have to come back next week to do it all over again,' he jokes, to Welby's relief.[12] The Queen's smile is genuine and very much broader than it had been at the start. Fiona Lansdowne later reflects on the importance of having family all around her: 'Having those grandchildren actually gave her something else to focus on because she wanted them to do it perfectly. And they wanted to do it perfectly for her, which was so lovely. I've never seen them sit up so straight. All those boys were completely marvellous. They rose to the occasion in a fantastic way.'

At the Great West Door, the last of the tweaks and innovations is completed as the King pauses to receive the pledge of minority faith leaders to 'acknowledge the value of public service' and 'unite for the common good'. The numerous multifaith and ecumenical elements in today's ceremony, along with all the female participation, do constitute an historic departure from all previous coronations. Yet none of this has felt forced or disrespectful to the past. Other religions and denominations have been delighted to join in. Back in 1953, for example, the Roman Catholic Cardinal Archbishop of Westminster was nowhere to be seen. Today, he has not only been part of the service, offering a blessing. He has also lent the abbey a set of six matching gold copes so that all the Anglican bishops on parade can look smarter.

Outside, the Gold State Coach has drawn up, pulled by eight Windsor greys. At just after 1 p.m., two hours after entering the abbey, the King emerges. He thanks the Earl Marshal and throws him a mischievous look that says: 'I think we just about pulled that off'. There will be no timing issues with the return procession. Not only is it the largest parade since the previous coronation, with more than 4,000 troops marching and another 3,000 in support, it will also be the first one in which all the bass drummers are linked electronically through earpieces so that the entire parade is synchronized, marching in step to the same tune, from front to rear. Eight separate marching sections will be supported by nineteen bands. The operation is so big that the first rehearsal required the use of both runways at RAF Odiham. Fleets of special trains have been ferrying troops in from a network of training bases spread around southern England where they have all been practising hard (each base was even equipped with a 'blister clinic'). After this is all over, one of the Princess Royal's favourite photographs of the entire Coronation will be a shot of a trainload of Royal Marines, in full ceremonial kit, marching through a crowd of baffled rail passengers across the concourse of Waterloo Station.

Charles III

Major General Chris Ghika has set the pace of the procession at 108 paces per minute. 'It's slightly slower than a normal quick march – which is 116 – because it's the Gold State Coach. But you'd have to be a real drill aficionado to notice,' he says.[13]

Garrison Sergeant Major Andrew 'Vern' Stokes sets the entire show in motion with the order: 'The Coronation Procession, by the Centre, Quick March.' Every section of the armed forces is here. So, too, are 400 troops representing all the King's realms and most of the countries of the Commonwealth, though not two of the most important – India and South Africa. No official reason has been given. However, both these nations abstained from a recent United Nations vote calling on Russia to leave Ukraine. They may not wish to be seen marching alongside one of Ukraine's staunchest allies.

Riding immediately behind the Gold State Coach is the King's closest bodyguard, otherwise known as Gold Stick, otherwise known as the Colonel of the Blues & Royals, otherwise known as his sister. Other members of the family will travel in carriages but the Princess Royal wishes to undertake the time-honoured duty which goes with being Gold Stick (and it does indeed include carrying a gold stick). 'They were the earliest senior personal protection officer, your last line of defence,' she says afterwards, explaining her role. 'Although whether the gold stick was ever really designed to do much damage, I'm not quite sure. But it was certainly an indication of who you were.' She is also well aware that there can be a genuine protection role for the closest outriders on occasions like this. 'They do an exercise every year on how the mounted escorts will behave if anything happens. I've done that – but I don't think you'd want me to draw a sword!'[14]

Behind the Gold State Coach, also in carriages, come the 'working' members of the family, led by the Prince and

Princess of Wales, with their three children. The front of the procession is already halfway down the Mall as the King and Queen set off and the rain begins to ease. The crowds are, for the most part, thrilled, not just by the sight of the Gold State Coach – last seen actually carrying a monarch at the Queen's Golden Jubilee celebrations in 2002 – but by military pageantry on a scale not seen for a generation. There are naysayers, too. The television cameras in Trafalgar Square will not spin round to capture several hundred republican demonstrators who are chanting 'Not My King' on the corner of Northumberland Avenue and feeling, with some justification, that they have been victimized. Their main organizer, Graham Smith, was among those six people arrested earlier in the day – under new and controversial public order legislation – on suspicion of 'going equipped to lock on'. It seems that he was, in fact, collecting bundles of placards from a van. In the run-up to the Coronation, he had been in contact with police liaison officers to explain what he and his fellow protestors were planning. Yet it seems that this liaison team were nowhere to be found when he and his colleagues were arrested. The 'Coronation Six' will spend much of the day in custody before being released without charge, as will three people arrested in possession of rape alarms. Palace officials roll their eyes when they hear the news. Smith may have been lugubriously bemoaning the evils of heredity and monarchy for years on any platform which offers him an invitation, but he is manifestly not a threat. 'Of all the people you don't want to arrest on a day like this, Graham Smith is one of them,' says a senior courtier. Within the republican movement, where some would prefer a more dynamic figurehead, there is a similar sense of astonishment. 'Graham's going to be a martyr now,' sighs one. Less is known of the other arrests, which will lead to more than forty people being bailed for public order offences. It soon emerges that a plot to throw paint, by people posing as stewards, has been foiled.[15] The day could have been a lot worse for the police – and for the monarchy, not to mention British national pride.

As troops reach the palace, those not on horseback march through into the garden for another Coronation innovation. They are all to form up on the lawn for a rousing finale in front of the King. After the Queen's funeral, the Earl Marshal and his team had been determined that everyone on parade should be given the chance to pay their respects and see their sovereign with their own eyes. Hence the final assembly in front of the coffin at Wellington Arch. The same thinking has been applied today and Garrison Sergeant Major Vern Stokes has planned it all meticulously. The only person who was not happy was the head gardener at Buckingham Palace, where thousands of troops are now marching across the grass. According to Vern Stokes, it required 'a charm offensive like no other' to win him round.[16]

No sooner has the Gold State Coach brought the King and Queen home, than the Master of the Household leads all the staff in a 'three cheers' as they come through the door. 'There was such an air of celebration. Everybody was sort of "Phew, take your shoes off",' says Annabel Elliot. Except that the King and Queen have yet to remove their crowns, let alone their shoes. They walk through the Bow Room and out onto the West Terrace overlooking the lawn. There the King receives an even more robust three cheers, led by the Garrison Sergeant Major. The noise carries over the palace and into the Mall. 'I could see the King's profile,' Fiona Lansdowne recalled. 'He loved that moment.'

The crowds are now being allowed to spill through the police barriers and down the Mall for the balcony appearance and the tri-service flypast. The weather has already forced the cancellation of what would have been one of the biggest airborne salutes in many years. It will now be helicopters-only today. The fixed-wing aircraft will have their turn soon enough, when they are invited back for the King's Birthday Parade in June. Today is unique. It is the only time the King will appear robed and crowned on the balcony, in front of the people. After today, the Imperial State Crown returns to the Tower, save for the occasional appearance in Parliament.

The Royal Family have to tread carefully on their way through to the Centre Room, just behind the balcony. The principal corridor is still a building site with bare floorboards, although the room itself has just been restored to its Queen Mary-era colour scheme of pale green walls, red carpet and swirling gilt cornices – plus a television for monitoring what is happening on the other side of the net curtains. From the age of two, Prince Charles would come out through these doors to see and hear the crowds, after the mandatory pep talk.* Today, for the first time, though, he is the one leading the rest of the family.

As in the abbey earlier, so the same principle applies here. Only those who are still undertaking official royal duties and appearing in the Court Circular are asked out onto the balcony. They are the 'working royals' in other words (plus the children of the Waleses and the Edinburghs). However, the King also extends the invitation to a few other guests, notably the Queen's two Companions and the pages. 'There were lots of photographs and lunch and drinks and just general happiness,' says Annabel Elliot later, 'and then this extraordinary thing –

---

* Recalling his own childhood balcony memories, the Queen's eldest grandchild, Peter Phillips, revealed to me the two golden rules drummed into younger royalty: 'Don't pick your nose. Don't yawn.'

which certainly we weren't expecting – of being called out onto the balcony. This really can't be true! This amazing noise and the sea of faces and the cheering – mind-blowing. I felt it was overwhelmingly positive. It seemed like something you see in a movie.' The royal wave, she says, is infectious. 'Me and the boys – we found ourselves waving as well. We were so caught up with the moment.'[17] The King and Queen are thrilled by the public response. 'Let's face it,' Elliot acknowledges, 'it wasn't the best day with the rain teeming down and yet so many people had turned out for them. I think he was very, very moved by it.'

The public appearances are now over. The royal couple now join the other members of the family who have remained inside, enjoying the drinks and the buffet lunch. All those who were in the royal seats at the abbey have been asked, including the Duke of York and the Middletons. The page boys, meanwhile, are happily back in the room full of video games. Everyone is invited to take part in the Coronation photographs and will receive copies for private use. Just a handful of official images will be released to the media, however. They will only feature those members of the family with public royal roles, so the argument goes, since the underlying theme of the day has been public service. One royal guest will not be in any of the photographs at all, even though he was invited back to the palace. The Duke of Sussex is already on his way to Heathrow Airport to catch a plane back to California. He has shown his support for his father and that is what he came to do. Today is not the moment to begin to patch up wounds still raw to the touch.

On the evening after her Coronation in 1953, the late Queen was expected to make repeated appearances on the balcony and also to broadcast to the Commonwealth. London would party on long into the night. There were balls, fireworks and special licences allowing pubs to stay open as late as 3 a.m. One source of particular excitement was the relaxation of the meat ration to permit ox roasts, the first since before the war. Lady Rosemary Muir recalls that, despite the privilege of being the senior maid of honour at the Queen's coronation, she was summoned straight home to Blenheim Palace. 'I was expected to get back and help,' she says. 'As far as my mother was concerned, her ox roast was much more important than the Coronation.'[18]

Seven decades later – and nearly three times the age of Elizabeth II at her Coronation – Charles III and Queen Camilla want an early night. There is no need to pack everything into Coronation Day, because this is a long weekend. The following evening, they welcome 20,000 people to a special Coronation concert at Windsor Castle, screened live via the BBC. It inevitably invites media comparisons with some of those great jubilee pop concerts of years gone by, like the 2002 show when Brian May of Queen burst onto the palace roof and the real Queen won a gold disc from the music industry – or her 2022 Diamond Jubilee concert when she starred in a comedy sketch alongside Paddington Bear. As long as everyone else was enjoying the show, she couldn't have cared less who was on the bill (in 2002 it included the bat-eating heavy metal legend Ozzy Osbourne of whom, it is safe to say, Elizabeth II was not a big fan). Tonight is another case of doing the same things a little differently. There are some big names (Take That and Katie Perry among them), but there is also a strong save-the-planet theme, without being too preachy. The show includes two of the King's great loves, Shakespeare and opera. There are no beacons and no fireworks. We can take it as read that those two stalwart elements of so many royal celebrations over so many years have now been consigned to royal history. However, there is a drone-borne light show of such epic proportions (despite the close proximity of Heathrow Airport) that no one talks about the lack of bonfires or rockets. As the King knows all too well, these are moments when the younger generation has to step forward. For years, he would round off these great celebrations by appearing on stage to salute 'Mummy'. Tonight, he has the relief of leaving it to his heir. The Prince of Wales steps out in front of the audience and praises the King for embracing the environment 'long before it was an everyday issue'. He declares that, 'most importantly of all, my father has always understood that people of all faiths, all backgrounds and all communities deserve to be celebrated and supported'. And he invokes the memory of the late Queen – 'I know she's up there, keeping an eye on us.' The following day, however, there is one line which will dominate most of the newspaper headlines at the end of a weekend which has very clearly stamped the 'CIIIR' imprint on the future of the monarchy: 'Pa, we are all so proud of you.'

Chapter Fifteen

'Doctor Who syndrome'

This is precisely the sort of event so many constitutional experts told us we would never see again: a gathering of eco-activists, scientists, business people and politicians with Charles the royal meddler stirring things up – as King.

It was a scene we saw so often in his princely days that people came to expect this sort of thing. The former Prince of Wales probably reached 'peak meddling' at the 2021 COP 26 summit in Glasgow as world leaders queued up for a meeting with the royal activist who had helped pave the way for COP 1.[*] Even US President Joe Biden wanted an audience. Once the Prince was King, however, everyone proclaimed that all this sort of activity would come clattering to a halt, for fear of 'crossing a line'.

So why is Charles III packing the Buckingham Palace Picture Gallery with politically partisan agenda-setters and plying them with champagne? Is he not straying dangerously close to the political cliff edge?

[*] In 1991, the Prince held an environmental summit with the Brazilian president and Senator Al Gore on board the royal yacht in Brazil to lay down targets for the 1992 Rio Earth Summit. This, in turn, led to the first Conference of the Parties (COP1) summit in 1995, the annual climate change summit which continues to this day.

Charles III

Having looked at those areas where the King has taken over, in some cases seamlessly, from the late Queen, it is important to examine others which were always uniquely his domain as Prince of Wales. Can he retain some residual control? Or should these aspects of his former life now be shut down, as some constitutional experts insist?

Certainly not in the view of the politicians present here tonight, notably several members of the current government. For Britain has just been holding a biodiversity conference at nearby Lancaster House. It is a very worthy, dry-as-dust gathering designed to follow up on the previous year's breakthrough biodiversity summit in Montreal, where 200 countries signed a deal to protect a third of the world's land and sea.

When the Department for the Environment originally assessed the level of interest for this conference, most foreign governments nominated a senior civil servant, a diplomat or a junior minister to attend. However, an idea then emerged via one of the prime minister's weekly audiences with the King. The monarch let it be known he would be delighted to invite all the delegates to come across the road after their deliberations and enjoy a reception at the Palace. Suddenly, the complexion of the conference changed completely. It could now perhaps even call itself a summit.

'It's very simple. If it wasn't for him, most of these people wouldn't be here,' says Lord [Zac] Goldsmith, the (then) Foreign Office minister for Commonwealth and climate.* 'You could put him on a round table with any of these people – the bankers, the charity foundations, the ministers – and he has authority. Without him, there would have been smaller delegations and a lot more heavy lifting for us.'

---

* He resigned from government four months later.

'Doctor Who syndrome'

Samuel Jinapor is a case in point. As Ghana's minister of lands and natural resources and the country's interim minister for trade and industry, he had recently been in Davos meeting the US climate envoy, John Kerry. His next scheduled overseas mission after that was to have been a mining summit in South Africa. He was not planning to go anywhere during the weeks in between. 'I was too busy and I wasn't going to come to this. I was going to send someone else,' he says. 'But then I saw the invitation. I came because of the King and I have not regretted that at all. I came on the basis that I was asked by him and that alone.'[1] Dozens of environment ministers, from France, Brazil and South Africa, among others, have done the same.

The King is clearly among friends tonight. Tony Juniper, former director of Friends of the Earth, has co-written books with him in pre-accession days and does not hold back: 'The King is recognized as a leader on the most pressing matters affecting humanity. He has been doing this for more than five decades. He is the most significant environmental figure in history.' That is quite a bold accolade from one of Britain's most prominent environmentalists. Juniper, a former Green party parliamentary candidate, has been a vocal critic of government policy over the years, although, like the King, he has had to rein in his opinions since taking a government sinecure as chair of Natural England. He acknowledges the double-edged sword which comes with being monarch. 'His convening power has grown even higher and now it is unparalleled,' he says. 'But, with that comes heightened sensitivity.'

The senior Cabinet minister present here is the environment secretary, Dr Therese Coffey. Does she not worry that the King might eventually find himself straying into political waters by hosting events like this? Saving the planet is perfectly noble and innocuous enough as an aspiration, but the route to delivering that is fraught with political hazards. When, say, should the country fix its target for 'Net Zero' carbon emissions? In short, should the King be doing this? 'Bring it on,' replies Coffey. 'When you have these conversations, he'll unlock things. That's the beauty of our constitution.'

Within the King's team, there is an insistence that the ex-Prince of Wales does not have to undergo some sort of character transplant and morph into his late mother. Her steadfast lack of political engagement, even in private, is sometimes cited as the necessary benchmark for King Charles and those who will succeed him. Yet the well-documented skirmishes between George VI and, before him, George V and their respective prime ministers on a range of issues – while still operating within the constitutional rules – show that Elizabeth II was the exception as much as the rule. Her father, for example, was happy to make interventions on issues such as the introduction of the welfare state or the appointment of a foreign secretary. George V had numerous spats with Downing Street. No one accused them of crossing a line. Each monarch is different – 'because people are different,' as the Princess Royal points out.[2]

One senior member of the King's team calls it 'Doctor Who syndrome,' after the long-running BBC television series. To date, Doctor Who has been played by thirteen different people while ostensibly remaining the same character. 'The monarchy has to reinvent itself in a similar way but not an identical way,' says his adviser. Receptions like these are a case in point. The Queen held themed events but they were always of a more mainstream nature – for the fashion world, for example – or else if Britain was staging a major gathering of heads of state, such as a G7 summit. 'Now, though, there is more thought given to working in a different way with government for a better return,' says one of the King's team. 'We've got these buildings so let's "sweat the assets" as they say.' One of the first examples was in the run-up to the COP 27 summit which was due to take place in Egypt within weeks of the late Queen's funeral. Some media reports suggested that the King was 'champing at the bit' to go and 'disappointed' when the government told him that he could not attend.[3] Ministers then attempted to paint it as the King's personal decision not to go. The King's officials were irked on both counts. First, he was quite content to abide by the ministerial advice and, second, it was not his personal decision. Both the King and the Foreign Office could see that the considerable diplomatic impact of his first overseas trip as sovereign would be diluted if not wasted were he simply to be one of more than 150 world leaders in a conference centre. What's more he had a plan for one of his new-style royal receptions. Why not invite all the big hitters heading for COP 27 to an event at Buckingham Palace en route? No matter if it had to be done at short notice. So, on the eve of the summit, the US climate envoy, John Kerry, and the head of the International Monetary Fund, Kristalina Georgieva, were among more than 300 guests at the King's party. He did not make a speech (he left that to the prime minister) but there was no doubt who was the main draw. The cast list merely underlined the power of his address book. It also made the COP organizers all the more determined to give the King star billing in future.

It was the success of this event which, in turn, has prompted semi-regular discussions with Downing Street on other ways of 'sweating the assets.' Back at the biodiversity reception (where, once again, the King makes no speech), the British politicians present say that the King should be encouraged to do as much of this sort of thing as he can. 'He does have that convening power. He believes that words don't butter many parsnips – you have to follow through,' says Lord [Richard] Benyon, minister for biosecurity. 'He is one of the great conveners. I'd put him alongside Mandela and Clinton in his day.'

Superficially, the King seems to be pursuing all the causes he used to champion only on an even grander scale, but without the speech-making. This sort of kingly 'activism-lite' might come as a surprise after all those warnings from royal experts that the King would have to take some monastic vow of constitutional abstinence, but it had actually been Prince Charles's plan all along. At the time of his sixtieth birthday, in 2008, he explained how he envisaged life as a semi-activist monarch. 'Eventually people might realize that some of the things I have been trying to do are not all that mad,' he told me, 'and that I might still have some convening power that could be brought to use for various purposes . . . like the halting of the deforestation of the rainforests.'

In other words, we can't say we weren't warned. We will no longer hear broadsides against modern architecture, of course, or stark warnings that 'we cannot have capitalism without nature's capital'[4] or that there are only 'eight years left to save the planet' (his doom-laden prediction ahead of the 2009 Copenhagen COP 15 summit). However, we can expect to see key players in most of these debates still crunching their way across the quadrangle of Buckingham Palace.

Just a day after acceding to the throne, the King was quite clear that things were going to have to change in terms of his personal causes and passions. 'I know this important work will go on in the trusted hands of others,' he said in his televised address to the nation. It would, self-evidently, be a wrench. In some cases, though, there would be no hands more trusted than his own. Nine months after his accession, he was still to be found walking the streets of Poundbury – the town he has created in his own image – with a full team of architects. Staff carried armfuls of plans so that the King could inspect the final stages of development for the nearly finished Dorset new town. It was, by this point, no longer his domain since the Duchy of Cornwall, which owns the undeveloped land and retains regulatory oversight of Poundbury, has passed to the new Prince of Wales. No one, though, is going to quibble if the King remains involved. It is, unquestionably, his handiwork, a town designed on classical lines around human rather than four-wheeled traffic. The residents were out in force to welcome the founding father on his tour of inspection with Queen Camilla. Even a couple enjoying a sauna at Poundbury's new beauty spa emerged in their bathrobes to say 'hello'. For centuries to come, Poundbury will stand (or fall) as a monument to Charles III. He had to fight officialdom and his own advisers to get the first houses off the ground in the 1990s and endure the barbs of modernisers routinely mocking his 'pastiche' architectural tastes. 'A deadly place, making up for what it lacks in soul and vitality with ogee curves and pop antiquarianism,' sniffed an *Observer* critic in 2009.[5] At around the same time, Labour Cabinet minister Hazel Blears said that Poundbury was about 'paternalism' and 'aggrandisement' rather than solving a housing shortage.[6] Yet, the King stuck to his guns and the buyers kept on coming. By the time of his accession to the throne, Poundbury had more than 5,000 residents, a growing school and more than 200 businesses (but still no yellow lines or traffic warden). Given that the 'deadly' project was close to completion and manifestly alive, its critics had given up sniping.

A building project, however, is finite. His broader network of charities and patronages, over his years as Prince of Wales, is not. To what extent is he now obliged, as King, to offload these concerns? And which aims and which organizations can he continue to claim as his own?

In the weeks after his accession, all 420 existing patronages were told that they were under review, that they should expect a few changes and that it would not happen immediately. Having spent the longest spell in history as heir to the throne, he came to the throne with a great deal of baggage. It was always going to take a long time to disentangle the network of all those princely patronages plus more than 600 in the name of the late Queen and then reallocate some while letting others go. Those with 'The Prince' in their name would, understandably, receive the closest attention, along with others he had also founded himself, like the British Asian Trust. It would not be until July 2023 that the first of these formally moved to a new post-princely modus operandi. He had created the Prince's Countryside Fund (PCF) in 2010 to help prop up what he regards as the backbone of the countryside, the small family-run farm. This was placed under the umbrella of the Prince of Wales's Charitable Fund, one of his three core charity networks (and the beneficiary of his Duchy Original Biscuits). Post-accession, the PCF would henceforth become entirely independent and eventually call itself the Royal Countryside Fund. It was all done with his blessing, though it was not down to him to approve the 'Royal' designation. This required government approval under the Companies Act 2006. Ministers retain a role in agreeing what may or may not present itself as a royal entity. It was the lack of such approval that compelled the Duke and Duchess of Sussex to take down their 'sussexroyal.com' business/charity franchise in 2020 and grudgingly rename it 'Archewell'. It also emerged that the Prince's Countryside Fund had considered the name 'The King's Countryside Fund', but the King himself advised against it.[7] He wanted it to look far beyond his own lifetime. So 'Royal' it was.

Another core network is the Prince's Foundation. This

focuses on heritage, regeneration and traditional skills based around the former Prince of Wales's biggest gamble. In 2007, he underwrote a £20 million loan to help buy Dumfries House in Scotland, a hitherto private stately home with one of the finest collections of Chippendale furniture in existence. Since then, the house and grounds have opened to the public, helping to drive the regeneration of a run-down, ex-coalmining corner of Ayrshire. Overgrown for many years, the estate has been rejuvenated, becoming a campus for arts, crafts and design while the nearby town of New Cumnock has enjoyed a complete makeover. Hundreds of jobs have been created as a result. A long list of educational and practical courses, ranging from integrated health to bricklaying, are now offered to all ages from primary school to post-graduate level. In so many ways, it has been a masterclass in regeneration – but at a cost. All this has been paid for by private donations, following years of dogged princely fundraising. In 2021, however, the foundation's chief executive, Michael Fawcett, resigned following press reports that a generous Saudi businessman had been offered help in securing a knighthood and British citizenship. An eighteen-month Metropolitan Police investigation ensued, investigating possible offences under the Honours (Prevention of Abuses) Act 1925 and the Bribery Act 2010. A file was sent to the Crown Prosecution Service in October 2022 but, in August 2023, the police concluded that 'no further action will be taken'.

Palace officials insisted that the King knew nothing of any offers of help to a potential donor. He was also aggrieved to lose Fawcett, a devoted long-serving former valet who had been instrumental in building up the Dumfries House operation. Other press reports of hefty cash donations from Middle Eastern sources many years earlier created further embarrassment.

The donations had all been accounted for with demonstrable results, but even the Prince's greatest admirers had acknowledged that this territory would be problematic when he became King. Of all the charities created in his name, the Prince's Foundation is now the most challenging when it comes to establishing an independent post-princely existence. The King still stays at Dumfries House and takes a keen interest in all its works. It has been a monumental achievement. In 2023, a new chief executive was appointed. Ahead of the King's 75th birthday, a new name was announced, too: The King's Foundation.

The greatest speculation was always going to centre on his philanthropic flagship, the Prince's Trust, the youth charity which he founded with his Royal Navy severance pay – £7,400 – in 1976. As with so many projects, it was not an easy start. The Queen's then private secretary, Martin Charteris, asked the Prince's private secretary to 'go easy on the trust Prince Charles has in mind', fearing that it would clash with other royal charities.[8] There was the ever-present anxiety that it might also stray into political territory. Not for the first time, this had the effect of both irritating the Prince and making him even more determined. His focus was on delivering tangible results at street level in the most deprived parts of his future kingdom. Initial grants included giving funds to two ex-offenders to help them set up a fishing club. There was a small grant for hiring swimming baths in Cornwall to train lifeguards. In 1977, he found himself in competition with the Silver Jubilee fund, created on the back of the Queen's twenty-fifth anniversary on the throne, which raised £14 million. The Prince, in contrast, had raised next to nothing. Indeed, it was only thanks to individual contributions like the £2,000 proceeds from a concert by his friend Harry Secombe that the trust even remained solvent.[9] The Prince stuck with it, though, and, ten years later, he was handing out grants of £300,000 a year. Offshoots like the Prince's Youth Business Trust evolved. By the mid-nineties, the trust had a turnover of £10 million and some of its pilot schemes were being copied by both the main political parties as policy initiatives. It would go on to become the largest charitable network of its kind, offering grants, training and mentoring to young people across the country. In 2020, it notched up its one millionth participant and in 2022 it had an annual income of £80 million (£50 million of that sum in government grants to run more than a hundred different programmes). The Prince's Trust had always known that it would need to prepare itself for a post-princely existence, although given the strength of the brand, there would inevitably be a vigorous debate about any change of name. In November 2023, however, the trustees decided that the charity should follow their founder and become The King's Trust. He might no longer be able to take executive decisions as of old, but the King would remain a devoted patron, amassing a healthy roster of celebrity ambassadors to bolster the trust's public profile.

There is a foretaste of this new arrangement just a couple of weeks after the Coronation. It is the day after the Prince's Trust Awards, a big annual show featuring plenty of famous faces at a theatre in London's West End. This year, though, there is an extra ceremony. The King has invited all of them to a reception at Buckingham Palace. In his days as Prince, he was able to stage the occasional event in the state apartments of St James's Palace, but not royal headquarters itself. Today's event is a pretty clear statement of intent in terms of his continued involvement with this core charity. The trust's chief executive, Jonathan Townsend, says that, in many ways, nothing has changed at all. He used to have a meeting with the Prince of Wales three times a year. Since the Prince became King, he has had three more.

One of the youngest award winners is Pearse Doherty, from Belfast. He has received the trust's education award for persevering with his dream of becoming a qualified youth worker, despite caring for his mother, coping with the suicide of his brother, becoming a father at the age of fourteen and a diagnosis of ADHD. The King has a long chat with him. Doherty is still trying to take it all in. He comes from a Catholic area of Belfast where there is little love for the monarchy. He has never been to London before and, all of a sudden, he is at the Palace having a drink with the King. 'It wasn't just one of those things where he shakes hands and walks off,' says Doherty afterwards. 'It was a real conversation, back and forth, as if you weren't talking to a King. He's here to congratulate you, not for you to congratulate him.'

The King is introduced to another teenage award-winner from Northern Ireland. Motaz Amer moved there after his family fled the civil war in Yemen and were granted asylum in the UK. The Prince's Trust has helped him with training programmes which have enabled him to get a part-time job while he works towards the qualifications he needs to get into dental school. Jonathan Townsend does the introductions. 'Motaz was originally from the Sudan,' he tells the King. 'Yemen!' interrupts the King, who has clearly read his briefing notes, adding: 'I always wanted to go there.' They discuss Motaz's journey from Yemen to the UK. ' It's amazing how many refugees end up in Belfast,' the King reflects, adding: 'Are your parents here? Will you give them my best wishes. I must come and visit the Yemeni community.' At the end, the young award-winner tells him: 'This belongs to you, Sir.' Afterwards, he says he is thrilled that the King actually knew – and corrected – his story.

The monarch formerly known as Prince is always thrilled, understandably, when he hears how the Prince's Trust has changed a life. Today's guests include two brothers, Graham and Mark Wray, who grew up in the Toxteth area of Liverpool in the 1980s. They were at school when Toxteth suffered some of the worst rioting seen in post-war Britain.* 'I left school soon after and there I was aged sixteen with a speech impediment,' says Graham. 'But we'd heard about the Prince's Trust so we went to see the lady with the diary and she opened it up.' The trust's regional co-ordinator came round to their mother's house, listened to their business plan and said it was 'a good idea.' 'You've no idea what it does to your confidence when someone says that to you at sixteen.' Armed with a grant of £3,000, they bought the boiler suits, scales and cutting machines required to start up a business making cloths and other cleaning products. Four decades later, they are still in the same area, currently employ twenty-eight people and have diversified into other areas, including commercial property. 'We're a genuine rags to riches story,' Graham jokes.

'Did I not meet you all those years ago?' says the King, trying to remember the nature of the original business. 'Rags and wipers,' Mark chips in. 'Wipers – that's fantastic,' the monarch replies. 'It's such a joy to see you. You look so distinguished.' He tells them how happy he is when Trust alumni 'come out of the woodwork.'

It is quite an emotional moment for the Wrays. 'We're here because that guy gave three thousand quid to two fellas with no skills in the middle of Toxteth four years after the riots,' says Mark afterwards. 'No one else was going to give us three thousand – but he did. We've been through five recessions.

---

* The Toxteth riots occurred days before Prince Charles's marriage to Lady Diana Spencer, and three months after major rioting in Brixton, south London. The Prince took a special interest in both areas for many years thereafter.

Woolworths and MFI and loads of others aren't there any more but we are. That money's still seeping into the local economy. Without him, the best I'd have managed in life is probably the assembly line at Ford's.'

There are plenty of celebrity 'ambassadors' for the trust here. Some have joined recently, like the UK's 2022 Eurovision star Sam Ryder. 'I've been to a few awards shows and most leave you feeling empty but this one fills your cup,' he says.

Television presenters Anthony McPartlin and Declan Donnelly, better known as Ant and Dec, reflect that they have been involved with the trust for so long that they will soon be marking their own silver jubilee. 'It's coming up to twenty-five years of being involved,' says Ant. The pair were born at around the same time as the trust and grew up hearing about it. 'People in our school knew that if you needed a grant to get into the workplace, you applied to the Prince's Trust,' says Ant. 'I have a friend, John, who started with a Prince's Trust grant and is still going strong. Now he has a pipe-fitting business here in London but he started out as a kid in Newcastle.'

It has inspired the two presenters to introduce their own Prince's Trust training programme within their production company, to help young people enter the television industry. They have come to know the King well over the years, but were still surprised to be asked to his Coronation. 'It was just mind-blowing. I don't get this feeling very often but I felt as if I'd climbed inside the TV,' says Dec. 'Our families couldn't quite believe we'd been invited – two working-class lads from the west end of Newcastle and we end up at a coronation. You never know which direction your life's going to take you.'

Unless, that is, you were born Prince Charles. His direction of travel was mapped out from the cradle. 'I have been told that the senior nanny at the time always referred to my senior brother as "the future King",' recalls the Princess Royal. 'So, presumably, I was brought up to believe that I had to know my place!'[10] The Princess hints that the King may now have to curb some of his former enthusiasms. 'Not everybody will share your particular interests. When you're a monarch, it's quite important that you don't have too many passions, because not everybody will feel them,' she says. 'I don't envy him this last year. To assume you can go on doing the things that you did before, it's probably not going to work because you suddenly find you just don't have that time available. And you don't have the choices available that you had before.'

There are, though, one or two areas where the King can break with the past, stamp his identity and experiment away to his heart's content. Gardening is one. Hence one of the first decisions after the accession was his plan to dig up the west lawn at Sandringham to make way for a new topiary garden. It would include the yew hedges which were used in and around the abbey at his Coronation. The King's grandfather, George VI, was an avid gardener who would regularly dragoon his protection officers into helping out in the grounds of Royal Lodge. However, no modern monarch has been quite as dedicated to gardening as Charles, whom some experts have called the 'Gardener King'.[11] 'My grandfather and my grandmother were very keen gardeners. Maybe there's a bit of heredity in this,' he told me when he was Prince of Wales. 'When my sister and I were small we had a little tiny plot – you know, hidden away at the back of a wall at Buckingham Palace. And we used to fiddle about and grow tomatoes.'[12]

This grew into a great passion after he moved to Highgrove in 1980, attracted to the place as much by the landscape as the house. 'It was the setting that I rather liked – the feeling of the fields around the house. And it had these rather wonderful old oaks dotted about.'

His garden designs, he said, would often come to him while asleep: 'It sounds perhaps silly to say but I have gardened to a certain extent from my dreams, which is very interesting. If you garden from your dreams, it's amazing the effect it has on other people.'

As Prince of Wales, he was sometimes accused of extravagance because of the ten gardeners he once had on the payroll at Highgrove. Friends acknowledge that gardens are his weak spot; quite apart from those at Highgrove and Birkhall, the restored walled garden at Dumfries House has been an astonishing, if costly, exercise. As monarch, he now has even more gardens to dream about and has recently embarked on a major new overhaul of the garden at Balmoral, complete with maze. Critics sometimes paint him as the big spender in contrast to the late Queen, with her love of cereal in Tupperware boxes and TV dinners. A senior ex-courtier veteran says this is unfair: 'He's accused of being extravagant because he likes to have the best things. She was more "Scottish frugal" in terms of her living style. The table would not be groaning under the weight of silver and gold whereas he loves to have the gold and silver on the table because it is in the cupboard anyway. When the Queen went to Balmoral or Sandringham, she would still take 117 staff with her. Some rich people spend their money on yachts, art, football clubs, that sort of thing. The King spends money on gardening. The late Queen spent her money – a lot more – on racehorses.'[13]

Gardens are a useful reflection of the character of their owners. Elizabeth II liked order, neat beds, roses and bright colours, even in the Highlands. Raymond Evison, whose clematis displays were always on her itinerary at the Chelsea Flower

Codename: 'Operation Patek'. St Edward's Crown is the centrepiece of every coronation. However, it needs to be stripped down, amid great secrecy and tight security, before it can be adjusted to fit the head of Charles III.

The King and Queen will each wear scarlet Robes of State for the initial stages of the Coronation and then depart wearing more elaborate purple Robes of Estate. The only new creation is the Queen's Robe of Estate, now taking shape at the Royal School of Needlework at Hampton Court.

US singer Lionel Richie and partner Lisa Parigi are among the 8,000 guests at the pre-Coronation garden party hosted by the King and Queen. Richie will be one of the stars at the Coronation Concert.

At the eve-of-Coronation reception at Buckingham Palace, the Princess of Wales greets the first lady of the USA, Dr Jill Biden, and her granddaughter, Finnegan.

Coronation Day, 6 May 2023. The Prince and Princess of Wales, with their two younger children between them, sit in the front row of the royal section in the South Transept. Prince Edward, now Duke of Edinburgh, sits in front of the Princess Royal, who, in turn, sits in front of the Duke of Sussex.

Bare-headed, Queen Camilla processes through Westminster Abbey accompanied by the 'Bishops Assistant', the pages of honour and the 'Queen's Companions'.

The Anointment. What the King's staff call 'the Solomon moment' will take place privately behind the Anointing Screen while the choir sings Handel's Zadok the Priest. Holy oil is dabbed on the King's hands, head and chest in a ritual rooted in the Old Testament.

The King is seated in St Edward's Chair and is finally invested with all the regalia. The Archbishop of Canterbury, Justin Welby, can now crown him with St Edward's Crown (which is only worn at this service).

The Prince of Wales pays homage to his father, promising
to be his 'liege man of life and limb'. He then kisses him.

One of many changes to the ancient ceremonial. As he leaves the abbey, the King is greeted
by leaders of all the main faiths in the name of 'public service' and 'the common good'.

The largest military parade in Britain since the previous coronation accompanies the Gold State Coach down the Mall and back to Buckingham Palace.

The King and Queen, wearing their crowns, plus their attendants and family members, appear on the palace balcony. The Duke of Sussex is already heading for the airport and a flight home to the USA.

As monarch, Charles III can no longer take an active role in organizations like the Prince's Trust, Britain's biggest charity in the field of youth opportunity. That does not mean he can no longer attend – or host – the annual celebration for winners of its awards. Buckingham Palace, 1 June 2023.

'C-Rex'. The King has been spotted wearing a number of ties which, say some, carry humorous coded messages. A particular favourite features a *Tyrannosaurus rex* motif.

To mark the 75th anniversary of the arrival in Britain of post-war workers from the Caribbean, the King commissioned a series of portraits of the 'Windrush generation' for the Royal Collection Trust. He then invited them to the palace with their families and friends for a grand unveiling.

Entente Cordiale. One year into the new reign, the King and Queen finally arrive in Paris for their delayed state visit. President Emmanuel Macron and his wife, Brigitte, welcome the royal couple to a state banquet at the Palace of Versailles. Over a dinner of blue lobster and chicken, the King tells his hosts: 'The United Kingdom will always be one of France's closest allies and best friends'.

Show, recalls the day she told him: 'I love clematis but they won't grow at Balmoral because they're not hardy enough.' When Evison said that they might, he was invited to Balmoral where, to her delight, he installed a sturdier variety that settled in happily. Charles III likes clematis, too (especially Evison's Duchess of Cornwall variety), but is equally passionate about his wildflowers, his hawthorn, his hostas, his hellebores and all the rest. A spot of verdant chaos is welcome. He loves his 'stumpery', a grove of gnarled old tree trunks which have sprouted their own ecosystems. Once popular with Victorian gardeners, the 'stumpery' has now enjoyed a modern revival thanks to the King. 'The stumps give it this rather extraordinary dream-like feel – almost Arthur Rackham-like,' he told me, referring to the early-twentieth-century book illustrator.[14]

The 2022 Chelsea Flower Show will go down in history as the last regular public engagement which was undertaken by Elizabeth II.* A year later, the King and Queen Camilla are the guests of honour. He might have been a semi-regular visitor in previous years, venturing only occasionally into an event which was identifiably his mother's patch. Now, that has changed. The Royal Horticultural Society has commissioned a special 'Garden of Royal Reflection & Celebration' to honour both the late monarch and the recent coronation of Charles III. The designer, Dave Green, has consulted the head gardener at Sandringham for the perfect selections for both. The result is a quiet, reflective space in the rear half of the garden, with orderly pinks, whites and a lot of roses, in honour of the late Queen. In the front section, Green has planted a riot of effusive blues, purples and

---

* Elizabeth II toured the site in a chauffeur-driven golf cart. She was delighted to see a Platinum Jubilee silhouette of herself made up of seventy pots of lily of the valley (her favourite).

busy woodland plants in keeping with the tastes of the King. Green describes the Elizabeth II section as 'tidy' while the Charles III area was 'more natural'. Others might even call it 'wild'. The garden is the natural place for the King to distribute a new RHS award called the Elizabeth Medal, for services to horticulture. The first three winners are here to be honoured. Afterwards, the King and Queen Camilla adjourn to the RHS reception where he can be heard earnestly dispensing one piece of advice to his hosts: 'Plant more trees!' Though the late Queen might have been less direct, she would surely have concurred with the sentiment – as, no doubt, would Doctor Who.

Chapter Sixteen

The Three Rs

The Buckingham Palace staff have rearranged the furniture once again. It is 14 June 2023 and the King is having yet another new-style bumper reception for 500. There is the usual mix of nerves and excitement as everyone flocks through the Grand Entrance, delighted to be here after all the anticipation, the worries about what to wear, the pride of their family in a loved one being summoned for drinks with the head of state. By no means all are royalists. No matter. This is a grand celebration of the guests, not the organizer.

It is an event which could easily feel distinctly political and synthetic. That it does not is down to the host. The seventy-fifth anniversary of the arrival of those destined to go down in history as the Windrush generation has prompted much soul-searching in the media, given the way some of them have been treated by the government in recent years.* The King, however,

---

*   In 2018, it was revealed that many post-war migrants from the West Indies, as well as some of their descendants – who had every right to be in Britain – had been deported or threatened with deportation over several years. The Home Office had kept no records of their status and their original entry papers had been destroyed. In 2020, the government's own Williams Report into the scandal found multiple failings and condemned a Home Office culture of 'disbelief and carelessness'.

had been an ally well before 'Windrush' had entered popular parlance in the way it is used now. It was in the year of his birth, 1948, that the first wave of migrants from the West Indies arrived in Britain, answering the call to help rebuild an ailing economy. Although people from the Caribbean had been in Britain for centuries, had fought in Nelson's navy and had served in both world wars, it was several hundred passengers on the troopship the *Empire Windrush*, travelling from Jamaica to Tilbury, who gave a name to this chapter in the story of modern Britain. Most of that generation would actually arrive in other ships or by other means, both before and long after the *Windrush* itself docked on 22 June 1948. In 1998, on the fiftieth anniversary, the Prince of Wales held a reception for them at St James's Palace to recognize their contribution to the UK. Now, a quarter of a century further on, their numbers are significantly smaller but their renown is considerably greater as Charles III welcomes them to royal HQ for the seventy-fifth anniversary.

He has also commissioned ten portraits of the Windrush generation from ten young black artists for the Royal Collection. This mirrors his previous projects to honour veterans of D-Day and survivors of the Holocaust. His idea is to capture the last witnesses to some of the key moments in modern history as well as to diversify and update the paintings within the Royal Collection.

The subjects of the new Windrush portraits and their families have all gathered in the main state apartments, together with the artists. There may be great masterpieces by Rubens, Vermeer and Van Dyck on the walls of his Picture Gallery, but no one is looking at those today. As a keen and accomplished watercolourist, the King has seen some of the preliminary Windrush sketches but today he will set eyes on the finished works for the first time.

'I hope it wasn't a great imposition,' he says to Delisser Bernard, ninety-four. Talk turns to Bernard's wartime service in the RAF. The King has done his homework and knows that Bernard's father served in the First World War. 'Your father was in the West Indies Regiment, wasn't he? Thank goodness he survived.'

Every one of these family groups tells a tale of grit, graft, love, hardship and modern Britishness. Delisser Bernard's daughter, Verona Elder, a former British Olympic runner who competed at the 400 metres during the seventies and won two Commonwealth gold medals, is wearing the MBE she received for services to athletics. Bernard's son, Roy, a businessman, is here with his wife, Caroline, who turns out to be the sister of Lucy Frazer, the Cabinet minister who played a key part in organizing the Coronation as secretary of state for culture. 'I hope she has survived,' the King jokes. It's just another reminder of the way in which the Windrush story overlaps, like a Venn diagram, with so many facets of national life.

Moments later the King is talking to Jessie Stephens, who arrived from St Lucia in 1955. She has devoted much of her life to liaison work between the police and the black community in the London borough of Haringey. She is here with her son Leee John, a member of the 1980s pop band Imagination. 'I'm just knocked off my feet that my mother's honoured with a portrait in Buckingham Palace in 2023,' he says. It turns out that he has actually met the King before, some years ago when his band was performing in aid of the Prince's Trust. Here too is family friend Leroy Logan, a retired superintendent in the Metropolitan Police and a founder of the National Black Police Association. He acknowledges that the monarchy faces challenges, not least in its appeal to young black Britain, but he believes that events like this show the way forward. 'You need to go out of your way to understand people in a different way, to identify their stories and speak with a degree of empathy – and that's what the King is doing,' he says. 'When you hear the same old same old, then people see through that. This is different.'

Today is in no way an attempt to gloss over past unhappiness. Baroness [Floella] Benjamin, the Trinidad-born broadcaster and author – whose nomination for the Order of Merit was one of the very last acts of the late Queen – has chaired the committee choosing both sitters and artists. She has been a stern critic of the government's handling of the Windrush scandal. She is adamant, however, that it should not be allowed to eclipse all that is being recognized today. 'The Windrush scandal is just part of the journey but we mustn't let this generation be defined by that. Today is a celebration.' She points out that the King's active support for Britain's minorities has always been a feature of his public work. She remembers her own first contact with him during the eighties when she wrote to thank the then Prince of Wales for recognizing the contribution of Britain's black community to public life. 'That was in 1984 and I reminded him the other day. He has always understood the importance of opportunities. Without opportunities you are nothing.'

Today is also a microcosm of what may yet prove to be one of the greatest challenges of the King's reign. All monarchs, to some extent, go down in history for issues or upheavals which have come to identify their reigns – empire and industrial revolution in the case of Victoria, prosperity and pomp under Edward VII, abdication in the case of Edward VIII, war and social upheaval with both George V and George VI, and the evolution of the Commonwealth in tandem with a multicultural Britain in the case of Elizabeth II. Charles III may well come to be remembered, if not judged, on his response to what one aide calls 'the three Rs' – race, realms and republicanism.

The Three Rs

On the day that he became King of the United Kingdom, Charles III additionally became King of fourteen other countries, known in royal and diplomatic terms as 'the realms'. From Canada to Australia and Tuvalu, they are independent countries once ruled by the United Kingdom as part of the British Empire but which have still chosen to retain the monarch as their head of state. In all of these, Charles III performs a constitutional role. Quite separately, he has also assumed the strictly non-constitutional role of Head of the Commonwealth. As such, he is the symbolic figurehead of an association of fifty-six nations, a uniquely mixed bag spanning every continent and every faith. They include all the realms, though many more are republics. Most were once British colonies. Some have their own monarchies.* A significant minority were nothing to do with the British Empire at all.

During the reign of Elizabeth II, the big question was whether the Commonwealth could survive deep divisions over some of the great international divides of the day, notably racial politics in Rhodesia and South Africa. For Charles III, there are – at present – no fears of a great schism. The organization is a paragon of unity compared to years gone by. In 2018, for example, its members were unanimous in endorsing the then Prince of Wales as future head. The role has never been hereditary. Elizabeth II was not appointed until the Indian prime minister, Jawaharlal Nehru, sent a telegram of condolence on the death of her father, adding that he 'welcomed' her as the new Head of the Commonwealth. The other member states then followed suit. Prince Charles was deemed to have earned it for his services both to the Commonwealth and to the environment over the previous half-century (for many low-lying

* Malaysia, Tonga, Brunei, Eswatini (formerly Swaziland) and Lesotho.

member states, climate change is now an existential threat).
'It was very clearly recognition of the personal role of the man
himself. They were not choosing the future King Charles III.
They were choosing Charles Windsor, in the light of his long-
term dedication both to the Commonwealth and to the planet,'
says one senior diplomat who was present. 'The view was that
the job would still be his, even if, for whatever reason, he did
not become monarch or even if he stopped being monarch.'[1]
It raises the intriguing (albeit highly improbable) possibility
that the King could, one day, cease to be sovereign of the United
Kingdom but continue as Head of the Commonwealth.

He faces a very different post-colonial challenge from that
which kept his mother awake at night. How should the King
deal with an increasingly vocal political narrative that Britain
(and, by extension, the monarchy and his royal ancestors) was
not, actually, on the right side of history and progress but,
rather, a force for bad – with debts still to pay? More to the
point, how should he navigate these arguments in his own
realms, especially among those descended from the enslaved
or from the indigenous populations who were conquered and
colonized? Indeed, might this be what finally prompts some
of them to abandon the monarchy altogether?

The last question was one familiar enough to Elizabeth II. In
the days after her death, it was suggested that many of her
realms had been reluctant to ditch the monarchy for as long as
she was alive, for fear of upsetting her or showing some sort of
disrespect. 'The era of warm, wave-and-smile relations between
the British monarchy and its distant realms has come to an end,'
pronounced *The New York Times* on the eve of the King's
Coronation. Hardly. By the time of her death, the late Queen
could count more ex-realms than existing ones. Countries had
been ditching her as head of state all through her reign, starting

with Pakistan in 1956 and Ghana in 1960. She lived to see eighteen countries dispense with her services, versus the fifteen (including the UK) which she handed on to her son. Her only caveat was always that any such change should be democratic. One aide recalls her reaction to the news that she was no longer going to be Queen of Barbados, following its parliamentary vote to become a republic in 2021: 'It was a shrug. As long as it was done properly, she would never take these things personally.'[2] That is because she always believed that her priority was to bolster the Commonwealth, not to worry about the number of nations within it which called her head of state. Her life's work, in Commonwealth terms, had always been focused on the future and on welcoming the new nation states into the 'family of nations'. After all, that had been the expectation when she came to the throne in 1952. The British Empire had come to an end in 1947, following the partition of India into the independent states of India and Pakistan. The modern Commonwealth was then specifically created with new rules to enable ex-colonies like India to become republics and still join the club.

It is this new and strongly political emphasis on the imperial past rather than the post-imperial future which marks an important difference between this reign and the last. Back in the days of decolonization, most newly independent nations had a forward-looking agenda rooted in self-determinism and self-confidence. Independence meant a seat at the United Nations for a new generation of home-grown leaders. As founding fathers of new nations, many were proud to stand as equals alongside a popular, glamorous and conciliatory figure like Elizabeth II, who shared their aspirations. On the Queen's first visit to India in 1961, for example, the Nehru government tried to expunge all references to the days of the Raj in favour of showing her the country's technological and industrial advances. Crowds of many millions turned out to see this almost mythical figure on her journey across the country. When Australia held a referendum on becoming a republic in 1999, the rallying cry was the need for a grown-up twenty-first-century constitution. It was not a plebiscite on a monarch who, in person, seemed dignified and affable. She would, in any case, return soon after the vote to make clear that there were no hard feelings. In the last few years, the arguments have pivoted through 180 degrees and intensified. A new generation of leaders, responding to social unrest, pandemics, global and environmental uncertainties and debates about race, have started to look in the opposite direction. With a mounting sense of historic injustice come growing calls for Britain to atone for imperial wrongs. Most troubling for the King is the underlying charge of historic racism in the name of the Crown. This is an issue which could have serious implications for perceptions of the modern monarchy overseas and, indeed, for the King's own role as Head of the Commonwealth.

For Charles III's accession coincides with concrete demands from states across the Caribbean for reparations from the UK and other former colonial nations for their part in 'native genocide' and the international slave trade, in which Britain played a major part until 1807 (with slavery itself not abolished until 1838). The debate had already started to gain prominence towards the end of the reign of Elizabeth II. The advent of the so-called 'culture wars' and social media's propensity for instant judgement simply gives it added potency. Within the Caribbean, it has received considerable added momentum through external factors. The rise of the Black Lives Matter movement in the USA, following the 2020 murder of George Floyd by a white policeman in Minneapolis, is one. The Windrush scandal has simply compounded a pan-regional sense of historic injustice. More recently, and more damagingly for the monarchy in particular, is a perception that the Duke and Duchess of Sussex have felt compelled to abandon their royal duties, in part, because of latent racism within the Royal Family and the Royal Household. 'Much of the Caribbean gets its news through US outlets and the US media were generally more sympathetic to Harry and Meghan,' says a former Palace aide. 'So Megxit plays directly into this debate.'

Collectively, these factors have unquestionably played a part in moves by some of the King's eight Caribbean realms to sever the royal constitutional link. This is often reported along the lines of 'Charles's Commonwealth crisis', when it is nothing of the sort. None of these nations has voiced any wish to leave the Commonwealth. None of them has (so far) expressed any issue with Charles III being Head of the Commonwealth either. At issue is whether he should remain as head of state of these individual nations. Though his presence is often painted as a remnant of imperialism, he is not their King for any other reason than this was the democratic will of the people at the time of independence.

While most ex-colonies opted for a republican constitution on becoming autonomous, some actively chose to retain the British monarch as head of state. In part, this was because the Crown was seen to confer greater stability and respectability on small nations taking their place on the world stage; in part, because the Crown offered various judicial functions – such as a court of appeal – free of charge through the Privy Council; in part, because it offered the people an added layer of protection from corrupt politicians and would-be dictators; in part, because it came with a ready-made honours system. It is harder to co-opt the military or the judiciary if they owe allegiance to the sovereign. Even Fidel Castro, the Marxist Cuban dictator, appreciated the merits of monarchy. In 1994, when the Antiguan prime minister Lester Bird told Castro that he wanted to remove the Queen as head of state, the dictator advised him to think again. 'Does she interfere?' he asked. She did not. 'So, why are you doing that?' argued Castro. 'You want to be a big tourist island and she's good for showing off your stability.'[3]

At the time of independence, this arrangement might have appealed to fledgling governments as a convenient transitional arrangement while they concentrated on more pressing matters. It was the British government which was actively discouraging it. As Professor Philip Murphy has revealed in his detailed study of the dismantling of the British Empire, UK officials were pressing departing colonies *not* to hang on to the Queen, describing it as a 'troublesome procedure.'[4] They much preferred to see a clean break and a republican constitution. Now, a couple of generations on from independence, a new political class is finally pushing for that constitutional change. This is not just on the grounds that it is demeaning to have an absentee white family automatically inheriting the role of head of state (Elizabethan republicanism, in other words). The more forceful and emotive argument is the claim that the monarchy was historically complicit in enslaving the ancestors of most of the population of the Caribbean and derived great wealth as a result. Previously, the emphasis in schools and popular history had been on the role of a young Queen Victoria in accelerating the end of slavery in 1838 (by overturning the 1834 Emancipation Act, which required slaves to serve as 'apprentices' for a further eight years). As for imperialism, by the time the Royal Titles Act formally created the British Empire with Victoria as Empress in 1876, slavery had already been abolished in British territories for more than forty years and the slave trade for nearly seventy. For all the faults of the British government, the monarchy was frequently portrayed through the prism of independence celebrations and the Commonwealth.

However, it is now the earlier actions of the original colonizers and their Tudor, Stuart and Hanoverian royal patrons which are being directly linked to modern-day grievances. This is shaping that new political narrative across the region. Royal support for the abolition of slavery, so the argument goes, can offer no hiding place for previous evils, which, in turn, must be linked to enduring inequalities suffered by today's descendants of the enslaved. For a twenty-first-century politician seeking to explain away current failings and also seeking potential future financial windfalls, the monarchy is, understandably, a tempting target. It certainly makes for an easier argument than disentangling the historic role of multiple governments and myriad commercial entities. Continuity, that all-important attribute of monarchy, works in both directions. If all historic injustices took place under the aegis of the Crown, then Charles III is now the obvious conduit for all retrospective justice.

Within British diplomatic circles, old Commonwealth hands also sense the covert influence of Chinese paymasters nudging the agenda. Having spent more than US $10 billion across six Caribbean nations (notably Jamaica and Guyana) since 2005,[5] Beijing is more powerful than ever and looking for diplomatic as well as financial returns. Any reduction of British soft power across the region is in its own interests. The late Queen was well aware of the rise of Chinese economic clout and influence in the region, and of the corresponding decline in British prestige. While Beijing could offer too-good-to-be-true financing for new roads, government buildings and grand sporting stadia through its 'Belt and Road' scheme, the UK's own overseas aid programmes looked minuscule. Instead, the former colonial power was generating dire headlines with its Windrush scandal and the Sussexes' allegations of racism. The signals were there for those who chose to look. In 2018, the same year as the Windrush saga was unfolding, the council of the University of the West Indies met behind closed doors and decided to amend its charter. After nearly seventy years, the Queen was to be removed as 'Visitor', the university's ultimate honorary position, and replaced by a Caribbean judge. Ironically, the decision required her own approval, through the Privy Council, which she duly granted.[6]

The King can do nothing to change history. However, perceptions of history are changing around him and, in the process, placing greater emphasis on uncomfortable truths about Britain's colonial past. The stories were always there – of the monstrous plantation owner, of the brutal quashing of a slave revolt, of murder, rape and unspeakable cruelty. In many cases, however, it is only now that they are receiving a wider audience and they are especially shocking to a new generation for whom human rights are seen as both universal and retrospective. The argument that every nation, European or African, lived by the entirely different moral codes of another age, offers the Crown no protection. How the King navigates this new mood will be a major test of his regal skills and authority. Though the manifest evil of the triangular trade involving human beings is beyond dispute, attempting to apportion liability several centuries later is bound to be complex and extremely divisive. 'It is a classic example of politicians setting up one community against another and that can never be good for cohesion,' says one very senior Caribbean ex-politician.[7] The King cannot know where the debate will go, nor how he is supposed to engage with it. He must abide by the advice of his prime minister in each of his realms. What happens if there is prime ministerial advice from one of his Caribbean governments to say something on this issue? If royal officials were then to shield the King behind the argument that this is a matter for the British government, then these realms could instantly argue that the King was no longer 'their' King anyway.

On the other hand, the King could find himself in constitutional trouble in the UK if he starts to take decisions or make statements which cut across British government policy, be it regarding slavery, reparations or ownership of museum artefacts. 'It's all very well people constantly demanding historic apologies from the King, but it is not always clear who should be apologizing for what,' says one adviser, pointing out that royal and government policy become increasingly blurred with the passage of time. Things perpetrated in the name of a Tudor autocrat, the adviser explains, cannot be judged to the same standards as policies enacted in the name of a Hanoverian monarch, like George III, who had relinquished executive control to his elected government (though, as his biographer Andrew Roberts notes, while the young George strongly opposed slavery, 'he did nothing to help abolish it when it became a practical political possibility . . . a moral blot on his reign').[8]

In July 2023, King Willem-Alexander of the Netherlands used the 160th anniversary of Holland's abolition of slavery to apologize on behalf of his country: 'On this day that we remember the Dutch history of slavery, I ask forgiveness for this crime against humanity.'[9] His words followed a formal apology by the Dutch prime minister, Mark Rutte. The Dutch government, however, has ruled out paying reparations.

This flatly contradicts the demands of the Caricom Reparations Commission, formally endorsed by the governments of all the

Caribbean member states in 2013, including all Charles III's realms. It explicitly calls for 'payment', 'debt cancellation' and 'monetary compensation' from governments of 'former colonial powers' and also from 'relevant institutions'. Its chairman, Professor Sir Hilary Beckles, vice-chancellor of the University of the West Indies, has stated that 'the movement for reparatory justice will become the greatest political and historical justice movement of the twenty-first century'. The monarchy, as well as the British government, is in its sights.

Regardless of his personal feelings, it is self-evident that the King has to tread extremely carefully as a constitutional monarch. One thing he can do of his own volition is to ensure that he is in full possession of the facts. As he told his hosts during his state visit to Kenya (his first, as monarch, to a Commonwealth nation) in November 2023: 'It matters greatly to me that I should deepen my own understanding of these wrongs'.

In 2022, before the death of the late Queen, a Manchester University academic, Camilla de Koning, had embarked on a PhD exploring the Crown's links to the early slave trade. She was supported by Historic Royal Palaces, the charity which runs five former royal residences, including the Tower of London. Due for completion by 2026, the project was granted access to the Royal Archives at Windsor Castle. HRP's role in de Koning's slavery study is significant given its close links to the monarch (who appoints four of the ten trustees). The research project only became public knowledge when it was reported in *The Guardian* in April 2023.[10] The Palace responded by saying that the Royal Household was 'supporting' the research, hence the access to the Royal Archives. Camilla de Koning was not the first academic to delve into royal links with slavery; many historians and several books have previously explored the monarchy's connection with slaving entities like the Royal African Company. However, the King was already developing more ambitious plans in this area. He wants a much broader investigation into the monarchy's role in the slave trade, in slavery and in the abolition of both. 'The HRP research is looking at one small piece of a much bigger jigsaw,' says one official. 'The King understands that this has to be done properly and objectively. He is absolutely not going to hide anything about the past.'

Even before *The Guardian*'s report, the King's officials had begun the process of assembling an eminent and authoritative panel to examine the subject and to begin working out a modus operandi. His staff have looked at the way in which academic institutions and charities have explored their own links to slavery – including universities, museums and heritage organizations. One blueprint under close scrutiny is the Church of England's approach to historic racial justice. Having conducted a forensic examination of Lambeth Palace's own slavery links, the Church Commissioners produced their response in January 2023. The Church's historic share portfolio had included lucrative investments in ventures involving the slave trade in the eighteenth century. This prompted a full and formal apology. 'It is now time to take action to address our shameful past,' declared the Archbishop of Canterbury, Justin Welby. 'Only by addressing our past transparently . . . can we face our present and future with integrity.'[11] Additionally, the commissioners pledged to invest £100 million over nine years to support further research and 'projects focused on improving opportunities for communities adversely impacted by historic slavery'. The Church has also established its own commission and directorate for racial justice. The commission is chaired by the former Cabinet minister and high commissioner to South Africa, Lord Boateng.

The directorate, which is charged with implementing the strategy, is led by Guy Hewitt, parish priest and London-born former high commissioner for Barbados to the UK. Both are well known to the King's team.

One senior British government minister, however, warns firmly against the King going down the Lambeth Palace route, arguing that these exercises ultimately satisfy no one and actually exacerbate ill feeling: 'Grievances can be addictive. But who is going to decide who has suffered, who caused it and who gets compensation? It's impossible. And once you start, it will never stop. The King has got to be very careful on this.'

Our instant revulsion upon hearing stories of centuries-past barbarism understandably lends itself to the campaign for twenty-first-century restorative justice. Seeking some sort of latter-day resolution is invariably not so simple. For example, another royal family in an awkward position is that of the former kingdom of Benin (now part of Nigeria and not to be confused with the republic of Benin). When British institutions, including Jesus College, Cambridge, and America's Smithsonian Museum, announced that they were returning stolen imperial artworks to the Oba (king) of Benin in 2022, it was heralded as the righting of a great wrong. The 'Benin Bronzes' had been taken by a punitive British military expedition in 1897. In 2023, however, geochemical analysis by German academics showed that the artworks were made from the European bronze rings or *manillas* with which Portuguese slave traders had been buying slaves from the rulers of Benin since the sixteenth century.[12] Separately, there has been an angry response and legal action in the USA. The New York-based Restitution Study Group has pointed out that the family to whom many of these bronzes are being returned had been among the richest and cruellest slave dealers on the West Coast of Africa. Since their wealth had come from selling their neighbours to 'Portuguese, Dutch, French and English traders,'[13] any restored treasures, the RSG claimed, should go to the descendants of the enslaved, not the heirs to the slavers.

It is one more reason for the King to insist on surrounding himself with all the facts. After a lifetime's support for modern Britain's evolution as a multi-cultural society, however, he sees the growing strength of these historic racial justice campaigns as an inevitability to be addressed with compassion rather than something to be feared or avoided. 'He understands that this has to begin somewhere,' says one of his staff. 'It's a journey that starts with the acknowledgement of pain and you can get a lot done once you have acknowledged someone's pain.'

His ready acceptance of the invitation to attend the transition of Barbados from realm to republic at the end of 2021 was an illustration of that. 'You had people in Britain – and at the Palace – viewing Barbados as a case of losing something,' says one of his team. 'We looked at it the other way and said: "He is a citizen of Barbados and how are most of the other citizens going to be feeling? They are going to be celebrating. So that is how the Prince should view it."'

The following summer, in June 2022, the debate about the British government's plans to send asylum-seekers to Rwanda exploded in the very month that the long-delayed 2020 Commonwealth summit finally took place in the Rwandan capital, Kigali. Newspapers reported that the Prince had privately described this key policy of Prime Minister Boris Johnson as 'appalling.'[14] These allegations did not elicit much of a denial from the Palace. The story eclipsed the significance of the Prince's speech at the summit's opening ceremony. After extolling the scope for the modern Commonwealth, and its appeal to nations (like Rwanda) with no historic ties to Britain, he was frank. 'I want to acknowledge that the roots of our contemporary association run deep into the most painful period of our history,' he said. 'I cannot describe the depths of my personal sorrow at the suffering of so many, as I continue to deepen my own understanding of slavery's enduring impact.'

In Barbados the year before, the Prince had spoken of the 'appalling atrocity of slavery' which 'forever stains our history'. Now, here in Rwanda, he was not just acknowledging it as a live issue but one with 'enduring' implications. As he put it starkly: 'Quite simply, this is a conversation whose time has come.'

That conversation was already well underway behind the scenes in the Prince's office long before his visits to Barbados or Rwanda. 'One of the first steps was his appointment of Eva Omaghomi,' says one official. Formerly a senior member of the Clarence House press team, Dr Omaghomi is a long-serving and popular straight-talking aide of Nigerian heritage who was seconded to the Prince's Trust network in 2019 to develop strategies for West Africa and the wider Commonwealth. In 2021, the Prince brought her back to his private office to take up a new post which he had created, with one eye on his future as monarch. She would (as noted previously) be his first 'director of community engagement'. The role would, very deliberately, avoid Royal Household terminology. Her mission was to ensure that the Prince's office was talking to the sort of people who wouldn't normally talk to the Prince's office. 'Eva's job was to be a bridge to the Household for people who might not know where to go to,' says a member of his team.

In the merger of the two households following the death of the Queen, Omaghomi was in the first tranche of those assigned to the King's new team, making her one of the most senior women and the most senior black person in the Royal Household. On any normal day of royal duties, she ensures that the schedule includes a broad and diverse cross-section of community groups, not just the usual suspects like mayors and council leaders. So, on a royal awayday to Leeds early in the reign, the itinerary included an engagement with 'The World Reimagined', a children's project designed to transform understanding of the Trans-Atlantic slave trade, and also a meeting with the Jamaica Society Leeds.

Omaghomi is also in contact with organizations like the Caricom Reparations Commission. As a senior Palace source explains: 'The King follows all these developments very closely. Eva's job is to get into that zone as it gets louder – as it will.'

'You don't want to be caught out. You have to do your homework,' says a senior ex-adviser from princely days. 'You have got to address slavery as the terrible thing it is before you can move on to talk about Britain at the forefront of both the abolition of the slave trade and slavery. And you also need to look forward: never forget the horror of what went before but also celebrate what these countries are doing today. Embrace the positive as well.'[15]

There is nothing new or tokenistic about any of this. The King has been an active promoter of what used to be called race relations and is now more usually called diversity for half a century. In the summer of 2022, while still Prince of Wales, he went to meet the organizers of the Notting Hill Carnival as they prepared to resume the largest street festival in Europe following the pandemic. Some of the younger staff were surprised to learn that, back in the 1970s and 1980s, when many people were calling for the closure of the event, it was the Prince of Wales who was writing forewords to the programme. 'Charles sent messages of support,' said Ansel Wong, Carnival veteran and former chair of the Notting Hill Carnival Board. 'When local politicians demanded the event be stopped, he came to our assistance.' When the editorial team at *The Voice*, Britain's leading black community news-paper, were looking for a guest editor for its fortieth anniversary edition in 2022, they talked to Omaghomi and asked the Prince. 'You have welcomed me into your communities with wonderful enthusiasm,' he wrote in a lengthy article, just days before becoming King. 'I am grateful that you have always been candid with me about the issues you continually face and how I might help.' The paper, in turn, carried a separate editorial, concluding: 'We know how far we have to go to make real progress on race equality, but we have an ally in Prince Charles and that is significant.'[16]

Similarly, few (if any) mainstream figures in British public life can match his track record when it comes to promoting a greater mutual understanding of Islam. In 1993, as Prince of Wales, he made a speech at Oxford University, entitled 'Islam and the West'. 'That which binds our two worlds together is so much more powerful than that which divides us,' he argued. It was a long, at times scholarly, speech, much of it overlooked in the ongoing drama of the collapse of his first marriage. Yet it was televised in full across the Middle East, where it resonated for years afterwards. At one point, his office was having to deny reports that he had actually converted to Islam.

Again, there was nothing tokenistic about this. The Prince would go on to become an active patron of the Oxford Centre for Islamic Studies, to learn basic Arabic, to read the Quran, to study Islamic geometry and even to sign his name in Arabic in some visitors' books as he does today.

It is a case of engagement in depth. When the old princely diary was being merged into the new regal one in the days after his accession, plenty of engagements fell out, but all the pre-existing engagements with minority faiths stayed in. These included his Advent service with the Ethiopian Christian

Fellowship Church and a day with London's Jewish community, culminating in a dance with Holocaust survivors. It rapidly went viral on social media. 'It was magical,' says Sir Lloyd Dorfman, who was there. 'It was entirely natural, not staged. There was music and he just started dancing with them. It left everyone on a high.' Though that was the joyful news image, the King also visited the leaders of the Community Security Trust, the charity which works to defend Britain's Jewish communities from anti-Semitism. 'The symbolism of him doing that, of coming to the headquarters of Jewish defence as King – that's sending a very strong, very reassuring message to British Jews,' says Dorfman.

If that Windrush seventy-fifth anniversary reception had been a major event for the Master of the Household and his team, it was a breeze compared to what happened at the Palace just weeks after the King's accession. Staff had already been preparing to welcome 200 athletes and officials from the British Olympic squad at the 2020 Tokyo Olympics to a long-awaited royal reception. Like the Games themselves, the reception had been delayed as a consequence of the Covid pandemic. Then staff were informed that the King wanted to hold another event on the very same day. While still Prince of Wales, he had agreed to attend a reception for the fiftieth anniversary of the arrival of the Ugandan Asian community in Britain. More than 30,000 had been expelled from their homes and businesses in Uganda in 1972 by the psychotic Ugandan dictator, Idi Amin. Unfortunately, that event had been scheduled for mid-September and had to be cancelled following the death of the Queen. The King had not forgotten his commitment, however, and had a fresh idea: he would stage the event at Buckingham Palace, since it would already be in hospitality mode for the Olympians.

Charles III

Not that too many introductions were needed when the Asian community came through the door. As Prince of Wales, he had been one of the founders of the British Asian Trust in 2007. Previously, on the twenty-fifth anniversary of the arrival of the Ugandan Asians in 1997, he had hailed them as 'a tremendous asset to this country'. At the Palace reception, he heard the actor Sanjeev Bhaskar commend his 'unsurpassed' support for British Asians, before joking: 'That was before he had to meet the same one every week'. This was just a few days after the King's appointment of Rishi Sunak as the UK's first prime minister of Asian heritage.

The King has grown up with stories of the Commonwealth, visiting it since his youth while watching the way in which Britain has been reshaped and enhanced by those over whom it once ruled. It is why he is a firm believer in the power of diasporas, as a way of reaching the Commonwealth when he cannot be there in person. Before heading for the Kigali summit in June 2022, the King held another bumper reception for 'the Commonwealth diaspora' at Buckingham Palace. On his very first day of engagements after the end of Court mourning, while still in Scotland, he held a British Asian Trust reception for 'the South Asian diaspora' at Holyroodhouse. It's a part of his work which may not make major headlines in Britain, yet it does not go unnoticed further afield.

There is certainly a different feel in Westminster Abbey on 13 March 2023 as the 2,000 guests arrive for the first annual Commonwealth Day service of the new reign. Not only is there a full turnout of all the senior working members of the Royal Family (which was not always the case in the past), but the King has decided to deliver his first Commonwealth Day speech live from the pulpit. The Queen usually issued her annual message in the form of a written statement or, on occasions, a recorded address.

'The Commonwealth has been a constant in my own life,' he tells the congregation. 'Its near-boundless potential as a force for good in the world demands our highest ambition; its sheer scale challenges us to unite and be bold.' This is ambitious talk but the King goes further. He links the organization to his own vision of a better future – 'one that offers the kind of prosperity that is in harmony with Nature.'

Critics of the Commonwealth point out that it is a shadow of the great organization which once helped bring down apartheid in South Africa and which was so revered by the late Nelson Mandela that his first major executive decision after being elected president was to rejoin the 'family of nations'. However, the King's words will have particular impact today. Usually, the member states send their London-based diplomats to this service. On this occasion, all the foreign ministers of the Commonwealth are in the abbey. They had been due to have their annual conference back in September during the United Nations General Assembly in New York but the death of the Queen forced a postponement. The new date was fixed for this week in London. It means that senior politicians from all over the Commonwealth are treated to the quirkiest church service in the royal calendar. This year's event features Maori conch-blowers, a Samoan choir and a dramatic entry by a troupe of Rwandan ballet dancers. Representatives of all the main religions deliver an invocation which ends: 'May the Commonwealth be blessed.'

The King underlines his enthusiasm later in the day. Usually, it is Marlborough House, the organization's headquarters, which hosts the annual Commonwealth Day reception. This year, as with so many events, he has invited everyone back to his place. Politicians, business leaders and emissaries of myriad Commonwealth associations – covering everything from education to dentistry – fill the state apartments of Buckingham Palace while the members of the Royal Family work the room. There is also a group photograph. The foreign ministers gather around the King as he signs a copy of the Commonwealth Charter. It is the tenth anniversary of the night the late Queen signed the original document 'reaffirming the core values and principles' of 'a compelling force for good'. Once again, everyone breathes a little more easily when the royal pen works properly.

How the Commonwealth achieves what the King calls its 'near-boundless potential' remains to be seen. The numbers are certainly strong. Its membership is at a record high of fifty-six, including several nations which were never part of the former British Empire, such as Cameroon and Togo. Others are waiting to join. Nations may now regard membership as useful rather than crucial. Its members include almost a third of the world's population, most of them with a shared language, legal code, parliamentary structure and sporting culture. In some nations, that includes rugby. In some, it includes cricket. In quite a few, it means both. Its role as a low-cost network of expertise in almost every field, and the opportunity for small and vulnerable nations to sit as equals with two G7 nations and a quarter of the G20,* make its future secure enough.

However, the same arguments about atoning for historic injustice could start to move up the agenda of this organization, since, self-evidently, most of its members were once colonized by Britain in the name of the Crown. 'That was not a problem for the late Queen because she personified change at a time

* Australia, Canada, India, South Africa and the UK are all members of the G20, while Canada and the UK are G7 members.

when countries were focused on independence, flags, the UN and so on,' says broadcaster and writer Wesley Kerr, British-born son of Jamaican parents. 'Issues from a troubled past and modern Britain's alleged responsibility were not to the fore in the way they are now. In countries where the institutions of slavery were deeply embedded, that deep history can be very emotive.'[17] In 2015, Indian opposition MP Shashi Tharoor delivered a passionate demand for compensation and an apology from Britain for '200 years of depredations' during an Oxford Union debate. The speech went viral and was even endorsed by the Indian prime minister, Narendra Modi, who said it 'reflected the feelings of patriotic Indians'. While that is clearly a subject for the British government, not the monarchy, there is much Indian resentment surrounding the continued presence of the Koh-i-Noor diamond as part of the Crown Jewels.

Otherwise known as 'the Mountain of Light', it remains mounted in the crown of the late Queen Mother, the last member of the family to wear it. As noted earlier, it played no part in the coronation of King Charles III, during which it remained under lock and key at the Tower of London. Its true origin is unknown but it enjoyed a fabulously bloody history as it passed through the hands of Persian, Mughal, Afghan and Sikh rulers. One Afghan warlord tortured another with a crown of molten lead in order to secure it.[18] In 1849, the defeated Sikh child king, Duleep Singh, was ordered to hand the stone over to the East India Company as part of the Treaty of Lahore. It was presented to Queen Victoria the following year and, at Prince Albert's suggestion, was recut from 191 carats down to its present size of 105.6. Any future plan for 'repatriation' would instantly raise a fresh debate. Several nations claim ownership, though India continues to shout loudest. The stone's royal provenance clearly makes this a problem for the King, even though the diamond sits within the Royal Collection and is not his to return (the collection holds it in trust 'for the nation'). However, there was a telling sign of fresh royal thinking when the Crown Jewels reopened to the public after the Coronation. The Historic Royal Palaces panel explaining the Koh-i-Noor no longer states that it had been 'given' to Queen Victoria. Rather, it now states that it was 'taken'.

Another area of reputational risk quite outside the King's control is the state of the Overseas Territories, those scattered parts of the globe which are still – of their own volition – British colonies. Some, like Bermuda, Gibraltar and the Falkland Islands are prosperous and stable. However, others, like the British Virgin Islands and the Turks and Caicos Islands, are seeing crime and drug-related corruption on an unprecedented scale, collapsing local government and no co-ordinated response from the colonial power. Their populations are also descended from victims of slavery. 'One of these places could simply implode. The Foreign Office is supposed to be in charge of them but they can't tell the Home Office to help with border controls or the Ministry of Defence to help with security so nothing gets done,' says one British diplomat. 'It would be highly embarrassing for the King if one of his own territories suddenly became a failed state. But I sense that he has already raised this with the prime minister because, since he became King, we have suddenly seen letters from Downing Street telling the relevant government departments to assign a minister for overseas territories.' It means that Britain, and by extension the King, will be accused of being too colonial in some places and insufficiently colonial in others.

A perennial issue is the future of the mainstay of the UK's honours system. The Order of the British Empire was groundbreaking when it was created by George V in 1917, opening up decorations for women and working-class civilians. It is not the medal, though, but the name which is the problem, as some royal representatives readily acknowledge. One possible solution currently under discussion is the idea of offering recipients an option either to join the current 'Empire' order or a parallel 'Order of British Excellence'. The actual medal, the acronym and the different tiers – from Member (MBE), Officer (OBE), Commander (CBE), Knight or Dame (KBE/DBE) up to Knight or Dame Grand Cross (GBE) – would remain the same. A similar thought process could be applied to the (separate) British Empire Medal. Another idea could be to rebrand the whole lot as the 'Order of Elizabeth', by way of a memorial to the late Queen.

So what are the prospects for Charles III's remaining thrones? Over time, three Caribbean realms have ditched the monarchy and have switched to a presidential model.* It seems highly likely that more will follow suit during the current reign. Politicians including the Jamaican prime minister Andrew Holness call this a question of 'independence', even though his country has been as independent as Canada or New Zealand or any other realm since it became autonomous in 1962. Many remain unconvinced, however. 'Jamaicans are certainly not known for their subservience but for their feistiness. Think Bob Marley, Michael Manley and all those sporting stars,' says Wesley Kerr. 'Even when I was reporting on the Queen as she toured Jamaica, it never occurred to me that this proud nation was anything other than independent.'[19]

Removing Charles III as head of state would be more straightforward in some places than others, depending on the

---

* Guyana, Trinidad and Tobago, and Barbados are former realms. Only Dominica opted to become a republic from the start.

threshold for constitutional change. Through the late Queen's reign, a certain pattern emerged.

In those Caribbean countries which have switched from realm to republic, it was the national parliament, not the people, who voted to remove the Crown. Why the reluctance to ask the people directly? In the last twenty-five years, when the issue has been put to a full public referendum in very different countries – Australia, St Vincent and the Grenadines and Tuvalu – the people have voted to retain the Crown rather than replace it with yet another politician. In Antigua, for example, the constitution means that a two-thirds majority would be needed to replace the monarchy. At present, that remains a high threshold. Jamaica requires a two-thirds majority in both parliamentary chambers followed by a 50/50 referendum, which is less of a hurdle. Ancient colonial atrocities, however, must be set against deep-rooted bonds. As one of the Caribbean's most illustrious sons, Grenada-born Warrant Officer Johnson Beharry, holder of the Victoria Cross, puts it: 'When you are in trouble, you want your friends with you. And who is going to be our friend in the future? The King and the UK? Or China?'[20]

It is not a case of the monarch trying to 'cling on'. The King cannot take part in anything approaching a debate on the subject. He can only say what he has said many times in the past, namely that constitutional reform is entirely down to the will of the people. As Prince of Wales, he said it in Sydney, on Australia Day, back in 1994: 'Personally, I happen to think it is the sign of a mature and self-confident nation to debate those issues and to use the democratic process to re-examine the way in which you want to face the future.'[21] On the very same day, Australia had dropped the Queen from the oath of allegiance for new citizens. The message was identical almost thirty years later, as he addressed Commonwealth leaders in Kigali: 'Each member's constitutional arrangement, as republic or monarchy, is purely a matter for each member country to decide. The benefit of long life brings me the experience that arrangements such as these can change, calmly and without rancour.'

How will the issue pan out beyond the Caribbean? There is still no great appetite for a republic in the largest of the realms, Canada. The monarchy is seen as a healthy point of difference with the great republic to the south and not as a constraint on Canada's place on the world stage. Although there were protests against the monarchy in French-speaking Quebec in the early years of the late Queen's reign, her obvious devotion to Canada (and her command of French) saw off the separatist threat during her lifetime. It has yet to resurface.

At the time of the King's Coronation, Australia had a republican prime minister, Labour's Anthony Albanese, who had also appointed the country's first 'assistant minister for the republic'.* He favours a much more conciliatory approach than his combative predecessor in the 1990s, Paul Keating, who allowed the issue to appear personal (even if the Queen and her staff always found him a model of good manners). Before tackling the issue of the Crown, Albanese tried to push through a different constitutional reform with his plan to give Australia's indigenous communities a special place or 'voice' in the country's constitution. In October 2023, it was overwhelmingly rejected in a referendum. Designating a putative 'republic' as a specific ministerial portfolio might send out an important signal. However, the country's 1999 referendum

---

* Matt Thistlethwaite was also appointed assistant minister for defence and assistant minister for veterans' affairs.

on the monarchy, like the 2023 vote on the 'voice', is a reminder of the challenge facing Australian republicans. Any change to the constitution requires not only an overall majority of voters, but a majority of voters in four or more of the country's six states.

Having spent the happiest part of his schooldays in Australia, the King has always felt a sense of belonging there. Former Australian diplomat John Dauth knows him well, having served as Australian high commissioner to the UK and, many years before, as Prince Charles's press secretary. In those days, Dauth recalls, the Prince was quite keen on the idea of becoming governor-general to Australia. 'He felt it would be liberating compared to the UK but it would not have been. It would have been a bad idea, dragging him into politics,' he says. Whenever he has been asked what the King should do to shore up the monarchy Down Under, Dauth has been blunt: 'I argue he should do nothing at all. It's not a given that it will happen soon and he should not be seen to intervene.' However, the King will be following it all very closely. 'He is probably very aware the monarchy won't last in Australia,' adds Dauth, 'but he would rather it was not in his reign.'

Constitutionally, it would be considerably simpler for New Zealand to abandon the Crown since a straight referendum result of more than 50 per cent would suffice. Few expect there to be an appreciable appetite for change in the foreseeable future. It was only in 2016 that a referendum to change the country's flag, replacing the Union flag element with the silver fern, was defeated by a clear majority. As for (much larger) Papua New Guinea, with its 800 languages and remote communities, it remains the only country which has actually invited the monarch to take charge.* There is no indication of republican rumblings. Of the two smaller Pacific realms, the Solomon Islands and Tuvalu, when the latter last had a referendum on removing the monarchy in 2008, fewer than 10 per cent were in favour. The one thing which all of the above have in common is that, whatever the change in their constitutions, they all remain committed to staying inside the Commonwealth. Nor has anyone voiced (or even whispered) any wish to change the Head of the Commonwealth, either.

Historians may note that, as a hereditary head of state, King Charles III automatically inherited the thrones of fourteen countries besides Britain. They landed in his lap. Yet it took decades of dedication to earn his appointment as head of an organization spanning fifty-six nations. For now, it is the latter which looks by far the safer bet.

---

* Previously a UN mandate run by Australia, PNG became autonomous in 1975. Unable to agree on a presidential model, its government invited the Queen to be head of state.

Chapter Seventeen

The Future and 'the Force'

Charles III was never going to be anywhere else on 8 September 2023. Just as Elizabeth II always liked to spend the anniversary of her accession quietly at Sandringham, the place where her father had died in the early hours of 6 February 1952, the King is marking his own accession day at Balmoral. He has released a short message recalling the late Queen's long life, devoted service and 'all she meant to so many of us', along with a beautiful and hitherto unpublished 1968 photograph of Elizabeth II (in full Garter robes but looking faintly amused by something going on just behind the photographer, Cecil Beaton). Buckingham Palace is keen to avoid any mawkishness. Down in London, as the international television networks gather outside the palace to discuss the anniversary, the crowds have gathered for the time-honoured morning ceremony of Changing the Guard. Those expecting a sombre and reflective atmosphere are somewhat surprised by the jaunty repertoire of the Band of the Welsh Guards. At one point, they suddenly burst into the theme tune of the BBC's old sports show *Grandstand*. The King remains out of the public gaze for most of the day, surfacing only for a short service of 'private prayers and reflection' at Balmoral's place of worship, Crathie Kirk. His own prayers will surely have included a particular word of thanks to the Almighty for the way the past year has gone.

So many of the doom-laden prophecies made in the autumn of 2022 have not been fulfilled. 'I think a lot of people thought, from one reign to another, it was going to be pretty choppy,' says Queen Camilla's sister, Annabel Elliot. 'And I don't see it like that at all.'[1] Predictable external factors may have come to pass, not least fresh and frequent interventions from the Sussexes and resurgent debates about royal finances and republicanism. Yet the polls and the public mood have remained stubbornly inert. The verdict of the royal commentariat in their first-year reports has either been broadly positive or else grudgingly non-committal. 'There have been no eye-catching reforms in his first year, and he can be fairly described as the "cautious" king,' reports *The Guardian*.[2] 'Any expectations of a modernizing monarch have so far been put on hold,' observes the BBC.[3] *The Daily Telegraph*, on the other hand, is more generous. 'The new King and Queen have performed their duties in a way that not even the institution's diminishing number of critics can find fault with,' says its anniversary editorial.[4] Ditto the *Daily Mail*: 'Charles and Camilla have performed their new roles with aplomb – impeccable in their public duties, compassionate, industrious and reassuring.'[5]

As the King and his officials had decided from the start, a careful change of gear in terms of tone and public interaction might be in order, but there has been no noisy rebranding. The former foreign secretary Lord [David] Owen has said that one of the great virtues of Elizabeth II is that she 'dared to be dull.'[6] She was merely emulating her father and grandfather. After H. G. Wells mocked George V's 'alien and uninspiring court', the King famously remarked: 'I may be uninspiring but I'll be damned if I'm an alien!' Now, Charles III was following suit. In other words, he was not the loose cannon that republicans longed to see. Those who predicted dire problems for the monarchy during a period of economic and political turbulence overlooked the intrinsic appeal of royalty in times of turmoil. As noted earlier, a walkabout by retirement-age royalty in suburban Britain may not be as glamorous or photogenic as a Los Angeles red carpet, yet it emphasizes that vital royal virtue: authenticity. There is nothing phoney about it.

One year into the new reign, all is calm on a sunny September morning in the run-up to the anniversary as the King and Queen prepare to welcome the prime minister and his wife for the traditional houseparty in the Highlands. By convention, there will also be a private audience. Whatever the subjects on the agenda ahead of Rishi Sunak's arrival, there will be no pressing issues involving the monarchy itself, beyond preliminary ideas for a national memorial to the late Queen.

Balmoral Castle still looks much as it did throughout her reign. The Grand Hall still has its racks of rods and boots plus a set of golf clubs and a pair of curling stones as door stops. The walls are still lined with estate maps, a portrait of Queen Victoria's dachshund, Deckel, and a Landseer study of a stag outwitting the hunt. Called *The Sanctuary*, it was a birthday present from Victoria to Albert in 1842. Overlooking it all is an 1867 bust of Queen Victoria herself. There is no other royal residence which bears the stamp of a single monarch quite like Balmoral. Victoria's successors might have made a few tweaks. The Sunaks, for example, will be steered to their room along a corridor lined with landscapes by Prince Philip. Elsewhere, they will find watercolours by the King. The walls behind these pictures, however, are still lined with the same heavy William

Morris flock wallpaper, featuring raised crowns, thistles and the initials 'V R I' in beige felt.

The King's sitting room is not very different from when the late Queen used to work in here. He has been rehanging a lot of pictures around the castle but portraits of Victoria and Albert still look down over the monarch's desk. Photographs stand to attention on the piano. Several feature the King with the late Queen Mother – as a boy or at a gathering of the Royal Company of Archers and so on. Elizabeth II used to have all the newspapers laid out in here. The King does not, preferring a selection of back issues of *Country Life* and regimental magazines. Her (very) old, chunky television has been replaced with a thinner model. The selection of books, however, is as eclectic as ever – a book on thoroughbred studs, a Ruth Rendell mystery, Charles Moore's *Path to Power* (the first in his three-part biography of Margaret Thatcher), the Church of Scotland's Book of Common Order . . .

Whenever he is here, the Supreme Governor of the Church of England is an ordinary parishioner of the Church of Scotland. 'The King has been coming to this area for all his life and his understanding of this place has been informed by the people around him, especially his grandmother,' says the Rev. Kenneth MacKenzie, the minister of Crathie Kirk, where the King has worshipped for longer than most of the parishioners. MacKenzie points out that the King is not just a regular here during the summer season when the church is full. 'All through the year, the King has been coming for as long as I've been here – nearly twenty years. He's come sometimes when there's just forty people.'

Just moments before he became King in 2022, the former Prince of Wales was out in the grounds of Birkhall picking mushrooms. One year on, he is doing the same, with a very specific purpose: he wants to serve them to his guests at dinner. Whether the Sunaks will have room for them is another matter. They arrive in time for Balmoral tea, which includes trays of cakes and sandwiches. Sitting down for his audience with the King afterwards, the prime minister is already struggling. 'I'm figuring out how to work up an appetite in the next two hours before dinner,' he jokes. 'I'm sorry about that. We ought to send you out for a run,' the King replies. Queen Camilla and the dogs, meanwhile, take the prime minister's wife, Akshata Murty, on a tour of the house. The Sunaks greatly enjoy the 'informal formality', as Sir Clive Alderton would call it, of this houseparty. The other guests include the Princess Royal, the chairman of the Victoria and Albert Museum, Sir Nicholas Coleridge and his wife, Georgia, and Sarah Troughton, Lord Lieutenant of Wiltshire, and her husband, Peter, both old friends of the King and Queen (Sarah is a distant cousin of the monarch). 'I think His Majesty foraging for mushrooms for guests to eat at dinner that night sums up a lot about what he's passionate about – the environment, farming, where our food comes from,' the prime minister reflects later.

The Sunaks join the royal party for Sunday service at Crathie Kirk, followed by lunch. Before they leave, they present the King and Queen with a pair of shepherd's crooks made by a champion stick-maker in Sunak's North Yorkshire constituency. On the same day, it is announced that the government has established a Queen Elizabeth Memorial Committee to consider all proposals for a permanent tribute to the late Queen. It is to be chaired by her former private secretary, Lord [Robin] Janvrin, and will announce its final plans on the centenary of her birth in 2026.

If there is one aspect of this first anniversary which does cause the King and his staff to bristle, it is commentators reheating those claims – made immediately after the Queen's death – that his will be a stop-gap reign. 'Charles the "caretaker king" for William,' declared the front page of *The Sunday Times* a few days before the anniversary, adding that the monarch found his new role an 'unexpected burden' and that his heir would be the 'change-maker.'[7] Those close to the King say that this is demonstrably wrong. 'He can't help but be different. When you start much later in your life, inevitably you've got more experience to fall back on and you will have more opinions,' says the Princess Royal.[8] 'People keep talking about "he's a caretaker". And I don't see that at all, knowing we'll see quite a few changes,' says Annabel Elliot. Within the offices of both the King and the new Prince of Wales, it is simply accepted that both will make their own changes according to their own tastes and personalities along with the circumstances of the moment. Prince Charles established his own modus operandi in his younger days and entirely understands that Prince William wants to do the same.

So, whereas the King likes to assemble panels of experts around him, Prince William does not. 'He will say: "Don't get me a meeting with an academic". He might want to meet a brilliant scientist who is doing something amazing but he doesn't seek intellectual company,' says one of those who has worked closely with him.[9] 'He is a very serious, pragmatic bloke and he doesn't want to make lots of speeches. The King liked amateur dramatics in his youth. His son does not have that same love of showmanship.' Prince Charles might have been happy to wade into the big social issues of the day with a provocative speech or foreword to a book, be it on architecture or education, sometimes risking a media backlash. He was happy to bend the ear of ministers on some issues, and challenge them on others. However, he knew he had gone too far in 1985 when the prime minister, Margaret Thatcher, objected to comments attributed to him about urban regeneration.[10] He was thirty-six at the time. Now in his forties, Prince William has been nothing like as combative. He has steered a more conventional and cautious path. Within the Palace, some see traces of an earnest, dutiful George VI. Another senior Kensington Palace official uses a *Star Wars* analogy. 'What is happening is that, like a Jedi Knight, he is starting to learn how to use "the Force" and make the most of his influence.' One such 'Jedi' encounter was a meeting at Windsor between the Prince and Michael Gove, secretary of state for levelling up and housing, shortly after the Coronation. 'He wasn't pushing a particular point. He wanted to discuss the ways in which his foundation was engaging with homelessness,' says one of those present. As a senior adviser puts it: 'He is one of the least ideological people I have met.' In many ways, therefore, the royal 'change-maker' is actually father, not son.

Prince William gets most of his news from online sources like the BBC website and briefings from staff. He prefers cogent, bullet-point memos to big bundles of documents and prefers to talk through agendas with a coterie of trusted advisers. Those to whom he might turn include, say, the former Tory leader Lord Hague, who now chairs the Royal Foundation of The Prince and Princess of Wales, as well as the former British ambassador to the USA, Sir David Manning, and Simon Case, the Cabinet secretary (who previously worked as the Prince's private secretary). On major constitutional and international issues, he will talk and defer to his father. Otherwise, though, he remains his own man. 'He has got agency. He really feels that. He takes his own decisions. I don't think I have ever heard him say: "Why the hell did you tell me to do this?" He owns things,' says one who has known him for many years.[11]

'He is a functional decision-maker, very intuitive. He is good at making judgement calls and is confident in his own judgement. If there is an important decision, he will normally ask three or four other people and that is an excellent trait.'

His instincts have served him well, with a preference for thoughtful, long-term engagement on a few carefully chosen fronts. Like his father and his grandfather Prince Philip before him, he has already made his own significant mark on the world's environmental stage with his Earthshot Prize. Sometimes described as a 'Nobel Prize' for the environment, it was launched by Prince William and Sir David Attenborough in 2020 with a £50 million prize fund and a mission to inject some 'positivity' into the (frequently doom-laden) climate debate. Each year, until 2030, five winners – from anywhere in the world – will receive £1 million every year for ground-breaking work in five categories, including 'Clean Our Air' and 'Revive Our Oceans'. By any measure, it is a substantial example of royal soft power.

Even before the King announced that he was making his elder son the Prince of Wales, the former Duke of Cambridge automatically became the 25th Duke of Cornwall upon the death of the late Queen. It is the Duchy of Cornwall, with its 200 square miles of agricultural and commercial property, which will now provide his income until he becomes King. Like his father before him, Prince William takes the role very seriously. He is a hands-on chairman of the Prince's Council* and a regular presence at gatherings of the finance and rural committees. He is, therefore, at a Duchy meeting of some sort every three or four weeks. Like the King, he detests unnecessary

---

* The Prince's Council is, in effect, the Duchy of Cornwall's board of non-executive directors. Its main role is to advise the Prince of Wales in his capacity as Duke.

waste and has decreed that all the old Duchy stationery and branding should be used up before any replacements are commissioned. Duchy staff are already noticing a few changes, however. The Prince has a special fascination with seaweed as a potential replacement for single-use plastics. So, for example, the Oval cricket ground, which is owned by the Duchy of Cornwall, now uses seaweed-based packaging from a company called Notpla (a past Earthshot winner).

His new role involves oversight of the Duchy's property portfolio, which includes the King's home at Highgrove (the King still has many years left on the lease). Prince William, however, does not share his father's fondness for accumulating new homes. The King's purchases of a farmhouse in Wales (another Duchy property) and one in Romania, not to mention Dumfries House in Scotland, are viewed with a certain degree of trepidation among the Prince of Wales's team. 'No more properties!' replies one adviser, only half-jokingly, when asked if the Prince might be thinking of any fresh acquisitions of his own.

Whereas his father operates his private office along the same lines as that of the late Queen – with a private secretary delegating downwards – the Prince and Princess of Wales have been developing a more lateral command structure at their Kensington Palace headquarters. 'The idea is to engender greater collective responsibility, strengthen the structure and avoid a single point of failure,' says one of the team. Previously, the Prince's right-hand man had been his private secretary, most recently Jean-Christophe Gray. A high-flying civil servant, Gray had previously worked for three chancellors of the Exchequer and a prime minister (David Cameron). He had arrived on loan from Whitehall to replace another civil servant, Simon Case. The fact that Case was leaving Kensington Palace to go back to the top job in the entire civil service, that of

Cabinet secretary, was indicative of the importance which the government attaches to the work of the heir to the throne. One of Gray's last tasks, before returning to the civil service himself in 2024, would be to split his job in two. The Prince and Princess of Wales would, henceforth, have both a 'chief executive', managing the whole show, alongside a private secretary covering the more constitutional side of things. These two would become part of the same 'leadership team', which would also include an assistant private secretary with specific responsibility for foreign affairs, in this case a former ambassador to Lithuania, David Hunt. It is seen as a priority to have another Welsh-speaking assistant private secretary who can handle Welsh interests. Sidestepping ancient terms like 'comptroller', the Waleses have additionally created the position of 'chief operating officer' (with a financial and human resources role). External recruitment consultants were summoned to ensure that the search for these vacant posts extended beyond the usual trawl of the armed forces and Whitehall. As Valentine Low has written, Prince William only hired an earlier press secretary after first checking that the applicant had *not* been educated at a top public school but, rather, at a comprehensive.[12] The Kensington Palace team, at the time of writing, also includes the acting private secretary to the Princess of Wales, Natalie Barrows, a 'KP' staffer for many years, and the 'Head of the Private Household', Lieutenant Commander James Benbow. The former Royal Navy helicopter pilot and equerry occupies a chief of staff/Master of the Household role, running life beyond the public gaze for both the Waleses and their children.

A constant refrain from the office of the Prince and Princess is the need to avoid things which smack of insincerity. So, when it comes to Wales itself, the new Prince of Wales made three early decisions which represent a break with his father's approach.

First, he would not spend months at university learning Welsh. Second, he would not be buying a home in Wales. Third, he had no wish for a grand formal investiture like the 1969 ceremony arranged for Prince Charles. Held at Caernarfon Castle, that was a Welsh quasi-coronation to coincide with the coming of age of the heir to the throne. It was also the first made-for-television royal spectacular, the first royal event screened live through the new medium of colour television and a primary target for an embryonic Welsh terrorist movement. Uncharacteristically, the late Queen found the whole event so stressful that she cancelled all her engagements for the following week and took to her bed.[13] There will not be a repeat. 'There's never going to be a Caernarfon,' says one of the Prince's team, 'unless the people of Wales want one. And they don't.'

Prince Charles's investiture was very much driven by the secretary of state for Wales of the day, George Thomas, and the prime minister, Harold Wilson. Both saw it as a way of drawing Wales closer to the Union in the face of increasing demands for some sort of devolution. Today, neither the Welsh nor the UK government has expressed any desire to hold a similar event, much to the relief of the current Prince of Wales. Nor, say his officials, does he intend to use the Welsh farm at Llwynywermod, even though he now owns it through the Duchy of Cornwall. He will allow it to become a permanent rental property. It is not because of any lack of interest in Wales. Far from it. Having spent their first years of marriage there, while Prince William was serving as an RAF rescue pilot in Anglesey, the former Duke and Duchess of Cambridge retain a profound love of Wales. 'They've been very clear that they respect the history that comes with the position and the relationship with the Welsh people that comes with that,' says an adviser, 'but they are going to do things their way. It's about building trust and respect over time.' So, on their increasingly frequent trips to Wales, the couple have preferred to stay at local guest houses. Rather than making speeches containing a few words of a language they clearly cannot speak, they have decided to appeal to Welsh hearts and minds through a solid, old-fashioned diet of walkabouts and community engagements. An early Welsh trip, as Prince and Princess of Wales, involved a visit to Aberfan, scene of that unimaginable horror in 1966 when a landslide killed 144, most of them children. The trip included a sombre, suited visit to the Aberfan Memorial Garden. But there was also a later visit to the local rugby club where the couple, in casual clothes, handed out pizza to local mountain rescue volunteers.

If the King's idea of dressing down is a tweed jacket instead of a suit, his son will favour more of a Boden-style look. 'I suppose our default is chinos and blazer if possible – often with no tie,' says one member of the Prince's staff, 'and there is not lots of changing.' One feature of royal life which often surprises newcomers to the Royal Household is the number of wardrobe changes in the course of a day. Those with the monarch on an overseas tour or at a weekend houseparty may be expected to change three or four times in a day (it was even more under the late Queen). Prince William, who does not take a valet on tour, travels relatively light.

Father and son have contrasting artistic tastes. Whereas the King adores classical music, especially opera and English choral works, the Prince of Wales does not. 'The King is a great nineteenth-century romantic. He loves Wagner,' says a family friend. 'His son loves AC/DC.'[14] Indeed, Prince William has said that he likes to kick off each week to the sound of the Australian rock band's hit 'Thunderstruck', calling it 'the best tonic for a Monday morning'.[15] The Prince is also a keen fan of nineties dance music, with a particular soft spot for The Chemical Brothers. 'He was very pleased to see Pete Tong [the veteran disc jockey] at the Coronation concert,' adds the friend.

As for books, the King has inherited his late father's love of reading, kickstarted by childhood bedtime stories like Pocohontas[16] and a passion for Shakespeare, first instilled during his teenage years at Gordonstoun. He has written four books and co-authored thirteen more. Prince William, by contrast, will dip into books for information, less so for pleasure. As previously noted, *Spare* is not to be found anywhere in the house.

Asked to name the Prince's favourite author, one official replies diplomatically: 'He's a box-set guy.' Superhero movies are, apparently, a particular favourite, especially all things Batman-related plus the (more violent) blockbuster *Deadpool*.[17] No doubt psychologists might be fascinated by the appeal of a caped crusader to an impossibly famous royal Prince. His friends put it down to something more straightforward. 'He just likes action flicks,' says one. The Waleses are always keen to take tips from the staff in the office, too. Says one: 'They heard us all raving about *Happy Valley** in the office so they went and watched it.' While a future King and Queen might be expected to lean towards historical fiction, this is not the case. Says another friend: 'They are not what you might call "period drama" people.'

One hit series which they will not be watching is the glossy Netflix royal drama *The Crown*. Its timeline has gradually been creeping ever closer to the present day, through the childhood of William and Harry and into the twenty-first century. Its plotlines and dialogue are fabricated but the Royal Family know

---

* Set in West Yorkshire, *Happy Valley* was a BBC crime drama running over three series between 2014 and 2023.

that large parts of the world regard the series to be broadly true. 'The Prince knows about it. He rolls his eyes when people say that "it's just drama". He knows what they [Netflix] are doing,' says a close aide.[18] 'Yet he will not give it any greater publicity by complaining. He doesn't like the idea of being seen as a complainer all the time.' There is, however, one particular media bugbear about which he will never cease to complain vigorously. 'The one thing which really makes his blood boil is Martin Bashir,' says a friend, referring to the television reporter who used faked documents to lure the Prince's mother into giving her devastating 1995 interview to the BBC's *Panorama*.

What may mark out the future King William V as a 'change-maker' is not what he does, so much as what he may *not* do. He is not, it seems, unduly fearful of losing the constitutional link between the Crown and the realms. Like his father, he believes that this is entirely a matter for the people of Australia, Jamaica and the other independent nations where, for now at least, he is the heir to the throne. His 2022 trip to the Caribbean to mark the late Queen's Platinum Jubilee remains etched in the memory at Kensington Palace. Having been invited to take part in a forward-looking expression of goodwill, the Prince found himself unwittingly cast as the repository for historic grievances, though he could hardly be expected to provide an answer.* However, as a realist, he is content to regard this as something beyond his control. One Commonwealth politician with whom he has a close connection, for example, is Jacinda Ardern, former prime minister of New Zealand and a trustee

* The prime minister of Jamaica, Andrew Holness, used the official welcome for the Duke and Duchess of Cambridge to declare that his country had 'unresolved' issues with the Crown. The Duke, who had not been forewarned, later released a statement saying that royal tours were a useful opportunity to learn 'what is on the minds of prime ministers.'

of the Earthshot Prize. Her stated aim is for a Kiwi republic one day in the future. 'He has clocked that you can still have a good relationship with a realm when it becomes a Commonwealth republic – like Barbados,' says an aide. 'And he can see that some leaders, like Jacinda, look in that direction.' The main thing – and the King would wholeheartedly agree – is that these nations, whether realms or republics, remain enthusiastic members of the Commonwealth.

Where Prince William can legitimately deploy a little more 'agency' – and where his position may diverge from that of his father – is when it comes to his future role within the 'family of nations.' In the case of Charles III, it had always been the aspiration that he would follow his mother and become Head of the Commonwealth. Since the role is not hereditary, it was not always clear whether Prince Charles would indeed take over. Ultimately, his dedication to both the organization and to the environment resulted in a unanimous endorsement, in 2018. The new Prince of Wales is not as steeped in the ways and the quirks of the modern Commonwealth as his father, who talks fondly of growing up around some of its founding fathers and has visited most of its member states. Prince William, say his team, is passionate about the Commonwealth's potential with regard to civic society and youth. He is more circumspect about whether future Commonwealth leaders will want to continue the royal connection. If the monarchy starts to be seen as a source of division rather than a unifying element within the organization, he may feel that a new arrangement is better for all parties. 'He is quite "third way" about it,' says a close adviser, adopting Blairite jargon for circumventing traditional either/or positions. 'He really wants the Commonwealth to succeed and there is a private frustration that it's not as active as it might be. But he is admirably open-minded as to whether his involvement in the Commonwealth has to translate into the headship. He'd be very nervous of being seen to assume he is the future head. It's something he thinks about a lot.' However, one idea which he certainly does not favour, says one who has discussed it with him, is the idea of being a 'co-head'.

The prospect of there being a future monarch who is not Head of the Commonwealth is not nearly as big a leap of the royal imagination, however, as having a monarch who is not Supreme Governor of the Church of England. It is no secret in royal circles that the Prince of Wales does not share the King's sense of the spiritual, let alone the late Queen's unshakeable devotion to the Anglican church. It was said, by her most senior staff, that her (and their) favourite annual fixture in the calendar was the Royal Maundy service with its eve-of-Easter distribution of 'Maundy money' to elderly churchgoers.[19] Indeed, she not only revived the 800-year-old tradition but was the first monarch to take it on tour around the country. Prince William has yet to attend. 'His father is very spiritual and happy to talk about faith but the Prince is not,' says a senior Palace figure. 'He doesn't go to church every Sunday, but then nor do the large majority of the country. He might go at Christmas and Easter, but that's it. He very much respects the institutions but he is not instinctively comfortable in a faith environment.'[20]

The Prince, however, surprised himself by the extent to which he was moved during his father's Coronation. 'He was very, very struck by what he called the "solemnity" of the anointing. That really brought home the uniqueness of this,' says one senior royal official. 'It was the fact that he couldn't actually see that moment and nor could anyone else except the Archbishop. He will want to preserve that.' The heir to the throne has since expressed a few private thoughts about how he envisages his own Coronation, according to one who has heard them. 'He thought it was brilliant but he is less instinct-ively spiritual than his father so he would want something a bit more discreet.' The future King William, it is understood, would like his ceremony to be shorter – 'ideally an hour and ten minutes' – and, with that in mind, he might dispense with some of the regalia. 'We may not necessarily bring out the armills and the ring,' says the official, adding that there was one brief scene in particular which jarred with the Prince: 'The glove was a moment he thought was a bit "Erm . . ."'[21] Having somehow survived from the Normans through to the twenty-first century – via the Lords of the Manor of Worksop, the Dukes of Newcastle and latterly Lord Singh of Wimbledon – it seems that the Coronation Glove may have had its final outing.

William V would not be the first modern monarch to be an unenthusiastic churchgoer. Edward VII would only attend church on Sundays if there was no communion and 'a short Sermon.'[22] Edward VIII was frequently chided for his erratic church attendance,[23] but even he managed to turn up more than twice a year. The new Prince of Wales is going to find that his attendance at church – and other places of worship – will have to increase anyway since he now takes on the mantle of chief national mourner. For decades, Prince Charles would be expected to drop everything and represent the late Queen at funerals.* Indeed, he was just nineteen when he undertook his first mourning mission. He had to set aside his studies at Cambridge and fly to Australia to attend the funeral of former prime minister Harold Holt in December 1967. Over the subsequent years, he has attended the formal farewells to many leaders,

---

* By tradition, monarchs do not travel to the funerals of other world leaders, not least because it could cause grave offence to attend one but not another.

including Presidents Mandela, Reagan and Bush. His elder son will now do the same, having already represented the late Queen at the funeral of Sheikh Khalifa of the United Arab Emirates in 2022. However, while Charles III still follows his mother's custom of inviting visiting clergy to Sunday lunch – be it at Windsor, Sandringham or Balmoral – that tradition may ease off in the next reign. Should the disestablishment of the Church of England ever become an issue in the reign of the future King William, it is safe to say that he may be less perturbed than his predecessors.

Quite apart from all his duties as Prince of Wales, the new heir to the throne has what he regards as one paramount duty. It is one which some of his predecessors virtually ignored: training one's heir. 'In his view, it's not far off the most important job he has – raising the next King but one,' says a family friend. Whereas Charles III had his future mapped out without consultation, Prince William had a significant degree of autonomy in his choice of university education, his engagement with the armed forces and his introduction to regular royal duties.[24] He is determined that Prince George should have a similar if not greater involvement in the way he develops his own royal role. 'There is no expectation that any royal duties are going to kick in until George is well into his twenties,' says a Kensington Palace veteran. 'Before he was even made a page at the Coronation, William and Catherine wanted to ask him if he felt comfortable about it because he was clearly the youngest. It turned out he was keen.'

As has been noted earlier, the Prince of Wales's relationship with the King has been strengthened by the twin burdens of their new roles and periodic broadsides from California. Also, the more that the heir to the throne becomes involved in the running of the Duchy of Cornwall and the royal estates, the more he has come to appreciate his father's dedication and his achievements over the years. 'They are as one when it comes to sustainability,' says one of Prince William's team. The King certainly finds it easier to discuss these issues with his son than he did with his late father. 'Prince Charles and Prince Philip were always quarrelling about the best way forward,' says a close aide, recalling meetings of the 'Chequers Group', which oversees the private royal estates. This would involve father and son plus the royal land agents and the Keeper of the Privy Purse. 'Prince Philip did have a tendency to treat his sons as if they were in short trousers. He was a modernist and Prince Charles was a post-modernist.' Now that Prince William is part of the Chequers Group, as he has been since 2019, meetings are a good deal more harmonious.* Prince William, however, is said to be closer to the late Prince Philip than to his father on farming issues. According to one adviser, this is especially true when it comes to the merits of organic farming. Whereas the King is a purist on the matter, his son, like Prince Philip, is more agnostic, given the difficulties facing many farmers in seeking to attain organic status. Both, however, have a strong admiration for what each other has achieved in terms of keeping the environment to the fore.**

It also helps that the King is a huge fan of the new Princess of Wales. 'He thinks Catherine is doing a wonderful job, not just with her royal duties but also bringing up his grand-children,' says a friend. In certain regards, the new Princess of

---

* The Chequers Group takes its name from the chequers board on which medieval royal finances were transacted. The post of chancellor of the Exchequer, custodian of the national finances, has the same origins.
** The King's passion for organic farming is matched by his dislike of genetically modified (GM) crops. For many years, visitors to Highgrove would be greeted by a sign saying: 'You are entering a GM-free zone.'

Wales perhaps shares more characteristics with the new Queen than the new Prince of Wales does with the King. Both Camilla and Catherine are keen readers of books. Unlike their husbands, both keep an eye on the press (including, in the case of the Princess, the Mail Online website).[25] Both have very strong, non-negotiable relationships with their own families which continue very happily in parallel to their respective royal roles. They even share similar artistic tastes, with a particular fondness for ballet (the Princess of Wales took Charlotte to watch the Royal Ballet's *Cinderella* for her eighth birthday). Both are also firm believers in the merits of gradual, thorough engagement with an issue or an organization rather than instant, headline-grabbing initiatives. In 2020, the then Duchess of Cambridge launched the largest survey of life opportunities and outcomes in the under-fives ever conducted in the UK (through the Royal Foundation). Some of those reporting on the occasion were surprised to discover that she had already been working extensively in the 'early years sector' for the previous six years.

Chapter Eighteen

'Virtues for all seasons'

Were the House of Windsor to fall in line with many of its counterparts, then the depiction of Charles III as a 'caretaker King' might have validity. As noted elsewhere, several European royal houses, including those of Belgium, the Netherlands and Spain, have now set a precedent for retirement when sovereigns reach their late seventies. Furthermore, Prince William is now anything but a trainee or apprentice. Born in 1982, he is not far short of the average age of accession of new monarchs in the post-George III era – forty-six. However, within the British monarchy, retirement equals abdication, and that continues to remain an unmentionable. The throne is occupied by a very active septuagenarian who lives on the sort of restrained and disciplined diet which might appear in the health pages of a newspaper or magazine. Charles III is very content to leave it to genetics and the Almighty to dictate the length of his reign. There will be nothing 'interim' about any of it as long as he has Queen Camilla at his side.

'She is his rock, and I can't actually emphasize that enough,' says Annabel Elliot. 'She is completely loyal and she isn't somebody who has huge highs and lows. They're like any couple who've been together for a long time. Lots of jokes and squabbles. They're both huge walkers – very fit, both of them. Her with her mad dogs; him gardening and planting all the time.' The Queen's sister puts the strength of their marriage down to the attraction of opposites: 'They're the yin and yang. They really are polar opposites, but I think it works brilliantly. And, you know, I go back to the thing of humour. Basically, she makes him laugh. And he brings to her, well, everything. He has such a knowledge and interest in so many different things, whether it's religion, other countries and whatever, which she wouldn't really have been open to if she hadn't met him.'

Also playing a key role in the new reign, in her customary understated way, will be the Princess Royal. One look at the official Coronation photographs is proof of that. While the King has the Queen to his left, it is his sister who stands at his right-hand side. One of the three members of the family who regularly performs investitures, along with the King and Prince of Wales, the Princess has also now been added to the roster of senior royal mourners. It means that she can attend important world funerals if the Prince of Wales is unable to attend (as happened after the death of ex-King Constantine of the Hellenes in January 2023). Even more understated is her husband, Vice Admiral Sir Tim Laurence. His distinguished Royal Navy career has been followed by multiple leadership roles in institutions ranging from the Commonwealth War Graves Commission to private sector bodies like the Major Projects Association, often during periods of change. As the National Trust found itself caught up in the full force of the 'culture wars' through its handling of issues such as slavery and the sexuality of former stately homeowners, its main rival, English Heritage, did not. It, too, looks after hundreds of castles, monuments and swathes of countryside plus all the blue plaques on important buildings. In addition, it was also undergoing a fundamental transformation from government agency to national charity. As its two-term chairman, Laurence was at the helm throughout what could have been a turbulent period – yet it proved not to be. While he has no official royal role, and has never sought one, he is widely respected across the Royal Household as a wise sounding board and the proverbial 'safe pair of hands'. In September 2023, with a minimum of fanfare, he received his first patronage when he was appointed patron of the International Maritime Rescue Federation. With the Princess now enjoying an enhanced role, life is unlikely to slow down for this low-key, non-royal, royal consort.

The Duke and Duchess of Edinburgh will, similarly, be no less busy, as the late Queen's cousins – the Duke and Duchess of Gloucester, the Duke of Kent and Princess Alexandra – gradually scale back their engagements. In May 2023, the Duchess of Edinburgh became the first member of the Royal Family to visit modern Baghdad. She was undertaking several engagements in support of the United Nations' campaign against sexual violence in conflict, a cause close to the heart of Queen Camilla. The Duchess also held a meeting with the Iraqi head of state, President Rashid. This was precisely the sort of delicate royal diplomacy which the late Duke of Edinburgh used to undertake on his visits to parts of the world where a state visit was out of the question. The new Duke of Edinburgh devotes much of his time to extending the reach of his father's award scheme into new parts of the world. As well as being re-appointed as a Counsellor of State, he now takes on some of the duties which might previously have been delegated to the old Duke. During the first state visit of the new reign, the King asked his younger brother to escort South Africa's President Cyril Ramaphosa on some of his engagements. Such are the subtle indicators of the elevated roles of those who make up that 'slimmed-down monarchy'.

There can be no slimming down the business of monarchy,

however. Nor is there any great appetite to do so. One year on from his accession, even on a Balmoral weekend there is a glimmer of excitement as the first red box of the day makes its appearance at the King's 11 a.m. meeting with his private secretary. Sir Clive Alderton is pleased to announce that this one contains what he calls 'quite an interesting crop'. Today's state business includes proposals for a new two-pound coin. The Royal Mint has sent the King three choices for an inscription, based on the Coronation theme of service to all. The King can have his message in English or Latin, Alderton explains, as long as he doesn't exceed thirty-nine characters. So the monarch plumps for '*In servitio omnium*'. 'Well, having done Latin at school, why not?' he adds, reflecting on the virtues of a classical education: 'It helps you understand English – and other languages.' By Alderton's reckoning, the King has had to approve more than 400 different coins and stamps in his first year, by dint of being head of state of so many nations. Today's box includes a set of Kiwi coins which also need his consent. They have been commissioned to mark the twentieth anniversary of filming the *Lord of the Rings* trilogy in New Zealand. This is the cue for some happy reminiscing about a bygone royal visit to see the films being made. 'I went to visit the studios,' the King recalls. 'It was extraordinary.' Alderton chuckles at the memory of the King being presented with a Bilbo Baggins prosthetic arm and making a joke about being given 'a big hand'.

There are also letters to be signed recalling the British ambassador to the Central African Republic and appointing a new one. The King wants to know where she served previously (Beirut). The box contains the latest lists of promotions and retirements from the armed forces, always a source of interest. 'It is quite fun looking through to see if I can find names which remind me of people I served with in the navy,' he murmurs.

'I did find one last year. I thought: "That's interesting, that name" – because he'd been a commanding officer of a mine-hunter at the same time as I had. It was his son – who'd become an Admiral! So I wrote to my old friend.' There are quite a few entries today. 'Why do I know that name?' he asks on seeing a new commissioner for the Royal Hospital Chelsea. He also spots two former equerries to the late Queen on the Royal Air Force list. It is a small world.

Looking further down the defence lists, he adds a little wistfully: 'A lot of people retiring . . .' It is not just members of the armed forces who are calling it a day. Another letter seeks the King's permission for the Bishop of Richborough to retire. 'I'm trying to remember which part of the country Richborough is in,' he says, but he is amused by a footnote: 'He's a flying bishop – such a splendid term.'* The King is especially impressed by the track record of a Vice-Lord Lieutenant of Lancashire who is up for reappointment, having visited every corner of the county. 'She did very well, didn't she, getting around every single secondary school and college . . .' He reads on: 'A member of the Burnley Municipal Choir. Just wonderful. I can never get over the numbers of people who take part in community music activities.' He is so enthusiastic that he puts his signature to the document even though it is not required. 'I've done the wrong thing. I've signed it,' he chuckles. 'Never mind.' It may be routine but he finds these granular details of the mechanics of public life not just interesting but, in many cases, inspiring. The late Queen felt much the same about the contents of her boxes, according to her staff.

---

* 'Flying bishops' – or 'Provincial Episcopal Visitors' – were created by the Church of England to administer to parishes which would not accept the ordination of women. The see of Richborough, which is in Kent, was created in 1994.

Charles III

The King is still learning what needs his signature, what needs initials and what just needs a nod. The pen and signature issues which were such a prominent feature in the early days of the reign have not gone away entirely. The King is constantly alert to the risk of smudging his name by mistake. 'You must not put your great finger on it – which has happened,' he mutters. 'It has indeed, Sir,' Alderton acknowledges knowingly. 'It's my fault,' says the King. 'Probably more mine, Sir,' the private secretary loyally insists.

There is also a spot of royal business today. The foreign secretary has asked the monarch to sign a message to the King of Sweden ahead of his upcoming Golden Jubilee. 'I didn't know if you might want to fiddle with that and to personalize it a bit, Sir,' says Alderton. 'Oh, gracious. Is this in Swedish?' the King replies, looking at the wording. It is indeed. He asks Alderton to have the wording double-checked because 'you never know if somebody's fed you something frightful to say' – and decides that it needs 'a bit of warming'. So he adds some more personal lines for King Carl XVI Gustav in his own hand. 'Having known him since we were very young,' he reflects, 'it's amazing how long he has done, isn't it.' After one year in this job, completing fifty of them seems unfathomable.

Like the red boxes, the problems and challenges will keep on coming. Were he content to remain a 'caretaker' monarch, the King could probably kick many of them into the next reign. In fact, he is rather enjoying dealing with some of them, not least Balmoral itself. As well as rehanging many of the pictures, he is busy replacing some of the more threadbare patches of tartan on walls and floors. He has even more ambitious plans for the grounds. Soon after his accession, he asked the estate office to begin work on a maze, like the one he has installed at Dumfries

House. Shaped like a thistle, it is not for his own pleasure (though he loved mazes as a boy). It is part of his plans to draw more members of the public to the estate. The King has now introduced free access to the grounds on certain days when the family are not in residence.

Balmoral is private property. However, it needs public footfall not just to help pay the bills but to bring benefits to the wider community and to remain in step with other stately homes. Critics and supporters of the monarchy alike have long complained that the castle is only open for a few months in spring and early summer. Even then, the public are only given access to the ballroom and stables. Why not offer them a good gawp at the main interior rooms all year round as long as the family are not in residence? After all, the King and Queen are much happier living at Birkhall, the Queen Mother's old home, when they are in these parts. They spent just three weeks at Balmoral Castle itself during the summer of 2023, whereas the late Queen would spend eight to ten weeks there each summer and autumn. Three weeks was long enough to ensure that all the King's siblings – including the Duke of York – could enjoy a spell at the family retreat. Inevitably, however, the turnover of guests was reduced (with many invited for one night rather than the traditional two). Similarly, the King held a single Ghillies' Ball,* whereas, in the past, there might have been two of them during the course of the sovereign's stay.

In theory, then, it ought to be quite easy to open up more of Balmoral Castle for more of the time. However, it transpires that the late Queen's officials looked closely at multiple

---

* Held in the Balmoral ballroom, the Ghillies' Ball is attended by the Royal Family, house guests, estate staff and neighbours. It traditionally opens with an eightsome reel. It certainly does not descend into a riotous bacchanal, as invented by the producers of the Netflix series *The Crown*.

options, including opening throughout the winter months, but the advice was not encouraging. As with projections for Buckingham Palace, greater access can sometimes mean greater costs. 'The problem is staffing it. You would need to train up a full-time workforce and the projected visitor numbers just do not support that during the winter,' says one former official.[1] 'So it only becomes logical to open for just a few months each year.'

Among old royal hands, there are those who wonder how much longer the King can divide his time between five main residences – Clarence House, Highgrove, Windsor Castle, Birkhall and Sandringham – without offering some movement elsewhere. Opening up Balmoral Castle and the Palace, two properties for which he has less affection, could provide the answer. 'The King may decide it is just better to take the hit and do it anyway,' says one veteran royal adviser. 'It's a bit like life in general. You have to give a bit to retain a lot.'

Similarly, the question of the two decommissioned royal Dukes is not likely to go away. In both cases, the King has decided to keep relations civil and pragmatic rather than confrontational. When the Duke of Sussex let it be known he was coming to Britain in September 2023, en route to his Invictus Games in Germany, the King invited him to stay at Balmoral. When Harry's Invictus commitments ruled out a trip up to Scotland, he was, according to royal officials, offered royal accommodation at Windsor. It was later reported that he had asked for a room at the castle and that this request was rejected because he had not given adequate notice. Not so. Windsor's skeleton summer staff did indeed offer Harry somewhere to stay, but, by the time this had been arranged, he had already booked a hotel. 'No one was snubbing anyone,' says a member of staff.[2]

The Duke of York, meanwhile, remains eager to be part of

any private family gathering. Whether he remains in residence at the Queen Mother's old house, Royal Lodge, is another matter. There will be no eviction order from the King. It will depend on whether the Duke can pay the separate security bill, estimated to be around £1 million a year. With no public duties to justify this from public expenditure, and no regular means of private income, the Duke may find it makes more sense to move to much cheaper accommodation inside the Windsor security cordon than deplete his remaining assets footing security costs. Royal officials would then look to secure a private tenant, subject to vetting. One year into the new reign, fresh details about Prince Andrew's friendship with dead convicted sex offender Jeffrey Epstein continue to surface with embarrassing frequency. For example, in June 2023, United States court proceedings brought by the government of the US Virgin Islands, where Epstein owned an island, against JP Morgan, Epstein's bankers, threw up previously unreported email correspondence. This suggested that the Duke was still communicating with the paedophile long after he claimed (during his disastrous 2019 BBC interview) to have severed all contact.[3] Such revelations might be incidental and offer no grounds for legal action. It is, though, precisely this potential for further surprises which make any prospect of public rehabilitation impossible for the Duke in the foreseeable future. Royal insiders point to two other considerations. First, he remains penitent and eager to please, though he might not remain so were he to be cast out of the royal fold. Second, there are those who fear for his mental well-being. One official who had known him over many years during his days as a working member of the family was astonished by the transformation in him after a meeting since his internal exile, describing him as 'almost incoherent'.[4] For as long as he has a (limited) number of family events to shape his year, and the presence of grand-children to occupy some of his time, he retains some sort of framework to life, albeit with no obvious direction. Fit, teetotal and still in his early sixties, the Duke of York seems destined to remain an unanswered question for many years to come.

On the world stage, meanwhile, the King has those challenges, previously discussed, with republican rumblings in some of his realms. Yet, despite being a relative newcomer to the heads of state club, he already commands the status of an international statesman. This is partly by dint of his position but also because of half a century of engagement at the highest levels of international diplomacy. There had been great sadness within the French presidency in March when civil disorder forced the cancellation of what was supposed to have been the King's first state visit overseas. The depth of that disappointment was reflected in the subsequent determination of President Emmanuel Macron and his wife, Brigitte, to make the rearranged event, in September 2023, as grand as the original, if not more so. The president had always wanted to hold the state banquet at the Palace of Versailles, not at the Élysée Palace where state visitors are usually entertained. The Macrons had also sought to sprinkle the guest list with some extra show-business glamour and sports stars on top of the usual establishment names. Rolling Stones singer Sir Mick Jagger, footballer Patrick Vieira, actress Charlotte Gainsbourg and actor Hugh Grant were among the additions lending a bohemian edge to the event. The tiniest touches did not go unnoticed by British diplomats, such as the inclusion of a British cheese, Stichelton,* among the trio served between the chicken (a uniquely

---

* Produced by a single farm in Nottinghamshire, Stichelton is a highly acclaimed blue cheese made from unpasteurized milk.

French specimen, the white-feathered *poularde de Bresse*) and the raspberry compote. The 170 guests had started with blue lobster and crab cakes, with Bâtard-Montrachet Grand Cru 2018, followed by Château Mouton Rothschild 2004 Grand Cru Classé with the chicken. In honour of such a special evening, there was even a modern twist to state banquet protocol as Madame Macron rotated one or two guests. She herself would have Mick Jagger next to her for one course and Hugh Grant for another. Though there would be no British wine served (France may be a secular state but some things remain sacred), the Macrons at least served arguably the most British of champagnes for the toasts, Pol Roger 'Sir Winston Churchill' 2013.

In his banquet speech, the King made light of Britain's earlier efforts at wine production as he recalled the Queen's 1972 state visit. Officials at the British embassy in Paris had wanted to import several cases of English wine for the Queen to serve to her hosts. However, the consignment had been blocked by a French customs official who refused to believe that there was any such thing as 'English wine'. The King went on to quote the observation of the French writer and cartoonist Roland Topor about French wine and British wit: '*Les Français ont du vin, les Anglais de l'humour*'. As if to prove the point, he added (in French): 'I think it was a French King who once said that he would rather be a wood-cutter than the King of England, dealing with our national complexities. As an avid forester, I am pleased to report that it is entirely possible to combine the two.'

As in Germany earlier in the year, the hosts were touched by the efforts of Charles III to speak their language and his evident appreciation of their efforts to make this an exceptional event. Over the course of three days, a combination of royal stardust, humour and self-deprecation, plus a good deal of charm (reciprocated by the president), left diplomats on both sides harking back to the Entente Cordiale, almost 120 years after Edward VII had coined the phrase with his own exercise in regal cross-Channel bilateral bonhomie. There was a palpable sense of a resetting of the diplomatic dial. Relations already strained by Brexit had been further soured by the 2021 UK/US 'AUKUS' deal to sell submarines to Australia behind the backs of the French. That was followed by an astonishing remark in 2022 by then foreign secretary Liz Truss, two weeks before she became prime minister. Asked on camera if France was friend or foe, she had replied: 'The jury's out.' It was, surely, no coincidence that the King used his speech at the French parliament to state very clearly (again, in French): 'Quite simply, the United Kingdom will always be one of France's closest allies and best friends.' As the King and Queen flew home, the reviews were unequivocally positive in both countries. 'His visit has accomplished tangible good, and proves him wholly attuned to the late Queen's legacy,' declared *The Times*.[5] Writing in *The Guardian*, French commentator Agnès Poirier concluded: 'This is what you call taking a country by storm . . . On a Richter scale of affability, Britain and France's heads of state scored high.'[6] A poll in the French newspaper *Le Figaro* had revealed that 62 per cent of French people had a 'good opinion' of the King overall (rising to 71 per cent among the centre-right Republican party, but still more than half – 51 per cent – even among supporters of Jean-Luc Mélenchon's far-left France Insoumise).[7] *Le Parisien* proclaimed that the King had 'captured the heart of France.' Writing in *Le Point*, Marc Roche, French-language biographer of the late Queen and doyen of French commentators on all things British, was emphatic: 'Charles III has imposed his style: more simplicity, less protocol. Faultless.'[8] While all this was very gratifying to diplomats on both sides, what no one was expecting was one additional plaudit: Charles III, the fashion icon. 'Le Roi Style,' proclaimed *Le Monde*, saluting the King's fashion sense, his tailoring and even his sunglasses. 'George Clooney? No,' wrote style writer Marc Beuagé. 'Better. Very much better.'[9]

One area of expected turbulence and possible trouble, however, would turn out to be nothing of the sort during this first year. The King has certainly not scaled back his passion for all things environmental. When his officials broached the subject of his seventy-fifth birthday in November 2023, he devised his own present to himself. He was well aware that the public's appetite for royal spectacles had been thoroughly sated after a jubilee, a state funeral and a coronation in the space of a year. He would celebrate, instead, with a new initiative to combat food waste. Called the Coronation Food Project, it aims to produce 200 million meals a year for vulnerable people. It would be launched with a single royal birthday photoshoot. Bypassing the usual candidates – either a glossy such as *Country Life* or a national newspaper – the exclusive went to the street magazine *The Big Issue*.

The King's passion for the global campaign against climate change has even led him into new territory – space. In the aftermath of the Coronation and the long weekend of festivities which followed it, the King and Queen withdrew to Sandringham for a few days to recuperate. It was barely noticed that the monarch did not actually go straight to Norfolk. He stopped off en route for what would be his first and only public engagement during that week. It was reported in an unusually verbose and technical introduction to the Court Circular for that day: 'The King today broke ground on the new Whittle Laboratory, 1 JJ Thomson Avenue, Cambridge, which aims to serve as the leading global public-private sector hub focused on rapidly progressing the development of zero carbon flight systems and technologies.' This was certainly considerably longer than the first item on the Court Circular three days earlier, which had simply stated: 'The Coronation of The King and Queen took place in Westminster Abbey today.'

The King's visit to Cambridge underlined a level of engagement with the scientific world that has grown deeper since the loss of both parents. As monarch, he can now dictate his own agenda in a way he could not while Elizabeth II was in charge. Furthermore, although he had always been interested in technology, this had been very much the preserve of the late Duke of Edinburgh, the longstanding chancellor of Cambridge (and several other universities besides). Although he would often wince at some of the comparisons made between himself and Prince Albert, the previous consort of a reigning queen, the Duke of Edinburgh was always proud to celebrate and continue his great-great-grandfather's support for science (along with his chancellorship of Cambridge). Charles III remains a fan of Albert, too. 'Following the death of his father in 2021, he was very keen to pick up those royal links with science and technology, and keep them going,' says one of the King's team. In that same year, George Freeman MP was appointed science minister and says that he was soon receiving regular communications from the office of the then Prince of Wales. 'I had only just started in the job when I met the Prince at the opening of the new AstraZeneca research centre in Cambridge,' says Freeman. 'Not long afterwards, his office were in touch saying that he would like to know if we had other labs we would like him to support.'[10] The Whittle* Laboratory was one, says

* Named after Sir Frank Whittle, the Cambridge-educated inventor of the jet engine.

Freeman, because of its commitment to 'disruptive innovation' rather than conventional thinking: 'There's a bit of him that knows that orthodoxies get stale.'

In January 2022, Freeman welcomed the Prince to Oxfordshire where he visited the UK Atomic Energy Authority and also a small company, Astroscale, which had big plans for clearing up man-made debris in outer space. Though Britain is a second-tier space nation, it has been in the vanguard of clearing up mankind's extra-terrestrial mess, including the 3,000 redundant satellites now littering Earth's orbit. The Prince was fascinated and then had an idea. In 2021, he had established his 'Terra Carta' as a seal of approval for companies signing up to his Sustainable Markets Initiative (which means pledging to put nature 'at the heart of global value creation'). Now, he had the idea of a similar 'Astra Carta' scheme. This would be a badge of sustainable good practice for companies operating responsibly in space.

He launched it in June 2023, in tandem with the government. George Freeman and his civil servants were planning a symposium for international space experts in London so the King (as he now was) offered to join forces. 'He knows that he can't do the government's job and that he can't cross political lines but he is incredibly politically savvy,' says Freeman. 'So he offered to bolt on a reception at the Palace. He was very serious about it.' Here was an exact repeat of that Palace reception which the King had organized alongside the government's biodiversity summit earlier in the year. Once again, a politician would host the crunchy, business end of a big international event. The King then would give the occasion the added kudos and glamour of an invitation to the Palace. It ensured a bumper crowd of academics, scientists, astronauts and industry figures from twenty space nations – including the former commander of the International Space Station and the astrophysicist and rock guitarist Sir Brian May – plus senior figures from NASA.* There was no big lectern-grabbing speech from the King, just a few words of welcome with a Charles-ish tweak: 'Nothing can give me greater pleasure than to unveil this Astra Carta seal in the hope . . . we can ensure the protection of outer space – having made rather a mess of this planet.' Here was another example of the King craftily deploying his 'convening power'. Even his harshest critics would struggle to describe this as 'meddling'. If both the elected government of the day and the opposition were on board, he could hardly be accused of crossing the proverbial 'constitutional line'. Events like these have served to normalize a level of kingly interplay with one of the major issues of our times in a way which seemed inconceivable just a year before. As world leaders gathered for the 2022 COP 27 climate change summit in Egypt, in those precarious weeks after the King's accession, it was no surprise to learn that he was not planning to attend. Ahead of COP 28 in 2023, it was no surprise to learn that he was – or, indeed, that he was even invited to make the opening address.

How much all this cuts through to a wider, younger generation in Britain, let alone in the other realms, remains to be seen. It is ironic that a King who has devoted more years to improving the life chances for both the planet and for young people than any of his predecessors is routinely described as having a 'youth problem'. For polls repeatedly show support for the monarchy at its lowest among young adults. The King has never been one for 'getting down with the kids' and is certainly not going to start now that he is in his mid-seventies. He knows that all he can do is play the long game and try to

---

* The USA's National Aeronautics and Space Administration

ensure that he is remembered as a decent King who did his duty. Historically, says one senior adviser, Palace polling has shown that youth support has always been lower when there are no young members of the family regularly on duty. That is a situation unlikely to change until the mid-2030s, assuming Prince George then embarks on a regular royal role. One happy by-product which the King has discovered since becoming monarch, says one senior Palace aide, is the number of people across government, civil society and the public at large who are only now waking up to the extent of his historic engagement on so many important apolitical fronts.

At home, he leads a kingdom united in name, though frequently divided along multiple lines. That is why, in the days immediately after his accession, he went on that instant tour of all the home nations. It is why the hospitality arm of Buckingham Palace has found itself as busy as it has ever been. It is why, having hit the ground running, he can hardly slow the pace. The monarchy may stand for continuity, but the nation over which Charles III reigns is an entirely different creature from the one that Elizabeth II inherited in 1952.

For proof of that, look no further than a single afternoon in July 2023. The King had come north for that ceremony where he would receive the Honours of Scotland, as his mother had done after her own coronation in 1953. Back then, as noted earlier, the only distraction had been the debate about her title in Scotland: was she Elizabeth I or II? Seven decades on, Charles III and Queen Camilla arrived at St Giles' Cathedral to find the Royal Mile packed with well-wishers and tourists. There was also a small but vocal 'Not My King!' contingent of anti-monarchists occupying a prime position just across the road. Inside, the King attended a Church of Scotland service during which the lesson from the Book of Psalms was read expertly by the First Minister of Scotland, Humza Yousaf. A stranger beamed in from 1953 might have been surprised to hear the lesson read by a Muslim Scottish Nationalist who seeks both to break up the United Kingdom and (as a republican) to replace the monarch with a president. The 2023 congregation would only have been surprised were Yousaf not there for an important state occasion like this. Such is the distance travelled in Scottish public life over seven decades. Yousaf's coalition partners from the Green Party, however, had boycotted the event altogether, in favour of an anti-royal rally elsewhere. Ancient ran alongside modern in terms of music, readings and even the Crown Jewels. Here, before the King, sat the oldest piece of royal regalia, the Crown of Scotland, dating back to 1540. Here, too, was the brand-new Elizabeth Sword, a hefty work of both art and arms weighing twice as much as Westminster's Sword of State (it needed an Olympic rowing champion, Dame Katherine Grainger, to carry it).

The whole event had been preceded by a celebratory 'Procession of the People of Scotland', featuring every strand of Scottish life from fishermen, golfers and kilt-makers to Edinburgh bus drivers and cabbies, all marching down to the cathedral. It concluded with a royal procession down a packed Royal Mile, led by the Household Cavalry, while the Red Arrows thundered overhead. Behind them came their famous vapour trails in the Union colours of red, white and blue.

Here, then, entwined at a single event on a single afternoon, was a perfect illustration of the sort of nation over which Charles III now reigns – from ardent royalists and loyalists to those who believe that the monarchy and the UK should be no more, plus every shade of opinion in between. As at his Coronation, all the main faiths and ethnicities of multicultural Britain had been included. And the King was clearly enjoying every minute of it all. Drawing the service to a close, the Moderator of the General Assembly of the Church of Scotland, Sally Foster-Fulton, concluded with a message both for the new King and for his people: 'The worship is over. Let the service begin.'

And so it has. Buckingham Palace staff have calculated that during the first year of the new reign, the King and Queen notched up 571 engagements between them. The monarchy has continued to provide reassuring familiarity while also adhering to a favourite Palace catchphrase, from Giuseppe di Lampedusa's *The Leopard*: 'If things are going to stay the same, then things are going to have to change.'

That churchgoing, hat-wearing nation of 1952, with its shared experience of war, its shared sources of news and information and its shared belief in containing one's emotions, has now vanished. The monarchy is there to promote both community and diversity; tradition and innovation; the conformist and the free spirit. If it is too much to expect it to be a force for unity in this fragmented, digital, secular age, it can at least play the role of referee, promoting togetherness amid disunity; a willingness to agree to disagree. The King has said as much himself. Shortly after the first anniversary of his accession, the King and Queen attended the traditional Mansion House banquet which the Lord Mayor of London hosts at the start of a new reign. Everyone in the media had been busy writing an end-of-year report card on the King. This was the cue for the man himself to reply with his own thoughts on the state of the nation. There was no attempt to gloss over the challenges ahead. He spoke of Britain as a 'community of communities' living through a 'watershed age' shaped by climate change, artificial intelligence and 'the rancour and acrimony' of 'the digital sphere'. People could draw on 'deep wells' to 'see us through good times and bad'. These included 'the deep well of civility and tolerance', the 'breathing space' to speak freely, the 'duty of care we feel for others', the 'cataract of science, innovation and scholarship' and the 'healing well' of humour, preferably with 'an invigorating dash of self-irony'. He offered up himself as an example, citing 'the vicissitudes I have faced with frustratingly failing fountain pens this past year'.

He called for greater 'appreciation' rather than the 'chill, demotivating scapegoating' of public services. 'Even in the most fractious times – when disagreements are polished, paraded and asserted – there is in our land a kind of muscle-memory that it does not have to be like this,' he argued. 'The temptation to turn ourselves into a shouting or recriminatory society must be resisted.' These were words which could only come from a constitutional monarch. Delivered by a politician or celebrity, they would have invited ridicule.

Nearly five years earlier, Elizabeth II had made a similar plea as Britain went through a foul-tempered post-Brexit political collapse. Since her audience was the Sandringham Women's Institute, she chose a culinary metaphor: 'As we look for new answers in the modern age, I for one prefer the tried and tested recipes, like speaking well of each other and respecting different points of view; coming together to seek out the common ground.'[11]

The late Queen had her recipes. The King has his wells. The deepest of them all, he concluded, should be the one which nurtures 'the sense of responsibility' and 'the decencies on which our institutions and our constitution depend, as well as our relationships, one to another.' In short: 'These are virtues for all seasons.'

For those seeking a blueprint for the reign of King Charles III, this would seem as good as any.

Acknowledgements

I am grateful to His Majesty the King for allowing me to make use of certain papers within the Royal Archives and for permission to reproduce certain images which are subject to Crown copyright. I also wish to thank both the King and Her Majesty Queen Camilla for special access to various royal residences and events in the course of my research.

This is not an authorized portrait of Charles III. It is, however, an authoritative one since I have been able to hear from those who have played a key role in this pivotal period in royal history. I am particularly indebted to Her Royal Highness the Princess Royal; the Archbishop of Canterbury, Justin Welby; the Dean of Westminster, Dr David Hoyle; Annabel Elliot; the Marchioness of Lansdowne; the Earl Marshal; the Duke of Norfolk; Prime Minister Rishi Sunak; the former prime minister, Liz Truss; the Governor-General of Antigua and Barbuda, Sir Rodney Williams; the former foreign secretary, James Cleverly; the Lord President of the Council and Leader of the House of Commons, Penny Mordaunt; the former Bishop of London, Lord Chartres; the former science minister, George Freeman; Lord and Lady Lloyd Webber; and two key architects of the pageantry of 2022 and 2023, Major General Sir Chris Ghika and Garrison Sergeant Major 'Vern' Stokes. I also want to thank the first lady of the

United States, Dr Jill Biden, for taking the time to share her reflections on the King's first year.

Many past and present members of the Royal Household at every level and across multiple royal departments have facilitated my research in different ways. They know who they are and I am extremely grateful to them all. Having also been the writer and co-producer of the separate BBC film *Charles III: The Coronation Year*, I am aware that I have tested the collective patience of Buckingham Palace on numerous occasions. I would, therefore, particularly like to thank the team in the press office. In the course of my research on the coronation of 1953, I have been indebted to Bill Stockting, Laura Hobbs and their colleagues in the Royal Archives. At Lambeth Palace, coronation planning director Danny Johnson has filled the gaps on everything from liturgy to anointing oil. At Westminster Abbey, the Precentor, Mark Birch and Duncan Jeffery have done the same. Coronations are the reason that we have the most famous jewellery collection in the world. My thanks to the Crown Jeweller, Mark Appleby, and to his predecessor, Martin Swift, who were generous with their time and knowledge at moments when they had more pressing things to do.

Many of those involved in the coronation of Elizabeth II and the early years of her reign have been kind enough to share their recollections with me and, in some cases, family photographs, papers and letters, too. I am indebted to Lady [Prue] Penn, Brigadier Andrew Parker Bowles, Lady Rosemary Muir, Sir Simon and Lady Bowes Lyon, Francis Dymoke, Lady [Anne] Glenconner, Jeremy Clyde, Brian Alexander, Julian James and James Drummond. Special thanks go to the late Earl of Airlie and Virginia, Countess of Airlie. Lord Airlie was the last witness to the coronation of 1937, having been there as a page to his father. He kindly shared his memories and photographs of that day with me. I want to thank Cosy Bagot Jewitt and the trustees of Lady Bagot's Will Trust for permission to quote from Nancy Bagot's account of 1953, and Lady Penn for permission to quote from the papers of Sir Arthur Penn. Similarly, I would like to acknowledge the assistance which I have received from Simon Doughty and the editorial team at the *Guards Magazine*.

My unflappable editor, Ingrid Connell, and the publishing team at Macmillan have been excellent throughout, in particular Laura Carr, Philippa McEwan, Lydia Ramah, James Annal, Lindsay Nash, Holly Sheldrake, Victoria Denne, Nicole Foster, Kate Berens and Caroline Jones. My thanks, too, to my American publishers, Jessica Case and Claiborne Hancock at Pegasus. No writer could be in finer hands than those of my agent, Georgina Capel, and her colleagues Simon Shaps, Irene Baldoni, Polly Halladay and Rachel Conway. They have been true allies. We are all grateful to Hugo Burnand for the superb photography which frames this work, fore and aft.

This book was conceived at the same time as the BBC documentary on the first year of the new reign, *Charles III: The Coronation Year*, for which I have been writer and co-producer. Throughout both projects, it has been a pleasure working with old friends at Oxford Films, Nick Kent, Ashley Gething, Faye Hamilton and Nikki Weston. My thanks, too, to the BBC commissioning editor Simon Young.

It is entirely down to journalism that I have been able to cover so many landmark royal moments of modern times, most recently the Platinum Jubilee, the global farewell to Elizabeth II and the accession and coronation of Charles III (all in the space of twelve months). My first duty has been to my editor at the *Daily Mail*, Ted Verity, and to many colleagues there, among them Richard Kay, Rebecca English, Liz Hunt,

Charles III

Andrew Morrod, Oliver Thring, Andrew Yates, Dominic Midgley, Clara Gaspar and Ulla Kloster. They are a pleasure to work with. I have also been lucky to have a front-row seat in various commentary boxes with the BBC Studios Events team and warmly thank Claire Popplewell, Kirsty Young, Huw Edwards, Sophie Raworth, Catherine Stirk, John Shirley and their colleagues.

For reasons too varied and numerous to mention, I am indebted to John Dauth, Harry Mount, Commodore Anthony Morrow, Lord Godson, Julia Mizen, David McDonough, John Bridcut, Lady [Sandra] Williams, Ralph Isham, Lois Fletchman, the Duke and Duchess of Beaufort, Antonia Romeo, Dame Joanna Lumley, Nicky Dunne, Algy and Blondel Cluff, Lord Goldsmith, Johnny McLaren, Con and Katherine Coughlin, Sir Lloyd Dorfman, Zaki Cooper, Nick Loughran, Lord Howell, Jonathan Isaby, Lord and Lady Egremont, Nick Ashmore, Lady [Susan] Roberts, Sarah Vine, Baroness Finn, Dr Amanda Foreman, Jonathan Barton, Lord Bilimoria, Lizzie Pitman, the Countess of Carnarvon, Rosie Bowes Lyon, Andrew Pierce, Russell Tanguay, Christopher and Natasha Owen, Todd and Dan Daley, Willie and Camilla Gray Muir, Peter and Annabel Wyllie, James Pembroke, Ian and Natalie Livingstone, Michael Gove, Henry Dallal, Catherine and Albert Read, Plum Sykes, David Oldroyd-Bolt, Polly Payne, Sir Alan and Lady [Jane] Parker, Geoffrey and Jane Gestetner, Rory and Nicky Darling, George Trefgarne, Anne-Marie McGrath, Iwona Whitaker, John Holland-Kaye, Sophie Barnes, Lev Murynets, Henry Robinson, Marcus Scriven, Mark Foster-Brown, Toby and Jessica Leslie, the Earl of Shrewsbury, George and Fiona Courtauld, Charles and Victoria Spicer, Lisa Barnard, Ollie Boesen and Kitty Abel Smith.

I am especially indebted to those great and prolific historians who have always been so generous with their thoughts, their

Acknowledgements

advice and their company whenever I have called upon them, especially Simon Sebag Montefiore, Andrew Roberts, William Shawcross, Peter Hennessy and Hugo Vickers.

Whatever the occasion, I have always been thankful for the insights, be they ceremonial or constitutional, of Sky's Major General Alastair Bruce of Crionach and Dr David Torrance at the House of Commons Library. With new formats reshaping our analysis of all things royal, it has been a great pleasure, too, to enter the world of podcasting, devising *Tea At The Palace* with my old friends Andy Goodsir at History Television International and writer, broadcaster and fount of royal knowledge Wesley Kerr. Once again, Wesley has been kind enough to read some of my chapters and offer some excellent feedback, not least on the realms and the Commonwealth, which is greatly appreciated. Likewise, I have again called on my old friend Melanie Johnson, a born editor whose unerring instincts and shrewd suggestions always make for a better book.

As ever, it is my family who have had to endure my semi-detachment during evenings, weekends and holidays while I have been writing this. With so much good material, this book has grown rather longer than originally intended and has taken up even more time. My wife, Diana, has borne the brunt. I cannot thank her – and our children, Matilda, Phoebe and Hal – enough. We have all been grateful to the wider family, especially Richard and Dinah Hardman, Harriet and Johnny Hewitson, Hugo and Victoria Hardman, Victoria and Justin Zawoda, Marion Cowley, and Fleur and Alex Evans.

It is family and friends who make such projects more bearable in the making and more satisfying at the end. With that in mind, I dedicate this book to my godchildren – Henry, Matthew, Angus, Tom, Lily, Isaac, Eliza, Isabella, Cailean, Charlie and Hero.

Notes

CHAPTER ONE: C-REX

1   Shakespeare, *Henry IV: Part II.*
2   Interview with author.
3   *The Times*, 14 December 1992; 19 June 2000; YouGov.co.uk biannual tracker 2019–2022.
4   Robert Hardman, *Our Queen* (Arrow, 2012), p. 377.
5   Interview with author.
6   Interview with author.
7   Interview with author/BBC.
8   Private information.
9   Private information.
10   D. R. Thorpe (ed.), *Who's In, Who's Out: The Journals of Kenneth Rose: Volume One 1944–1979* (W&N, 2018), p. 375.
11   Interview with author, 2011.
12   Interview with author.
13   Interview with author.
14   Interview with author.
15   Interview with CBC Canada, 2 May 2023.
16   Jonathan Dimbleby, *The Prince of Wales: A Biography* (Little, Brown, 1994), p. 69.
17   Sally Bedell Smith, *Elizabeth The Queen* (Penguin, 2016), p. 19.
18   Dimbleby, *The Prince of Wales*, p. 114.
19   Interview with author.
20   Interview with author.
21   Cambridge University website.

Charles III

22   ITV, 29 June 1994.
23   Interview with author.
24   Interview with author.
25   Interview with author.
26   Interview with author.
27   Interview with author, 2008 (*Charles at 60*, BBC/Crux).
28   Private information.
29   Interview with author, 2008.
30   Interview with author, 2008.
31   *Horse & Hound*, 4 May 2023.
32   Interview with author.
33   Interview with author.

CHAPTER TWO: QUEEN CAMILLA

1   Interview with author.
2   Interview with author.
3   Private information.
4   Interview with BBC/Oxford.
5   Angela Levin, *Camilla: From Outcast to Queen Consort* (Simon & Schuster, 2022), p. 4.
6   *Daily Mail*, 24 December 2002.
7   Interview with author/BBC.
8   Gyles Brandreth, *Charles & Camilla: Portrait of a Love Affair* (Arrow, 2006), pp. 104–5.
9   Interview with author/BBC.
10   Interview with author.
11   Interview with author.
12   Interview with author/BBC.
13   Private information.
14   Prince Harry, *Spare* (Penguin Random House, 2023), p. 100.
15   *60 Minutes*, 8 January 2023.
16   *Wiltshire Gazette & Herald*, 14 December 2007.
17   *Country Life*, 13 July 2022.
18   Interview with author/BBC.
19   Interview with author/BBC.
20   Interview with author.
21   Interview with author/BBC.

22   Interview with author/BBC.

23   Interview with author.

24   *Country Life,* 7 July 2022.

25   Interview with author.

CHAPTER THREE: LONDON BRIDGE

1   Interview with author.

2   Interview with author.

3   Interview with author.

4   BBC, 12 September 2023.

5   Private information.

6   *Daily Mail,* 2 September 2023.

7   Interview with author.

8   Interview with author.

9   Interview with author.

10   Interview with author.

11   Interview with author.

12   Interview with author.

13   Interview with author.

14   Private information.

15   Prince Harry, *Spare* (Penguin Random House, 2023), p. 403.

16   Interview with author.

17   Prince Harry, *Spare,* p. 403.

18   Interview with author.

19   Interview with author.

20   Private information.

21   Interview with author.

22   Private information.

23   Private information.

24   Interview with author.

25   Private information.

26   Private information.

27   Interview with author.

28   Interview with author.

29   Interview with author.

30   William Shawcross, *Queen Elizabeth, The Queen Mother* (Macmillan, 2009), p. 932.

Charles III

CHAPTER FOUR: D-DAY

1   Interview with author.
2   Prince Harry, *Spare* (Penguin Random House, 2023), p. 403.
3   Interview with author.
4   Interview with author.
5   Interview with author.
6   Interview with author.
7   Interview with author.
8   Private information.
9   Private information.
10 Interview with author.
11 Interview with author.
12 Private information.
13 Interview with author.
14 YouGov, 13 September 2022.
15 *Guards Magazine,* No. 206, p. 82.
16 Private information.
17 HO 290/60.
18 Interview with author.
19 Interview with author.
20 Interview with author.
21 Interview with author.
22 Interview with author.
23 Interview with author.

CHAPTER FIVE: 'IT'S FINISHED'

1   Interview with author.
2   Interview with author.
3   Private information.
4   *People* magazine, 20 April 2023.
5   Interview with author.
6   Interview with author.
7   Interview with author.
8   Interview with author.
9   Interview with author.
10 Interview with author.

11   Interview with author.

12   Interview with author.

13   Interview with author.

14   CNN, 14 September 2022.

15   Interview with author.

16   Interview with author.

17   Interview with author.

18   Interview with author.

19   *Guards Magazine*, No. 206, p. 86.

20   Interview with author.

21   Interview with author.

22   Private papers of Sir Arthur Penn.

23   Interview with author.

24   Interview with author.

25   Interview with author.

26   Interview with author.

27   Interview with author.

28   DCMS figures.

29   Interview with author.

30   Interview with Oxford Films.

31   Interview with author.

32   Interview with author.

33   Private information.

34   *Guards Magazine*, No. 206, p. 96.

35   Prince Harry, *Spare* (Penguin Random House, 2023), p. 405.

36   Interview with author.

37   Interview with author.

CHAPTER SIX: TRANSITION

1   Interview with author/BBC, 2023.

2   *The Guardian*, 14 September 2022.

3   Interview with author.

4   Interview with author.

5   Private information.

6   Robert Hardman, *Queen of Our Times* (Macmillan, 2022), p. 588.

7   *Daily Mail*, 18 March 2023.

8   Robert Hardman, *Queen of Our Times*, p. 121.

9   Interview with author.

10   Hansard, 15 April 1953.

11   PREM 11/31.

12   Hazell: Review of the UK Constitution 2022.

13   Interview with author.

14   Interview with author.

15   Interview with author.

16   Interview with author.

CHAPTER SEVEN: 'HEADWINDS'

1   *The Late Late Show*, 26 February 2021.

2   *The Times*, 15 December 2022.

3   Private information.

4   Institute for Government: 'A crossroads for diversity and inclusion in the civil service', December 2022.

5   Government-backed Parker Review 2023.

6   Private information.

7   Valentine Low, *Courtiers* (Headline, 2022), p. 325.

8   Jonathan Dimbleby, *The Prince of Wales: A Biography* (Little, Brown, 1994), p. 443.

9   Private information.

10   *Harry & Meghan* (2022), Netflix, Episode Three.

11   Jessie Thompson, *Independent*, 15 December 2022.

12   *The Times*, 9 January 2023.

13   Interview with author.

14   Interview with author.

15   Prince Harry, *Spare* (Penguin Random House, 2023), p. 41.

16   Ibid., p. 406.

17   Ibid., p. 75.

18   *The Times*, 10 January 2023.

19   Private information.

20   Private information.

21   Private information.

22   yougov.co.uk – YouGov Royal Family Opinion Tracker.

23   Robert Hardman, *Queen of Our Times* (Macmillan, 2022), p. 348

Notes

CHAPTER EIGHT: DOING THE SAME – DIFFERENTLY

1   Interview with author.
2   Interview with author.
3   *Horse & Hound*, 5 May 2023.
4   Private information.
5   Private information.
6   Interview with author.
7   Interview with author, 2007.
8   Interview with author, *Charles at 60*, 2008.
9   Robert Hardman, *Queen of the World* (Century, 2018), p. 477.
10 Ibid., p. 271.
11 Interview with author, *Charles at 60*, 2008.
12 Forces.net, 28 April 2023.
13 Jonathan Dimbleby, *The Prince of Wales: A Biography* (Little, Brown, 1994), p. 194.
14 Interview with author.
15 Interview with author.
16 *Stern*, 29 March 2023.
17 *Frankfurter Allgemeine Zeitung*, 1 April 2023.

CHAPTER NINE: OPERATION PATEK

1   PREM 11/38.
2   MRH/MRH/QEII/FUNC/O453/1.
3   RA PPTO/PP/QEII/COR/CSP.
4   Peter Butler (ed.), *The Wit of Prince Philip* (Leslie Frewin, 1965), p. 28.
5   Letter from Ronald Beaty. RA QEII/ADD/COPY/MISC.
6   Vickers, quoting HRH the Duke of Windsor, *The Crown and the People, 1902–1953* (Cassell, 1953), p. 50.
7   CAB 128/25/46.
8   Simon Heffer (ed.), *Henry 'Chips' Channon: The Diaries (Volume 3): 1943–57* (Hutchinson Heinemann, 2022), p. 826.
9   From 'The Duke of Devonshire: Memories of a Coronation Page Boy (Aged 9 ¼)', Sotheby's, May 2022.
10 Letter from Lady Bagot, 24 June 1953. RA QEII/ADD/COPY/MISC.

11 RA QEII/ADD/COPY/MISC.

12 Letter from Denise Boyle, 7 June 1953. RA QEII/ADD/COPY/
    MISC.

13 Interview with author.

14 Joanna Lumley, *A Queen for All Seasons* (Hodder & Stoughton,
    2021), p. 1.

15 Interview with author.

16 Hugo Vickers, *Coronation: The Crowning of Elizabeth II* (The
    Dovecote Press, 2023), p. 105.

17 Palace statement, 14 February 2023.

18 QEII/ADD/MISC.

19 Oxford Films/BBC.

CHAPTER TEN: NO PLUS-ONE

1   *Daily Telegraph*, 1 November 1997.

2   PREM 11/320, 3 April 1952.

3   Ibid.

4   Private information.

5   Interview with author.

6   Interview with author.

7   Coronation Joint Committee sub-committee, 17 July 1952.

8   PREM 11/319.

9   Coronation Committee of the Privy Council (CCPC),
    16 February 1953.

10 CCPC, 24 February 1953.

11 Interview with author.

12 Interview with author.

13 Interview with author.

14 CAB 124/1206.

15 PREM 11/319.

16 Simon Heffer (ed.), *Henry 'Chips' Channon: The Diaries
    (Volume 3): 1943–57* (Hutchinson Heinemann, 2022), p. 872.

17 Ibid.

18 CAB 124/1206.

19 RA F&V COR /1953.

20 PPTO/PP/QEII/COR/BILLS.

21 PPTO/PP/QEII/COR/CSP.
22 PPTO/PP/QEII/COR/BILLS.
23 Ibid.
24 PREM 11/32.
25 Interview with author.
26 Private information.

CHAPTER ELEVEN: THE HENRY V TEST

1 LCO 6/3479.
2 Ibid.
3 Interview with author.
4 Jonathan Dimbleby, *The Prince of Wales: A Biography* (Little, Brown, 1994), p. 642.
5 Interview with author.
6 Private information.
7 Interview with author.
8 Robert Hardman, *Queen of Our Times* (Macmillan, 2022), p. 488.
9 Interview with author.
10 Interview with author.
11 Interview with author.
12 Coronation Joint Committee, 7 July 1952.
13 PREM 11/34.
14 Ibid.
15 Ibid.
16 Ibid.
17 *Daily Telegraph*, 24 October 1952.
18 Hansard, 23 October 1952.
19 PREM 11/34.
20 Ibid.
21 Coronation Commission minutes, 5 December 1952.
22 Hugo Vickers, *Coronation: The Crowning of Elizabeth II* (The Dovecote Press, 2023), p. 107.
23 CAB 195-10-29.
24 *The Times*, 1 May 2023.
25 BBC *Today*, 5 May 2023.

Charles III

CHAPTER TWELVE: 'JAM IT ON'

1   BBC, 18 May 2023.
2   CAB 130/75.
3   PREM 11/320.
4   RA F&V/COR/1953.
5   RA PPTO/PP/QEII/COR/BILLS.
6   Author interview with Royal Mews staff.
7   RA PPTO/PP/QEII/COR/BILLS.
8   Ibid.
9   Interview with author.
10   PREM 11/319.
11   Interview with author.
12   PREM 11/364.
13   Ibid.
14   Ibid.
15   Interview with author.
16   Interview with author.
17   Interview with author.
18   RA PPTO/PP/QEII/COR/CSP – 6-20.
19   Anne Glenconner, *Lady in Waiting* (Hodder & Stoughton, 2019), p. 60.
20   *The Coronation*, BBC, 2018.
21   Interview with author.
22   Interview with author/BBC.
23   Interview with author.
24   Interview with author.
25   Interview with author/BBC.
26   Interview with author/BBC.
27   *The Washington Post*, 21 April 2023.
28   RA PPTO/PP/QEII/COR/CSP.
29   RA MRH/MRH/QEII/FUNC/0453/1-8.
30   RA FPPTO/PP/QEII/COR/CSP.
31   Interview with author.

Notes

CHAPTER THIRTEEN: 'A DECENT-SIZED HAT'

1   *The Spectator*, 6 May 2023.
2   RA MRH/MRH/QEII/FUNC/O453/1.
3   Private information.
4   PA News, 5 May 2023.
5   Interview with author.
6   Interview with author.
7   Rowley letter to Mayor Sadiq Khan, 11 May 2023.
8   Metropolitan Police statement, 3 May 2023.
9   Interview with author.
10   Hugo Vickers, *Coronation: The Crowning of Elizabeth II* (The Dovecote Press, 2023), p. 12.

CHAPTER FOURTEEN: 'I WAS GLAD'

1   Interview with author/BBC.
2   Interview with author.
3   Interview with author/BBC.
4   Interview with author.
5   Private information.
6   Interview with author/BBC.
7   Interview with Oxford Films.
8   Interview with author.
9   Interview with author/BBC.
10   Interview with author/BBC.
11   Private information.
12   Private information.
13   Interview with author.
14   Interview with author/BBC.
15   Private information.
16   *Guards Magazine*, Coronation edition, p. 11.
17   Interview with author/BBC.
18   Interview with author.

Charles III

CHAPTER FIFTEEN: 'DOCTOR WHO SYNDROME'

1   Interview with author.
2   Interview with author.
3   *The Times*, 29 October 2022.
4   Speech to COP 15, Copenhagen, 15 December 2009.
5   *The Observer*, 10 May 2009.
6   *Evening Standard*, 3 April 2008.
7   Private information.
8   Jonathan Dimbleby, *The Prince of Wales: A Biography* (Little, Brown, 1994), p. 286.
9   Ibid., p. 290.
10 Interview with author.
11 *Gardens Illustrated*, 1 May 2023; *Tea at the Palace* podcast, 5 May 2023.
12 Interview with author.
13 Interview with author.
14 Interview with author.

CHAPTER SIXTEEN: THE THREE RS

1   Interview with author.
2   Interview with author.
3   Robert Hardman, *Queen of Our Times* (Macmillan, 2022), p. 462
4   Philip Murphy, *Monarchy and the End of Empire: The House of Windsor* (Oxford University Press, 2014), p. 91.
5   US Foreign Affairs Committee, 14 November 2022.
6   Privy Council minutes, 7 November 2018.
7   Interview with author.
8   Interview with author; Andrew Roberts, *George III: The Life and Reign of Britain's Most Misunderstood Monarch* (Penguin, 2021), p. 501.
9   Reuters, 1 July 2023.
10 *The Guardian*, 6 April 2023.
11 Lambeth Palace statement, 10 January 2023.
12 Tobias Skowronek et al., 'German brass for Benin bronzes', PLOS One, 5 April 2023.
13 Submission to District Court, Washington DC, 7 October 2022.

14   *The Times*, 11 June 2023.

15   Interview with author.

16   *The Voice*, September 2022.

17   Interview with author.

18   William Dalrymple and Anita Anand, *Koh-i-Noor: The History of the World's Most Infamous Diamond* (Bloomsbury, 2017), p. 90.

19   Interview with author.

20   Interview with author.

21   *Daily Telegraph*, 27 January 1994.

CHAPTER SEVENTEEN: THE FUTURE AND 'THE FORCE'

1   Interview with author.

2   *The Guardian*, 8 September 2023.

3   BBC website, 8 September 2023.

4   *The Daily Telegraph*, 8 September 2023.

5   *Daily Mail*, 8 September 2023.

6   Interview with author.

7   *The Sunday Times*, 20 August 2023.

8   Interview with author.

9   Interview with author.

10   Jonathan Dimbleby, *The Prince of Wales: A Biography* (Little, Brown, 1994), p. 392.

11   Interview with author.

12   Valentine Low, *Courtiers* (Headline, 2022), p. 335.

13   Robert Hardman, *Queen of Our Times* (Macmillan, 2022), p. 196.

14   Interview with author.

15   *Time to Walk* podcast for Apple Fitness+, 5 December 2021.

16   Interview with author/BBC, 2021.

17   Private information.

18   Interview with author.

19   Robert Hardman, *Our Queen* (Arrow, 2012), p. 325.

20   Interview with author.

21   Interview with author.

22   Jane Ridley, *Bertie: A Life of Edward VII* (Chatto & Windus, 2012), p. 531.

23   Philip Ziegler, *King Edward VIII: A Biography* (HarperCollins, 2012), p. 162.

24   Hardman, *Queen of Our Times*, p. 471.

25   Private information.

CHAPTER EIGHTEEN: 'VIRTUES FOR ALL SEASONS'

1   Interview with author.

2   Private information.

3   *Daily Mail*, 20 June 2023.

4   Private information.

5   *The Times*, 23 September 2023.

6   *The Guardian*, 23 September 2023.

7   *Le Figaro*, 21 September 2023.

8   *Le Point*, 29 September 2023.

9   *Le Monde*, 1 October 2023.

10   Interview with author.

11   Robert Hardman, *Queen of Our Times* (Macmillan, 2022), p. 535.

Selected Bibliography

Allison, Ronald and Riddell, Sarah (eds.), *The Royal Encyclopaedia* (Macmillan, 1991)

Bedell Smith, Sally, *Elizabeth The Queen* (Penguin, 2016)

——, *Charles: The Misunderstood Prince* (Michael Joseph, 2017)

Bower, Tom, *Rebel Prince* (William Collins, 2018)

Bradford, Sarah, *Elizabeth: A Biography of Her Majesty the Queen* (William Heinemann, 1996)

Brandreth, Gyles, *Charles & Camilla* (Arrow, 2005)

——, *Elizabeth: An Intimate Portrait* (Penguin, 2022)

Butler, Peter (ed.), *The Wit of Prince Philip* (Leslie Frewin, 1965)

Channon, Henry 'Chips', *The Diaries 1943-57*, Vol. III, edited by Simon Heffer (Hutchinson, 2022)

Dalrymple, William and Anand, Anita, *Koh-i-Noor: The History of the World's Most Infamous Diamond* (Bloomsbury, 2017)

Dimbleby, Jonathan, *The Prince of Wales: A Biography* (Little, Brown, 1994)

Glenconner, Anne, *Lady in Waiting* (Hodder & Stoughton, 2019)

Hardman, Robert, *Queen of Our Times: The Life of Elizabeth II, 1926-2022* (Macmillan, 2022)

——, *Queen of the World* (Century, 2018)

——, *Our Queen* (Arrow, 2012)

Prince Harry, *Spare* (Penguin Random House, 2023)

Keay, Anna, *The Crown Jewels* (Thames & Hudson, 2011)

Levin, Angela, *Camilla: From Outcast to Queen Consort* (Simon & Schuster, 2022)

Charles III

Low, Valentine, *Courtiers* (Headline, 2022)

Lumley, Joanna, *A Queen for All Seasons: A Celebration of Queen Elizabeth II* (Hodder & Stoughton, 2021)

Murphy, Professor Philip, *Monarchy and the End of Empire* (Oxford University Press, 2013)

Pimlott, Ben, *The Queen: Elizabeth II and the Monarchy* (HarperPress, 2012)

Ramphal, Shridath, *Glimpses of a Global Life* (Hansib Publications, 2014)

Ridley, Jane, *George V: Never a Dull Moment* (Chatto & Windus, 2021)

Roberts, Andrew, *George III: The Life and Reign of Britain's Most Misunderstood Monarch* (Allen Lane, 2021)

———, *The Royal House of Windsor* (Kindle edition, 2011)

Rose, Kenneth, *The Journals*, Vol. I (Weidenfeld & Nicolson, 2018)

———, *The Journals*, Vol. II (Weidenfeld & Nicolson, 2019)

Shawcross, William, *Queen Elizabeth, The Queen Mother* (Macmillan, 2009)

Strong, Roy, *Coronation: A History of the British Monarchy* (HarperCollins, 2022)

Vickers, Hugo, *Coronation: The Crowning of Elizabeth II* (The Dovecote Press, 2023)

Wilkinson, James, *The Queen's Coronation – with a foreword by HRH The Duke of Edinburgh* (Scala, 2011)

Ziegler, Philip, *King Edward VIII* (HarperPress, 2012)

Sources

With the kind permission of His Majesty The King, I have been granted access to a number of files and boxes held in the Royal Archives (RA) at Windsor relating to the Coronation of 1953. These include:

RA MRH/MRH/QEII/FUNC/0453/1–8 – Master of the Household Central Office files re: the Coronation of Queen Elizabeth II, 1953

RA PPTO/PP/QEII/COR/CSP – Privy Purse and Treasurer's files re: the Coronation of Queen Elizabeth II

RA PPTO/PP/QEII/COR/BILLS – Privy Purse and Treasurer's files re: the Coronation of Queen Elizabeth II

RA QEII/ADD/COPY/MISC – Recollections of guests and onlookers at the Coronation of Queen Elizabeth II

RA F&V/COR/1953 – Lists of the Royal Family and of Royal and Foreign guests for the Coronation; 'Ceremonial to be observed', 1953

RA QEII/ADD/MISC – Letter and notes concerning the preparation of Coronation anointing oil, *c.* 1902–1952

Under the Open Government Licence, I have drawn extensively on the files held (both physically and digitally) by The National Archives (TNA) at Kew. They include papers from:

The Cabinet Office (CAB)

The Foreign Office (prior to its merger with the Commonwealth Office) (FO)

Charles III

The Home Office (HO)
The Lord Chamberlain's Office (LCO)
The Prime Minister's Office (PREM)

Picture Credits

Charles III

Index

Index

Index

Index

About the Author

Robert Hardman is a renowned writer and broadcaster, specializing in royalty and history for more than twenty-five years. He is the author of several international bestsellers. His latest, *Queen of Our Times: The Life of Elizabeth II*, was the 2022 *Sunday Times* Biography of the Year and was presented by Prime Minister Boris Johnson to Ukrainian president Volodymyr Zelensky in the same year. Hardman has also written *Monarchy: The Royal Family at Work*, *Our Queen* and *Queen of the World*, along with globally acclaimed television documentaries of the same names. He has interviewed the then Prince of Wales for several films, including the BBC's *Charles at 60*, Prince William for his book *Our Queen*, the late Duke of Edinburgh for the BBC's *The Duke: In His Own Words*, and the Princess Royal for ITV's *Anne: The Princess Royal at 70*. Most recently Hardman has written and co-produced the BBC films *Charles III: The Coronation Year* and *Prince Philip: The Royal Family Remembers*, for which he interviewed a dozen members of the Royal Family. A member of the BBC commentary team at all the major state occasions of recent times, including the Coronation of Charles III and the funerals of Elizabeth II and Prince Philip, Hardman is an award-winning journalist for the *Daily Mail* and lives in London. *Charles III: New King. New Court. The Inside Story* is his fifth book.